Late Victorian Flow Blue

Other Ceramic Wares

A Selected History of Potteries & Shapes

William H. Van Buskirk

4880 Lower Valley Road, Atglen, PA 19310 USA

Dedication

This book is dedicated, first and foremost, to my wife, Sheila, and my daughter, Sarah. This work would not have been possible without their extended patience and their help with so many tedious tasks.

Dedication is also made to those determined collectors, who diligently seek answers to questions on late Victorian Flow Blue, for they understand the intrinsic value and recognize the simplistic beauty and rich history it represents.

Library of Congress Cataloging-in-Publication Data

VanBuskirk, William H.
Late Victorian flow blue, other ceramic wares : a selected history of
potteries & shapes / by William H. Van Buskirk.
p. cm.
ISBN 0-7643-1509-9
1. Blue and white transfer ware. 2. Pottery, Victorian. I. Title.
NK4277 .V358 2002
738.2'0942'09034--dc21
2001008055

Designed by Bonnie M. Hensley
Cover design by Bruce M. Waters

Type set in ShelleyAllegro BT/ZapfHumnst BT
ISBN: 0-7643-1509-9
Printed in China
1 2 3 4

Published by Schiffer Publishing Ltd.
4880 Lower Valley Road
Atglen, PA 19310
Phone: (610) 593-1777; Fax: (610) 593-2002
E-mail: Schifferbk@aol.com
Please visit our web site catalog at **www.schifferbooks.com**
We are always looking for people to write books on new and related
subjects. If you have an idea for a book, please contact us at the
above address.
This book may be purchased from the publisher.
Include $3.95 for shipping. Please try your bookstore first.
You may write for a free catalog.
In Europe, Schiffer books are distributed by
Bushwood Books
6 Marksbury Ave. Kew Gardens
Surrey TW9 4JF England
Phone: 44 (0)20 8392-8585; Fax: 44 (0)20 8392-9876
E-mail: Bushwd@aol.com
Free postage in the UK. Europe: air mail at cost.
Please try your bookstore first.

Contents

Foreword

As we enter the twenty-first century, we note hundreds of books written in the field of ceramics, covering aspects of Oriental, European, and North American wares. By far, most of these works stop with the 1850s. Late Victorian and twentieth century research is basically few and far between, and even the later researchers deal primarily with ceramics that date to pre-1850.

Bill Van Buskirk's love of ceramics, and in particular Flow Blue of the post 1850 period, is the reason for this work. The nineteenth century gave rise to some fascinating and important British potters, amongst whom are the Meakins, Johnson Brothers, and Grindley; about whom very little has been written. A scant amount of documented, primary source material existed for Bill's research. Yet, a story and history had to be told for these major Victorian potters. The foundation of Bill's research lies in the earthenware bodies and shapes of these potters and their manufactories. From these bodies and shapes, as well as through available primary source material that he plumbed, Bill developed a detailed storyboard, which includes economics of the period, the emergence of catalog sales, and the expanding English world market. He also added a human touch by providing a personal history of the potters, as well as adding faces to these potters through the inclusion of photographs.

We can all learn from Bill Van Buskirk's research on this truly vast area of ceramics.

Arnold A. Kowalsky
Yonkers, New York
March, 2001

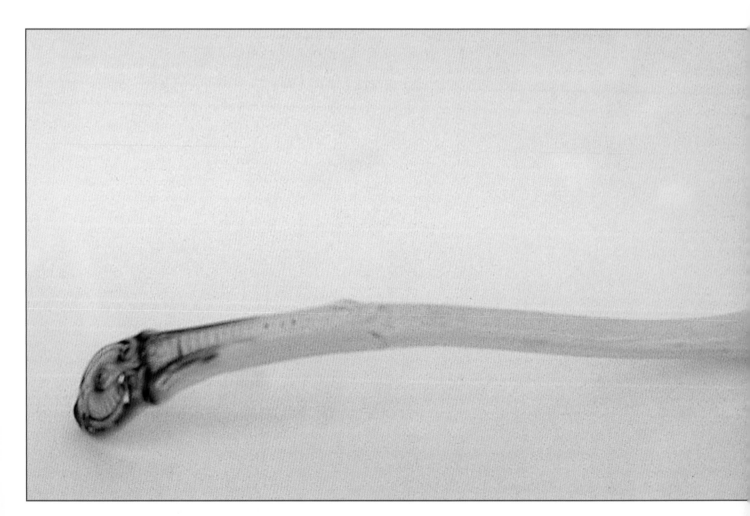

Acknowledgments

I am very fortunate to have had so many dedicated and skilled friends who helped me with this project. I would like to thank Ann Potts for her beautifully detailed line drawings of the different body styles. Ann recognized the importance of her work to this study and endeavored to create her drawings with great accuracy. I would like to thank Lynn Miller and the Wedgwood Museum for their help with photos. John Potter for his help with research and photos on the W.H. Grindley, and J.&G. Meakin projects. Neil Ewens for his tedious research on the Johnson Bros. and Alfred Meakin projects, and for his wonderful photos of the potteries and canals. To Robert Copeland for his answers to my questions, and his article on Flow Blue. Arnold and Dorothy Kowalsky for their patience in supplying me with detailed answers to the mountain of questions I posed to them, and allowing me to print their article on attribution. Their dedication to factual representation is unparalleled, and their massive library on ceramics was always at my disposal. Their constant prodding helped to keep me on the straight and narrow path, and the responsibility of any deviation from that path that I may have taken falls squarely on my shoulders. A generous thank you to Jonathan Goodwin, Assistant Archaeologist, Potteries Museum and Art Gallery, Stoke-on-Trent, for taking the time from his work to write an article about his excavations at the Grindley and Johnson Bros. potteries. To the Sears Roebuck & Co. for their help with researching their catalogs. A warm thank you to Shelley Lewis for her help with many aspects of this project. Shelley is a dedicated Late Victorian Flow Blue collector who can always be counted on for her help and support with educational projects. The Staffordshire Sentinel for articles researched, and use of the William H. Grindley photo. I also would like to thank the wonderfully dedicated experts who offered insight through their articles on the different fields of ceramics: Henry Kelly, Mulberry; Ernie & Bev Dieringer, White Ironstone/Granite; and Dale Abrams, Tea Leaf. Special thanks to Tom and Murline Georgeson of Auntie M's Antiques, Eureka, California, for their dedication and continual support of my research. A most deserved thank you goes to all those collectors who offered pattern photos and who allowed me into their homes to take pictures of their collections. Their patience and understanding of my goals for this book have not gone unnoticed by me. I thank each and every one of you for allowing me to share your collections with others so that they might learn more about this beautiful ceramic we call Late Victorian Flow Blue.

Preface

I have never been satisfied, while looking at anything, that what I am told about it is all there is to know or completely accurate. I always have more questions. For example, I have been compelled since birth to seek answers to questions about my family's genealogy. This interest led me, in 1988, to begin a serious study that took six years and eventually led me to write two books on my genealogy, one on my father's side and one on my mother's side. The study was most fulfilling. Always, during my research, I wondered what each newly discovered person in my past had looked like. For me, the knowledge of that person's existence and the incidental information I discovered about them was not enough; only the eventual discovery of a picture brought that person into reality.

When I began to collect Flow Blue in 1988, this quest for detail did not change. I always had more questions than there were answers. That same year I bought my first piece of Flow Blue. Produced by the W. H. Grindley & Co. Ltd. pottery; it was a 10" plate in the pattern FLORIDA. When I viewed this plate, I looked at the mark on the back and my first and second questions were: "Who was W. H. Grindley?" and "What did he look like?" Those questions led me on a search for more information about this pottery. I discovered that the five leading Late Victorian English potteries that exported to America were Doulton & Co. Ltd., W. H. Grindley & Co. Ltd., Johnson Bros. Ltd., Alfred Meakin Ltd., and J. & G. Meakin Ltd. Soon thereafter, my research was broadened to cover these potteries and the Late Victorian period in general.

The W. H. Grindley & Co. pottery is used extensively throughout this book because it best represents the Late Victorian period of ceramic production in England, especially where Flow Blue is considered.

I became very interested in the body styles that Late Victorian Flow Blue was produced on. Their shapes are distinctly different from those made in the earlier two periods of production. This fascination with shapes led me on a mission of acquiring line drawings of as many different body styles as I could identify. Then, I began to categorize the patterns that were applied to each style of dish, and then progressed to categorize the wash sets as well. Gradually, light was shed on Flow Blue's evolution through the Late Victorian period. It was only by categorizing the research that I was able to recognize trends in shapes as well as patterns. Other interesting data evolved that enabled me to develop a formula to help date Late Victorian Flow Blue. With this type of research, answers to the many questions began to come forth.

This book is the culmination of subsequent discoveries born from a need for answers. It is about the people of the potteries and the goods they created. I have tried not only to give the reader many technical aspects of Late Victorian Flow Blue, but, just as important, a description of the era in which it was produced. The Late Victorian period was a most glamorous time and one that was constantly changing. The cultural changes became most apparent at the dining table. Late Victorian Flow Blue fit into this cultural event with the ease and grace of a natural occurrence, and brought its exquisite beauty to that table. Today, collectors bring this same beautiful china to their tables, and it is my hope that through this book they can realize the full history it represents.

Introduction

Petra Williams is one of the pioneer researchers of Flow Blue china, and is the author of several ceramic reference books. In Petra's book, *Flow Blue China An Aid to Identification*, Fountain House East 1971, she very aptly segments and then details through dates three periods of Flow Blue china production. They are:

Early Victorian, 1835-1840 to 1850s

Mid-Victorian, 1860s to 1870s

Late Victorian, 1880s-1890s to early 1900s

Each period is distinctly different from the other and each period is definable by those differences. In this enormous field of Flow Blue ceramics, at least for this author, Late Victorian Flow Blue stands out as the true jewel. This period of Flow Blue production has woefully few reference books and even fewer researchers. This mostly comes as a result of the high interest in eighteenth and early nineteenth century ceramics, primarily porcelain. There is a voluminous amount of books written on this period that deals with every aspect of a potter and his wares. David Crowley, in his book *Introduction To Victorian Style* (Shooting Star Press, New York) brought out an interesting point when he wrote, "Victorian values, however, were not firmly entrenched until the late 1840s and were already breaking down by the 1870s. This is the age that has come to be known as the 'High Victorian period.' These years saw the height of British economic dominance, intense innovative activity in industry and communications, and the untrammeled growth of the British Empire."

The Early Victorian period of Flow Blue, which is distinctly different from the other two periods and coincides with this era, may also be called the "High Victorian Period." There are many serious and dedicated collectors of early Flow Blue and it is easy to see why. The shape of the early wares and the flow of the blue are extremely beautiful. We must remember, however, that every new style of dish or pattern design came as a result of a cultural movement that affected clothing, furniture, art, and, in general, the world around us. A company's ability to be successful and even to remain in business, came as a result of its ability to recognize and follow current trends that were being determined by cultural styles. So it is through cultural trends, formed by customer demand, by which we transgressed from Early to Late Victorian Flow Blue. Whether a person collects Early, Middle, or Late Victorian Flow Blue today, is really a matter of what past trend they prefer.

The purpose of this book is to bring to the forefront the history and exquisite beauty of the Late Victorian Flow Blue potteries and their wares. And while the main theme will be Flow Blue, many other forms of Late Victorian ceramics also will be covered. It is noted here also, that this book will focus on England's Staffordshire District and their wares. Stoke-on-Trent (considered the Staffordshire potting district) covers thirty-six square miles and consists of six towns: Burslem, Fenton, Hanley, Longton, Stoke, and Tunstall. Several other countries produced Late Victorian Flow Blue and they will, to some degree, be dealt with systematically as the book unfolds.

A goal of this book is to paint a broad picture of the Late Victorian potter, his wares, and the times in which he lived to give readers a broad view of the ceramic world during a transitional period. This was a period of economic adjustment. The American Industrial Revolution that helped bring about Middle Class America was in full swing and saw, for the first time, a decline in farming and increase in the populations of cities. The American Industrial Revolution created new jobs and the promise of a better life for city dwellers. The movement of people from rural areas to cities helped create the middle class in America. Families that had been poor found themselves with steady jobs and regular income. In an effort to emulate wealthy neighbors, they cultivated elaborate meals with many courses served by hired domestic servants. The new widespread preference for elaborate dining created a need for additional pieces of china that did not exist before. For example, the 1880s saw, for the first time, the use of individual butter pats, vegetable servers, and bone dishes. Even though such pieces were not used in England, the English potteries, in the business to make money, were more than happy to supply these new forms to their Yankee cousins.

Throughout the research for this book, every effort has been made to acquire all possible detail and historical fact and to record it accurately. Each chapter is placed in order of importance, with each being the building block for the next. This book employs a systematic approach that will carry the reader from modest beginnings to a more advanced field of learning. While the intent is to instruct, it is my hope also to dispel many of the misconceptions about Flow Blue so that the myths and distortions of fact can be recognized.

My intentions here are to give the reader a better understanding of English ceramics and the ability to distinguish between the old and the new Flow Blue. Who were England's competitors and how effective were they? As only the true answer could, these issues deal with economics. The phrase "There are no absolutes in the world of ceramics" has been drilled into me by many experts in the field. This is a hard fact to accept when you are trying to clearly define a subject. I recognize the importance of that statement's finality, and have been confronted with it many times during my research; it can be most frustrating and, if allowed, a hindrance to one's research. My goal, then, was to find a balance between absolute fact, assumption, and areas where there clearly was no answer.

The first chapter deals with what is and what is not Flow Blue. This is an important basic step in understanding the premise of the book, and will give the reader basic knowledge to recognize the real Flow Blue. This is of timely importance today when the market is so congested with the influx of "new" Flow Blue. This chapter lists other wares associated with Flow Blue, or what is to be considered the Flow Blue family. This chapter also describes the manufacturing process, including basic potting procedures from bisque to the final glazed product. For those interested in deeper study, further reading would be required. Suggested reading would be C. F. Binns' book *The Story of the Potter* (George Newnes Ltd., London, England, 1898) and two books by Robert Copeland, *Spode's Willow Pattern and other designs after the Chinese* (Courier International, Essex, England, 1980) and *Blue and*

White Transfer-Printed Pottery (Shire Publications Ltd., Buckinghamshire, England, 1982).

The potters, the potteries, and the Staffordshire potting district come alive in the second chapter. Biographies of the potters give insight to the people, the buildings, and the towns. Great detail has been given to the history of the people through pertinent facts as well as incidental stories. They were people who had lives, goals, and families in good and tragic times. This chapter presents the products they made through both line drawings and photographs of their wares. This section also contains complete pattern lists, explanations of how other colors were used on Flow Blue body styles and that other colors replaced the blue on known Flow Blue patterns. It presents shapes in each of the potteries' body styles, discusses other ceramic products, and provides a current price guide in the captions.

The third chapter deals with the wares. It is divided into two sections, one for dish body styles and the other for wash set body styles, with lists of what was made and what they were called. For this chapter, hundreds of catalogs were consulted and the name of each piece was recorded. I listened to many ceramic dealers and noted what they named each piece. Through this method I drew conclusions about the proper names for each piece. Most of the pieces made for a Late Victorian Flow Blue set of dishes were standard for the industry; there are many elegant and beautiful pieces, but not many surprises. The "What was it called?" section was the most difficult part of the book to write. Because there are various cultures in the world, there are no absolute names to some pieces.

Collectors always want to know, "Is this a rare piece and what is it worth?" Chapter Four deals with this subject. It is divided into sections that lead from the most common pieces to the extremely rare. Each piece in a set of dishes and in a wash set are placed into one of the listed categories. This chapter will aid collectors in prioritizing pieces by their values. For the past two years, I have kept track of the prices paid in a variety of markets, including internet auction sites, antiques shows, antiques malls, private conversations with dealers, and specialty shows such as the International Flow Blue Collectors Club convention. Through all these numbers, I have been able to determine for each item what I believe to be a fair value.

The people who made up the pottery workforce are examined in Chapter Five. Who were the workers; male or female? What were their ages? What was it like to work at a pottery? Were there health concerns? What were their wages and working conditions? All these questions I sought to answer. Also, in this chapter is a brief history and tour of the all-important transportation canals that connected the workers as they passed by the potteries from just north of Tunstall on the Trent River and Mersey Canal to just west of Hanley on the Caldon Canal. The canals enabled the ceramic wares to travel from the inland potteries to Liverpool, England's west-coast shipping port. The canals were built through Josiah Wedgwood's and James Brindley's innovative ideas of a system to link the potting district to markets throughout the world. The canal system launched England's development as a leader in both the design and the manufacture of ceramics, but just as important was its role as a transportation cost-cutting measure that helped to keep the manufacturing companies in England.

In Chapter Six, the marketing techniques and export destinations are considered. England's position, compared with other countries that exported ceramic wares to the United States, is reviewed. While the potteries sold their wares by the piece, the marketers had a different view of how those same pieces should be sold. In the 1890s, dinner sets, tea sets, ice cream sets, etc. were sold to the public by marketers who were imaginative, and at times simplistic, in their approaches to selling English wares abroad. Here again, research in the sales catalogs helped to determine what was included in a set of Flow Blue dishes and wash sets, as first discussed in Chapter Three.

The age of each piece is important to most collectors, not only as an aid to determining value, but also for its historical perspective. In Chapter Seven, the examples discussed demonstrate how Late Victorian (from 1880 through 1925) wares followed then-current social trends. Fortunately, the potteries of this late period (as opposed to the early and middle periods) marked their wares in an assortment of ways that are understood today. Therefore, with reasonable accuracy, the date of a given body style or pattern can be determined within a finite "dating window" of time, instead of an era. An example is provided in the pattern FLORIDA by W. H. Grindley & Co. In most reference works until now, this pattern is given a dating period of circa 1891. Now it is known that the body style used for the pattern FLORIDA was first put into production in 1902; the circa date is actually 1902. For some people, this circa date may be disappointing. For the majority of Late Victorian Flow Blue pieces, the blistering truth is that it was produced post-1900. The reality of this came very early in the research. Attempts to make this a complete study to determine the age of an item led to the use of pottery marks, English registration numbers, United States patent dates, patent numbers, the shapes of the pieces, and the individual body styles.

The line drawings are provided to help identify a particular body style. The photographs, accumulated from many sources and displaying a variety of backgrounds and quality of lighting, illustrate individual patterns or shapes.

Chapter One — A Foundation

What is Flow Blue?

origins of the color blue

One of the most esthetic auras known to man is the color blue. The blue seen on Flow Blue ceramic ware is derived from cobalt oxide. Cobalt is a shiny silver-white magnetic metal element found with iron and nickel. Cobalt, when separated and reduced to a powder, can be from tan to dark black in color. It is only after this powder has been applied and fired in a kiln that it will turn blue in color. It is used for coloring many different types of wares such as glass, ceramics etc. In England, cobalt was even used in the textile industry to whiten linens. When cobalt oxide is given the addition of other metallic oxides, such as nickel or silver, different shades of blue are attained. This spectrum of blue can be from a dark black blue and will progress from the most brilliant to the lightest of shades.[1] In general, a deeper blue color is achieved, with the purest of cobalt.

The use of cobalt as a coloring agent can be traced back as far as 2000 BC. The Egyptians used it to color items in their pyramids. The Chinese, however, brought cobalt blue colored earthenware to the forefront. Robert Copeland states that cobalt was used to decorate pottery in China during the T' ang Dynasty (AD 618-907).[2] Mr. Copeland further states that he believes this cobalt was exported from Persia, giving us the indication of Persia's use of this substance on and before these dates. The blue decorated earthenware produced by the Chinese had a profound affect on Europe, and soon after the first pieces of Chinese porcelain arrived there, the search for mines there ensued, and was discovered as early as the 1500s in Bohemia. The Dutch purchased large quantities of this Bohemian mined ore at the turn of the 17th century.

It is believed that the first furnace used for extracting cobalt in England was in use by Roger Kinnaston in 1772.[3] Cobalt as a commodity was growing rapidly. As its use broadened, the demand became ever stronger. The expansion of more mines in England increased the amount of cobalt available, but the need was so great that it was still importing cobalt from other countries. It should be noted here that cobalt at this time in history, when fired in a kiln, was the only known substance that could be applied to a ceramic body and be stable enough to withstand the extreme high heat. It wasn't until after the 1820s that other stable colors were discovered.[4] Some of these other colors, such as red from ocher, were used as polychrome decoration on Flow Blue. These other colors, and how they relate to Flow Blue, will be discussed as the need arises throughout the text.

We can conclude from this that the use of cobalt in the worldwide ceramic industry in the eighteenth century was expanding at a massive rate. In England, the Spode and Wedgwood potteries were leading the way on the use of cobalt. The color blue, when used as a decorating agent on ceramics, was creating a steadily increasing market.

the ceramic body

The use of clay as a hardened substance has been with us for centuries. The Romans used clay mixed with straw to make bricks that were merely dried in the sun.[5] The first earthenware forms were made from clay, fired at low temperatures, and used mostly for utilitarian purposes such as jugs or bowls. The first designs used on these vessels were simple inscribed lines that formed a pattern. It appears that even in those times a basic utilitarian item was not enough, it also had to be esthetic. Over the centuries, improvements in the style of ceramics as well as the body of clay were steadily made.

The British were using a new way to decorate their basic earthenware in the first half of the eighteenth century.[6] This new improvement was in the form of a salt glaze. It was discovered that sprinkling sodium chloride over the clay body before it was fired in the kiln would produce a very hard, shiny surface. During this firing process, the salt would volatilize and create a vitreous glaze. It is to be noted here that unglazed earthenware, with the exception of true porcelain, even after it has been fired in a kiln, can still absorb moisture. Porcelain is fired at such a high temperature (around 2000 degrees) that it is rendered non-porous. This new salt glaze helped to prevent this. With the invention of the salt glaze, new refinements were destined to occur.

Using salt glazed earthenware as a prototype, the English led the way to new improvements. Sometime between 1720 and 1740, John Astbury of Shelton mixed Devonshire clays with calcined flint and coated these earthenwares with a lead glaze instead of salt. After the final firing, the wares came out a creamy off-white color. However, this was not the desirable pure white body that eventually would evolve. The new "creamware," in spite of that fact, became very popular, and sold widely in an assortment of decoration.[7] The popularity of creamware was further supported by the fact that it was reasonably inexpensive to buy; especially when compared to Chinese Porcelain. The body of this new creamware should be considered earthenware and not stoneware, which was a term merely used to advertise and enhance it for sale.[8]

This new creamware was perfected and immortalized by Josiah Wedgwood. In 1765, Wedgwood was given an order for a coffee service from Queen Charlotte. The coffee set was completed by the end of that year and was so well taken that future orders from the Queen were given. This led Wedgwood to change the label of his creamware to "Queensware."[9] Soon the new creamware was being widely produced by many potteries all over England. For a further perspective, we reference the *Historical Archaeology Vol.25, No.1, 1991,* by George L. Miller. He states, "During the second half of the 18th century, a revolution took place in the English ceramic industry in Staffordshire. Developing technology, transportation, introduction of new raw materials, glazes, and marketing culminated in the Staffordshire industry becoming one of the dominant suppliers of ceramics to a world market. One of the major products of that revolution was creamware, which was introduced in the early 1760s and went on to become the dominant ceramic ware used during the rest of the century. By the late 1790s, however, the demand for creamware was declining, and it had become the cheapest refined ware available." This volume further states that, "While it consistently remained the cheapest ceramic, its appearance changed over that period. By the 1830s, creamware was considerably lighter in color and would be classed as a whiteware by most archaeologists."

With the trend set by creamware, the development that followed was a goal to have a pure white ceramic body that was light yet strong for the blue, as well as other forms of decorations to be applied on. Here again, Wedgwood comes to the forefront as an innovator in the ceramic world. In 1779, Wedgwood added a small amount of cobalt to the glaze and introduced "pearlware."[10] This new innovation was not so much to improve the main body of the piece, but rather, this addition of cobalt to the glaze made it appear whiter.

In 1813, Charles Mason took out a patent (#3724) for his new "ironstone." This new ware was much stronger than normal earthenware and was probably created to compete against the Chinese and their porcelain. This new ware proved to be very durable and was exported to the United States and other countries. Yet as durable as it was, it was much too heavy and cumbersome. Mason's patent ended in 1827, which left other English potteries free to improve on Mr. Mason's original formula. However, other English potteries had already formulated their own "stone" wares. Spode had "stone china" circa 1813, and "newstone" circa 1820. The salability of the term "ironstone" is deeply imbedded in our subconscious. It gives way to the thought of a highly durable, ever-lasting set of dishes. Even though there persists a controversy over the workability of Mr. Mason's formula, his icon of "ironstone" remains with us to this day.[11] For further reference I offer another description that I have read, "Ironstone china, fine felspathic ware made by C. J. Mason in the early 19th century, sometimes referred to as Mason's ironstone. Not a china in the sense of a bone china, but more accurately described as a white stoneware. Early indications that the body contained prepared iron stone are now considered to be fallacious. It is generally supposed that the name was adopted merely as a highly successful commercial trade name to introduce this very strong tableware body."

The popular white ironstone/granite was a continuation of the stonewares being produced, including creamwares.[12] This all white, white ironstone/granite demonstrated the potter's art as never before. Because it was not decorated with a transfer print, its beauty and salability relied strictly on its artistic shapes. White ironstone/granite proved to be a very strong and durable ware.

White ironstone/granite changed in style as we progressed from the Early to Late Victorian Periods. To better describe this to you, I have sought the help of experts Ernie and Bev Dieringer to explain what they feel were changes white ironstone/granite transgressed as it arrived in the late period.

A new process that improved the strength of earthenware in relation to creamware, and was lighter than Mason's ironstone was soon discovered. It was found that by taking clay and mixing it with calcined flint stones that had been ground in water, a new tougher lighter body was produced. The process to calcine flints was first discovered in 1720 by Robert Astbury. To calcine the flints, they were fired at a high enough temperature to remove impurities, but not so high as to melt or fuse the flints. They also discovered that this process left the flint, even after it was mixed with the clay, a pure white in color. This new stoneware/ironstone type of body was a perfect match for many types of decoration.

The differences between this stoneware/ironstone type of body and porcelain are three fold. One, in porcelain the clay mixture con-

---

White ironstone China, Under Flow Blue

Under most flow blue there is a world-famous Patent Ironstone China. The term Ironstone was coined by Charles James Mason and patented in 1813 as a clever way to market this new China which was harder, more durable, and less likely to chip. Over a hundred other potters developed their own formulas but used names like Granite, Stone Granite or Pearl Stone which all soon became a major part of the China produced in England primarily for export. It was made to compete with the Chinese blue painted China on the world market. Its heavy body was formed in the simple shapes of the Chinese wares and lent its self to a newly created cheaper way of decorating done with engraved designs that were transferred on rather than hand painted. That transfer ware done in blue had been popular long before Ironstone was introduced and continued its popularity. Eventually the blue glaze was intentionally made to flow. It created a market in America that lasted almost a century. The body and the formulas changed over that period of time, starting with heavy, simple shapes to the more geometric panel shapes of the 1830-1840s. During the 1840s a market was found in America for those shapes left in plain undecorated white ironstone, and during the mid Victorian period it dominated their export market. Between 1855 and 1865 the modelers and their potters created hundreds of richly embossed designs, which became almost as elaborate as the transfer and painted designs. Some of the paneled bodies changed to ribbed melon like shapes and they included fruits, grains, vegetables, flowers, vines, and leaves. All intentionally aimed at the tastes of Americans whose population at that time was over eighty percent agricultural. They were usually of the same heavy body as the earlier period but the quality of the glazes varied, some being very crazed. By 1870 the fashion reversed and the new shapes became simpler. New technology allowed potters to gradually make the body shapes thinner and lighter weight with clean craze free glazes. Body styles developed into an almost stark plainness. Eliminating much of the embossment, simplifying the handles and finials to functional forms and the body shapes to oval, round, and rectangular forms. This was a China with a Puritan aesthetic and chosen by the Shaker communities in America. By the 1890s embossing is again added, but of a finer more delicate manner. During this later period, flow blue became very popular again and decorated much of the white ironstone produced as well as some porcelain.

Ironstone china is opaque earthenware as opposed to porcelain, which is translucent. The difference can be seen if a piece of ironstone is held up to a strong bright light while moving the other hand behind it. Movement of the hand cannot be seen through opaque ironstone, while translucent porcelain allows it to show through.

Ernie & Bev Dieringer
W. Reading, CT
April 2, 2001

tains kaolin.[13] This kaolin is plastic in nature and can withstand the high temperature required to produce porcelain, without melting. Kaolin is also the whitest form of clay, and is sometimes called Cornish clay. The second reason is that porcelain is fired to a temp at around 2000 degrees, while stoneware is only fired at about 1200 degrees. Porcelain is fired at such a high temperature that true vitrification occurs. This is where, during the firing stage, the body and the glaze become one and render the piece non-porous. Since stoneware is fired at a lower temperature, it does not reach the point of true vitrification. Thus the biscuit body remains porous to some extent, even though the outer glaze is non-porous. This is why you will see stains on a piece of stoneware where the outer glaze has crazing. Food oils will seep through the fine cracks in the glaze and stain the biscuit body below. The nemesis for porcelain is stoneware's lack of true vitrification, even though it was marketed "semi-porcelain."

Glaze misses on the surface, or a poor or uneven glaze, are two reasons that will cause a piece to craze. However, in many cases crazing occurs because the glaze and biscuit body are of different substances. As a result, they will react differently to a sudden change in extreme hot or cold conditions. If the biscuit body expands from heat or contracts from cold faster that the outer glaze, crazing will occur. The glaze should have a lower thermal expansion than the main body. In this way, during the glost firing, the body will shrink more than the glaze and force the glaze to compress. A glaze will become stronger when it is compressed. Age may make a piece more brittle and provide more opportunities for crazing to occur, but age as a sole factor does not cause crazing. Rather, it is caused from a sudden change in extreme temperatures or improper handling.

You will see some pieces of stoneware marked semi-vitreous or semi-porcelain. These terms do not indicate that a piece of ceramic is porcelain, but rather these were marketing terms used to sell the product. We must remember that the English potteries were in strong competition with China and France, countries that produced enormous amounts of porcelain. From the English standpoint, it would make marketing sense to label their wares semi-porcelain.

The third reason is porcelain is translucent, which means that you can see light through it. On the other hand, stoneware is opaque, meaning you cannot see light through it. Although it should be said here, that thinly potted stoneware may appear to be translucent, which can fool you into thinking it is porcelain. England also produced porcelain of the highest quality. It was, however, very expensive for the consumer. This new stoneware was less expensive to make and helped the English gain their share of the market place. Let's face it, the pottery owners were in the business to make money, and with this new ware they were given the opportunity. This stoneware/ironstone body is what Late Victorian Flow Blue was produced on and is the core of this book.

the flow process

Flow Blue ceramic ware is manufactured by using transfer printing and hand applied decoration. This technique becomes apparent after the final glost firing (when the pattern and glaze are applied), and will leave the pattern somewhat blurred with a halo effect. In some cases, the flowing of the blue is so extreme that the pattern is almost obliterated. This flowing of the blue was achieved by adding a volatile chloride to the saggar during this final firing. While it is true that all Flow Blue is blue and white, the reverse cannot be stated accurately. All blue and white is not Flow Blue. It also can be further stated that all blue and white colored ceramic ware was not intended to be Flow Blue. Cobalt oxide, by nature, is unstable when fired in the kiln and some unintentional flowing of the blue can occur. This "accidental" blurring does not designate a piece to be Flow Blue. More accurately speaking, the blue is a color and the flowing of the blue is achieved with the intentionally applied process stated above. Flow Blue is, in

fact, an exploitation of cobalt oxide's instability and its tendency to run when fired at high temperatures. This process saw change made by the potteries as it progressed from the Early to Late Victorian periods.

In a search through reference works for Flow Blue, you will find the earliest Flow Blue pattern produced to be CHENSI in 1835 by John Meir.[14] There is some confusion as to the real maker of this pattern.[15] It also could have been manufactured by John Maddock who used the same printed or impressed initials for a factory mark, as did John Meir. John Maddock was in production from 1842 thru 1855 when the factory name was changed to John Maddock & Sons (1855-1987). There may have been some experimentation in the development of the Flow Blue process late in the 1830s, wherein pieces of true Flow Blue "may" be found. But most researchers today agree that Flow Blue was first being produced in the very early 1840s.

The differences between Early, Middle, and Late Victorian Flow Blue are many. They include, but are not limited to, patterns or designs, thickness of the body, the shape of the body style, clarity of the pattern, and different shades of the blue. All share equal importance and help to balance the transfer from one period to the next. The key to a better understanding of all Flow Blue comes when you realize, and can recognize, the differences between the three eras of production. Let's look at some of the more obvious differences between the three periods of Flow Blue production, as far as shapes are concerned.

In the early period, we find most patterns manufactured were Chinoiserie, in imitation of the Chinese. Oriental scenes dominate almost exclusively the designs produced. The pieces are thickly potted, and plates have paneled or flat sided edges. Platters, bowls, and tureens are rectangular in shape. Teapots, sugars, creamers, and pitchers are hexagonal in form, with very little embossing applied. The flow of the blue is very heavy and obvious. See Plate 1 for an example of Early Victorian Flow Blue.

Plate 1. AMOY plate, 1844, by W. Davenport & Company, 10 1/2" in diameter. This plate shows the typical traits of the Early Victorian Flow Blue period. This plate has a paneled edge, heavy flowing of the blue, body thickness, and a Chinese type pattern. *Courtesy of Terry and Ann Potts, Illinois.* $150+

As we enter the middle period, subtle changes occur. The wares are potted somewhat thinner than before and we see an influx of scenic, floral, geometric or abstract types of designs that reflect the aesthetic movement being applied. Smooth gentle scallops are applied to plate edges; hollowware begins to appear rounder; sugars, creamers, and teapots are somewhat reduced in size. Slate and brown colored patterns are very popular and Flow Blue production is reduced to some degree. We find, for whatever reason, less Flow Blue produced in the middle period than any other era of production.

If the middle period was the least in Flow Blue production, then most definitely the late period saw the highest. In the late period, floral patterns dominate heavily and Art Nouveau had its debut. Pieces are now potted very thinly and are heavily embossed. The paneled look is gone with scallops now dominating the edge of plates, platters, and tureen lids. The scallops are deep and clearly defined. Bowls, tureens, platters, cups, sugars, creamers, and pitchers become more round or oval in shape. Because of new machinery and control techniques, the flowing of the blue is reduced and the patterns are clearer or more distinct in clarity. Please see Plate 2 for an excellent example of Late Victorian Flow Blue.

Plate 2. MELBOURNE plate, 1903, by W. H. Grindley & Co., 10" in diameter. This plate shows the typical traits of the Late Victorian Flow Blue period. This plate has a deeply defined scalloped edge, clearly defined pattern, heavily embossed, and thinness of body. *Courtesy of Shell and Jim Lewis, Blue Heaven Antiques, Geneva, Illinois.* $100 - $125

How the "process" of producing Flow Blue changed, and its affect on the "flowing" of the blue from the Early to Late Victorian period is of strong importance to this book. As we have stated before and in general, as Flow Blue ware progressed through its three periods of production, it went from a strong blurring of the pattern in the Early Victorian period, to a more refined clearer image of the pattern in the Late Victorian era. To better understand this process change and its impact on the flowing of the pattern, we need to look at the differences in the "flow process."

In the Early (and most of the Middle) Victorian eras, there are two parts to the flowing process we need to look at. The flowing of the blue was achieved by the use of two coordinating processes. In the first, the blue used to print the pattern was a special mix or recipe, and secondly, a chemical mix was put in the saggar during the glost firing. Most potteries that produced Flow Blue, during any period of production, had their own recipes to achieve the flow effect. Geoffrey Godden referenced the following example as found in Sheridan Muspratt's *Chemistry, Theoretical, Practical and Analytical*, W. Mackenzie, Glasgow, 1860.[16]

---

flow powder (chemical recipe) placed in the saggar

Quicklime	5 parts
Salt	2 parts
Nitre	¼ parts
Borax	¼ parts

The ingredients were mixed and placed evenly at the bottom of each saggar. This volatile chloride mix would change to a gas during the high heat achieved in the kiln and caused the flowing or blurring of the pattern.

recipe for the blue color

Black prepared oxide of cobalt	12 lbs
Flint glass	4 lbs
Oxide of Zinc	2 lbs

In this recipe for the color pigment of the pattern, each ingredient had its effect. The cobalt oxide created the color blue. The flint glass was used as a fluxing agent to adhere the printed pattern to the ceramic body, and helped to make the blue either lighter or darker. The oxide of zinc helped to determine the shade of blue.

Another way the chemicals were added to the saggar was putting them in a cup that was merely placed in the saggar. This probably came as a later innovation. The amount of pattern flow each piece received depended on where it was placed in the saggar. For example, plates were stacked in the saggar separated by stilts (small tripods of hard ceramic used to create space between each piece). With this method of filling saggars, the plates on top flowed the most because they were more exposed to the elements. Manufacturing Flow Blue through this type of process created very unpredictable results. Because there was no way of controlling the extent of the flow when the wares were removed from the saggars after the glost firing, each piece was somewhat different than the rest. Catch as catch can, if you will.

It has been stated in many reference works that the potteries used seconds, thirds, and otherwise defective bisque fired wares (an undecorated item after its first firing to harden the clay) for the production of their Flow Blue. After my observations of Early Victorian Flow Blue, I find no disagreement with this statement. I have seen many pieces that were warped, had glazed over chips, glazed over clay cracks, and many other less than perfect attributes. Yet Americans loved, and took to this Flow Blue china readily and with relish. The English were more than happy to have this market, and by the use of seconds, they were able to keep the cost down and remain competitive for the American market. But as the American market increased, so did the demand. As this high demand increased the potteries production, first run pieces were needed to help fill the orders.

This new attraction to Flow Blue by the Americans came at a time when they were romancing the use of the highly durable white ironstone/granite. All white ware was immensely popular then, as it still is today. In fact, since all white ceramic ware was first produced, there has never been a time in American history that all white sets of china were not available or desired. However times were changing, and with those changes came an inevitable change in fashion. Early Victorian Flow Blue was a part of those fashion changes.

Flow Blue lagged in popularity during the Middle Victorian period, but became immensely popular as we approached the Late Victorian era. However, its appearance would change. If Late Victorian Flow Blue had been manufactured under the same process as the earlier versions had, the flowing of the blue would have been the same, but it is not. Flow Blue produced at the Spode factory never had too much diffusion of the blue, no matter what period it was produced. What were they doing different? I posed this, along with other questions to Mr. Robert Copeland, the author of, *Spode's Willow Pattern and other designs after the Chinese*, Artillery House, 1990, who was kind enough to write me with his views on Flow Blue, and has permitted me to publish the text of his letter.

Dear Mr. Van Buskirk

Thank you for your letter of June 1 and your enquiry about Flow Blue.

I do not know about the practices in the pottery industry in general. My knowledge is limited in this respect to what I "think" was practiced at the Copeland manufactory.

I am not surprised that you find the flow blue patterns better defined in the later Victorian period. The market must have become weary of the awful blotchy patterns that started as 'seconds' and were dumped on the American market in the early 1840s. I imagine that the use of the separate cup of flow powder gave way to modified recipes of the blue colour itself.

Copeland's had always, as far as my knowledge of examples goes, exercised restraint in their flow blue patterns. These showed a gentle diffusion of the blue from the printed lines and stipple dots.

Here are some recipes of about 1870:

Flow Blue Flux
> Feldspar
> Tin Oxide
> Flint
> Paris White (Whiting)

Another Flow Blue Flux
> Flint
> 1 ½ Cornish Stone
> ½ Paris White (Whiting)
> Tin Oxide

Flow Blue Calx
> Cobalt Oxide
> Flux (no note as to which flux)

Strong Flow Blue
> Cobalt Oxide
> Flux

Flow Blue for Painting
> 4 ½ Cobalt Oxide
> Flux

A recipe of about 1935 – 1940 Flow Blue
> Black Cobalt Oxide
> Flint Glass
> 1 ½ Zinc Oxide
> Whiting

Mix whiting, Zinc oxide and glass all together and muller them. Taking a saucer full at a time, dry, then sieve, mix with the Cobalt, then sieve four times more.

Calcine in the earthenware Biscuit oven; bottom of the Forebung (about 1100 C)

I believe we produced some College and other special plates for the United States market in the 1930s.

As you see there is no amount of chorine in these recipes so they will not flow beyond the fluxing property of the cobalt and flint itself.

Blue is blue, so 'flow blue' is an "effect." This effect is achieved by the fluxing nature of cobalt in a lead glaze and this may be achieved by a process but more especially by the choice and proportions of the ingredients. Certainly the addition of flow powder in a cup within the saggar is part of a process.

I hope that these observations may help you.

Robert Copeland
20 June 2000

The production of Flow Blue is no different than the production of any other manufactured item. If you change the manufacturing process, you have changed the product. The manufacturers will call this change research and development. This change to the flow process was a necessary development to bring Flow Blue into the Late Victorian period. I believe this change of the flow process from the early to the late periods, as Mr. Copeland describes it, is the key to how it changed. It is my contention that Late Victorian Flow Blue should be considered just that, Flow Blue. The flow process may have changed, as well as the extent of flow, but the term Flow Blue and what it represents to the ceramic world, I believe is reflected equally in all three eras. There are some purists who look at the early period as the true era of Flow Blue. Their reasoning is the age, shape, and extent of flow on the pieces for that era. However, Late Victorian Flow Blue, as it evolved, will continue to stand on its own merits; even though there are differences, and in obvious form. We find reference to this fact in many forms. The catalogs of that era including, Sears Roebuck & Co. and Montgomery Ward & Co. refer to this china in their ads as Flow or Flown Blue. Most Late Victorian potteries include an "FB" on the back of their Flow Blue wares. The obvious reference for this "FB" is to indicate that piece to be Flow Blue, and should be further noted here that the only pieces that do have the "FB" applied to them are ones with a cobalt blue pattern. In at least one example, Alfred Meakin goes a step farther by putting "Flown Blue" above the pottery mark applied to his pattern COBURG. With these facts behind us, it becomes known that it is not the extent of the flow that makes a piece Flow Blue, but rather the intent of the "process" that produced it.

other flow colors

Besides cobalt blue, other colors were used in the flow process. It becomes evident that not only was the color blue popular, but its appeal was the flowing of the color. The English potteries recognized this American attraction to the "flow" in Flow Blue and viewed it as an opportunity to expand. Other colors were selected and had limited use and acceptance. The 1899 Montgomery Wards Catalog, page 24, lists a pattern by W. H. Grindley & Co. called ALLIANCE. The ad states: "*The design is of small flower sprays in new-flown green, a real sea green, put on under the glaze and will not wear off. The body is a very close approach to china.*" The Grindley body style illustrated in this ad is what I call, Gr-M. This coding will be fully explained in the next chapter, which covers the W. H. Grindley & Co. pottery. This ad also helps to verify for us that Late Victorian Flow Blue was not porcelain, but was instead: *a very close approach to china.* You will find that a pottery not only produced a pattern in Flow Blue, they also made it in other colors such as Flow Green. An example would be the Grindley pattern, ARGYLE. It was made in three colors including Flow Green, and on the back of a piece you will see the initials "FB." This was done, as in the case of Flow Blue wares, to indicate that the pattern on this piece had been intentionally flown. Green was first possible for under glaze transfer prints, 1822-1825.

Brown was another color, but it had very limited use. In all of my research I have only seen about three or four pieces of Flow Brown that had the code "FB" on the back. Pink was made possible in 1832, with the addition of chromium. However, I do not believe that it was ever made to flow.

Another type of flow ware similar to the color brown was Flow Mulberry. Flow Mulberry was produced primarily from 1840 thru 1860, and obtained its brown/purple sepia color from manganese carbonate. Mulberry has the same body composition and was made to flow under the same process as Flow Blue. Flow Mulberry was being sold in Late Victorian catalogs and was manufactured primarily by the Johnson Bros. Ltd. and the J. & G. Meakin Ltd. potteries. Here again, as in the case of Late Victorian Flow Blue, there are questions as to the legitimacy of Late Victorian Flow Mulberry. On every piece of Johnson Bros. Ltd. and J. & G. Meakin Ltd. mulberry I have seen, the letter code "M" is printed on the back. This would give us the indication, that at least as far as the potteries were concerned, it was Flow Mulberry. In the catalogs it is listed as Flow Mulberry and the color is listed as a "rich Heliotrope color." The color tends to lean towards purple in the examples of Late Victorian Flow Mulberry that I have seen, and the feeling is that because of this color change, it is not true Flow Mulberry. Once again, I have enlisted the help of an expert on the subject. I wrote to Henry Kelly, the author of *Scottish Ceramics*, Schiffer Publishing ltd., 1999, for his views on the subject. Mr. Kelly has graciously allowed me to publish the text of his returned letter.

Mulberry wares

The mulberry bush is probably best known nowadays as part of a children's rhyme but was formerly of great importance in Europe and Asia since mulberries are the principal food of silkworms. Presumably the plant is still of immense importance in the Far East. In Britain certainly the berries themselves were used and to a certain extent still are used, as a source of jams and jellies, which have a beautiful dark purple color.

In the pottery trade mulberry is principally famous as being one of the first underglaze colors to be used successfully after blue. Underglaze blue had been known for some time, made from cobalt oxide and very popular, but inevitably other colors were wanted for variety's sake. The trouble was that most of the known colors used on pots were unstable at the temperature at which the pot was to be fired. A very limited range of high-firing colors was known and can be seen on Pratt Ware, comprising blue, yellow, green, brown, and black. Mulberry first appeared as an underglaze color on ironstone around 1830, was immensely popular and then, around 1860, disappeared almost completely. Named after the fruit it was a very dark purple, verging on black. It was based on manganese dioxide and was, like blue, able to flow, which seems to have been a particularly popular phenomenon-in the U.S.A. However, unlike flow blue, flow mulberry was just as popular in Britain as in America.

Recipes for underglaze mulberry have appeared in print in trade magazines and below are two from the Pottery Gazette:

May 1, 1884

oxide of tin 8; prepared oxide of cobalt 5; borax 4; manganese 10; stone 4. Calcine in biscuit oven.

It will be noticed that both of these recipes come from a period after the heyday of mulberry. This is perhaps less impor-

tant than it seems since most of the recipes given in the Pottery Gazette would have come from old recipe books, particularly as virtually no one was using underglaze manganese in the 1880s.

In Scotland, manganese was replaced in popularity with purple underglaze, which was used also in England but seems to have been less popular. This lasted until the late 1870s.

May 1, 1884

Prepared oxide of cobalt 1; pink (No.1) 16. No. 1 has the following recipe: oxide of tin 26; whiting 11; bichromate of potash 1. Calcine twice.

March 1, 1887

4 lb. Pink; ½ lb. Oxide cobalt. Grind together.

The two recipes are not dissimilar. The color obtained was much brighter than mulberry and not to be confused with it. It certainly was not so confused by the Scottish public who bought the purple color for more than ten years with great enthusiasm. However, by the late 1870s purple was being succeeded by brown, a color not to be confused with sepia or mulberry. This was a full reddish brown and many patterns, which had been popular in blue, were also at this time produced in brown. The recipes are again quite different from any of the above.

May 1, 1884 – Common Brown

oxide of zinc2; red lead 1. Top of glost oven.

March 1, 1887 – Common claret brown.

40 lb. oxide of zinc; 6 lb. bichromate potash; 4 lb. red lead; 5 lb. iron scales. Calcine in hardest part of glost oven. Obviously this required a higher temperature than the others to mature.

Of the three great rivals to blue and white, mulberry is still the favorite with collectors.

Henry Kelly
April 10, 2000

Times change, and with those changes came different recipes and processes for the production of Flow Mulberry. Esthetically, there are differences between the late and early mulberry, in addition to the changes in recipes Mr. Kelly gives us. I believe as I did for Flow Blue, that there is room in this world for the two different versions of Flow Mulberry. It is hard for a researcher looking at Late Victorian catalogs to deny that Flow Mulberry was being produced in that period. But it is my guess, that each version of Flow Mulberry will have its dedicated collectors.

associated wares

There are other associated Flow Blue wares that used different colors and pattern techniques. They each have their own special style and add a different dimension to Flow Blue collecting.

Slate blue is merely a variant of Cobalt Oxide that had other oxides mixed with it to create a darker, almost black blue image. In many cases, a halo effect is present. During the Middle Victorian period and through the 1880s, the slate wares were simple lines forming branches with flowers and geometric abstract designs. In the Late Victorian period, starting with the 1890s, we find that the pattern techniques to create designs were advanced. With the improved quality of stipple dots and fine lines, large shaded areas are created, and the pattern tends to cover a larger area than in the Middle Victorian period. In general, the patterns are more sophisticated and detail oriented.

Brush Stroke is where cobalt oxide is made into a liquid pigment and the design is stenciled, brushed or hand painted and then fired in the kiln. We find that because each piece was hand done, not only was each pattern unique, but every piece in each pattern was a one of a kind. Brush Stroke's popularity was mostly in the 1850s and 1860s. We find very little, if any, Brush Stroke during the Late Victorian period.

Polychrome is when more than one color was applied to an existing transfer or brush stroke pattern. In most cases this polychrome was applied over the glaze and seldom under the glaze. When polychrome was applied over the glaze it created the need for an additional firing to harden on the color pigment. Large amounts of polychrome wares were produced in the Middle Victorian period and extended itself into the late period. In the Late Victorian period, we find that most of the polychrome has been applied under the glaze, with red being the main color used.

Gaudy is a term that describes a Brush Stroke pattern that has polychrome decoration applied.

Copper Lustre is copper oxide or copper oxide mixed with gold. It was usually brushed on and applied most commonly to Brush Stroke or Gaudy wares.

other related wares

Even though I am listing these wares as related to Flow Blue, caution is the key word here. Many of the following were intended, and indeed are true Flow Blue wares. However, many of the pieces are not. Because of the uncertainty of these wares caution is advised, and your reasoning for purchasing the item should be thoroughly determined. In general, lower prices should prevail for these items.

Commemorative ware has been around for a very long time. For this type of ware, many different types of items were made and were produced originally to commemorate a special event or person (c1880s).

Series ware is a series of plates showing different scenes of a related subject. During the Late Victorian Period, the subject matter had a wide spectrum that included game birds, waterfowl, wild flowers, etc.

Relief Molded jugs are typically Toby jugs or steins with faces or other designs molded onto the surface of the jug.

Souvenir ware was very common throughout the Middle and Late Victorian periods. Typically, with this type of ware there would have been different scenes from a town or city on it, and pieces were either purchased or given as a premium. We know that with Souvenir ware many pieces were made and intended to be Flow Blue, but there are still many uncertain pieces to include them all as Flow Blue. Your discretion is advised.

myths, misconceptions, and untruths

If a falsehood is innocently believed and stated for a long enough period, it will eventually become accepted as fact. This scenario is the haze that covers Flow Blue. Anytime a collectible item such as Flow Blue becomes enormously popular, the doors will always be open for innocent or well-intentioned misconceptions to occur. The following is intended to be an attempt to correct the myths, misconceptions, and untruths that surround Flow Blue.

The body of Flow Blue is a fired, hardened ceramic, and when the pattern and glaze is fired on in the kiln, the pattern cannot "soak" or "bleed" through to the back. The blue pigment is, however, diffused with the glaze on the surface of the piece. The color pigment seen on the back of a piece came from the one below it in the saggar during the glost firing. During this glost firing, the pattern is being diffused with the glaze and gases are created. These gases will contain some of the cobalt oxide, which will rise up to the one above it in the saggar. In most cases, this will result simply in a blue haze with no definition of pattern. However, the closer the pieces are in the saggar, the greater definition of the pattern can occur. I have seen many broken pieces of Flow Blue, which will expose the center core, and I can attest to the fact that the color does not "soak" through. I can attest further to this misconception. I have a cake plate in the pattern DENTON by Grindley, which has a very close replication of the pattern on its underside. However, the two do not match up. The underside replication does not correspond directly to the pattern above it. If on the top surface a particular part of the pattern was at 12:00 o'clock, that same part of the pattern on the underside is at the 2:00 o'clock position. This clearly represents that any colorization on the underside of an item comes from the one below it in the saggar.

While there are some pieces of porcelain that were intended to be Flow Blue, porcelain is intentionally excluded from this category. We must, as collectors, look at what we collect. Flow Blue is a stoneware/ironstone ceramic and was made with a different approach, style, and intent than porcelain. They were made from different substances and fired differently in the kiln. Porcelain, such as that made by Limoges, has many patterns that contain cobalt oxide. Should we include them all as Flow Blue? To do this would leave the doors wide open for anything to be called Flow Blue, and the only true result would be to muddy the waters of an otherwise exquisite collectible. One of the greatest errors is that Flow Blue, on many of the Internet Auction sites, is listed under the porcelain category. Flow Blue is not porcelain, but some porcelain pieces can be considered Flow Blue.

I heard the comment once that a fellow said he had two plates in a slate colored pattern with one of those plates having some flow, and that he knew some time soon that the other one would start to flow too. We need to remember that we are talking about one hundred year old, or older plates here, and there exists a misconception that the pattern could still begin to flow, as though it were a living thing. This idea could not be further from the truth. Once a piece of Flow Blue is fired in a kiln, there is no going back. What you see is what you get.

It is believed that the majority of Late Victorian Flow Blue is circa 1890. The truth is that the majority of all Late Victorian Flow Blue was made in the first quarter of the 20th century, and in a later chapter of this book, this myth will be dispelled in detail.

I know of no hand painted patterns, or designs if you prefer, that were produced during the Late Victorian period. There was some polychrome decoration applied by hand, but the patterns were transfer printed. Transfer printing was the cost cutting technology of that period, and helped to keep England ahead of their competition.

Historic Blue is Flow Blue, and was manufactured using a pearlware body. Historic Blue was produced in the 1810s, 1820s, and 1830s and was not intended to be Flow Blue. It is merely an all over pattern and colored using cobalt blue. The process for making Flow Blue was not in use at this time and wouldn't be until the late 1830s or very early 1840s.

Because a piece of ceramic is blue and white, does not designate it to be Flow Blue. The case in point here is the pattern BLUE WILLOW and all variations of this pattern. BLUE WILLOW is a separate category by itself, just like Historic Blue. The only known pottery that produced BLUE WILLOW, with the intent of being Flow Blue, was Doulton & Co. Ltd.

A common belief is that crazing is normal and harmless on a piece of Flow Blue. Normal in this case is a misuse of terms; the term common would be better. Is crazing harmless, or can it cause harm? The answer is yes. The truth is that crazing only occurs where there is glaze misses, a poor or uneven glaze, or when an item is mishandled. The chances are greater that if crazing exists on a piece, it came as a result of mishandling. This can happen when an item is subjected to extreme cold weather conditions and heat is allowed to warm the piece too quickly. This will cause the glaze to crack (craze) because the bisque body will contract faster than the outer glaze. Age may make a piece of Flow Blue more brittle, but crazing usually occurs from the improper handling of the glazed ceramic ware. Buying through the mail is a common way today for an opportunity of crazing to occur. If it is very cold outside when your item is being mailed to you, and you open the package right away, this warm touching of a very cold item with your hands is enough to cause crazing. Think of the glaze as a very thin fragile glass, which is what it really is. If you purchase a cup with staining on it, and you have it professionally cleaned, the stain will return if you use it. A stain on any item of Flow Blue comes only as a result of the crazing of the glaze. With the glaze crazed, it will allow liquids and other deteriorating chemicals to seep through the tiny cracks in the glaze and be absorbed by the bisque body where stains and further damage will result.

I have heard and seen the comment "a tight hairline crack," and that the hairline was "on one side only." The existence of a hairline/crack that does not go through to the other side, is really a misuse of terms. A piece of ceramic has a hard brittle body, and if a crack occurs in that body, it will remain a brittle body but with a crack in it. If an item of ceramic has a crack, that crack will be all the way through the body of the piece. If you see what appears to be a hairline crack on one side only, it more than likely is a crack in the glaze, which is really crazing. To prove this theory, try to crack a piece of glass on one side only. There is one area that may look like an exception to this rule. Occasionally, a piece during its manufacturing can have what is known as a clay crack, but this is really not the type of crack we are discussing here. This type of crack will occur in the form of a crease on the surface, and comes as a result of an abnormality in the clay during its drying time. It will separate to form a line similar to a crack, but you will know this for what it is because you will see that it was glazed over and given its final firing by the pottery.

The main body of Late Victorian Flow Blue is painted white before the pattern is applied is incorrect. The English in fact, spent many years perfecting an all white body for their ceramic ware. I have seen many broken pieces, and in every case the pure white body prevails. It only achieves its glossy look after the glaze has been applied.

In describing a piece of Flow Blue, I have heard people say that "most of the pattern was still intact." When the pattern is applied under the glaze, as all Late Victorian Flow Blue was, it becomes impervious to wear. In fact, after the pattern has been applied to a piece and has had its final firing, the pattern color pigment becomes one with the glaze. They are fused permanently together, and even if left in the sun, the pattern will not fade. This is the beauty of under glaze-applied patterns. However, any over glaze applied enamels or polychrome decorations are subject to wear.

Manufacturing Process

It is not my intent to present myself as a master potter. That is a true art that takes years of apprenticeship to acquire. I have, however, researched this field extensively and through this research, it is my hope that I can give you a better understanding of how Flow Blue was made. Many methods of operation were standard for the industry, but I'm sure that each factory had some things they did differently. I would further state, that almost every book I have read on this subject portrays the process somewhat differently than others. Because of these differences, the reader is advised to use the following as a general guide.

In the beginning, all pottery was made by hand; it was a time for the true potters art. Every piece was thrown on a wheel and molded by hand. But as most things were guided by economics, this would soon change. As the pottery market grew and the need for uniformity of like pieces prevailed, the need for faster mechanical means became necessary.[17] Machines were first introduced to the potteries around 1845, which threw an immediate scare into the workers because they felt that they were being replaced.[18] This fear would always be present as new automated production developments were put into practice. One of the greatest innovations was the introduction of the automated flat presser that made plates and similar flat ware. This machine could make six hundred dozen plates per day. These machines had two arms for pulling down two revolving heads. One would flatten the ball clay to a circular bat similar to a pancake. This bat was then placed on the second head containing the plate mold. When the second arm was pulled down pressing the bat into the mold, the plate had been formed, and the whole procedure was ready to start again.[19] These freshly molded pieces were set aside to air dry to the consistency of leather.

For hollow ware, such as teapots, sugars, pitchers, gravy boats, a different method was used. To better illustrate how hollow ware was made, we need to go back to the beginnings of when a new style of dish was produced by a pottery. As the need arose, a pottery would create a new shape/body style of dish to put on the market. Each piece in this new set of dishes would be coordinated together by using the same scalloped edge, embossing, handle shape etc. For each piece in this new set of dishes, an artist would have to draw it on paper. The mold makers would then take these drawings and make a clay model. To further illustrate this, let's look at the process for making the body of a teapot. After the artist made the drawing, the clay modeler would make an exact replica in clay. This clay model was cut in half to make the permanent mold used for production. A plaster of paris mold would be made and both halves of the mold were constructed in such a way that allowed them to be rejoined to produce the final product.[20] With the two halves of the mold put together, slip was poured in and worked around the insides of the mold. After the walls of the teapot in the mold had been built up enough, the excess slip would be poured out. The pot would be removed from the mold only after it had dried enough for safe handling. During this drying period, the plaster would absorb the excess moisture from the slip, and the clay that remained hardened somewhat as it dried. At the appropriate time, the mold would be removed and the seams and rough spots were smoothed by fettling (rubbing the surface) with a wet sponge. The pot was then set aside to further air dry. Slip consisted of similar clay used for other pieces in the set, but was liquefied by adding water to the clay in a container called a "blunger." The consistency of slip is similar to a pancake batter.

To make one teapot, five different pieces had to be first drawn on paper, clay models made, and then the final molds used for production. These five parts to a teapot are the finial, teapot lid, main body, handle, and spout. All the individual parts of the teapot were molded separately and assembled using a small amount of slip to adhere each piece. Calipers were used to make sure the lids fit just right. As you can see, a lot of time and effort went into the making of a single teapot. It is interesting to note here, that the process for making a teapot also made each one unique. Even though each part of the pot was molded the same, all the parts were applied by hand. I have had as many as six teapots in the same pattern and shape, and none were exactly the same. Today that uniqueness is gone because with the exception of the lid the entire teapot would have been mold injected as one piece. This is one way you can tell the difference between the new or modern Flow Blue from the old. It is interesting to note here that so many people call this new Flow Blue a replica. The new Flow Blue wares should not be considered replicas at all, but in fact, should be considered what it really is, "new" Flow Blue. Here are some things to check that will help you to detect a new piece of Flow Blue from an old one. Where the spout is applied to the body of the teapot, several holes are pierced that will allow the liquid to enter the spout. On most new wares, the hole in the pot is as big as the base of the spout. This is because they were molded as one piece. Also the base of the spout will appear to be part of the teapot body. You would never see this on an old teapot because the spout was added after the pot was made. This same rule applies to the teapot handle and the lid finial. I believe that the old and new Flow Blue wares each have their place in this world, but because of values, I also believe in knowing the differences between the two.

Once the wares had air dried sufficiently, and the need arose for them, they were placed in saggars, which were stacked in the kiln for the first or "Bisque" firing. For this firing, the kiln would be brought to a temperature of 950c – 1100c degrees. The fireman, who had exclusive control of the kiln, had a very demanding job. It was his responsibility to bring the temperature up to its proper level and also to control the cooling off period. Timing was everything. If the kiln got too hot too fast the clay could melt, and if it cooled off too fast the wares could crack. The pottery's livelihood was literally in this mans hands. Too much loss from breakage could curtail profits extensively. Once the kiln had cooled sufficiently the wares were removed and were ready for the next step. Once a piece of clay ware has been bisque fired, the process cannot be reversed.[21] If it was porcelain in this bisque state, it would have been fired at a higher temperature and been rendered non-porous. That means that it was virtually impossible to be stained by liquids. This also is what is known as Bisque Porcelain. However, because our example was stoneware and fired at a lower temperature it is not non-porous; thus it is still susceptible to be stained by liquids. It took a great deal more fuel to fire at higher temperatures such as that needed for porcelain. The British were brilliant in their marketing of Late Victorian Flow Blue. They produced it on an ironstone/stoneware type body, which saved on firing costs; potted the wares delicately thin; and then called it semi-porcelain. With their wares so marked and placed in the main market stream, they did very well against their porcelain competition.

Now let's look at how the pattern was applied to this bisque body. With the pattern design drawn on paper, it was traced onto a copper plate. Once the pattern was drawn onto the copper, it was carved into the copper by using a V shaped tool. If the line being carved needed to be a darker shade of blue, it was carved deeper. If the line being carved was to be a lighter shade, it was not carved as deep. Engraving small lines and stipple dots created shaded areas. As the quality of engraving improved so did the quality of the pattern, as well as the variance of color tones. Once the copper plates were finished, they were given to the print shop. When you realize the various sizes of objects in a set of dishes, you realize how many copper plates had to be made in order to create the different sizes of the pattern being produced. In other words, you could not use the same size pattern on a 6" plate that was used on a 10" plate. It had to be reduced in size in order to fit. Mixing the cobalt oxide with its fluxing component and printing oils produced the color. The color was then applied to the copper plates in such a way that insured all the engraved lines were filled; then the surplus wiped off. Strong fiber free tissue paper was applied to the copper plate and rubbed thoroughly to ensure the transfer of all the color to the tissue. The printed transfer was now ready to be applied. The worker would place the printed-paper onto the piece being done and would rub it evenly and with pressure to insure the transfer of color. The paper was then slowly peeled off leaving the transfer print. The newly printed piece was then fired a second time at a temperature of 680c-700c to burn off the oils and harden on the color print. Afterwards, it was dipped into a liquid glaze containing silicates and left to dry. It was now ready to be placed back into the saggars in the kiln for its third or "glost" firing. For this glost firing, the glaze had been removed from the bottom rim of the wares to prevent it from adhering to the saggar. During this glost firing, which was done at a temperature of about 1050c, the glaze was rendered into a clear glass that enveloped the piece. The kiln had been brought by slow stages to its highest temperature and then the procedure was done in reverse for the cool down. We must consider for this glost firing that the wares now consisted of two elements, the bisque body and the glaze. If the ware was cooled down too quickly, the bisque body could contract quicker than the glaze and crack the piece. One of the highest paid workers was the fireman in control of the kilns, and with their extreme responsibilities, we can see why. If this glost firing had been for porcelain wares, it would have been done at a higher temperature that would have infused the glaze to the bisque body. This infusion would have made the bisque body and the glaze as one, rendering it non-porous. Our example, however, is ironstone/stoneware, and even though the glaze is non-porous, the bisque body below is still porous and susceptible to liquid stain if the glaze becomes crazed. If this glost fired ware needed to have gold gilding, it would have been applied by hand artisans and would have required a fourth firing to adhere the gold to the glaze. This fourth firing would have been at a much lower temperature.

England's Competition

In the late 1700s in the United States, you were either rich or a member of the vast majority, the poor. The rich were buying Haviland & Co. porcelain from Limoges, France and the poor were buying Wedgwood's creamware with a blue featheredge. There was very little else to be had. Most went without or merely had a few plates and maybe a bowl. After the turn of the century in the 1810s and 1820s, England was producing patriotic ware that depicted scenes from the American Revolutionary war, and had pictures of our war and political leaders as part of the patterns. It was a marketing move to help them compete against the French and their porcelain wares. We now call these patriotic dishes, Historic Ware. It was a good marketing tool and sold very well. There were no trains or transportation to speak of, and Canadian agents used this to exploit the American market by importing china from France and England, and shipped the wares by boat down the Great Lakes to be sold at seaports along the way.

Possibly in the late 1830s, but more realistically in the early 1840s, Flow Blue began to enter the market stream. This new Flow/Flown Blue ware evolved from the Historic Ware that England had been producing. They applied oriental designs to emulate Chinese Porcelain. The Americans took readily to this new "Flow/Flown Blue," and the dishes sold very well. During the Middle Victorian period, Germany entered the fray to compete for the American market. They went head to head with England making very similar types of wares. Their potteries were producing similar Flow Blue patterns on similarly constructed bodies of ceramic. However, they never reached the high volume of production or sales that England did because England would always under cut their prices.

The Industrial Revolution, originally begun in England in the first half of the 18th century, made it to the American shores just prior to the mid 19th century. For America, the timing was perfect, and the country was ready for a change. England's Industrial Revolution was sparked in part by Thomas Newcomen's invention of the "steam engine" in 1705. James Watt, an instrument maker from Glasgow University, began to make improvements on Newcomen's invention, in 1763. Watt changed the steam engine to be reciprocating and added a crank and flywheel to provide rotary motion.[22] This steam engine invention helped to revolutionize England's pottery manufacturing processes. Steam power was first introduced to drive the flint mills. The glaze grinding mills, the pumps, and lawn sifters were next to be steam powered.[23] After 1850, machinery was used extensively in the pottery industry. As a result, the price of ceramic ware fell and eating and drinking became more hygienic.

As for the American Industrial Revolution, it was being propelled in part by the newly developed railroad system. Railroads began to cover the American landscape in the 1820s and by the 1860s over 30,626 miles of railroad track had been laid. As America entered the Late Victorian period, a new phenomenon-was occurring. A new middle class America was being born. The sole contributing factor that created this new middle class was the American Industrial Revolution. New factories were springing up almost daily and looking for people to employ. The new railway system would help to facilitate the shipping of these new factory's products, and the employment opportunities these factories offered created a massive move of people from rural areas to the city. America was also experiencing a population explosion, which was due mostly to immigration from other countries, and they all were seemingly headed for the cities. The cities held an exciting aura of lights and new adventures. The British author Sir John Lang when speaking of American cities in 1876 stated, *"The thoroughfares are crowded, busy and bustling; and abounding signs of life and energy in the people are everywhere apparent."*[24] Between the years 1870 and 1900, Detroit grew in population from 79,500 to 285,700, Los Angeles grew from 5,700 to 102,400, Atlanta went from 21,700 to 89,900, Philadelphia went from 674,000 to 1,293,000, and the population of the entire United States in 1890 was 62,979,766 souls. Farms and rural residency was beginning to decrease, and towns were swelling with their promises of a better life and streets lined with gold. In the 1880s alone, 5 million immigrants entered this country, and nearly all of them moved to the cities. In the 1860s the journalist Horace Greeley stated, *"We cannot all live in the cities, yet nearly all are determined to do so."*[25] The people were eager to buy the new factory-made goods ranging from machine made shoes to canned meats that were being produced in large quantities at reasonable prices. In order to buy these goods, the average worker in the year 1900 was making .22 cents an hour, and working an average of 59 hours a week.[26] Skyscrapers had been built in cities that reached twenty stories and had electric elevators by the end of the 1890s. The city streets now had electric lights at night, and trolley cars could go 20 miles per hour. In 1883, the new Brooklyn Bridge made it possible for New York and Brooklyn to join as one metropolis that reached a population of 3.4 million by 1900, and was the wealthiest in the country. In the year 1900, there were 16,188,000 families in America, with an average of 4.7 per family. In that same year, a male could expect to live 46.3 years and a female would live an average of 48.3. In the entertainment field, Ethel Barrymore had her first hit in 1901, and in that same year at the age of 6, Buster Keaton was starting in Vaudeville.

The American Industrial Revolution also sparked western migration that pushed the countries boundaries further west, and helped relieve crowding in the swelling cities. Actually America was growing up, by moving west. Two of the catalysts for this western migration were the gold rush in California and the offering of free land by the government. The new developing railway system helped to facilitate this migration. With this push to the west a new industry was created with department stores and mail order catalog warehouses such as Sears Roebuck & Co. and Montgomery Ward & Co. All the small rural towns west of the Mississippi river was their market, and through their catalog sales, they helped to shape the western American culture. To help with getting their goods to the customers that bought them, the mail-order catalog warehouses turned to the railroad. The railroad system offered better economy, speed, and reliability. Life was moving along at a rapid pace in the United States.

As we entered the Late Victorian period, the three big ceramic producing countries that imported to the United States were England, France, and Germany. The new American mail-order stores were creating a tremendous amount of competition for the English. The catalogs offered French and German porcelain (the French spelled it porcelaine) and American china for sale. For the English to compete, they had to sell a similar product, and sell it cheaper. For the Americans, this was all good news. For without competition there is no change. Many ceramic innovations were made as a result of this competition for the American market. The French really never got into producing much Flow Blue. Even though the Germans and Americans were producing Flow Blue, they could not compete against the English on pricing or in the quality of the clays used. English clays were known to be superior, and the beleaguered American potteries that were competing against the English for their own market, in an attempt to upgrade the quality of American ceramics, began to purchase English clay for their wares. In one example, Dick Southern in his research paper, *A Look at La Belle and Wheeling Potteries*, (self published), lists England as one of the sources the Wheeling pottery purchased clay from.

Geoffrey A. Godden, in his book *Godden's Guide to Ironstone Stone & Granite Wares*, Antique Collectors' Club, Suffolk, England, 1999, sums up very well the problems experienced by the American potteries. In the late 1870s, the American pottery workers were being paid at a higher rate than the English, as well as other foreign countries were. This meant the American potteries had to charge more for their wares. The English believed in not paying any higher of a wage than their business could tolerate and still be successful. The American potteries were too caught up in their imitation of the English. They played more the role of a "copy cat" than the creators of their own style. Even the marks they used were in imitation of the English "Lion," and many even used their initials if they were the same as that used by a famous English pottery. In some cases, the Americans drew on the English for direct help. In the Fall/Winter, 1907/1908 Montgomery Ward & Co. catalog, bottom of page thirty-eight, there is an American set of dishes being advertised that was manufactured in Ohio. The pattern is NEW CENTURY and in the description it states, "The New Century is one of the best efforts of a noted English modeler. It is graceful in shape, made of fine American semi-porcelain, heavily glazed and decorated in a dainty border…" The American potteries knew that they needed to equal, or imitate the quality and style of the English potteries in order to be successful. In this case, they went straight to the source by using an English modeler.

One of the greatest problems facing the American potters was the quality of the clay they used for their wares. The President of the American Pottery Association stated at a meeting, "There is scarcely an even American clay that we can buy…The only clay we are able to get at present (1878), is from Pennsylvania, and all know that these clays are not good. They are refractory, unyielding to the fire; they do not fire easily. We need a better clay. We do not get a regular article. You cannot depend upon the quality being at all times uniform." The Chairman of a committee to look into the quality of materials and their prices, stated at a meeting, "Clays, flint and spar have not yet, in the opinion of your committee, reached that point which will enable us to compete successfully with foreign manufacturers…we must procure these articles at less prices than we are now paying. In the fierce fight now going on between the American and English for control of the American market, it is of the utmost importance that the production cost of our goods should be reduced…so long as imported English clays can be sold in our markets at less prices than our own American clays, we shall certainly labor under great disadvantages." The problems faced by the American potteries were many. The success being enjoyed by the English came as a result of their ceramic innovations, superior clays, trend setting wares and their lower prices.

To help compete against the French Porcelain, the British potteries using their same Flow Blue body styles, applied similar patterns that the French were applying on their Haviland wares. For examples of these patterns see Plates 3, 4, and 5.

To help further their cause, the British potted their quality wares thinly, and called it semi-porcelain. What a tremendous marketing tool! To look at the two products side by side, you would be hard pressed to tell the difference. In the china section of the Montgomery Ward & Co., catalog No.58 for Spring and Summer 1898, you will see an all white set of dishes being sold with the pattern name of VICTORIA and manufactured by the Johnson Bros. (the body style of dish used for this white set of dishes was also used by the Johnson Bros. for Flow Blue). In the descriptive caption for this set of dishes you will read, *Semi-porcelain, resembles pure, white French China. It is thin and has a finish not easily detected from china. For those desiring a service of pure white ware of a better and more modern style than regular ironstone, there is nothing better.* The new middle class Americans, who wanted to emulate the rich, bought the English Late Victorian "semi-porcelain" china because it was cheaper and had the same "look" as Haviland porce-

Plate 4. ROSLYN sugar, circa 1915, by W. H. Grindley & Co., 4 ½" high x 6" handle to handle. The pattern on this covered sugar represents one of the attempts made by the Grindley pottery to compete against Haviland china, with a very similar type of pattern. Note the small dainty flowers. *Author collection.* $35+

Plate 5. Unidentified floral pattern plate, circa 1900, by W. H. Grindley & Co., 10" in diameter. The pattern on this plate represents another attempt by the Grindley pottery to compete against Haviland china, using a similar type pattern. *Author collection.* $25+

Plate 3. Unidentified floral pattern plate, circa 1905, by J. & G. Meakin Ltd., 10" in diameter. Using a very similar type pattern, this plate represents one of the attempts made by J. & G. Meakin to compete against Haviland china. *Author collection.* $25+

lain. Even the term "china," translates to porcelain in one's mind. Yet today it is merely an umbrella term used to describe all ceramic ware. Realistically, when you consider the competition for the American market, the greatest competition an English pottery had was another English pottery.

About Absolutes

What is an absolute? An absolute is an item of fact that is stated firmly, without any exception or possibility of error. To say there are no absolutes in the ceramic world is a very strong statement to make, yet I am constantly hearing it from experts in the field. One of my goals in writing this book was to clearly define Late Victorian Flow Blue, and to find answers that no one else had before. This statement of no absolutes would appear to shackle my efforts, yet I am determined to try. I decided that in my research I would try to find clear-cut facts that were undeniable and to build on those. These clear-cut facts would form the foundation of my research, but I would continue the observance of the all-encompassing statement, "there are no absolutes." Let me give you an example of this. We know for an undeniable fact that the W. H. Grindley & Co. Ltd. Pottery applied for a patent for one of their Flow Blue body styles on December 29, 1896, and that the actual patent date was approved and dated February 2, 1897. Yet it is still possible that the Grindley pottery may have made this style of dish somewhat earlier than it was patented. This last sentence relates to the "there are no absolutes" part of the equation. Deciding that it was still a solid date to go by, I researched further. In that research, I discovered that the pattern registration numbers on six of the patterns applied to this body style showed actual dates of 1896 to 1898. With these facts in tow, we now have more corroborating evidence to prove the actual patent date of the body style was its accurate start-up date. The fact that the body style may have been made before the patent is the reason for the no absolutes. The second corroborating set of facts helps to verify with strong certainty that the actual start-up date is in fact the patent date given. Using this new found certainty, I can reasonably assume, because of facts researched, that any pattern applied to this style of dish was made post December 29, 1896. Here is another fact that I feel can be gleaned from my research of this body style. I have seen some pieces of this style of dish that have on the back "U.S. patent applied for." Knowing the two dates that I list for you, I feel that I can make the following statement. Any of the representative pieces from this body style that has "patent applied for" on them were made after December 29, 1896 and before February 2, 1897, or within a very close proximity to those dates. You can begin to see, I think, how I maneuvered around the no absolute part, of every facts equation.

Let me give you another example. The English registration number for a pattern or design, I believe, can be used to accurately date the pattern. The no absolute part of the equation says that it may have been made before its registration date. Look at this example as the opposite of the one listed above. In this case we have a body style of dish with no patent date, but we have several pattern registration numbers that range from 1893 to 1895 that were applied to this style. With this data in mind, it is my belief that we can accurately date this body style of dish to be 1893. The no absolute part of this equation says that we may find a pattern made in 1892, which would falsify the 1893 date, and that the body style may have been made earlier than the patterns would indicate. All of these scenarios are quite possible, and can make for a shaky foundation, but at times, however, those corroborating facts are all we have to go on without researching the company's records.

Let me give you one final example. In the course of researching a particular pottery, I will accumulate a complete list of known patterns. Because there are always more patterns to be discovered, the list is not an absolute one. Let's assume now that I have discovered one hundred patterns for a pottery, and of those patterns I discover the pattern registration number, and the subsequent date it represents for eighty-five of those patterns. I feel that I can list those eighty-five patterns numerically, by their registration numbers, and use this data to show pattern trends during the Late Victorian period. I realize that some patterns were made for a longer period than others, but it is the start-up date that I am considering here. The facts that I have listed for you here, while not absolutes, I believe to be very sound, and can be used for the foundation for further learning and research.

Endnotes – Chapter One

[1] Robert Copeland, *Spode's Willow Pattern and other designs after the Chinese* (Essex, England: Studio Vista 1980),79

[2] Ibid., 17

[3] Ibid., 18

[4] Robert Copeland, *Blue and White Transfer-Printed Pottery* (Pembrokeshire, England: CIT Printing Services Ltd. 1982),9

[5] C. F. Binns, *The Story of the Potter* (Strand, England: George Newnes Limited 1898),13

[6] Geoffrey A. Godden, *Ironstone & Granite Wares* (Suffolk, England: Antique Collectors' Club Ltd. 1999),162

[7] Donald C. Towner, *English Cream-coloured Earthenware* (London, England: Faber and Faber 1957),1

[8] Geoffrey A. Godden, *Ironstone Stone & Granite wares* (Suffolk, England: Antique Collectors' Club Ltd. 1999),58

[9] Donald C. Towner, *English Cream-coloured Earthenware* (London, England: Faber and Faber 1957),40

[10] Geoffrey A. Godden, *Ironstone Stone & Granite wares* (Suffolk, England: Antique Collectors' Club Ltd. 1999),8

[11] Ibid., 72

[12] Ibid., 162

[13] C. F. Binns, *The Story of the Potter* (Strand, England: George Newnes Limited 1898),190

[14] Petra Williams, *Flow Blue China An Aid to Identification* (Jeffersontown, Kentucky: Fountain House East 1971),17

[15] Arnold Kowalsky & Dorothy Kowalsky, *Encyclopedia of Marks On American, English, and European Earthenware, Ironstone, and Stoneware* (Atglen, PA: Schiffer Publishing, Ltd. 1999),281

[16] Geoffrey A. Godden, *Ironstone Stone & Granite wares* (Suffolk, England: Antique Collectors' Club Ltd. 1999),165

[17] C. F. Binns, *The Story of the Potter* (Strand, England: George Newnes Limited 1898),196

[18] Harold Owen, *The Staffordshire Potter* (Throwbridge & London, England: Redwood Press Limited 1901),63

[19] C. F. Binns, *The Story of the Potter* (Strand, England: George Newnes Limited 1898),200

[20] Ibid., 202

[21] Robert Copeland, *Blue and White Transfer-Printed Pottery* (Pembrokeshire, England: CIT Printing Services Ltd. 1982),11

[22] Professor Gerhard Rempel, *Article: The Industrial Revolution* (Department of History, Western New England College)

[23] Josiah Wedgwood, *Staffordshire Potter* (New York, New York: McBride & Co. 1947)144

[24] Editors of Time-Life Books, *This Fabulous Century 1870-1900* (Time-Life Books, New York, New York 1970)

[25] Ibid.

[26] Ibid.

W. H. Grindley & Co. Ltd.

a personal history

William Harry Grindley was born c.1857 approximately 15 miles south of Stoke at Weeping Cross, near Stafford, England. Every record examined indicates that Mr. Grindley spent his entire life living and working in the Staffordshire district of Stoke-on-Trent. We know very little of his childhood, except that he started in the pottery field c.1875 as an apprentice to George Turner at the Albert Works, built by Turner and Tomkinson about 1858.[1] In later years, the Victoria Pottery was added to the Albert Works. The Victoria and Albert potteries traded under the name Turner & Tomkinson from 1861 until 1873, when Mr. Tomkinson retired. From 1873 to about 1895, it continued under the trade name of G. W. Turner & Sons.

Very early in 1880, in partnership with Alfred Meakin, William Grindley acquired the Newfield Pottery from William Adams the 5th. Here they commenced in the manufacturing of general earthenware.[2] Alfred stayed until March 1883, and Grindley alone from there.[3] Soon his business outgrew the Newfield's capabilities and in 1891 he bought and completely rebuilt the Woodland Pottery. The Newfield works lay vacant until Grindley sold it to Thomas Rathbone in 1896. At the Woodland Pottery, remarkable developments were made. In 1926, it was one of the best-known factories in the world.[4] Through the Woodland firm, Mr. Grindley extensively developed the export market, and was still known to some extent in the home market.

Plate 6. Photo of a mature William Harry Grindley c.1858-1926. *Courtesy of the Staffordshire Sentinel Newspapers Limited, Stoke-on-Trent, England*

In 1908, Grindley went into partnership with Sir James Fleming of Scotland in hotelware manufacturing. A new building was erected and was located on Scotia Road, Tunstall. The firm was named "The Duraline Hotelware Co. Ltd." Their hotelware partnership developed strong markets in Australia, Canada, and the United States. In speaking about Mr. Fleming it was stated, "Sir Fleming was well known for his public services. He was esteemed by everyone connected with the pottery industry not only in Scotland but also in Staffordshire, where he was for many years a partner with Mr. W. H. Grindley in the Woodland Pottery, Tunstall. He took a deep interest in Education as a member of the School Board of Glasgow and as Governor of the Royal Technical College, and similar institutions. His chairmanship of the School of Art, whose destinies he guided so admirably for twenty-five years, and which became recognized as one of the best art training centers in Britain, was considered his best work. For these faithful services he received the honour of knighthood in 1906."[5] According to Mr. Grindley's obituary in the Staffordshire Sentinel, March 9, 1926, Grindley relinquished his interest in the hotelware division in 1921.

During WW I, both Mr. Grindley's youngest son, Captain Harry Grindley, and Mr. Fleming's son, Captain Fleming, were members of the 5th North Stafford (a member of the R. E. 14th Division). Tragically both men fell at Ypres salient, with the 5th North Stafford's heroic attack on the Hohenrollern Redoubts in October of 1915.

Mr. Grindley was a justice of the peace for many years for the counties of Staffordshire, Chesire, and Stoke-on-Trent. He was a member of the Stoke-on-Trent Council for a few years, but only after Federation. He was known to donate to any undertaking that contributed to the progress and welfare of Tunstall and gave generously to charitable causes in the district. Most of his contributions will never be known, but an example was in 1925 he made a contribution of 1000 pounds to the North Staffordshire Royal Infirmary. He was a member and past vice-president of the Ceramic Society and was one of the original members of the British Pottery Manufacturers Federation.

Mr. Grindley was known and well liked throughout the potting district, but none knew him as well as the people that worked for him. He was a man that got "involved" with his employees. On many occasions he was seen sitting at the potters bench, working and chatting with all.

In the pottery industry, Mr. Grindley was an incredible and savvy businessman. He knew how to extend his business, by knowing what his customers wanted. Of his products it was said, "At the Woodland Pottery he conceived and matured new designs both in body, modeling, and engraving. So careful must be the preparation in the sliphouse and leadhouse, &c., that the body and glaze compares equally with transparent china. The Embossed edge on the rims and shoulders of flat ware, is preserved in its distinctions to a marvelous degree. Finally, in the placing and firing, as well as in the care of selection to an almost minute degree, is shown a taste that places this firm in a high position."[6] Later in this section, when we cover Grindley's products, you will see this mans genius laid out before you.

An illness caused his retirement in 1921, and contributed to his death March 8, 1926. Mr. Grindley was 68 when he died at his home,

The Cedars, in the town of Stone, which is 7 miles south of Stoke. Mrs. Charles Bowers stated at a town gathering March 9th, "Mr. Grindley's love for the town of Tunstall was unique, and he always did his level best for it."[7] His funeral and internment was March 12th, and kept very private. Immediate relatives and a few personal friends were in attendance. His obituary in the Staffordshire Sentinel states, "Mr. Grindley leaves a widow, one son William Harry Jr., one daughter (Miss Grindley)." We also know that his son Captain Harry Grindley preceded him in death.

the pottery history

The Newfield Pottery at Sandyford was originally an estate built c.1764. In 1795, it was known as the Newfield Pottery and owned by John and Caleb Cole. By 1802, it was under the ownership of Caleb and his brother-in-law William Adams, who died in 1805. In 1806, the owner of the Newfield estate, Admiral Smith Child, was working it. Child, in 1809, entered partnership with John Henry Clive. After the Admirals death in 1813, Clive managed until 1824, the estate and the firm on behalf of Smith Child, the Admirals heir. The products produced there by Clive and Child was good quality creamware. The succeeding owners of this famous pottery were Joseph Heath from 1824 to at least 1841, and Podmore Walker from 1848 to 1853. The Newfield re-entered the Adams family when in 1857, William Adams the 5th, bought the pottery. This is the way it remained until Adams sold the pottery to Grindley in 1880. When Grindley removed to the Woodland Pottery in 1891, it remained vacant until it was sold to Thomas Rathbone in 1896. Rathbone held the Newfield until he sold it to Alfred Meakin in 1918. This ownership was held until 1960. The Newfield Pottery has since been demolished and new office buildings constructed over the site. The following pictures (plates. 7, 8, and 9) show the current buildings and the site where the Newfield pottery once stood.

In Geoffrey A. Godden's book, *Ironstone, Stone & Granite Ware* (Antique Collectors' Club Ltd., Suffolk, England, 1999), an old advertisement for the Newfield pottery is shown. It states that the wares were, "Suitable for the United States, Canadian, South American, and Australian markets." It also states that, "No agent represents this firm at home or abroad," and "Write direct for prices and samples." This was a very large, independent, and well-established firm.

Plate 8. This photo shows one of the current buildings located on the former Newfield pottery sight. *Courtesy of John Potter, England*

Plate 7. This photo shows one of the current buildings located on the former Newfield pottery sight. *Courtesy of John Potter, England*

Plate 9. This photo shows one of the current buildings located on the former Newfield pottery sight. *Courtesy of John Potter, England*

The Woodland Pottery was located on Woodland St. to the north, and Lower Woodland St. to the west in Tunstall. It was originally built and owned by a Mr. Littler c.1756 and was operating as a pottery at that time. J. Wedgwood was operating this pottery from 1841 until his death in 1857. Edmund T. Wood, brother to J. Wedgwood, continued the business until1875 when he sold the pottery to the partnership of Hollinshead & Kirkham. They would occupy the building until they sold it to Grindley in 1891. Shortly after buying the Woodland Pottery, Grindley made "great structural changes" in order to extend his business.[8] It was laid out, almost wholly, for the American market. We also know that it was at this pottery that Grindley produced all of his beautiful cobalt Flow Blue.

WWII brought increasing restrictions on trade, and in 1941 the government enforced a "Concentration Scheme," on the pottery industry. The government closed seventy-seven businesses and "concentrated" them on seventy-eight "nucleus" firms. Grindley's pottery was considered a nucleus, with Rigby & Stevenson pottery being concentrated there. The thought was that this would liberate the other potteries for a different use.

After Mr. Grindley's death in 1926, the pottery changed ownership several times, and the trade name of "W. H. Grindley & Co." was changed to "Grindley of Stoke" or just "grindley." In 1999, the Grindley pottery fell on hard times and the firm entered into voluntarily liquidation. The May 5, 1999 issue of the Staffordshire Sentinel lists the loss of 130 jobs and the auction of Woodland pottery's equipment & ware.[9] The auction was held shortly thereafter, and signifies to all Grindley china collectors the end of a fabulous era of ceramic production. The Sentinel further states in their article, "The building will be torn down, and a super market is to be built on the site." After 119 years of production, the doors are not only closed, but have vanished.

Plate 11. This photo shows the Woodland Pottery's main entrance. All of Grindley's beautiful Flow Blue wares would pass through these doors. *Courtesy of John Potter, England, 1996*

Plate 10. This photo shows most of the front façade of the Woodland Pottery. The arched sign states "Woodland Pottery – Rebuilt 1891". *Courtesy of John Potter, England, 1996*

Plate 12. This photo shows two additional buildings that were part of this marvelous pottery. *Courtesy of John Potter, England, 1996*

Jonathan Goodwin, Assistant Archaeologist at the The Potteries Museum & Art Gallery, Stoke-on-Trent, discussed in the following article some archaeological work he was doing at the Grindley and Johnson Bros. potteries. It is reproduced here with permission.

Since the late 1960s, archaeological work in Stoke-on-Trent has done much to clarify the history, operation and output of the north Staffordshire pottery industry during its 19th to 20th century heyday. Excavations of the hundreds of factory waste dumps that lie beneath the City have revealed the truly extensive range of standardized wares produced by factories operating in the locality during this period. Furthermore, the examination of these deposits, composed of misfired examples of the typical ceramics that formed the mainstay of north Staffordshire's output, has served to illustrate the deficiencies inherent in most private and public ceramic collections formed within the narrow parameters of connoisseurship. This latter approach is one, which has too often denied the importance of such mundane wares and has instead been influential in over-emphasizing the importance of the more aesthetically pleasing, higher-status wares.

The scope of archaeological work in Stoke-on-Trent has been greatly increased over the last ten years, with the introduction of closer ties between archaeology and the local planning and development process. Archaeological involvement in construction projects and road building schemes, for example, has provided the opportunity for more deposits than ever before to be identified, recorded and sampled.

One recent project typical of the relationship between developers and archaeologists, centered on the site of the Woodland Pottery and Pinnox Works, located in Tunstall, the most northerly of the six towns that comprise the modern City of Stoke-on-Trent. As is so often the case in the City today, the development involved the demolition of the existing potworks and the building of a retail outlet, with the archaeological work limited to the observation of ground works, such as foundation trenching.

Even with this somewhat restrictive brief, seven substantial groups of mid 19th/early 20th century pottery waste were discovered during the nine month project, amongst which was a significant collection of wares produced by W. H. Grindley & Co. of the Woodland Pottery.[I] The sherds were scattered in one corner of the site and as such appeared to represent a single deposit of pottery, perhaps laid as leveling material, rather than a gradual accumulation of waste over a lengthy period of time (Plate13Gr1.). This initial observation was confirmed by the presence of marked pieces amongst the sherds, which indicate the wares to have been made between 1915 and 1925.[II]

The finds can be split more or less equally between undecorated and transfer-printed earthenware's. The sherds represent a range of elaborately moulded vessels including numerous examples of plates, soup plates, cups, saucers, bowls and dishes, with less frequently occurring forms such as tureens, ewers, platters, ladles and compotes. The decorated earthenware's appear in all of the aforementioned forms, whilst the undecorated wares are largely confined to bowls and shallow dishes. Moulded detail is prevalent to varying degrees throughout the forms, appearing in the body styles – scalloped plate edges, scrolled handles etc. – and in the guise of embossed decoration such as beading and swags.

The transfer-printed wares, in all but one example, are of the distinctive flow-blue variety, exhibiting a subtle diffusion between glaze and print. Although some patterns remain anonymous, others are identifiable either from the presence of a printed mark with integral pattern name or from comparable surviving examples. Such patterns include 'Beaufort', 'Portman', 'Melbourne', 'Syria', 'Keele', 'Lorne' and 'Derwent' (Plate13Gr2.). The latter design is the sole recovered example to be printed in a style other than flow blue, appearing instead in green.

Of equal, if not greater archaeological interest to the wares themselves is evidence of the way in which they were produced. Fragments of kiln furniture illustrate one aspect of production, being the apparatus used to separate and support wares inside the refractory clay saggar, mostly during glost firing.[III] The Grindley material from Tunstall features two standard forms of kiln furniture for the time, namely thimbles – moulded clay cones with a protruding tab at the base, and saddles – v-shaped clay bars (Plate13Gr3.). The two were used in conjunction in the firing of flatwares such as plates, saucers and dishes, which were placed on end across the apex of two parallel saddles. To hold these wares in place, a column of thimbles was formed by stacking one inside the other, with the tabs on one side only. This was then positioned across the top of the row of flatwares, the upper edges of which were each held in place by one of the thimble tabs. The use of this placing technique is obvious amongst the Grindley flatwares, typically as small tell-tale scars on the rims – usually an area free from glaze where the flatware rested upon the saddles and a small mark on the opposite rim where the thimble tab made contact with the vessel. Other sherds displayed the use of this method even more dramatically, most notably a stack of fused plates and one of dishes which had clearly shifted on their saddles during firing and collapsed into each other (Plate13Gr4.).

Endnotes – Jonathan Goodwin Article

[I]Jonathan Goodwin, 2000, *Archaeology Watching Brief at Scotia Road* (Potteries Museum Archaeology Unit Report 92, Tunstall, Stoke-on-Trent, England)

[II]W. H. Van Buskirk, *William Harry Grindley and His Flow Blue Dishes* (F.B.I.C.C. private publication 1996)

[III]D. Barker, *Bits and Bobs – The Development of Kiln Furniture in the 18th Century Staffordshire Pottery Industry* (English Ceramic Circle, England)16

[IV]Jonathan Goodwin, *Archaeological watching Brief on Waters Mains renewal Work* (Potteries Museum Field Archaeology Unit Report 85, Tunstall, Stoke-on-Trent, England)

[V]Geoffrey A. Godden, *The Encyclopedia of British marks* (Bonanza Books, New York, New York 1964)355-6

[VI]S. Tarlow, & S. West, *The Familiar Past?*, article S. Tarlow, *Strangely Familiar* (England 1999)263-72

[VII]Neil Ewens, *Supplying the Present Wants of our Yankee Cousins, Staffordshire Ceramics and the American market 1775-1880* (George Street Press, Stafford, England 1997)8

The Grindley deposit is only one of a growing number of groups of later 19th/early 20th century wares that have recently been found through development control work within Stoke-on-Trent. Just a month before the development of the Woodland Pottery began, a scheme to relay water mains, again in Tunstall, had brought to light an assemblage of wasters produced by the firm of Johnson Brothers, one of, if not the most prolific manufacturers in the Potteries at the turn of the 19th/20th centuries.[IV] The sherds were recovered from an area, which from the cartographic evidence, was open waste ground between 1900 and, at the very latest, 1912. The Johnson Brothers' material must have been dumped here during this period to level the area in preparation for the construction of the modern street. This suspected date-range for the deposition of the wares corresponded very satisfactorily with a production date of between 1899 and 1913, suggested by those excavated sherds which bear printed manufacturer's marks.[V]

The sherds are once again exclusively earthenware, although some are of a durable ironstone variant. The moulded vessel forms mirror the more standard types represented amongst the Grindley finds, comprising of plates, saucers, cups, bowls, ewers and tureens. Applied decoration is transfer-printed, whilst undecorated wares occur most amongst the ironstone types, which also monopolize the larger tableware forms, such as bowls and tureens. Moulded decoration is again conspicuous, both in form and embossed detail. Flow blue is the prominent style of transfer-printed decoration, although other colors, primarily blue and green, are present. Individual printed patterns are not restricted to one color, with examples of the 'St. Louis' design recovered in both flow blue and standard green (Plate14JB1.).

Assemblages of this date provide a clear opportunity to further the archaeological study of ceramics, as until now the potential of later 19th/early 20th century material has remained comparatively unexplored. The relative modernity of these groups has fostered a false sense of familiarity with the material contained within them, encouraging us to downgrade their worthiness as subjects for study.[VI] It is crucial, however, to remember that these wares represent an important phase in the history of the north Staffordshire pottery industry that has already slipped beyond living memory and which consequently needs to be examined through every available source.

It is only in the past decade that pottery production in the earlier years of the 19th century has been lifted from a similar obscurity to its present position of prominence. How an understanding of the Staffordshire industry was ever likely to be reached without the inclusion of this period is now difficult to imagine. The themes that have subsequently been developed for the 19th century can surely be continued into later phases of production. A number of avenues await exploration, but one, which readily presents itself for the W. H. Grindley & Co. and Johnson Brothers' groups, is an examination of their position within the Staffordshire export trade with the United States.

Research into the 19th century American export trade has seen archaeology come into its own, invariably standing as the only source of material evidence to be found for this aspect of the Staffordshire manufacturers' output in Britain. Wares, which by the mid 19th century were representative of specific American ceramic preferences, the so-called *white granite* ironstones and flow-blue and flow-mulberry printed earthenware's, for example, have been encountered widely in excavations throughout Stoke-on-Trent. In contrast, British collections of extant wares, whilst supposedly representative of the Staffordshire industry, offer little or no indication of the significance of this trade – one which constituted as much as 97% of British wares exported to America.[VII] The intrinsic interest of American export wares is heightened by their explicit display of changing consumer tastes. This adds an extra dimension to their use as mere production evidence, instilling within them the means to relay information on the active links between the manufacturer and customer.

W. H. Grindley & Co. and Johnson Brothers represent two firms that were heavily involved in the American export trade well beyond the later 19th century boundary at which present study has halted. Their respective excavated assemblages show a high incidence of wares that are to American taste, most notably flow-blue printed earthenware's, and exhibit stylistically comparable applied designs and moulded details. It is reasonable to suppose that these traits betray similar producer-consumer dynamics to those of earlier groups, and with the discovery of other assemblages of this date, it should be possible to assess the response of Staffordshire producers to the demands of American consumers in the early 20th century. Archaeologists working in Stoke-on-Trent are uniquely placed to further the study of later 19th and early 20th century ceramics. Sustainable development in the City promises a bright future, with the potential for future significant discoveries high.

Jonathan Goodwin
Assistant Archaeologist, The Potteries Museum & Art Gallery, Stoke-on-Trent

Plate 13Gr1. Scatter of W. H. Grindley & Co. sherds at the Woodland Pottery site. *Courtesy of Jon Goodwin, England*

Plate 13Gr4. Fused earthenware. *Courtesy of Jon Goodwin, England*

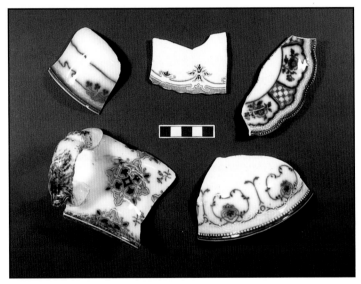

Plate 13Gr2. Printed earthen wares of W. H. Grindley & Co., top left LORNE, DERWENT, and MELBOURNE, bottom left SYRIAN, and BEAUFORT. *Courtesy of Jon Goodwin, England*

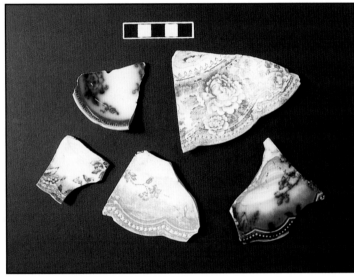

Plate 14JB1. Printed earthen wares of the Johnson Brothers Ltd., top left RICHMOND and MONTANA, bottom ST. LOUIS. *Courtesy of Jon Goodwin, England*

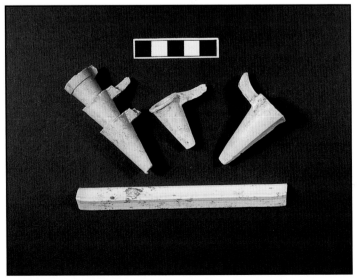

Plate 13Gr3. Earthenware kiln furniture, bottom thimbles, top saddle. *Courtesy of Jon Goodwin, England*

pottery marks

For the marks listed below, when possible, I have given the reader "code numbers" applied to the marks from two reference works. They are: Geoffrey A. Godden, *Encyclopedia of British Pottery and Porcelain Marks*, New York, N. Y.: Bonanza Books, 1964, and Arnold A. & Dorothy E. Kowalsky "KAD," *Encyclopedia of Marks On American, English, and European Earthenware, Ironstone, and Stoneware 1780-1980*, Atglen, PA: Schiffer Publishing, Ltd. 1999.

Plate 15. This form of the globe mark was used from 1880-1883, and enlists the use of the diamond registry symbol, and incorporates "Tunstall" in the lower banner. The pattern name is usually put in the top banner. The diamond form of registry was in effect from 1842-1883. It may or may not have "Trade Mark" displayed.

Plate 16. Godden No. 1842A - KAD No. B1127 - The globe mark with "Tunstall" incorporated into the lower banner was used 1880-c.1891. It also symbolizes the Newfield Pottery production as this mark was used concurrently with its operation. It may or may not have "Trade Mark" displayed. Usually the pattern name is put in the top banner.

Plate 17. This form of the globe mark incorporates "England" in the lower banner and replaces "Tunstall". The pattern name is usual put in the top banner. This mark was used c.1891-1914.

Plate 18. KAD No. B1129 - The Royal Coat of Arms mark, which incorporates "Royal Ironstone China" was in use from 1880-c.1925. This mark was used on White Granitewares, and Tealeaf/Copper Luster.

Plate 19. KAD No. B1130 - This mark, an oval with four crowns, has only been seen on Grindley body styles Gr-M c.1898 and Gr-W1 c.1897. This mark can also include the U. S. patent date and will be found within the oval.

Plate 20. Godden No. 1843 - KAD No. B1131 - The wreath mark was used from 1914-1925, and can be seen printed in either blue or green. Generally speaking, if the wreath mark is printed in blue, it is an earlier piece. The pattern name in many cases is printed just below the wreath. If there is a registration number printed above the wreath, it usually represents the English body style registry number.

Plate 21. There are several variations of Grindley's hotelware mark. They were in use from c.1908-1979. In some cases, the pattern name and/or the importer name will be printed just below the mark.

Plate 22. Godden No. 1850 - KAD No. B1133 - This mark was used from c.1936-1954. This mark can be seen printed in either blue or green. There are several variations of this mark that were used on non-Flow Blue patterns.

a pottery chronology

The following is a chronology of the W. H. Grindley & Co. Ltd. Pottery. The dates listed will include all pertinent, as well as incidental facts, and factory marks.

1857 - Grindley is born.

1875 - Grindley enters into apprenticeship with George Turner at the Albert Pottery.

1880 - Acquires the Newfield pottery in partnership with Alfred Meakin.

1880 - Globe mark with "Tunstall" used till 1891

1883 - Alfred Meakin leaves the partnership.

1891 - Acquires the Woodland Pottery from the partnership of Hollinshead & Kirkham.

1891- Globe mark with "England" used till 1914.

1891 - Royal Coat of Arms mark with "Royal Ironstone China" used till 1925.

1896 - The Newfield pottery is sold to Thomas Rathbone.

1897 - Oval mark with four crowns in use.

1908 - Grindley enters into partnership with Sir James Fleming in the hotelware manufacture under the trade name, "The Duraline Hotelware Co. Ltd."

1914 - Green/blue wreath mark is used till 1925.

1921 - Grindley retires.

1925 - Becomes "Limited."

1926 - Grindley dies March 8th from illness.

1929 - Susie Cooper chose Grindley as one of the potteries she bought from for her artwork.

1936 - Ship in rectangle mark used till 1954.

1960 - Bought out by Alfred Clough Ltd.

1976 - Alfred Clough is acquired by Newman Industries.

1978 - Trade name is changed to "Grindley of Stoke" and/or "grindley."

1982 - Newman Industries sells to Federated Potteries Co. Ltd.

1987 - Federated Potteries sells off Grindley hotelware division to Royal Stafford from Burslem.

1988 - Grindley management purchases the pottery from Federated potteries.

1999 - Grindley Pottery engages voluntary liquidation of equipment and wares.

dish body styles – specifics

The following few paragraphs are an introduction to the body style section, and will not be repeated for each of the potteries covered in this chapter. It will help the reader gain a better understanding of what this section hopes to accomplish.

Each manufacturer periodically would create a new body style/shape of dish or wash set to put on the market. They also would create new transfer patterns/designs that would be applied to these new body styles. What I have done here is an attempt to identify all the different body styles that each pottery created, and then catalog what patterns were applied to them.

Generally speaking, once a pattern was assigned to a particular style of dish or wash set, it was considered a marriage for the life of the pattern. Through this method, a pottery gave their customers consistent quality and uniformity. There was, whether done by intent or by error, some variation to this system. In the "pattern details" section for each pottery, I have tried to cover what patterns were applied to multiple body styles.

To date, I have only seen three instances of cross over from a dish to a wash set body style. Except in the three cases stated above, which are very rare, a pottery did not make a new set of dishes and then create a wash set to match it. However, in a few cases, I have seen the same pattern applied on both a dish style and on a wash set. Once again, in the "pattern details" section, I will list for you all known patterns that were used this way.

Another rare thing that a pottery would do was to apply an old pattern on a newer body style of dish. Let me further explain this to you. Let's assume a new body style of dish and a new pattern for it are created today and put on the market. In some cases, and it may be as much as 15 years later, this same pattern is brought back onto the market and applied to a new or current style of dish. I have made an attempt to identify those patterns applied to multiple body styles and will list them for you.

It is through this type of categorization research, that we can track a pottery's production. We find that there are few body styles made, but many new patterns that were applied to them. For a dish body style, it can be as many as fifteen or twenty patterns per body style. We find, however, that only three to five patterns were created for each wash set body style. The life of a new style of dish or wash set was about five years, and for patterns, it was about one or two years. In some cases, a pattern was so popular that it was left on the market as open stock for several years. We can take these "time windows" of a pottery's production and place them in date order. It is with this method that we are allowed a first hand view of trends and styles of a potteries line of wares. This topic will be covered in depth in a later chapter.

For each of the following potteries covered in this chapter, there is a section for each of the dish and wash set body styles. During my research, when I would discover a new body style I gave it a code. For a dish body style, I used letters such as "Gr-A." The "Gr" stands for Grindley and "A" represents body style A. For wash sets, I used numbers such as "Gr-W1." The "Gr" stands for Grindley and the "W1" represents wash set body style number 1. So far, the potteries I have body style codes for are W. H. Grindley & Co. "Gr," Johnson Bros. Ltd. "JB," J. & G. Meakin Ltd. "J&G," and Alfred Meakin Ltd. "AM." I have given them labels for the purpose of identification. With these codes, for example, a buyer and seller can have a common ground for discussing a potteries ware, especially when done over the phone. Because a wash set body style has the number code of "W1," or a dish body style with the code "A," does not mean that it is the oldest or the newest. They were merely labeled as discovered. As a new body style was discovered, I gave it the next consecutive number or letter.

For a dish body style, I took a plate and had a line drawing done. This line drawing represents the shape of the piece without a pattern applied and shows what embossing and edge treatment it received. For a wash set body style, I took a pitcher and had a line drawing done. This line drawing shows what embossing and what handle and spout treatment it received. These line drawings are the "body style finger prints." For each of the following pottery body styles, I give a line drawing of each style and show what patterns were applied. If known, I also give the English body style/shape registration number and/or the U. S. Patent date. Also, if known, I list the factory name of the body style.

A pottery applied many different patterns to a given body style, and that can include patterns that are not Flow Blue. In the "shapes" section of each body style given, you may see patterns other than Flow Blue. I ask the reader to remember that it is the "shape" I'm concerned with, and not the pattern. However, I think for the reader to see these non-Flow Blue patterns will be of benefit to them. It will help to give a better understanding of the vast spectrum of product variation a pottery produced. In this same line of thinking, because a pottery produced a pattern in Flow Blue, doesn't mean that Flow Blue will be the only color you find that pattern in. The pattern ARGYLE by Grindley, for example, was made in three colors, Flow Blue, slate blue, and green. They are all the same identical pattern, but printed in a different color. Color variation by a pottery was trend marketing. The English potteries were tremendous businessmen, and whatever trend color was "in," they produced it for their customers.

In addition to my reasons for this type of research, there are many ways that a collector can personally benefit. Realistically, collecting Flow Blue is not an inexpensive venture, especially if you want to collect a whole service. There are actually two elements in collecting a set of Flow Blue dishes: the pattern and the shape of the dishes. It can be very disheartening if you start by collecting a few plates in a desired pattern and discover at a later date that you don't care for the looks of the hollowware. If from the outset you know that you like the pattern, as well as the shape of the dish, you can feel confident in your purchases.

Some collectors enjoy acquiring a service of twelve, in twelve different patterns. I have seen this done, and it makes for a beautiful setting. Now let's assume that the same collector would like all twelve of the patterns to be different, but would like the pieces to be the same shape. All you would have to do is to look up a desired body style, from one listed in the book, and select twelve patterns in that style to collect.

Another true benefit for the collector is identification. How many of you have bought a piece of Flow Blue because you really liked it, but there were no factory marks on it? This can be very frustrating, especially if you would like to collect more pieces in that pattern. The answer to this frustrating problem is simple. All that is necessary is to compare the embossing and edge treatment from the plate you have purchased with the line drawings provided in this book. When you find a match, you will at least know what pottery made the piece, and with luck, your pattern will be listed there as well.

I realize that I have not covered every body style from every Late Victorian pottery that produced Flow Blue. What I do have here is a beginning, and when you consider the enormous contribution made by the potteries covered here, I'd say it was a very large beginning. My plans for the future are to continue this type of research and encompass more potteries.

The following information will be listed for each body style given: a picture of the line drawing, available photos of Flow Blue/Slate Blue patterns applied to this style, photos to represent the shapes, and any known non-Flow Blue patterns applied that were also applied to that body style. For each photo of the body style line drawing, you will be given the following information, if known.

Body Style:
Factory Name:
U. S. Patent Applied/Dated:
English Registry:
First year Catalog:
Late Victorian Dating Label:
Flow Blue Patterns Applied:

For "Body Style," I list the code I have given it. The "Factory Name" is the name the factory gave the body style. Under "U. S. Patent Applied/Dated," I list the date when that body style patent was applied for and the date it was approved. In some cases, the factory listed their "English Registry" number instead of the U. S. Patent date. In those cases, I list that number and the date it represents. For "First Year Catalog," I give you the year and the catalog that the body style first appears in. For this information, I used the catalog from two companies, Sears Roebuck & Co. and Montgomery Ward & Co. I have researched catalogs from other companies, and if used, I list them. If "circa" is given for the catalog date, it means that it could be before this date, but not after. Let me explain further why "circa' will be used. If the earliest date that I could research a particular company's catalog was 1895, and in that year there is a body style being researched, then there exists the possibility that the same body style could have been in the previous years catalog. Also for "First Year Catalog," "SS" before the catalog date is Spring/Summer, and "FW" is Fall/Winter.

The "Late Victorian Dating Label" is really getting ahead of myself. This subject is dealt with in the chapter on dating Late Victorian Flow Blue by body styles, and a better understanding will be had at that time. I have included this information here merely as a quick reference when researching a particular body style.

For "Flow Blue Patterns Applied," I list all known Flow Blue and slate blue patterns that were applied to this style of dish.

Gr-A

Plate 23. *Courtesy of Ann Potts, Illinois*
Body Style: Gr-A
Factory Name: -
U. S. Patent Applied/Dated: December 28,
1896/ February 2, 1897
English Registry: -
First Year Catalog: FW 1896/1897 Montgomery
Ward & Co.
Late Victorian Dating Label: Scroll
Flow Blue Patterns: ARGYLE, CHATSWORTH,
GIRONDE, JANETTE, MERION, MILTON, and
STRATFORD

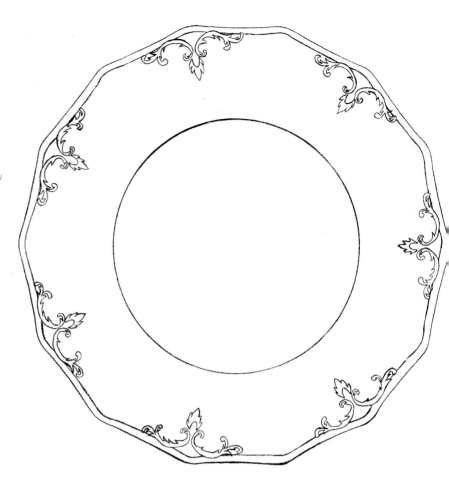

Gr-A pattern identification:

Plate 24. ARGYLE plate, 10" in diameter. *Courtesy of Shell & Jim Lewis, Illinois* $90-$125

Plate 25. GIRONDE plate, 10" in diameter.
Courtesy of Steve & Cindy Marut, Texas
$90-$125

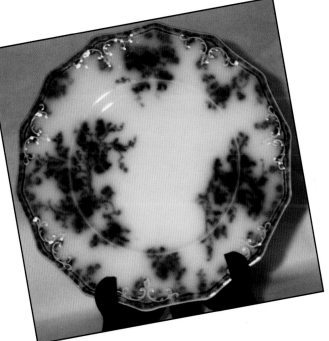

Plate 26. JANETTE plate, 10" in diameter.
Courtesy of Dave & Isabelle Long, Florida
$90-$125

Plate 27. MERION flange soup bowl, 9 7/8" in diameter. *Courtesy of Glynn & Shirley Jones, Illinois* $75 +

Gr-A body style shapes:

Plate 28. Butter pat, ARGYLE left, GIRONDE, 3" in diameter. *Courtesy of Shell & Jim Lewis, Illinois* $50+

Plate 31. Cake Plate, ARGYLE, 10 ½" x 9 ½" wide. *Author collection* $225+

Plate 29. Relish dish, ARGYLE, 8 ½" long x 4 ¾" wide. *Author collection* $175+

Plate 32. Nest round open bowls, ARGYLE, 10 ½" x 9 ½", 9 ½" x 8 ½", 8" x 7 ½". *Author collection* $225-$325

Plate 30. Oval platter, ARGYLE, 12 ¾" long x 8 ¾" wide. *Author collection* $175+

Plate 33. Nest oval open bowls, ARGYLE, 10" x 7", 9" x 6 ½". *Author collection* $175-$225

Plate 34. Round covered tureen, ARGYLE, 9 ¾" x 8". *Author collection* $300+

Plate 37. Oval covered sauce tureen & ladle, ARGYLE, tureen 8 ½" x 5", true undertray 8 ½" x 7 ½". Ladle handle 5". *Author collection* set $750+

Plate 35. Oval covered tureen, ARGYLE, 11" x 7 ½". *Author collection* $275+

Plate 38. Covered butter & drainer, ARGYLE, bottom tray 7 ½" in diameter x 3 ½" high. *Author collection* $425+

Plate 36. Oval covered soup tureen & ladle, ARGYLE, 13" x 9" x 7" high. Ladle handle 9 ½". *Author collection* set $1200+

Plate 39. Gravy boat & undertray, ARGYLE, gravy boat 7 ½" x 4" high, undertray 8 ½" x 5 ½". This is the true undertray because it has the indent for the gravy boat to rest in. *Author collection* set $275+

Plate 40. Coffee cup ARGYLE, teacup & saucer JANETTE, coffee cup 3" x 2 ¾", tea cup 4" x 2". *Author collection* $90-$125 ea.

Plate 41. Waste bowl, ARGYLE, 5 ½" x 3 ½" high. *Author collection* $275-$350

Plate 42. Bone dish, ARGYLE, 6" x 3 ½". A bone dish was never specifically made to match the Gr-A body style. The shape shown is the one used for Gr-A, but was also used for Gr-J, and also has been seen as part of a Newfield body style set of dishes. It is probably the first style of bone dish that Grindley produced. *Courtesy of Shell & Jim Lewis, Illinois* $95+

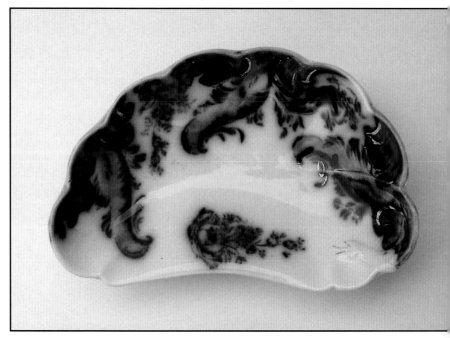

Plate 43. Spoon holder, ARGYLE, 5" high. *Author collection* $300+

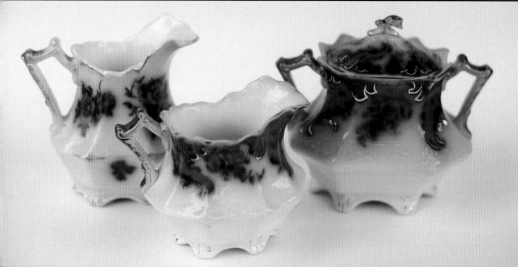

Plate 44. Sugar & small creamer, ARGYLE, large creamer, GIRONDE, Sugar 5 ½" high, creamers 4" & 5" high. *Author collection*, sugar $275+, creamers $225+

Plate 45. Pitchers, seven were available for a set of dishes. I show the smallest four here. Back ARGYLE 5 7/8" & 6 ½", front GIRONDE 5", ARGYLE 4". *Author collection $225-$350*

Plate 47. Eggcups, ARGYLE, these are the only ones I have ever seen. *Anonymous collector* $250+ ea.

Plate 46. Pedestal compote, ARGYLE, a very rare piece to find. *Anonymous collector* $1200+

Non-Flow Blue patterns applied to Gr-A body style:
STRATFORD II: Pink/yellow floral
VASSAR: Blue/yellow floral
WHITE: Whiteware
WHITE: Whiteware/gold tracings

Gr-B

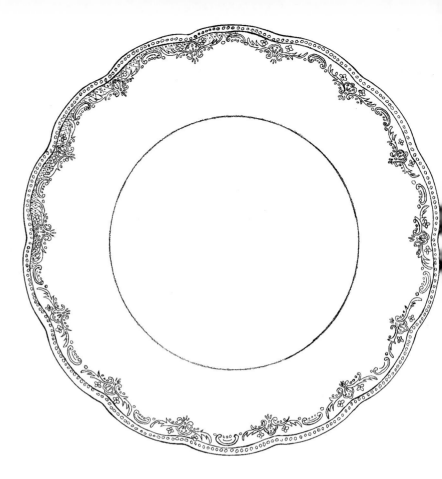

Plate 48. *Courtesy of Ann Potts, Illinois*
Body Style: Gr-B
Factory Name: -
U. S. Patent Applied/Dated: - /1902
English Registry: -
First Year Catalog: 1903 Sears Roebuck & Co.
Late Victorian Dating Label: Lace
Flow Blue Patterns: ALTON, ASTRAL, BEAUFORT, DELFT, EILEEN, FLORIDA, GIRTON, HADDON, KEELE, LORNE, MELBOURNE, WAVERLY, WOODBINE, and WOODVILLE

Gr-B pattern identification:

Plate 49. ALTON plate, 10" in diameter. *Author collection* $90-$125

Plate 50. BEAUFORT platter, 16" long. *Courtesy of Jerry & Margaret Taylor, Indiana* $225+

Plate 51. DELFT plate, 9" in diameter. I have seen this pattern with much better color and flow. *Author collection* $80-$100

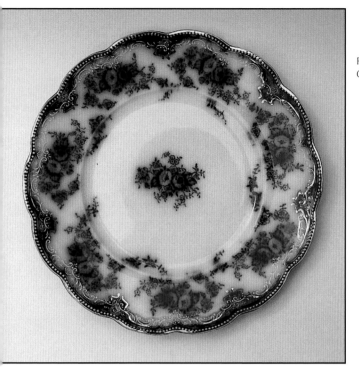

Plate 52. FLORIDA plate, 10" in diameter.
Courtesy of Shell & Jim Lewis, Illinois $90-$125

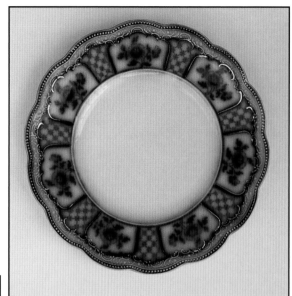

Plate 55. MELBOURNE plate, 9" in diameter. *Author collection* $80-$100

Plate 53. KEELE plate, 10"
in diameter. *Author
collection* $90-$125

Plate 56. WAVERLY plate, 10" in diameter.
Courtesy of David Long, Florida $90-$125

Plate 54. LORNE plate, 10" in
diameter. *Courtesy of James &
Phyllis Utick, California* $90-$125

Gr-B body style shapes:

Plate 57. Butter pat, top left FLORIDA, HADDON, bottom left MELBOURNE, WAVERLY, 3 ¼" in diameter. *Courtesy of Shell & Jim Lewis, Illinois* $50+

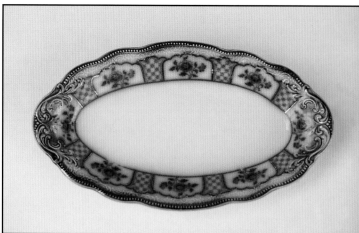

Plate 59. Relish dish, MELBOURNE, 9" x 5" wide. *Author collection* $175+

Plate 60. Platter, FLORIDA, 14" x 10' wide. *Author collection* $200+

Plate 58. Bone dish, MELBOURNE, 7 ½" long. *Courtesy of Shell & Jim Lewis, Illinois* $95+

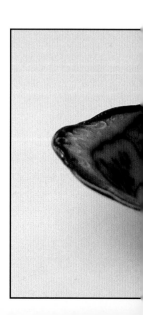

Plate 61. Cake plate, MELBOURNE, FLORIDA, 9 ½" x 9" wide. *Author collection* $225+

Plate 62. Salad bowl, MELBOURNE, approximate 12" x 5" high. *Courtesy of Dean & Victoria Hashimoto, Massachusetts* $300+

plate 63. Nest oval open bowls, MELBOURNE, 9" x 6 ½", 8" x 6". *Author collection* $175-$225

Plate 64. Individual oval bowl, MELBOURNE, 6" long. *Courtesy of Shell & Jim Lewis, Illinois* $90+

Plate 65. Round covered tureen, MELBOURNE, 8 ½″ x 10″ handle to handle. *Author collection* $300+

Plate 66. Oval covered soup tureen, MELBOURNE, tureen 14 ½″ long x 7 ½″ high, true undertray 14″ x 10″, ladle handle 9 ¾″. *Author collection* set $1200+

Plate 67. Oval covered sauce tureen with attached undertray, and ladle, MELBOURNE, undertray & tureen handle to handle 9″long, ladle handle 5″. This is a very rare sauce tureen because the undertray is attached. *Author collection* set $850+

Plate 68. Covered butter & drainer, MELBOURNE left & HADDON, bottom tray 7 ¼″ in diameter x 3 ¾″ high. *Author collection* $425+

Plate 69. Eggcups, l to r MELBOURNE, LORNE, COUNTESS, HADDON. Even though COUNTESS, is a Gr-C pattern, it was applied to the universal small eggcup. The shape of this small eggcup was used on all Grindley body styles, large eggcup 3 ¾" high, small eggcup 2 ¼" high. *Courtesy of Shell & Jim Lewis, Illinois* both sizes $175+

Plate 70. Waste bowl, MELBOURNE, 5 ½" x 3 ½"high. *Courtesy of Shell & Jim Lewis, Illinois* $275-$350

Plate 71. Oyster bowl, l to r MELBOURNE, HADDON, and WAVERLY, 5 ¾"x 3". *Author collection* $200+

Plate 72. Spoon holder, MELBOURNE, 5" high. This shape of spoon holder was made specifically for Gr-B body style. *Author collection* $300+

Plate 73. Covered sugar, FLORIDA, BEAUFORT, 7" handle to handle x 4" high. *Author collection* $275+

Plate 74. Teapot, MELBOURNE, 9 1/5" handle to tip of spout x 4 ¾" high. *Author collection* $1100+

Plate 75. Pitchers, I show the two largest in the seven pitcher series, left MELBOURNE 8 ½" high, WAVERLY 9 ½" high. *Author collection $500+ & 400+*

Plate 76. Covered mustered jar/attached undertray, MELBOURNE, 4" high. With the lid intact, this becomes a very rare piece. *Courtesy of Arnold & Dorothy Kowalsky, New York $275-$375+*

Plate 77. Double salt, HADDON, 5" long. *Author collection $250+*

Plate 78. Pedestal Compote, MELBOURNE, 9 ½" x 4 ¾" high. *Author collection $350-$750*

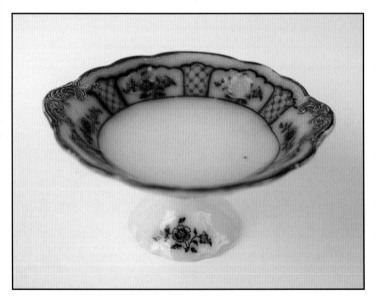

Plate 79. WHITE/gold tracings plate, 10" in diameter. This plate shows the ever popular all white set of dishes, on a Gr-B body style. *Author collection $25*

Non-Flow Blue patterns applied to Gr-B body style:
BUTE: Pink floral
LUXOR: Pink rose beneath green edge
WHITE: Whiteware
WHITE: Whiteware/gold tracings (see Plate 79.)

Gr-C

Plate 80. *Courtesy of Ann Potts, Illinois*
Body Style: Gr-C
Factory Name: -
U. S. Patent Applied/Dated: - /October 31, 1899
English Registry: -
First Year Catalog: SS 1900 Montgomery Ward & Co. & Sears
Roebuck & Co.
Late Victorian Dating Label: Lace
Flow Blue patterns: ALASKA, ALBANY I, ASHBURTON,
BLUE ROSE, CLARENCE, COUNTESS, DERBY, DORIS,
ISMAY, MARLBOROUGH, OCHIS, OSBOURNE, and
PORTMAN

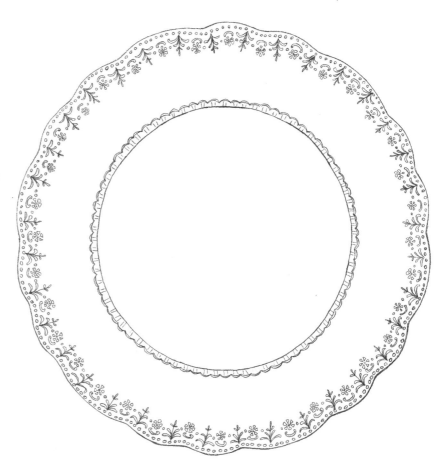

Gr-C pattern identification:

Plate 81. ALASKA plate, 10" in diameter. *Courtesy of
Lou & Molly Dubiel, Texas* $90-$125

Plate 82. ALBANY plate, 10" in diameter. *Courtesy of Lou
& Molly Dubiel, Texas* $90-$125

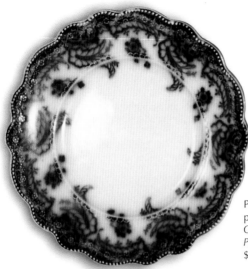

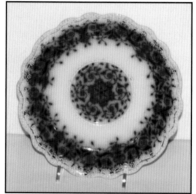

Plate 83. ASHBURTON plate, 10" in diameter. *Courtesy of James & Phyllis Utick, New York* $90-$125

Plate 86. DERBY plate, 10" in diameter. *Courtesy of Terry & Ann Potts, Illinois* $90-$125

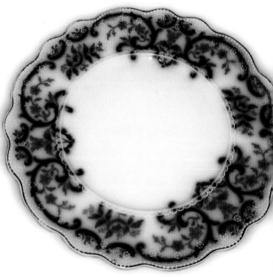

Plate 87. DORIS/OCHIS plate, 9" in diameter. *Courtesy of Irene Beer, Pennsylvania* $80-$100

Plate 84. BLUE ROSE plate, 8" in diameter. Courtesy of *Anonymous collector* $60-$80

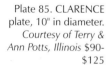

Plate 85. CLARENCE plate, 10" in diameter. *Courtesy of Terry & Ann Potts, Illinois* $90-$125

Plate 88. PORTMAN plate, 10" in diameter. *Courtesy of Jean & David Stelsel, Wisconsin* $90-$125

Gr-C body style shapes:

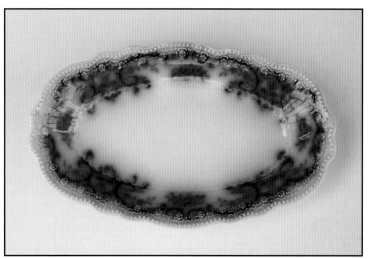

Plate 91. Relish dish, PORTMAN, 8 ¾" long x 5 ¼" wide. *Author collection* $175+

Plate 89. Butter pat, top left, COUNTESS, ALBANY bottom left, PORTMAN, ALASKA, 3 ¼" in diameter. *Courtesy of Shell & Jim Lewis, Illinois* $50+ ea.

Plate 92. Oval platter, PORTMAN, 18" long. *Author collection* $275+

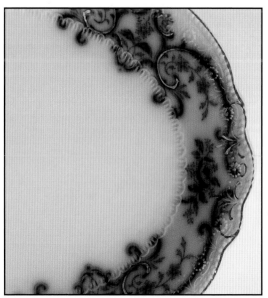

Plate 93. Same PORTMAN platter as Plate 92. This is one of the few body styles Grindley manufactured where the serving platters do not have tab handles, but instead have extra gold tracings in effigy. *Author collection* $275+

Plate 90. Bone dish, ALASKA top, PORTMAN, 7" long. *Courtesy of Shell & Jim Lewis, Illinois* $95+ ea.

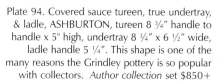

Plate 94. Covered sauce tureen, true undertray, & ladle, ASHBURTON, tureen 8 ¾" handle to handle x 5" high, undertray 8 ¾" x 6 ½" wide, ladle handle 5 ¼". This shape is one of the many reasons the Grindley pottery is so popular with collectors. *Author collection* set $850+

Plate 95. Covered butter & drainer, PORTMAN, bottom tray 7 ½" in diameter, 3 ¾" high. *Author collection* $425+

Plate 96. Teacup, PORTMAN, left, ALASKA, 3 ¾" x 2" high. *Courtesy of Shell & Jim Lewis, Illinois* $90-$125+ ea.

Plate 97. Waste bowl, l to r CLARENCE, OCHIS, and PORTMAN, 6" x 3 ½" high. *Author collection* $350 ea.

Plate 98. Oyster bowl, ALASKA left, PORTMAN, 6" x 3" high. *Author collection* $200+ ea.

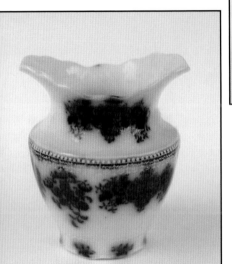

Plate 99. Spoon holder, CLARENCE, 4 ¾" high. *Author collection* $300+

Plate 100. Spoon holder, ALASKA, 4 ¾" high. In most cases, the pattern is applied exactly the same for each piece produced. However, in some cases through worker error the pattern is applied differently. *Courtesy of Shell & Jim Lewis, Illinois* $300+

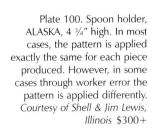

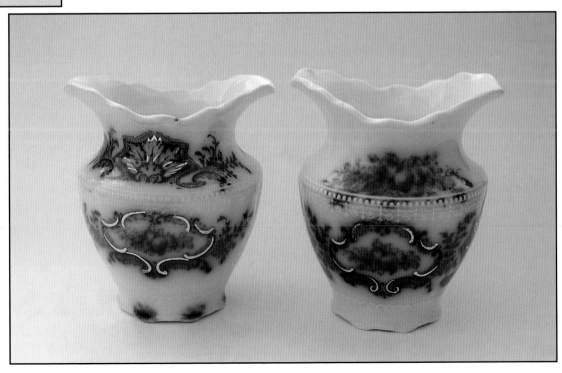

Plate 101. Large creamer, left to right PORTMAN, ALASKA, and CLARENCE, 4 ½" high. *Author collection* $225+ ea.

Plate 102. Covered sugar, left to right PORTMAN, MARLBOROUGH, and ALASKA, 7 ½" handle to handle x 5 ½" high. *Author collection* $275+ ea.

Plate 103. Covered sugar, COUNTESS, 7 ½" handle to handle x 5 ½" high. *Courtesy of Joseph & Nancy Padilla, Texas* $275+

Plate 104. This plate shows three pitchers that are number three in the seven pitcher series. They are one pint in size. left to right PORTMAN, COUNTESS, and MARLBOROUGH, 5 ½" high. *Author collection* $275 ea.

Plate 105. Teapot, PORTMAN, 9 ¾" handle to tip of spout x 6 ½" high. *Author collection $750+*

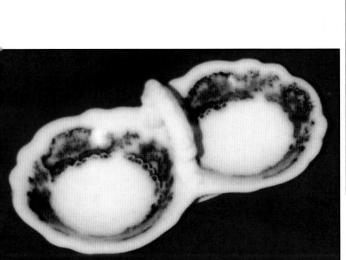

Plate 106. Double salt, ALASKA, 5" long. *Courtesy of Jim & Kathy Jalensky, Wisconsin $250+*

Plate 107. Pedestal compote, PORTMAN, 10" wide x 4 ½" high. *Author collection $350 - $1200*

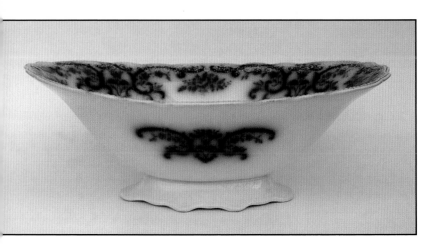

Plate 108. Pedestal fruit bowl, PORTMAN, 12 ½" long x 9" wide x 4" high. A very rare and exquisite bowl. *Author collection $500 - $750*

Non-Flow Blue patterns applied to Gr-C body style:
CECIL: Floral light blue edge
CYRIL: Pink flowers and green leaves
GREEN WREATH: Rd.No. 487049 (1906)
HOLLY: Green holly leaves and red berries
IVY: Green ivy border
KENWOOD: Green edge and pink flowers
MAYBELLE: Green F/AN
ROSA: Pink floral
TIVOLI: Pink flowers and green leaves
WHITE: Whiteware
WHITE: Whiteware/gold tracings
WILD ROSE: Pink floral
WOODLAND: Green edge with white/pink flowers

Gr-D

Plate 109. *Courtesy of Ann Potts, Illinois*
Body Style: Gr-D
Factory Name: -
U. S. Patent Applied/Dated: - / -
English Registry: -
First Year Catalog: circa 1894 Sears Roebuck & Co.
Late Victorian Dating Label: Scroll
Flow Blue Patterns: ANTIQUE, CATHERINE, CATHERINE
MERRETT, GARLAND, IDEAL, MARIE, OLYMPIA, PROGRESS,
RICHMOND, ROSE, UNIQUE, and UTOPIA

Gr-D pattern identification:

Plate 110. IDEAL plate, 10" in diameter. *Courtesy of Luanne Eisler, Pennsylvania* $45-$70

Plate 111. MARIE plate, 10" in diameter. *Courtesy of Shell & Jim Lewis, Illinois* $90-$125

Plate 112. PROGRESS plate, 10" in diameter.
Courtesy of Steve & Cindy Marut, Texas $90-$125

Plate 113. RICHMOND plate, 9" in diameter. *Courtesy of Jeanne Mueller, California* $80-$100

Plate 114. ROSE plate, 9" in diameter. *Courtesy of Jerry Hunsaker, California* $80-$100

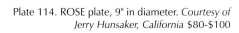

Gr-D body style shapes:

Plate 115. Butter pat, MARIE, 3" across. *Courtesy of Shell & Jim Lewis, Illinois* $50+

Plate 117. Individual oval bowl, MARIE left, ROSE, 5 ½" long. *Courtesy of Shell & Jim Lewis, Illinois* $90+

Plate 116. Relish dish, IDEAL, 8" x 4 ½" wide. *Author collection* $80+

Plate 118. Gravy boat, WHITE ware, 8" spout to handle x 3 ¾" high. *Author collection* $25+ because of color

Plate 119. Cup & saucer, PROGRESS, cup 3 ¼" x 2 ½" high, saucer 5 7/8" wide. *Author collection* $90-$125

Plate 120. Creamer, small & large, small OLYMPIA in green, 3 ¼" high, large PROGRESS, 4 ¾" high. *Author collection* large $225+, small $25+ because of color

Plate 121. Covered sugar, MARIE. *Courtesy of Terry & Ann Potts, Illinois* $275+

Plate 122. Teapot, IDEAL left, PROGRESS. *Courtesy of Warren & Connie Macy, Indiana* $550+

Plate 123. Covered mustard jar, ROSE, 4" x 1 ¾" high. Undertray is missing, but a rare find with lid in great shape. *Courtesy of Arnold & Dorothy Kowalsky, New York* $275-$375

Non-Flow Blue patterns applied to Gr-D body style:
ARCADIA: Yellow floral
DORA: Yellow floral, Rd.No. 268500 (1895)
WHITE: Whiteware
WHITE: Whiteware/gold tracings

Gr-E

Plate 124. *Courtesy of Ann Potts, Illinois*
Body Style Gr-E
Factory Name: -
U. S. Patent Applied/Dated: - /October 19, 1897
English Registry: -
First Year Catalog: FW 1898/1899 Montgomery Ward & Co.
Late Victorian Dating Label: Scroll
Flow Blue Patterns: ARGOS, BELMONT I, BRUSSELS, CELTIC,
CLYTIE, DOROTHY, GRACE, and WREATH

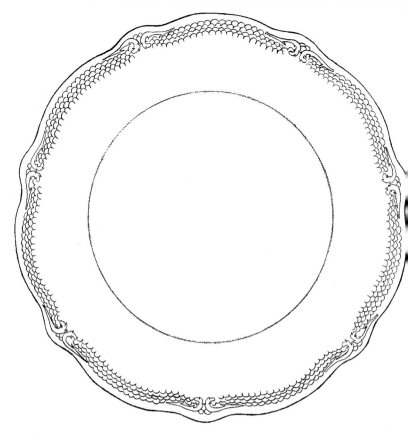

Gr-E pattern identification:

Plate 125. BRUSSELS rimmed soup plate, 9" in
diameter. *Courtesy of Glynn & Shirley Jones, Illinois* $80-
$100

Plate 127. GRACE platter,
10 ¾" x 7 ½" wide.
Author collection $150+

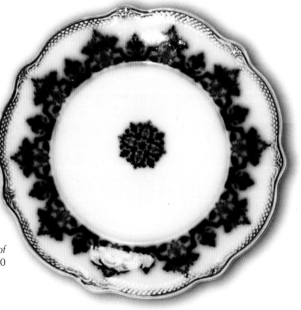

Plate 126. CELTIC plate, 9" in diameter. *Courtesy of
James & Phyllis Utick, New York* $80-$100

Gr-E body style shapes:

Plate 128. Butter pats, CELTIC left, GRACE, 3 ¼" in diameter. *Courtesy of Shell & Jim Lewis, Illinois* $50+

Plate 129. Bone dish, GRACE, 7" long. *Courtesy of Shell & Jim Lewis, Illinois* $95+

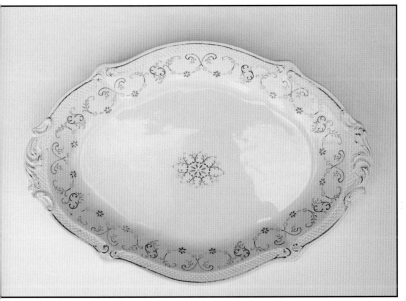

Plate 130. Platter, CLYTIE, shown in teal blue, 19" long. *Author collection* $130+ due to color

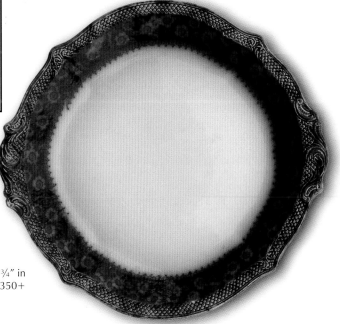

Plate 131. Round charger, GRACE, 14 ¾" in diameter. *Author collection* $350+

Plate 132. Covered butter, CELTIC, 7 ¼" in diameter x 4" high. *Courtesy of Lee & Betty Hochstetler, Indiana* $425+

Plate 133. Gravy boat, CLYTIE, 8 ¾" spout to handle x 3 ¾" high. *Author collection* $60+ due to color and no undertray

Plate 134. Eggcup, GRACE, 3 ¾" tall. *Courtesy of Shell & Jim Lewis, Illinois* $175+

Plate 135. Large teacup BRUSSELS left, 3 ¼" x 2 ¼" high, coffee cup, CELTIC, 4 ¼" x 2 ½" high. *Author collection* $90-$125, coffee cup $45+ due to color

Plate 136. Teacup, small and large, CELTIC. *Courtesy of Lee & Betty Hochstetler, Indiana* $90-$125

Plate 137. Spoon holder, CELTIC, 4 ¾" tall. *Courtesy of Lee & Betty Hochstetler, Indiana* $300+

Plate 138. Covered sugar and creamer, GRACE, sugar 7" handle to handle x 5" tall, creamer 5" tall. *Author collection* sugar $275+, creamer $225+

Plate 139. Teapot, GRACE, 7 ¼" tall. *Courtesy of Shell & Jim Lewis, Illinois* $1000+ due to popularity of pattern

Plate 140. Pitchers, this plate shows three of the seven pitchers in the series, left to right CELTIC, 5" tall, GRACE, 7 ½" tall, CELTIC, 6" tall. *Author collection* $225-$500+

Non-Flow Blue patterns applied to Gr-E body style:
WHITE: Whiteware
WHITE: Whiteware/gold tracings

Gr-F

Plate 141. *Courtesy of Ann Potts, Illinois*
Body Style: Gr-F
Factory Name: -
U. S. Patent Applied/Dated: - / -
English Registry: -
First Year Catalog: SS 1896 Sears Roebuck & Co.
Late Victorian Dating Label: Scroll
Flow Blue Patterns: DAISY II, DELMAR, LE PAVOT, LOUISE, and MARECHAL NEIL

Gr-F pattern identification:

Plate 142. MARECHAL NEIL plate and individual oval bowl, plate 10" in diameter, oval bowl 5 ½" long. *Courtesy of David Long, Florida* $90-$125 plate, $90+ oval bowl

Gr-F body style shapes:

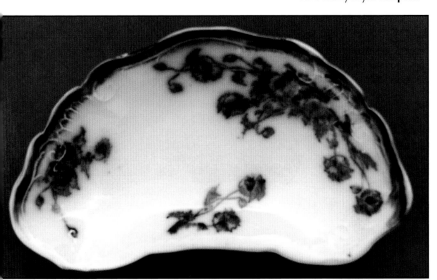

Plate 143. Bone dish, LE PAVOT, 6" long.
Author collection $95+

Plate 144. Platter, MARECHAL NEIL, 12" long.
Courtesy of Jerry & Margaret Taylor, Indiana
$175+

Plate 145. Covered sauce tureen and undertray, LE
PAVOT. *Courtesy of Bill & Nancy Lorne, Florida* $500+
because ladle is missing

Plate 146. Oyster bowl, MARECHAL NEIL, 5 ¾" x 3"
high. *Author collection* $200+

Non-Flow Blue patterns applied to Gr-F body style:
FLEUR D'OR: Pink/yellow floral, Rd.No. 268498 (1896)
WHITE: Whiteware
WHITE: Whiteware/gold tracings

Gr-G

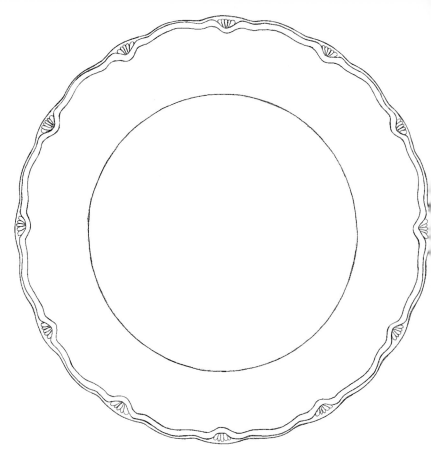

Plate 147. *Courtesy of Ann Potts, Illinois*
Body Style: Gr-G
Factory Name: The Imperial
U. S. Patent Applied/Dated: - / -
English Registry: -
First Year Catalog: 1906 Sears Roebuck & Co.
Late Victorian Dating Label: Transition
Flow Blue patterns: BELGRAVE, CLOVER, LOTUS, LYRIC,
SOMERSET, and THE HOFBURG

Gr-G pattern identification:

Plate 148. CLOVER saucer, 5 7/8" in diameter.
Author collection $20+

Plate 149. LOTUS plate, 10" in diameter.
Courtesy of Marilyn Harding, Missouri $90-$125

Gr-G body style shapes:

Plate 153. MELBA, covered sugar and creamer, sugar 5" to top of finial, creamer 4" tall. *Author collection* $50+ creamer, $75+ sugar, because of color.

Plate 150. Cake plate, THE HOFBURG, 10" handle to handle. *Author collection* $225+

Plate 154. WHITE ware, gravy boat, 8 ¼" spout to handle x 3 ¼" high. *Author collection* $25+

Plate 151. Gravy boat, THE HOFBURG, 8 ¼" spout to handle x 3 ¼" high. *Courtesy of Jerry & Judy Hunsaker, California* $150+ because it is missing undertray

Plate 152. Cup and saucer, CLOVER, cup 3 ¾" x 2" high, saucer 5 7/8" in diameter. *Author collection* $90-$125

Non-Flow Blue patterns applied to Gr-G body style:
CRYSTAL: Pink floral edge
NEVADA: Green clover border
ROSELAND: Green clover border
WHITE: Whiteware (see Plate 154.)
WHITE: Whiteware/gold tracings

Gr-H

Plate 155. *Courtesy of Ann Potts, Illinois*
Body Style: Gr-H
Factory Name: The Regal
U. S. Patent Applied/Dated: - / -
English Registry: 568951 (1910)
First Year Catalog: FW 1910/1911 Montgomery ward & Co.
Late Victorian Dating Label: Transition
Flow Blue Patterns: BISLEY, BLYTHSWOOD, BOMBAY, DENMARK, DENTON, GLENMORE, GLENTINE, LAWRENCE, and LYNTON

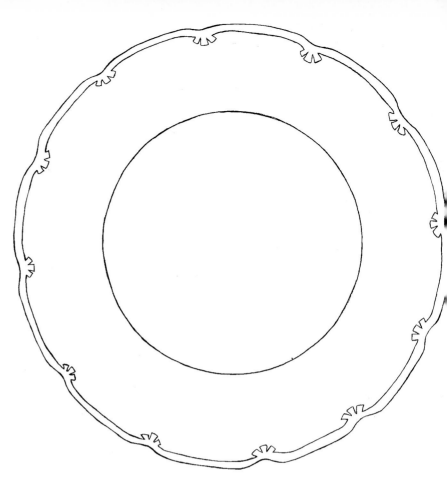

Gr-H pattern identification:

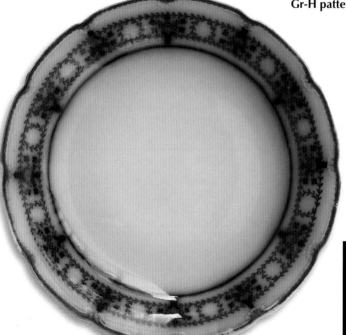

Plate 156. BLYTHSWOOD coupe soup, 8" in diameter. *Author collection $70+*

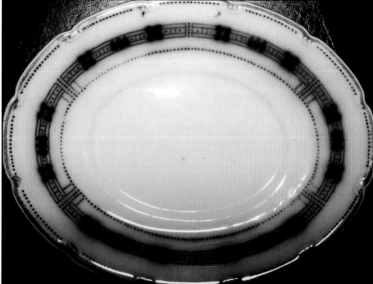

Plate 157. DENMARK platter, 11" x 8 ¼" wide.
Anonymous collector $150+

Plate 158. DENTON plate, 10" in diameter. *Courtesy of Steve & Cindy Marut, Texas* $90-$125

Plate 159. GLENMORE plate, 10" in diameter. *Anonymous collector* $90-$125

Plate 160. LAWRENCE plate, 8" in diameter. *Courtesy of Nancilee M. Van Buskirk, Illinois* $60-$80

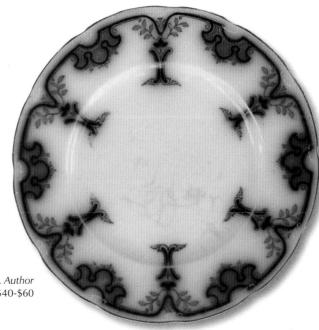

Plate 161. LYNTON plate, 7" in diameter. *Author collection* $40-$60

Gr-H body style shapes:

Plate 162. Platter, LAWRENCE, 11" long. The platters for Gr-H body style, round or oval, do not have tab handles. *Author collection* $150+

Plate 163. Round charger, DENTON, 12" in diameter. *Author collection* $350+

Plate 164. Cake plate, BISLEY left, DENTON, 9 ¾" handle to handle. For this particular body style, Gr-H, the cake plate is the only piece to have tab handles. *Author collection* $225+

Plate 165. Eggcup, DENTON, 2 ¼" high. *Courtesy of Debby Hagara, Washington* $175+

Plate 166. Cup and saucer, BLYTHSWOOD, cup 3 ¼" x 2 ½" high, saucer 6"in diameter. *Author collection* $90-$125

Plate 167. Waste bowl, DENTON, 5" x 3"high. *Author collection* $275-$350

Plate 168. Creamer and sugar, DENTON, creamer 3 ½" tall, sugar 5 ½" handle to handle x 4" high. *Author collection* set $250+ because of pattern color and quality

Plate 169. Pedestal compote, BLYTHSWOOD, 9 ¾" in diameter x 4 ¼" high. *Author collection* $350-$1200

Non-Flow Blue patterns applied to Gr-H body style:
DAINTY: Pink floral
WHITE: Whiteware
WHITE: Whiteware/gold tracings

Gr-I

Plate 170. *Courtesy of Ann Potts, Illinois*
Body Style: Gr-I
Factory Name: The Olympic
U. S. Patent Applied/Dated: - / -
English Registry: -First Year Catalog: circa 1922 Montgomery Ward & Co.
Late Victorian Dating Label: Transition
Flow Blue Patterns: BEAUTY ROSE, BURTON, HARTINGTON, IDRIS, LYNDHURST, RAMSGATE, SHANGHAI, SHANGRILA, THE LAHAYA

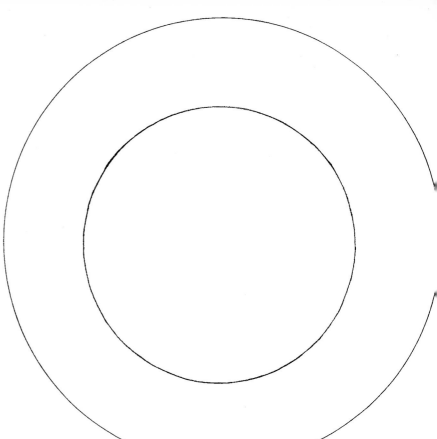

Gr-I pattern identification:

Plate 171. IDRIS platter, 12" long. *Anonymous collector* $175+

Plate 173. LYNDHURST plate, 10" in diameter. *Anonymous collector* $90-$125

Plate 172. HARTINGTON platter, 16" long. *Courtesy of Dave & Isabelle Long, Florida* $225+

Plate 174. SHANGHAI plates, 10" and 6" in diameter. *Courtesy of Bob & Bonnie Hohl, Pennsylvania* 10" plate $90-$125, 6" plate $40-$60

Gr-I body style shape:

Plate 175. Nappy, SHANGHAI 6 ½" in diameter. *Courtesy of Nancy Headen, Illinois* $50+

Plate 176. Round charger, SHANGHAI, 11" in diameter. This is one of Grindley's body styles where the platters do not have tab handles. We know this is a charger because of the size, and note there are five sets of the design. Normally there are four on a plate. *Courtesy of Nancy Headen, Illinois* $350+

Plate 177. Round and oval covered tureens, SHANGHAI. *Courtesy of Nancy Headen, Illinois* round tureen $300+ much harder to find, oval tureen $275+

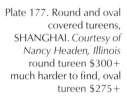

Plate 178. Covered butter and butter tub, SHANGHAI. *Courtesy of Bob & Bonnie Hohl, Pennsylvania* $425+, butter tub $500+

Plate 179. Double spout gravy with attached undertray, LYNDHURST. *Anonymous collector* $325+ because of double spout

Plate 180. Eggcup, IDRIS. *Courtesy of Shell & Jim Lewis, Illinois* $175+

Plate 181. Cups left to right cream soup with two handles, large tea, demi, large coffee, demi, small tea, and large tea, SHANGAI, *Courtesy of Bob & Bonnie Hohl, Pennsylvania* Large cups $135+, small cups $90-$125, demi's $150+

Plate 182. Cup and saucer, SHANGHAI, in this plate, we show you the saucer. *Courtesy of Bob & Bonnie Hohl, Pennsylvania* $90-$125

Plate 183. Teapot, SHANGHAI, This teapot represents one of two styles that were made for Gr-I. *Courtesy of Bob & Bonnie Hohl, Pennsylvania* $750+

Plate 184. Creamer, teapot, and sugar, sugar and creamer RIVIERA, teapot unidentified pattern. This tea set represents the other shape made for Gr-I, even though these are non Flow Blue patterns. Potentially, any Gr-I, Flow Blue pattern could be found on either tea set in Plates 183 & 184. I have seen SHANGHAI and IDRIS patterns on this shape. This shape could also be a universal one, for I have also seen MELBOURNE a Gr-B pattern applied to it.

Plate 185. Pitcher, SHANGHAI, 8 ¼″ tall. *Courtesy of Nancy Headen, Illinois* $400+

Plate 186. Pedestal compote, SHANGHAI. *Courtesy of Nancy Headen, Illinois* $350+

Plate 187. This photo shows a nice variety of pieces produced in the Gr-I shape.

Below, for Gr-I body style, are listed non-Flow Blue patterns that were applied to this style of dish. Many of the following patterns are typical Botanical type designs. Botanical patterns were very popular during the 1910s and 1920s, and this gives us a very strong indication of the popularity of this body style. It had a very long run at the factory. I list "first catalog" as circa 1922, but it would not surprise me at all to find out this style of dish, was being mass-produced during the 1910s.

Non-Flow Blue patterns applied to Gr-I:
BRISTOL: Floral
CRANBY
CUBA: Botanical border
DINART: Green festoon border
EASTBOURNE: Green botanical edge
GRECIAN ROSE: Pink flowers and green Greek key edge

LILY: Red floral
LINCOLN I
MIKADO
RIVIERA: Green edge design
ROSEMEATH: Green edge
SANTANGEL: Brown festoon border
STELLA: Checkered border
THE LANDSEER
THE OLAF: Red border
TILBURY: Brown festoon border
TROY: Green Greek key border
WHITE: Whiteware
WHITE: Whiteware/gold tracings
WICKLOW: Red rose floral on border
WRENBURY: Gold border with pheasants in center

Gr-J

Plate 188. *Courtesy of Ann Potts, Illinois*
Body Style: Gr-J
Factory Name: -
U. S. Patent Applied/Dated: - / -
English Registry: -
First Year Catalog: circa 1895 Montgomery ward & Co.
Late Victorian Dating Label: Scroll
Flow Blue patterns: BROCKLYN, DUCHESS, FERN, HUDSON, LA GLORIA, MARGUERITE, MARSEILLES, MILAN I, POPPY, PREMIER, and WILDFLOWER

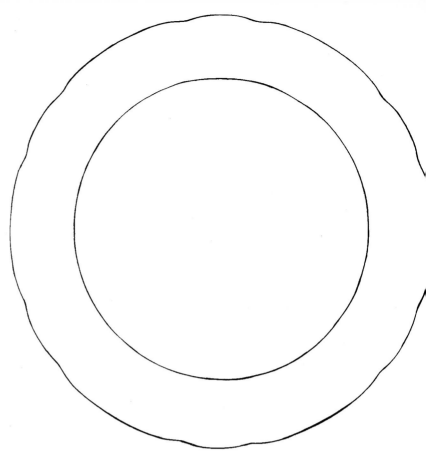

Gr-J pattern identification:

This body style, Gr-J, represents the transition style of dish from the Newfield to the Woodland Pottery. At the Newfield Pottery, so typical of the 1880s, square and oblong shaped body styles were made. This new for its day shape was the first attempt by Grindley at making his ware round in definition, and with a heavier use of embossing and edge scallops. In the transition from the Newfield to the Woodland Pottery, there were many "old" already manufactured pieces that were brought to the new facility. Several of the new patterns first made at the Woodland pottery were applied to these "old" shapes, rather than discarding them. That is why you will see several of Gr-Js patterns applied to two different styles of dishes. The two styles are the last one made at the Newfield Pottery, and the first one made at the Woodland pottery.

Plate 189. ARABIC coupe shaped bowl, 7 ¾" in diameter. The shape of this dish is from the Newfield pottery, but this pattern was also applied to the Gr-J body style. *Author collection* $30+ due to slate color

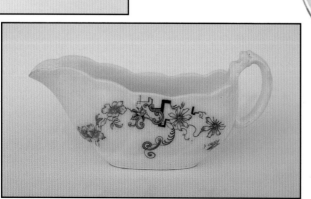

Plate 190. BROCKLYN gravy boat, 8 ¾" spout to handle. *Author collection* $60+ due to slate color

Plate 191. DUCHESS plate, 10" in diameter. *Courtesy of Steve & Cindy Marut, Texas* $90-$125

Plate 192. MARGUERITE plate, 10" in diameter.
Anonymous collector $90-$125

Plate 193. MARSEILLES oval bowl, 8 ¾" x 6 ¼" wide. *Author collection $60+ due to slate color*

Plate 194. POPPY bowl, 8 ¾" x 6 ¼" wide. *Courtesy of Bill & Nancy Lorne, Florida $175-$225*

Plate 195. POPPY plate, 10" in diameter. This plate is the same pattern as Plate 194, but in slate color. *Author collection $60+ due to slate color*

Gr-J body style shapes:

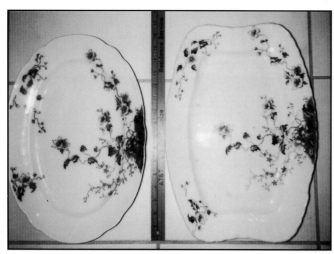

Plate 196. Platter, DUCHESS, left 14"long, 16"long. This is an excellent example of my previous comments. One pattern is applied to two styles of dish. On the left is Gr-J shape, which was the first new shape at the Woodland Pottery, and on the right is the "old" and last shape made at the Newfield Pottery. *Courtesy of Richard Dodd, New York* left $200+, right $100+ due to slate color

Plate 197. Round tureens, DUCHESS, left to right round covered soup and ladle, small round covered tureen, regular size round covered tureen. Only the round covered vegetable tureen came in two sizes, with the smallest one being the hardest to find. *Courtesy of Richard Dodd, New York* l to r $750+, $350+, $300+

Plate 198. Cup & saucer, DUCHESS. *Author collection* $90-$125

Plate 199. Oyster bowl, DUCHESS, 5 1/2" in diameter x 2 7/8" high. *Author collection* $200+

Plate 200. Round bowls, DUCHESS, four in back row are the round open vegetable bowls, left front are the two sizes of waste bowl, and right are the two sizes that the oyster bowl came in. *Courtesy of Richard Dodd, New York* back row $225-$325, left front $275-$325+, right front $200+

Plate 201. Sugar and creamer, MARGUERITE. *Author collection* sugar $275+, creamer $225+

Plate 202. Teapot, MARGUERITE, *Author collection* $750+

Plate 203. Pitcher, 8 ½" high. MARGUERITE, *Author collection* $400+

Non-Flow Blue patterns applied to Gr-J body style:
WHITE: Whiteware
WHITE: Whiteware/gold tracings

Gr-K

Plate 204. *Courtesy of Ann Potts, Illinois*
Body Style: Gr-K
Factory Name: -
U. S. Patent Applied/Dated: - / -
English Registry: Rd. No. 412411 (1903)
First Year Catalog: circa 1905 SS Sears Roebuck & Co.
Late Victorian Dating label: Lace
Flow Blue Patterns: BALTIC, BRAZIL, and CRESCENT

Gr-K pattern identification:

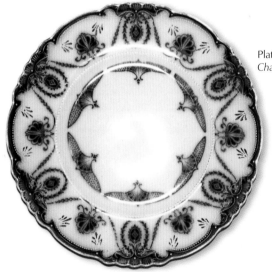

Plate 205. CRESCENT plate, 10" in diameter. *Courtesy of Charles & Dorothy Washer, Illinois* $90-$125

Plate 206. BALTIC plate, 10" in diameter. *Courtesy of Shell & Jim Lewis, Illinois* $90-$125

Gr-K body style shapes:

Plate 207. Platter/undertray, BRAZIL. Plate 207 will show you the shape of the oval platters, even though it is the undertray for the sauce tureen. *Author photo* $125+

Plate 208. Round charger, CRESCENT, 13 ¼" in diameter. *Courtesy of Charles & Dorothy Washer, Illinois* $350+

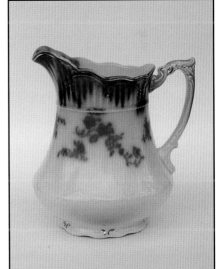

Plate 209. Sugar, teapot, and small creamer. Sugar & teapot BRAZIL, small creamer BALTIC, left to right 3 ¾" high, 5 ½" high, 4 ½" high. *Author collection* left to right $275+, $750+, $225+

Plate 210. Pitcher, BRAZIL, 5 ½" high. *Author collection* $275+

Plate 211. Pedestal compote, CRESCENT, 9 ½" in diameter x 3 ¼" high. *Courtesy of Charles & Dorothy Washer, Illinois* $350-$1200

Non-Flow Blue patterns applied to Gr-K body style:
SARATOGA: Pink floral
SYLVIA: Pink floral
VIRGINIA: Pink floral
WHITE: Whiteware
WHITE: Whiteware/ gold tracings

Gr-L

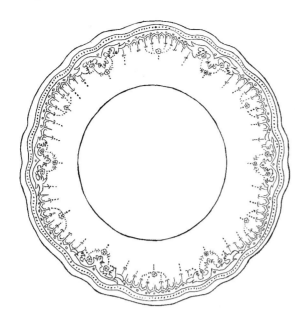

Plate 212. *Courtesy of Ann Potts, Illinois*
Body Style: Gr-L
Factory Name: -
U. S. Patent Applied/Dated: - / -
English registry: Rd.No.457049 (1905)
First Year Catalog: FW 1905/1906 Montgomery Ward & Co.
Late Victorian Dating Label: Lace Flow Blue Patterns: ATLANTA, DOVER, HAMPTON, HAMPTON SPRAY, KENT, THE ATHENS, and VICTORIA

Gr-L pattern identification:

Plate 213. DOVER saucer, 5 7/8" in diameter. *Author collection* $25+

Plate 215. HAMPTON SPRAY saucer, 5 7/8" in diameter. *Courtesy of Marilyn Harding, Missouri* $25+

Plate 214. HAMPTON plate, 10" in diameter. *Courtesy of Sue Otteman, Texas* $90-$125

Gr-L body style shapes:

Plate 216. Cup & saucer, DOVER. *Author collection* $90-$125

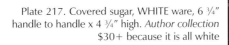

Plate 217. Covered sugar, WHITE ware, 6 ¾"
handle to handle x 4 ¾" high. *Author collection*
$30+ because it is all white

Plate 218. Covered sauce tureen and undertray, HAMPTON.
Courtesy of Sue Otteman, Texas set $550+ because ladle is missing

Non-Flow Blue patterns applied to Gr-L body style:
CEDRIC: Floral
WHITE: Whiteware
WHITE: Whiteware/gold tracings

Gr-M

Plate 219. *Courtesy of Ann Potts, Illinois*
Body Style: Gr-M
Factory Name: -
U. S. patent Applied/Dated: - /November 8, 1898
English Registry: -
First Year Catalog: FW 1899/1900 Montgomery Ward & Co.
Late Victorian Dating Label: Scroll
Flow Blue Patterns: ALDINE, EATON, FESTOON I, MANILA, TERESA, and THE HAVANA

Gr-M pattern identification:

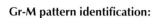

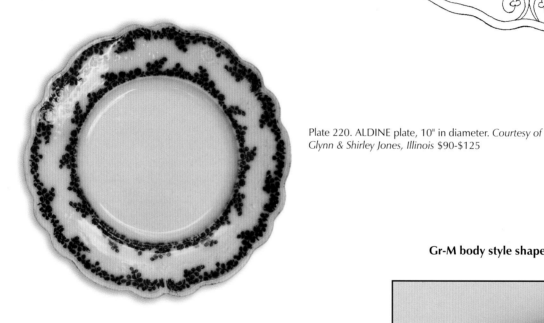

Plate 220. ALDINE plate, 10" in diameter. *Courtesy of Glynn & Shirley Jones, Illinois* $90-$125

Gr-M body style shapes:

Plate 221. Plate, GREEN airbrush, 10" in diameter. *Author collection* $25+ due to color

Plate 222. Platter & creamer, ALDINE, platter 18" long. *Courtesy of Irene Beer, Pennsylvania* platter $275+, creamer $225+

Plate 223. Oval covered tureen, PINK airbrush. *Courtesy of John Hauserman, Michigan* $125+ due to color

Plate 224. Oval covered sauce tureen & ladle, PINK airbrush. *Courtesy of John Hauserman, Michigan* $150+ due to color

Plate 225. Eggcup, ALDINE, 3 5/8" high.
Author collection $175+

Plate 226. Cup, BLUE airbrush. *Courtesy of John
Hauserman, Michigan* $25+ due to color

Plate 227. Pitcher, PURPLE unidentified
floral, 6" high. *Author collection* $50+
due to color

**Non-Flow Blue patterns applied to
Gr-M:**
BLUE: Airbrush border
GREEN: Airbrush border
LINCOLN: Green floral, Rd.No.
326054 (1898)
PINK: Airbrush border
WHITE: Whiteware
WHITE: Whiteware/gold tracings

Gr-N

Plate 228. *Courtesy of Ann Potts, Illinois*
Body Style: Gr-N
Factory Name: The Marquis
Factory Name: White Marquis, for whiteware
U. S. Patent Applied/Dated: - /May 9, 1906
English Registry: Rd.No.473130 (1906)
First Year Catalog: -
Late Victorian Dating Label: Transition
Flow Blue patterns: CAMERON, GRANBY, and THE MARQUIS

Gr-N pattern identification:

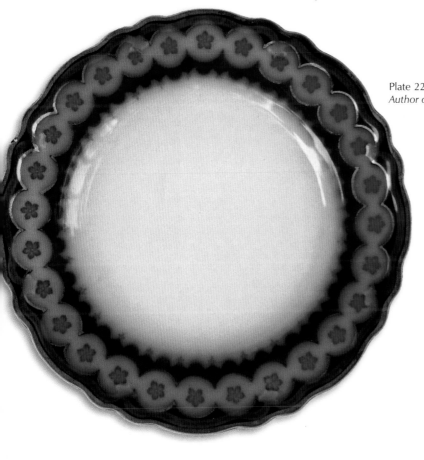

Plate 229. GRANBY plate, 7 ¾" in diameter.
Author collection $60-$80

Plate 230. THE MARQUIS plate, 6" in
diameter. *Courtesy of Edna C. Anderson,
Illinois* $40-$60

Gr-N body style shapes:

Plate 231. Cup & saucer, GRANBY, cup 3 5/8"
x 2 ½", saucer 6" in diameter. *Author
collection* $90-$125

Plate 232. Pedestal compote, THE MARQUIS, 9 ½" in diameter x 4"
high. *Author collection* $350-$1200

Non-Flow Blue patterns applied to Gr-N body style:
WHITE: Hand painted lady/flowers
WHITE: Light blue edge, Rd.No. 521192 (1908)
WHITE: Whiteware
WHITE: Whiteware/gold tracings

Gr-O

Plate 233. *Courtesy of Ann Potts, Illinois*
Body Style: Gr-O
Factory Name: The Duchess
U. S. patent Applied/Dated: - / -
English Registry: -
First Year Catalog: -
Late Victorian Dating label: Transition
Flow Blue Patterns: CLIFTON, BERLIN, DERWENT, MADRID, and WENTWORTH

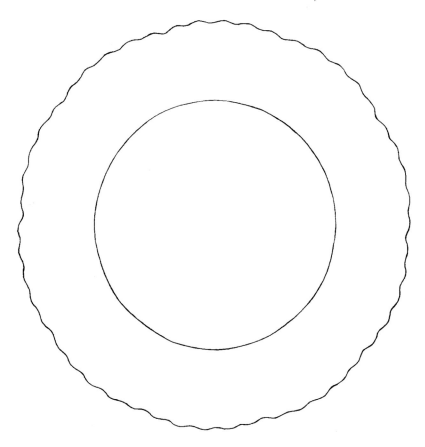

Gr-O pattern identification:

Plate 234. DERWENT plate, 10" in diameter.
Author photo $90-$125

Gr-O body style shapes:

Plate 235. Butter pat, CLIFTON. *Courtesy of Shell & Jim Lewis, Illinois* $50+

Plate 236. Round covered tureen bottom, CLIFTON. *Courtesy of Jerry & Judy Hunsaker, California* $125+ because of missing lid

Plate 237. Cup & saucer, CLIFTON. *Courtesy of JoAnn Woodall & Paul Woolmer, Illinois* $90-$125

Plate 239. Covered sugar, WENTWORTH, 6" handle to handle x 4 ½" high. *Author collection* $275+

Plate 238. Oyster bowl, WENTWORTH, 5 ¾" x 3" high. *Author collection* $200+

Plate 240. Pitcher, WENTWORTH, 5 ¼" high. *Author collection* $275+

Non-Flow Blue patterns applied to Gr-O body style:
BERLIN: Green AN
JEWEL: Pink floral
ROSLYN: Pink floral
WHITE: Whiteware
WHITE: Whiteware/gold tracings

Plate 241. 10" Plate, unidentified pattern. *Author collection*
Body Style: Gr-P
Factory Name: -
U. S. Patent Applied/Dated: - /October 2, 1900
English Registry: -
First Year Catalog: 1903 Sears Roebuck & Co.
Late Victorian Dating Label: Lace
Flow Blue Patterns: Two unidentified, floral

Gr-P is a newly discovered Grindley Flow Blue body style. I have seen two unidentified floral patterns being sold over one of the Internet auction sites. The hollowware in this style of dish is a cross between Gr-B and Gr-C. It is very similar to both of those styles. Plate 233 shows an unidentified pink floral plate, which is on the Gr-P body style. Just when you think you have discovered all the Flow Blue body styles that Grindley made, up pops another one. The research I am doing is very exciting, and seemingly, never ending. Collectors who may have a piece from this Gr-P body style are encouraged to contact me through my publisher, Schiffer Books, Ltd.

wash set body styles – specifics

I would like to reiterate and add some additional information here from what I gave you in the beginning of the "dish body styles." Wash set body styles, in my research, appear to be totally separate from dish body styles. Separate both in style and patterns.

The reason I have had a line drawing done of a pitcher from each style is that the pitcher will contain all the necessary markings to recognize all pieces in a wash set. What ever scallop, spout, handle or body treatment it received, so did the other pieces in the set. That is why they are a "matched" set.

In some cases, a pottery did make a wash set to match a dish set. I will as we go along, point these out to you. A pottery also did use some patterns on both a wash set and a dish set. I will also point these

out to you. Wash sets are easy to research, but very hard to acquire a pitcher to have a line drawing done. I have been very fortunate to have many willing friends loan me their pitchers to be drawn for the Grindley and Johnson Bros. projects. The two Meakin projects have suffered from lack of drawings. More research is needed, and many more line drawings need to be completed. I will endeavor to do my best in the future.

There are twelve pieces to a wash set. If you own a complete set with all twelve, you are a very lucky and envied collector. Treat your set as one of the most sacred things you own. One thing we must always remember is that every time any piece of Flow Blue is broken irreparably, there is one less in this world. When it comes to Flow Blue wash sets, there are too few now to handle carelessly – guard them!

Plate 242. *Courtesy of Ann Potts, Illinois*
Body Style: Gr-W1
Factory Name: -
U. S. Patent Applied/Dated: - /September 21, 1897
English Registry: -
First Year Catalog: FW 1901/1902 Montgomery Ward & Co.
Late Victorian Dating Label: Scroll
Flow Blue patterns: CLEMATIS, SYRIAN, and UNIDENTIFIED floral

Plate 243. CLEMATIS pitcher & bowl. Even though the first catalog date is 1901, we know that it was produced before this date because of the 1897 patent date. *Courtesy of Irene Gill, England* $900+

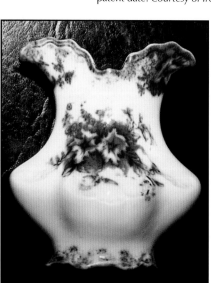

Plate 244. CLEMATIS toothbrush holder.
Courtesy of Irene Gill, England $225+

Plate 245. SYRIAN wash set complete except for slop jar.
Courtesy of Kenneth Franks, Kentucky $2800+

Plate 246. *Courtesy of Ann Potts, Illinois*
Body Style: Gr-W2
Factory Name: -U. S. Patent Applied/Dated: - / -
English Registry: -First Year Catalog: -
Late Victorian dating Label: Scroll
Flow Blue Patterns: ALBANY II

Plate 247. ALBANY II large pitcher. *Courtesy of Jerry & Margaret Taylor, Indiana* $600+

Plate 248. ALBANY II chamber pot no lid & master slop jar. *Courtesy of Jerry & Margaret Taylor, Indiana* chamber pot $100+, master slop jar $275+

Plate 249. ALBANY II mug. *Courtesy of Arnold & Dorothy Kowalsky, New York* $225+

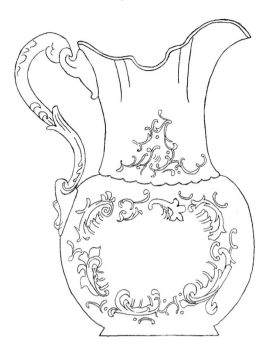

Plate 250. *Courtesy of Ann Potts, Illinois*
Body Style: Gr-W3
Factory Name: -
U. S. Patent Applied/Dated: - / -
English Registry: -
First Year Catalog: SS circa 1895 Montgomery Ward & Co.
Late Victorian Dating Label: Scroll
Flow Blue patterns: BOSTON, LA BELLE, PRIMULA, and TRIUMPH

Plate 251. PRIMULA small pitcher. *Author collection* $275+

Plate 253. BOSTON mug 3 ¾" high. *Author collection* $225+

Plate 252. LA BELLE master slop jar, no lid. *Courtesy Ron & Dee Pine, Illinois* $75 because of damage & no lid

Plate 254. BOSTON in pink/yellow. This is a good example of the use of other colors to replace the blue. This pattern is identical to and called BOSTON. From this, we can determine that the pottery registered the pattern and not the color. *Courtesy of Shell & Jim Lewis, Illinois* $30+

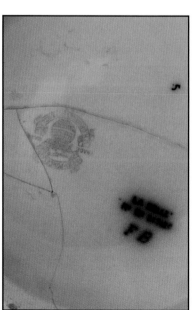

Plate 255. I have included this plate to show you by example how Grindley marked some of his wash sets. Notice that the globe mark is brown, and in the banner at the top of the globe it states "Semi-Porcelain". This is normally where the pattern name goes, but because that area is filled, the pattern name is applied separately as shown, and in blue. If you see an Rd.No., as in this case, it represents the pattern registration number. If there were an Rd.No. in brown, and by the globe mark, it would be the body style registration number. Why was this done? Because with "Semi-Porcelain" included in the mark, it became more attractive to a buyer who was made to "think" that they were buying Porcelain. Marketing, pure and simple. *Courtesy of Ron & Dee Pine, Illinois*

Plate 256. This pitcher is from Body Style Gr-B. This line drawing was done because a wash set was made in this body style, and has been seen only in WHITE. This, however, creates the potential for a Flow Blue pattern to be applied. *Courtesy of Ann Potts, Illinois*

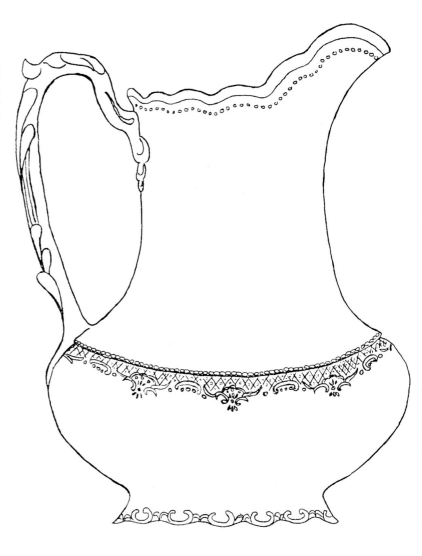

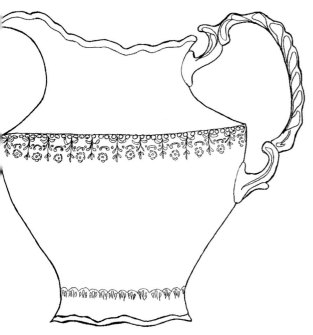

Plate 257. This pitcher is from Body Style Gr-C. This line drawing was done because a wash set was made in this body style, and seen in WHITE, and in the Flow Blue pattern OSBORNE. *Courtesy of Ann Potts, Illinois*

Plate 258. This pitcher is from Body Style Gr-E. This line drawing was done because a wash set was made in this body style, and has been seen only in WHITE. This, however, creates the potential for a Flow Blue pattern to be applied. *Courtesy of Ann Potts, Illinois*

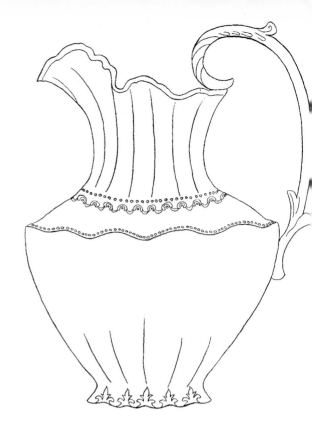

Plate 259. *Courtesy of Ann Potts, Illinois*
Body Style: Gr-W7
Factory Name: -
U. S. patent Applied/Dated: - / -
English Registry: -First year Catalog: -
Late Victorian Dating label: Lace
Flow Blue patterns: FESTOON II, PERTH, and UNIDENTIFIED floral

Plate 260. FESTOON complete wash set. This body style Gr-W7 is very close to Grindley's dish body style of Gr-C, but they are different. Plate 260 shows all twelve pieces available for a wash set. They are large pitcher, bowl, small pitcher, mug, toothbrush holder, soap dish (3), chamber pot (2), and master slop jar (2). *Courtesy of Ronald Morley, Missouri* $3000+

Plate 261. FESTOON large pitcher and toothbrush holder. This plate shows a little more detail of the shape of these two pieces. Not all toothbrush holders will have the two spouts on either side of the top rim. Some are straight sided and do not have any at all. *Courtesy of Ronald Morley, Missouri* $600+ large pitcher, $225+ toothbrush holder

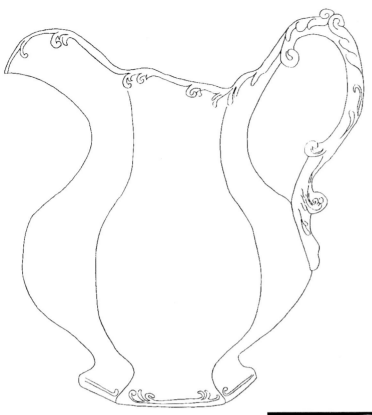

Plate 262. *Courtesy of Ann Potts, Illinois*
Body Style: Gr-W8
Factory Name: -
U. S. patent Applied/Dated: - /February 16, 1897
English Registry: -
First Year Catalog: FW 1897/1898 Montgomery Ward & Co.
Late Victorian Dating label: Scroll
Flow Blue Patterns: DOREEN

Plate 263. DOREEN wash set complete except for chamber pot. *Courtesy of Al & Marge Jager, Michigan* $2800+

Plate 264. DOREEN in a usual setting for a wash set, and shows the chamber pot for identification. Minus only the small pitcher. *Courtesy of Jerry & Margaret Taylor, Indiana* $2600+

Plate 265. DOREEN large pitcher for a clearer, close up look. *Courtesy of Jerry & Margaret Taylor, Indiana* $600+

Plate 266. *Courtesy of Ann Potts, Illinois*
Body Style: Gr-W9
Factory Name: -
U. S. Patent Applied/Dated: - / September 21, 1897
English Registry: -
First Year Catalog: SS 1896 Sears Roebuck & Co.
Late Victorian Dating Label: Scroll
Flow Blue Patterns: ATHENA I

ATHENA I pitcher & bowl. *Courtesy of Bill & Nancy Lorne, Florida* $900+

Plate 268. *Courtesy of Ann Potts, Illinois*
Body Style:Gr-W10
Factory Name: -
U. S. Patent Applied/Dated: - /March, 1897
English Registry: -
First Year Catalog: -
Late Victorian Dating Label: Scroll
Flow Blue Patterns: HARLEY

Plate 269. HARLEY complete wash set. *Courtesy of Mark & Sarah Cotrupi, Nebraska* $3000+

Plate 270. HARLEY large wash pitcher. This plate will show the pitcher in better detail. *Courtesy of Mark & Sarah Cotrupi, Nebraska* $600+

Plate 271. HARLEY wash bowl and mug. This plate offered for a better display of detail, for items shown. *Courtesy of Bill & Nancy Lorne, Florida* $225+ mug, $300+ wash bowl

Plate 272. *Courtesy of Ann Potts, Illinois*
Body Style: Gr-W11
Factory Name: -
U. S. patent Applied/Dated: - / -
English Registry: -
First Year Catalog: -
Late Victorian Dating Label: Scroll
Flow Blue Patterns: ALBANY I, and MAY

Plate 273. MAY pitcher &
washbowl. *Courtesy of
Adele Kenney, New Jersey*
$900+

Plate 274. ALBANY I mug. This is a
dish pattern crossover from Gr-C
body style. *Author collection* $225+

Plate 275. *Courtesy of Ann Potts, Illinois*
Body Style: Gr-W12
Factory Name: -
U. S. Patent Applied/Dated: 1896 / -
English Registry: 269020 (1896)
First Year Catalog: SS 1898 Montgomery Ward & Co.
Late Victorian Dating label: Scroll
Flow Blue Patterns; CHATSWORTH, and MARGOT

Plate 276. MARGOT wash set minus the soap dish and the master slop jar.
Courtesy of Joe & Sandy Evers, Canada $2400+

Plate 277. CHATSWORTH mug. A Gr-A crossover pattern,
and very close to the MARGOT pattern design. It may even
be the same pattern. *Author collection* $225+

Plate 278. *Courtesy of Ann Potts, Illinois*
Body Style: Gr-W13
Factory Name: -
U. S. Patent Applied/Dated: - /-
English Registry: - /
First Year Catalog: FW 1899/1900
Montgomery Ward & Co.
Late Victorian Dating label: Scroll
Flow Blue Patterns: ATLAS

Plate 279. ATLAS wash set minus the master slop jar. In the Montgomery Ward & Co., catalog it specifically states that the soap dish came without a drainer. I would be curious if anyone has one. *Courtesy of Charles & Louise Loehr, Pennsylvania* $2700+

Plate 280. ATLAS large pitcher 13" high x 10 ½" wide. This plate shows the pitcher in great detail. *Courtesy of Irene Gill, England* $600+

Plate 281. *Courtesy of Ann Potts, Illinois*
Body Style: Gr-W14
Factory Name: -
U. S. Patent Applied/Dated: - / -
English Registry: Rd.No.245999 (1894)
First Year Catalog: SS 1896 Montgomery Ward & Co.
Late Victorian Dating Label: Scroll
Flow Blue Patterns: CAMPION

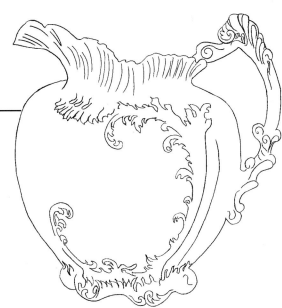

Plate 284. CAMPION large pitcher for better detail. I discovered a very interesting thing about this pitcher from the Montgomery Ward & Co. catalog. This same shape was sold in three sizes as a fancy water pitcher. The three sizes, sold separately in the catalog were, 1 pint, 1 quart, and 2 quart. The color for these three pitchers was an all over Royal Blue. Has anyone seen any of these? *Courtesy of Jeanne Mueller, California* $600+

Plate 282. CAMPION wash set minus the chamber pot, master slop jar, and the soap dish lid. *Courtesy of Jeanne Mueller, California* $2300+

Plate 283. CAMPION chamber pot. *Courtesy of Brad & Jane Nelson, Washington* $175+

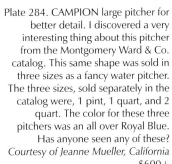

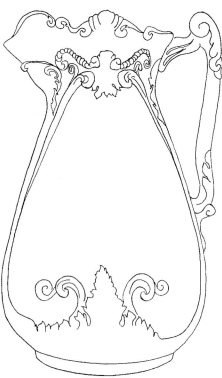

Plate 286. BELMONT II wash set minus the small pitcher, mug, chamber pot lid, and master slop jar. *Courtesy of Sue Otteman, Texas* $1900+

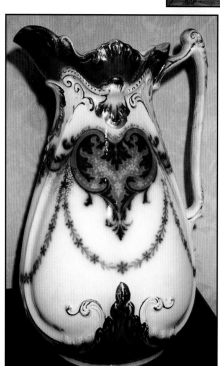

Plate 287. BELMONT large pitcher for better detail. *Courtesy of Sue Otteman, Texas* $600+

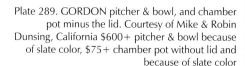

Plate 285. *Courtesy of Ann Potts, Illinois*
Body Style: Gr-W15
Factory Name: -
U. S. Patent Applied/Dated: - / -
English Registry: -
First Year Catalog: -
Late Victorian Dating Label: Scroll
Flow Blue Patterns: BELMONT II, and GORDON

Plate 288. BELMONT toothbrush holder and mug shown here for better detail. *Courtesy of Glynn & Shirley Jones, Illinois* $225+ ea.

Plate 289. GORDON pitcher & bowl, and chamber pot minus the lid. Courtesy of Mike & Robin Dunsing, California $600+ pitcher & bowl because of slate color, $75+ chamber pot without lid and because of slate color

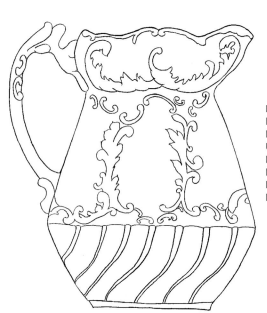

Plate 290. *Courtesy of Ann Potts, Illinois*
Body Style: Gr-W16
Factory Name: -
U. S. Patent Applied/Dated: - / -
English Registry: -
First Year Catalog: -
Late Victorian Dating Label: Scroll Flow
Blue Patterns: SIENE

Plate 291. SIENE smaller pitcher. This is a very elusive wash set, which is very hard to locate. The chamber pot and lid has also been seen. *Courtesy of Roger & Virginia Buckaloo, Wisconsin* $275+

complete pattern list

The following is a complete pattern list for W. H. Grindley & Co. These patterns may also have been printed in other colors, but to get on this list they must have been printed in Flow Blue, Flow Mulberry or Slate Blue. The reason I have included Slate Blue is that I consider this color to be in very close association with Flow Blue and many of the catalogs will call this color, "flow." There are no known Flow Mulberry patterns produced by the Grindley pottery. The following information will be given, if known, for each pattern:

"Pattern" is the name of the pattern.

"Category" is one of the following: "AN" Art Nouveau, "F" Floral, "M"

Miscellaneous, "O" Oriental, "S" Scenic.

The "Body Style" is the code I have given the body style of dish the pattern was applied to. In some cases, you may see more than one body style code. This means that this pattern was applied to more than one style of dish or wash set. The first code given will be its original and the others will represent secondary body styles. All patterns were produced at the Woodland Pottery, unless "Newfield" is put for Body Style code. When "Newfield" is used it means that these patterns were produced at the Newfield Pottery and these will be covered in the next section.

"Rd.No." and "(date)," these will show the English pattern registration number and the "start up" date it represents.

PATTERN	CATEGORY	BODY STYLE	Rd.No. (DATE)
AGRA	-	-	-
ALASKA	M/AN	Gr-C	-
ALBANY I	F	Gr-C	-
ALBANY II	F	Gr-W2	-
ALDINE	M/F	Gr-M	325874 (1898)
ALLEN	-	-	-
ALTON	AN	Gr-B	-
ANTIQUE	F	Gr-D	250386 (1895)
ARABIC	F	Newfield	154743 (1890)
ARGOS	AN	Gr-E	303724 (1897)
ARGYLE	M/AN	Gr-A	289457 (1896)
ASHBURTON	F	Gr-C	-
ASTORIA	AN	-	-
ASTRAL	AN	Gr-B	426592 (1904)
ATHENA I	M	Gr-W9	303231 (1897)
ATHENA II	F	Newfield, Gr-J	149525 (1890)
ATLANTA	M/AN	Gr-L	-
ATLAS	F	Gr-W13	-
BALTIC	AN	Gr-K	433097 (1904)
BEAUFORT	AN	Gr-B	408448 (1903)
BEAUTY ROSE	F	Gr-I	690339 (1922)
BELGRAVE	F	Gr-G	-
BELMONT I	AN	Gr-E	-
BELMONT II	AN	Gr-W15	-
BERLIN	F	Gr-O	-
BISLEY	AN	Gr-H	-
BLUE ROSE	F	Gr-C	-
BLYTHSWOOD	M	Gr-H	568951 (1910)
BOMBAY	F	Gr-H	-
BOSTON	F	Gr-W3	219411 (1893)
BRAZIL	F	Gr-K	-
BROCKLYN	F	Gr-J	-
BRUSSELS	F	Gr-E	303723 (1897)
BURTON	M	Gr-I	-
CAMERON	F	Gr-N	-
CAMPION	F	Gr-W14	245688 (1894)
CATHERINE	F	Gr-D	233436 (1894)
CATHERINE MERRETT	F	Gr-D	233436 (1894)
CELTIC	AN	Gr-E	310588 (1897)
CHATSWORTH	F	Gr-A & Gr-W12	274727 (1896)
CHINESE	O	-	-
CLARENCE	F	Gr-C	-
CLEMATIS	F	Gr-W1	303250 (1897)
CLIFTON	AN	Gr-O, B, & C	-
CLOVER	M/AN	Gr-G	-
CLYTIE	AN	Gr-E	304006 (1897)
COUNTESS	M/AN	Gr-C	-
CRESCENT	AN	Gr-K	433102 (1904)
DAISY I	M	Newfield, Gr-W17	-
DAISY II	M	Newfield	39562 (1885)
DAISY III	F	Gr-F & N	268499 (1896)
DELFT	M	Gr-B	-
DELMAR	M/F	Gr-F	-

PATTERN	CATEGORY	BODY STYLE	Rd.No. (DATE)
DENMARK	M	Gr-H	-
DENTON	AN	Gr-H	-
DERBY	F	Gr-C	-
DERWENT	AN	Gr-O	-
DOREEN	F	Gr-W8	-
DORIS	AN	Gr-C	-
DOROTHY	M/F	Gr-E	305973 (1897)
DOVER	M/F	Gr-L	457049 (1905)
DUCHESS	F	Gr-J	184834 (1891)
EATON	F	Gr-M	326056 (1898)
EILEEN	F	Gr-B & C	-
ENGLAND	M	Newfield	Diamond mark
FERN	F	Gr-J	214257 (1893)
FESTOON I	F	Gr-M	326058 (1898)
FESTOON II	AN	Gr-W7	-
FLORA	F/M	Newfield	152444 (1890)
FLORIDA	F	Gr-B	-
GARLAND	F	Gr-D	250388 (1895)
GEM	F	Newfield	-
GIRONDE	F	Gr-A	293169 (1897)
GIRTON	AN	Gr-B	457960 (1905)
GLENMORE	AN	Gr-H	-
GLENTINE	AN	Gr-H	-
GORDON	F	Gr-W15	-
GRACE	F	Gr-E	303495 (1897)
GRANBY	M/AN	Gr-N	473130 (1906)
HADDON	AN	Gr-B	-
HAMPTON	AN	Gr-L	457049 (1905)
HAMPTON SPRAY	AN/F	Gr-L	457040 (1905)
HARLEY	F	Gr-W10	-
HARTINGTON	AN	Gr-I	-
HUDSON	F	Gr-J	-
IDEAL I	F	Gr-D	213154 (1893)
IDEAL II	M	Newfield	Oct. 6, 1883
IDRIS	AN	Gr-I	-
ISMAY	AN	Gr-C	-
JANETTE	F	Gr-A	292398 (1897)
KEELE	M/AN	Gr-B	-
KENT	M/AN	Gr-L	-
LA BELLE	F	Gr-W3 & Gr-J	213120 (1893)
LA GLORIA	F	Gr-J	-
LAWRENCE	M	Gr-H	568951 (1910)
LE PAVOT	F	Gr-F	277089 (1896)
LORNE	AN	Gr-B	-
LOTUS	AN	Gr-G	-
LOUISE	F	Gr-F	269029 (1896)
LYNDHURST	AN	Gr-I	-
LYNTON	AN	Gr-H	-
LYRIC	M	Gr-G	-
MADRID	S	Gr-O	484496 (1906)
MALTA	M/F	Newfield	69160 (1887)
MANILA	M	Gr-M	-
MARECHAL NEIL	F	Gr-F & K	269030 (1896)
MARGOT	F	Gr-W12	269028 (1896)
MARGUERITE	F	Gr-J & K	-
MARIE	AN	Gr-D	250387 (1895)
MARLBOROUGH	M/AN	Gr-C	-
MAY	F	Gr-W11	256165 (1895)
MELBOURNE	F	Gr-B	-
MELBA	AN	Gr-G	-
MERION	F	Gr-A	292307 (1897)
MERSEY	F	Newfield	135130 (1889)
MILAN I	M/F	Gr-J	213153 (1893)
MILTON	AN	Gr-A	299397 (1897)
MISSOURI	AN	Newfield	150034 (1890)
NATIONAL	F	Newfield	184829 (1891)
OCHIS	AN	Gr-C	-
OLYMPIA	F	Gr-D & B	233436 (1894)
OSBORNE	F	Gr-C & W5	-

PATTERN	CATEGORY	BODY STYLE	Rd.No. (DATE)
OXFORD I	M	Newfield & Gr-W17	-
OXFORD II	M	Newfield	-
PENSHURST	-	-	-
PERTH	F	Gr-W7	-
POPPY	F	Gr-J	-
PORTMAN	AN	Gr-C	-
PREMIER	F	Gr-J	-
PRIMULA	F	Gr-W3 & J	218422 (1893)
PROGRESS	F	Gr-D	233435 (1894)
RAMSGATE	M	Gr-I	-
RICHMOND	F	Gr-D	-
ROSE	F	Gr-D	213117 (1893)
RUSTIC	F	Gr-J	-
SEINE	F	Gr-W16	-
SHANGHAI	S	Gr-I	-
SHANGRILA	F	Gr-I	-
SOMERSET	F	Gr-G	-
SPRING	F	Newfield	51058 (1886)
STRATFORD	F	Gr-A	287328 (1896)
SYRIAN	M/AN	Gr-W1	303260 (1897)
TERESA	F	Gr-M	326059 (1898)
THE ATHENS	M	Gr-L	-
THE HAVANA	F	Gr-M	326055 (1898)
THE HOFBURG	M/AN	Gr-G	-
THE LAHAYA	F/S	Gr-I	Has Ltd. Mark 1926+
THE MARQUIS	M	Gr-N	473130 (1906)
TRIUMPH	F	Gr-W3	219413 (1893)
TROY	M/AN	Newfield	64490 (1886)
UNIQUE	F	Gr-D	-
UTOPIA	F	Gr-D	-
VICTORIA	AN	Gr-L	-
VICTORY	AN	-	-
WAVERLY	AN	Gr-B	-
WENTWORTH	M	Gr-O	-
WILDFLOWER	F	Gr-J & O	-
WOODBINE	F	Gr-B	-
WOODVILLE	M	Gr-B	-
WREATH	F	Gr-E	305976 (1897)

Now let's look at the above pattern list a little differently. This time we'll put the patterns in "start up" date order. Because we do not have registration numbers for all patterns, this list will not be as complete. By putting the pattern list in date order, we can attempt to show trends in patterns and body style shapes. The reader should note that in this list we find the body styles are now fairly grouped together, and each pattern applied to that shape are now in order of production. We can also note when a body style starts, how it over laps the next body style and when each body style production ends. This is a marvelous tool that we can use to analyze a potteries production. The large gap between the patterns TERESA and BEAUFORT is because we do not have a single pattern registration number for body style Gr-C, even though we know Gr-C was patented October 31, 1899. This is one of the problems that occur with incomplete data. However, we show what we can and move forward.

PATTERN	BODY STYLE	Rd.No.	YEAR
IDEAL II	Newfield	-	1883
DAISY II	Newfield	39562	1885
SPRING	Newfield	51058	1886
TROY	Newfield	64490	1886
MALTA	Newfield	69160	1887
ARABIC	Newfield	134743	1889
MERSEY	Newfield	135130	1889
ATHENA II	Newfield	149525	1890
MISSOURI	Newfield	150034	1890
FLORA	Newfield	152444	1890
NATIONAL	Newfield	184829	1891
DUCHESS	Gr-J	184834	1891
ROSE	Gr-D	213117	1893
LA BELLE	Gr-W3	213120	1893
MILAN I	Gr-J	213153	1893
IDEAL I	Gr-D	213154	1893

PATTERN	BODY STYLE	Rd.No.	YEAR
FERN	Gr-J	214257	1893
PRIMULA	Gr-W3	218411	1893
BOSTON	Gr-W3	219411	1893
TRIUMPH	Gr-W3	219413	1893
PROGRESS	Gr-D	233435	1894
CATHERINE	Gr-D	233436	1894
CATHERINE MERRETT	Gr-D	233436	1894
OLYMPIA	Gr-D	233436	1894
CAMPION	Gr-W14	245688	1894
ANTIQUE	Gr-D	250386	1895
MARIE	Gr-D	250387	1895
GARLAND	Gr-D	250388	1895
MAY	Gr-W11	256165	1895
DAISY III	Gr-F	268499	1896
MARGOT	Gr-W12	269028	1896
LOUISE	Gr-F	269029	1896
MARECHAL NEIL	Gr-F	269030	1896
CHATSWORTH	Gr-A	274727	1896
LE PAVOT	Gr-F	277089	1896
STRATFORD	Gr-A	287328	1896
ARGYLE	Gr-A	289457	1896
MERION	Gr-A	292307	1897
JANETTE	Gr-A	292398	1897
GIRONDE	Gr-A	293169	1897
MILTON	Gr-A	299397	1897
ATHENA I	Gr-W9	303231	1897
CLEMATIS	Gr-W1	303250	1897
SYRIAN	Gr-W1	303260	1897
GRACE	Gr-E	303495	1897
BRUSSELS	Gr-E	303723	1897
ARGOS	Gr-E	303724	1897
CLYTIE	Gr-E	304006	1897
DOROTHY	Gr-E	305973	1897
WREATH	Gr-E	305976	1897
CELTIC	Gr-E	310588	1897
ALDINE	Gr-M	325874	1898
THE HAVANA	Gr-M	326055	1898
EATON	Gr-M	326056	1898
FESTOON I	Gr-M	326058	1898
TERESA	Gr-M	326059	1898
BEAUFORT	Gr-B	408448	1903
ASTRAL	Gr-B	426592	1904
BALTIC	Gr-K	433097	1904
CRESCENT	Gr-K	433102	1904
DOVER	Gr-L	457049	1905
HAMPTON	Gr-L	457049	1905
THE ATHENS	Gr-L	457049	1905
GIRTON	Gr-B	457960	1905
GRANBY	Gr-N	473130	1906
MADRID	Gr-O	484496	1906
HAMPTON SPRAY	Gr-L	497040	1907
BLYTHSWOOD	Gr-H	568951	1910
LAWRENCE	Gr-H	568951	1910
BEAUTY ROSE	Gr-I	690339	1922

pattern details – additional information

The patterns below are from the complete pattern list, but with additional information. Not all patterns will be represented, as further information is not known for all patterns. The additional information will include different colors used, catalog data, and the unusual.

AGRA: Also seen in slate color.

ALBANY II: Also seen in slate or green colors.

ALDINE: Also seen in slate color.

ALTON: Has been seen with MELBOURNE stamp.

ANTIQUE: Also seen in slate or green colors.

ARABIC: Also seen in slate color.

ARGYLE: Also seen in slate or green colors. Was first sold in the FW 1897/1898 Montgomery Ward & Co. catalog. ARGYLE had the longest run of any pattern I tracked in the catalogs and was sold under the pattern name of "STRATFORD." It sold an unbelievable eight years and finally closed out in the FW 1904/1905 catalog.

ATHENA I: Was first sold in the SS 1896 Sears Roebuck & Co. catalog under the pattern name of "GRETCHEN." It sold for one year.

ATHENA II: Also seen in brown color.

ATLAS: Was first sold in FW 1899/1900 Montgomery Ward & Co. catalog and was sold under its correct pattern name. It sold for two years.

BELMONT II: Also seen in slate color.

BLUE ROSE: The same pattern and body style of ware was apparently sold to Arthur J. Wilkinson, Royal Staffordshire Pottery. They called it "IOWA."

BOSTON: Also seen in green color.

BROCKLYN: Also seen in slate color.

BRUSSELS: Also seen in slate or green colors. Was first sold in the FW 1898/1899 Montgomery Ward & Co. catalog under the pattern name "BELMONT." It sold for two years.

BURTON: Is the same pattern as SHANGRILA.

CAMPION: Also seen in green color. Was first sold in the SS 1896 Montgomery Ward & Co. catalog under the pattern name of "MYRTLE." It sold for three years.

CATHERINE: Is the same pattern as CATHERINE MERRETT and OLYMPIA. Also seen in green and red colors.

CATHERINE MERRETT: Is the same pattern as CATHERINE and OLYMPIA. Also seen in red color.

CELTIC: Also seen in green color.

CHATSWORTH: The identical pattern also seen but with purple flowers. Also seen in slate or green colors. May be the identical same pattern as MARGOT, which was used for a wash set, but both patterns have different registration numbers.

CLARENCE: Was first sold in the SS 1902 Montgomery Ward & Co. catalog under the pattern name "CHARLESTON." It sold for two years and was advertised in the catalog as being sold without gold tracings to reduce the cost.

CLEMATIS: Also seen in violet color.

CLYTIE: Was first sold in the FW 1898/1899 Montgomery Ward & Co. catalog under its correct pattern name. It sold for two years.

COUNTESS: Was produced with and without polychrome.

DAISY III: Also seen in slate, green or red colors.

DERBY: Was produced with and without polychrome.

DERWENT: Also seen in green color.

DOREEN: Also seen in slate color. Was first sold in the FW 1897/1898 Montgomery Ward & Co. catalog under its correct pattern name. It sold for one year.

DORIS: Is the same pattern as OCHIS.

DOROTHY: Also seen in green color.

DUCHESS: Also seen in slate color.

EILEEN: Also seen in slate or green colors.

FESTOON I: Also seen in slate color.

FESTOON II: Also seen in slate color.

FLORA: Also seen in slate color.

GARLAND: Also seen in green color.

GIRONDE: Was first sold in the SS 1897 Montgomery Ward & Co. catalog under the pattern name of "CHATHAM" and "OAKLAND." It sold for four years, a very long run.

GLENMORE: Is the same pattern as GLENTINE.

GLENTINE: Is the same pattern as GLENMORE.

GORDON: Also seen in slate color.

GRANBY: Was formally known as "THE MARQUIS II."

HAMPTON: Also seen with yellow/pink/white flowers.

HAMPTON SPRAY: Same pattern but flowers in pink.

HUDSON: Also seen in slate color.

IDEAL I: Also seen in slate color.

IDRIS: Also seen in green color.

ISMAY: Also seen in slate or green colors (see plate 292.).

KEELE: Was first sold in the FW 1904/1905 Montgomery Ward & Co. catalog under the pattern name of "FLEUR-DE-LIS." It sold for four years, a very long run.

LE PAVOT: Also seen in slate color.

LOUISE: Identical pattern but with pink flowers/green leaves.

MADRID: Also seen in slate color.

MALTA: Also seen in slate color.

MARECHAL NEIL: Also seen in slate or green colors.

MARGOT: Was first sold in the FW 1897/1898 Montgomery Ward & Co. catalog under the pattern name of "CHATSWORTH." It sold for four years, a very long run.

MARGUERITE: Also seen in slate color.

MAY: Also seen in slate color.

MELBOURNE: Same blue pattern but with pink flowers added to center. Also same blue pattern but with multi-colored fruit in center (see plate 293.) Has been seen with rectangle ship mark. Was first sold in the F 1903 Sears Roebuck & Co. catalog under the pattern name of "WELLINGTON." It sold for two years. Two seven inch plates were seen with this faint inscription on back, "21st Anniversary Nov. 21st 1908 (a picture of an acorn, then) Oakdale Castle No. 50 K.G.E.."

MELBA: Also seen in green color.

MERION: Also seen in slate or green colors. Was first sold in the SS 1896 Sears Roebuck & Co. catalog under the pattern name of "MELROSE." It sold for one year.

MERSEY: Also seen in slate color.

MILAN I: Also seen in green color.

MISSOURI: Was used for a dish and for a wash set. Has been seen in slate or brown color only.

NATIONAL: Has been seen in slate color only.

OCHIS: Is the same pattern as DORIS.

OLYMPIA: Is the same pattern as CATHERINE and CATHERINE MERRETT. Also seen in red color.

OXFORD I: Seen in slate color only.

OXFORD II: Seen in slate color only.

POPPY: Also seen in brown or green colors.

PRIMULA: Also seen in brown or red colors.

PROGRESS: Also seen in slate color.

RUSTIC: Also seen in slate or brown colors.

SHANGHAI: Has been seen with rectangle ship mark.

SHANGRILA: Is the same pattern as BURTON.

SPRING: Also seen in slate, brown, or brown/pink colors.

STRATFORD: Also seen in slate, green, or pink/yellow.

SYRIAN: Also seen in slate or green colors.

TERESA: Also seen in slate color. Was first sold in the FW 1899/1900 Montgomery Ward & Co. catalog under the pattern name of "ALLIANCE." It sold for two years.

THE MARQUIS: Has been seen with hand-painted portrait in center.

TRIUMPH: Also seen in red color. Was first sold in the SS 1895 Montgomery Ward & Co. catalog under its correct pattern name. It sold for two years.

TROY: Also seen in slate color.

UTOPIA: Also seen in slate color.

VICTORIA: This pattern was used as a commemorative plate for the "1807-1907 Primitive Methodist Centenary" (see plate 294.).

WAVERLY: This pattern and the Gr-B body style that it was printed on were apparently sold to Petrus Regout of Holland and they sold it as the pattern "SUPERIOR."

WREATH: Also seen in green color.

Plate 292. ISMAY a Gr-C pattern seen here in green, 8 ¾" x 5" wide. *Author collection* $75+ because of color

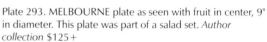

Plate 293. MELBOURNE plate as seen with fruit in center, 9" in diameter. This plate was part of a salad set. *Author collection* $125+

Plate 294. VICTORIA commemorative plate. The two men are Hugh Bourne left, and William Clowes. The plate with its Flow Blue design was sold to John P. Humphreys, Park Pottery, who applied the center decoration, his mark, and the over glaze. This information came courtesy of Geoffrey A. Godden. Other patterns used for this purpose were HAMPTON SPRAY, THE MARQUIS, and WENTWORTH. *Courtesy of Phil & Cindy Neff, Connecticut* $150+

other wares produced

TEA LEAF/COPPER LUSTRE: shapes
BAMBOO: Also seen with brown BURMAH transfer pattern on it.
FAVORITE Rd.No. 51059 (1885) (see Plate 295.)
Gr-A bone dish has been seen with Tea Leaf applied.

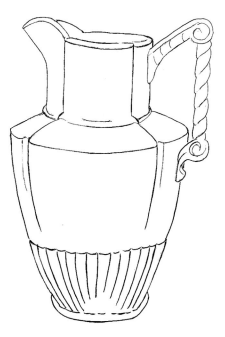

Plate 295. Line drawing of
the pitcher to a wash set.
Courtesy of Ann Potts, Illinois

WHITE IRONSTONE/GRANITE: shapes
BAMBOO
FAVORITE Rd.No. 51059 (1885) (see Plate 296. & Plate 297.)
FLOWER GARDEN BORDER

Plate 296. "FAVORITE" shape, large pitcher to a wash
set, 12" high. *Author collection* $175+

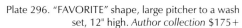

Plate 297. MOSS ROSE open oblong vegetable
bowl. 9 3/8" x 6 ¾" wide. Alfred Meakin
produced the identical pattern. *Author collection*
$50+

Shapes and patterns of the 1880s are different from those of any other period of production. The wares made at the Newfield Pottery fit into this era perfectly because Grindley was in production there from 1880 to 1891. I know of no Flow Blue that was produced at the Newfield, but rather, the patterns were black, brown, slate, green, and red in color. The 1880s is also the first of four segments that I will divide the Late Victorian period for dating purposes. I state this now so you may begin to formulate in your mind the look of the 1880s.

There were several different shapes made at the Newfield Pottery and I have not attempted to acquire line drawings to identify them individually. The reason is that they are not the main theme of this book, which is Late Victorian Flow Blue. The following Plates are a random selection to give you an idea of the type of shapes and patterns that were produced at the Newfield Pottery during the 1880s. The diamond mark of registry was used from 1842 thru 1883. This means that the first three years of Grindley's production was under this form of registration. For this three-year period (1880 thru 1883) Grindley had ten known registration dates, they are:

DATE	PATTERN
April 22, 1880	-
June 22, 1880	JAPANESE (see Plate 298.)
November 2, 1880	-
January 7, 1882	DAFFODIL
January 19, 1882	SHAKESPEARE (see Plate 299.)
May 30, 1882	COLUMBIA
January 17, 1883	BURMAH
January 29, 1883	-
February 14, 1883	-
October 6, 1883	IDEAL II

Plate 298. JAPANESE plate, 9" in diameter. *Author collection* $75+

Plate 299. SHAKESPEARE plate, 8" in diameter. *Author collection* $60+

Newfield Pottery "Flow Slate" & non-Flow Blue patterns 1884 thru 1890

Rd.No./DATE	PATTERN	PATTERN COLORS
154743 (1890)	ARABIC	Slate
149525 (1890)	ATHENA II	Slate, Brown (see Plates 300 & 301)
120138 (1889)	BLOSSOM	Brown
-	COLUMBUS	Brown
-	DAISY I	Slate
39562 (1885)	DAISY II	Slate, Brown
-	ENGLAND	Slate, Brown
152444 (1890)	FLORA	Slate
-	GEM	Slate (see Plate 302.)
39560 (1885)	GREEK	Brown, Red
69160 (1887)	MALTA	Slate (see Plates 303, 304 & 305.)
135130 (1889)	MERSEY	Slate
19561 (1885)	MILAN II	Brown
150034 (1890)	MISSOURI	Slate
184829 (1891)	NATIONAL	Slate
-	OXFORD I	Slate
-	OXFORD II	Slate
51058 (1886)	SPRING	Slate, Brown (see Plate 306.)
64490 (1886)	TROY	Slate (see Plate 307.)

Plate 300. ATHENA demi saucer for pattern & shape identification, 4 ¾" in diameter. *Author collection* $10+

Plate 301. ATHENA demi cup & saucer, cup 2 1/8" high. *Author collection* $30+

Plate 302. GEM platter, 11" long. *Author collection* $30+

Plate 305. MALTA teapot, Favorite shape, 8 ½" tall. *Author collection* $200+

Plate 303. SPRING, a nice selection of different items to show their shapes. *Courtesy of Betty F. Stadler, Louisiana*

Plate 306. SPRING plate in Brown, 10" in diameter. *Author collection* $30+

Plate 304. MALTA gravy boat, 8" spout to handle x 3 ¾" wide. *Author collection* $40+

Plate 307. TROY plate, 10" in diameter. *Courtesy of Irene Beer, Pennsylvania* $50+

The following is a list of body styles and the patterns printed on them at the Woodland Pottery. I will first list the body style name and any registration numbers/dates that apply and then list all known patterns applied to that style of dish. None of these body styles have any known Flow Blue patterns, but rather, are very typical 1900-1920s all over floral, Greek key edge, and botanical edge type of designs.

We must remember that the English were up against many forms of competition. They not only had to compete against other countries, but they also had to keep abreast of trends in patterns, no matter who was producing them. If the following patterns became more popular, than fewer Flow Blue patterns were manufactured. We know that the following eventually won out and Flow Blue passed into history.

Woodland Pottery non-Flow Blue body styles & patterns 1900-1930:

Athens Rd.No. 692647 (1922): no patterns identified
Carlton Rd.No. 697579 (1923):
    DELAMERE: Flower basket center
    THE HEREFORD
Chelsea Ivory Rd.No. 714550 (1925):
    ALTON
    AUDREY
    AVIGNON
    BARBARA
    CARVIVAL Rd.No. 714660 (1925)
    DARTMOUTH
    DORSET
    ELLESMERE: Red floral/yellow border
    HENLEY: Blue/yellow floral
    LICHFIELD: Large orange/violet/red flowers
    MARJORIE
    NAVARRE Rd.No. 714650 (1925)
    PENELOPE
    PENRITH
    ROCHESTER
    TANJORIE: Cobalt band/floral edge
    THE ARCADIA
    THE ASHBOURNE
    THE CANNES
    THE CHAIRMAN
    THE CORONA
    THE CRAWFORD
    THE MARENGO
    VENICE: Blue lined border
    VIRGINIA
    WENTWORTH: Floral border
    WINTHROP
Country Inns:
    THE PEACOCK
Country Style: no patterns identified
Cream Petal: (see Plate 308.)
    ALISON: Autumn colored flower border
    AUTUMN PRIDE
    BUNDARRA: Autumn colored border
    CARMONA: Botanical border
    CHELSEA BOUQUET
    CLAREMONT: Floral
    CLYDE: Orange/black piping edge
    CORONATION of HENRY VIII
    DEVONSHIRE ROSE: Red/blue roses stripe edge
    DORCHESTER: Blue border
    ENSIGN: Fruit border
    FALKIRK: Brown/yellow/blue border
    LILAC

    LYNTON: Red/brown floral border
    MAY CLUSTER: Green leaves, white bellflowers
    POMPADOUR
    STRATHCONA
    SWANSEA ROSE
    TEWKSBURY: Blue floral center & edge
Cries of London:
    FINE BLACK CHERRIES
    SWEET ORANGES
    WHO'LL BUY MY LAVENDER
    YELLOW PRIMROSE
Dickens Coaching Stages:
    THE LEATHER BOTTLE
    THE WHITE HORSE
    NICHOLAS NICKLEBY
English Country Inns:
    GEORGE & DRAGON
    THE BEARS HEAD
    THE LAMBERT ARMS
    THE PEACOCK
    THE TALBOT
English Rural Scenes:
    PRINCESS HOUSE
Excelsior Rd.No. 501256 (1907):
    CADORE
Georgian Jbore Rd.No. 707597 (1924):
    BELVEDERE
    CHELMSFORD
    MONTCALM Rd.No. 707970 (1924)
Hamilton Rd.No. 697579 (1923): no patterns identified
Laburnum Petal: all yellow ware
Marlborough Royal Petal: (see Plates 309 & 310)
    CAMBRIA
    CATHAY: Red/yellow/rust floral
    CELIA: Large blue/pink/yellow floral
    CONNAUGHT: Multi colored floral
    GREENWAY: Flowered border
    INDIAN TREE
    LORRAINE
    MONMOUTH
    OAKLAND: Red acorn border
    PENROSE
    PERTH
    SPRINGFIELD
    STRATHCONA
    SYLVAN: Yellow floral border
    WARWICK: Multi colored floral
Old Chelsea: no patterns identified
Royal Tudor: (see Plate 311)
    BOUQUET
    CROWN HARVEST
    FLEUR SAUVAGE
    VELVET: All over brown leaf
Satin White: (see Plates 312 & 313)
    ASCOT
    AVON
    RHAPSODY
    SYLVIA
Scenes of London:
    ST. PAUL'S CATHEDRAL
    TOWER BRIDGE
Sheraton Ivory Rd.No. 723436 (1927) patent #D71528 (July 15, 1928):
    PENRITH

POPPY
Sunday Morning: no patterns identified
The Victory Rd.No. 669667 (1919) (see Plate 314.): no patterns identified
The Zenith Rd.No. 639798 (1914):
    RUGBY: Green/burgundy edge stripes
Windsor Ivory:
    BATHURST Rd.No. 737555 (1928)
    MATHURST Rd.No. 737553 (1928)
    THE ASTORIA: Red flowered botanical border
    THE CHARMIAN: Blue/red botanical border (flower)
    THE DORSET: Blue/red/yellow flower border
    THE ELIZABETH
    THE FLEURETTE Rd.No. 737554 (1928)
    THE PATRICIA: Yellow floral/green edge
The After Constable series:
    A COTTAGE IN A CORN FIELD
    A LOCK ON THE STOUR

ARUNDEL MILL
CANAL BANKS NEWBURY
FLATFORD MILL
HAMPSTEAD HEATH
SALISBURY CATHEDRAL
THE CORNFIELD
THE GLEBE FARM
THE HAY WAIN
THE LEAPING HORSE (see Plate 315.)

The After Constable series was based on the paintings by the English painter John Constable (1776-1837). The engraver for this series was Henry Fennell (c1854-June 1934). Henry married the daughter Elisha Pepper, who also was an engraver. Henry's workshop was first on Jasper Street, and then on Mollart Street, Hanley. At one time he employed nineteen journeymen and apprentices. This business was closed down in 1943.[10]

Plate 308. Cream Petal bowl, unidentified floral. 8 1/2" in diameter. *Author collection* $30+

Plate 309. Marlborough Royal Petal, unidentified floral covered sugar & INDIAN TREE pitcher. *Author collection* $25+ sugar, $30+ pitcher

Plate 310. Marlborough Royal Petal, OAKLAND teapot. 10" spout to handle x 5 ¾" high. This teapot shape is very close to the Gr-I shaped teapot, yet there are differences. Note the acorn finial. *Author collection* $100+

Plate 313. Satin White, "BOY IN CREEK" plate, 10" in diameter. On the back of plate, in addition to the Grindley mark, is one that says, "Supplied by Harry Hancock (Tunstall Ltd.) Stoke-on-Trent". This same shape of plate was also used for a wild fowl series. *Author collection* $50+

Plate 311. Royal Tudor, MERRY OLDE ENGLAND creamer, 3 ¼" high. *Author collection* $20+

Plate 314. The Victory, unidentified botanical pattern, double spout gravy boat, with attached undertray. This body style of dish was named after the allies' victory in WW I. *Author collection* $75+

Plate 312. Satin White, ASCOTT cereal bowl, 5 ¾" in diameter. Satin White apparently is a trade name, as several different shapes exist with this name. *Author collection* $5+

Plate 315. After Constable, THE LEAPING HORSE, sandwich tray, 11 ½" x 5 ¾" wide. This tray originally came with six square plates. *Author collection* $30+

The following is a list, in date order, of both Flow Blue and non-Flow Blue dish and wash set body styles. The list will not be a complete one because we do not know the registration number for all body styles. The list will, however, give you a good sense of how trends changed the shape of dishes and when the changes occurred. It will also emphasize the high production year of 1897 and when the end of Flow Blue came, the middle 1920s. This body style list will cover the Woodland Potteries production from 1891 to 1928. You will see similar trends in the other potteries covered in this book.

Note: The dates of Mr. Grindley's retirement and his death have been included to show what was produced under his leadership.

BODY STYLE	START-UP YEAR
Gr-J	1891
Gr-D	1893
Gr-F	1896
Gr-A	February 2, 1897
Gr-W8	February 16, 1897
Gr-W10	March 1897
Gr-W1	September 21, 1897
Gr-W9	September 21, 1897
Gr-E	October 19, 1897
Gr-M	November 8, 1898
Gr-C	October 31, 1899
Gr-P	October 2, 1900
Gr-B	October 1902
Gr-K	1903
Gr-L	1905
Gr-G	1906
Gr-N	May 9, 1906
Excelsior	1907
Gr-H	1910
The Zenith	1914
Gr-O	1915
The Victory	
Athens	1922
Gr-I	1922
Carlton	1923
Hamilton	1923
Georgian Jborie	1924
Grindley retires	
Chelsea Ivory	1925
Grindley dies	March 1926
Sheraton Ivory	1928
Windsor Ivory	1928

Grindley's hotelware, "The Duraline Hotelware Co. Ltd." Below are lists of importers, hotels, restaurants, organizations, body styles, and patterns. None of the following are Flow Blue body styles or patterns.

Hotelware Importers, Wholesalers:
Alfred Stahel & Sons Inc., San Diego, CA
Boston China and Equipment Co.
Burley & Company, Chicago, IL
C. W. S. Longton
Cassidy-Buscombe Ltd., B.C., Alberta, Yukon
Cassidy's Ltd., Montreal, Toronto, Vancouver & Winnipeg, Canada
Dohrmann Hotel Supply Co.
Gibson & Paterson Pty Sydney, Australia
H. S. Barney Company of Schenectady, NY
Higgins & Leiten
Higgins & Ruiten

Horton & Wade Inc., Albany, NY
John R. Thompson Co.
L. Strauss & Sons, NY
Loftus Moran Pty. Ltd., Melbourne, Australia
M. Sellers & Co., Portland, Seattle & Spokane
Mitchell Woodbury & Co.
Nathan K. Stauss & Son's Inc., NY (could be affiliated with Abraham & Strauss Department Stores, NY, early 20s)
Nerlich & Co.
St. Louis Glass & Queenware Co., St. Louis, MO
T. Wiley & Co., Montreal, Canada
Taylor Smith Taylor U.S.A.
Wright, Tindale & VanRoden

Hotel, organization or restaurant:
Ambassador Hotel
Ashland 944 B. P. O. E.
Baltimore Dairy Lunch, J.A. Whitcomb
Bowles Lunch Inc.
CN Railroad
Chateau deBlois Trois Rivieres, Canada
Canadian Coast Guard
Canadian National System
Childs Restaurant
Clinton Hotel
Croatian Educational Home
Dalhousie University, Nova Scotia, Canada
Department of Marine & Fisheries
Elenara Restaurant
Elks lodge 652 B.P.O.E., Eureka
Frys Restaurant
Gibsons & Patterson
Goodrich Steamship Lines
Harvard Club of Boston
Hotel East's Pump Room, Chicago, IL
Hotel Morrison
Hotel Savoy, Seattle, WA
Hotel Waskada, Lake Rosseau, Muskaka
Islesworth Hotel
LaSalle Hotel, Regina, Saskatchewan, Canada
Labrador Cruise Lines
Leonard's Restaurant, since 1892
Lower Canada College
Luft & Luft, New York
Maxim's
McGill University, Montreal, Quebec, Canada
Moana Hotel
Natalby's Restaurant
Neal's Cafeteria
Parade Restaurant
Peter Pan Café, Vancouver, B. C.
Richelieu & Ontario Navigational Company
Royal Canadian Air Force
Shrine Ladies Auxiliary
Southern Pacific Railroad
Staffordshire County Police
Standishall Hotel
Swiss Chalet in Canada & Buffalo, NY
Texas & Pacific Railroad
The Alberts Hotel
The Australia Hotel
The Beaumont Hotel, Green Bay, WI
The Buttery Restaurant

The Goodall Hotel, Marion, IL
The Hamilton Hotel
The Hotel Windsor, Melbourne, Australia
The New Sherbrooke Hotel
The Pink Shell
The Rossmore
Virginia Golden Brown

Body styles used for Hotelware:
Duraline
Hercules
Lupin Petal: Solid blue color
Peach Petal: Solid peach color

Hotelware patterns (see Plates 316 & 317.):
ALTON
APPLE BLOSSOM: Pink flowers/green leaves on border
BLUE MEISSEN: Onion
BORDEAUX
CAIRO
CARLTON
CARNIVAL
CORNFORD
COUNTRY FAIR
DUNDEE
EL PASO
GRASSE: Botanical border
HANFORD (see Plate 318.)
IVORY
KARNIVAL: Gray/maroon stripe on border
LENNOX
LOUISE
LYONS
LYNTON
MANDALAY
MODERN Rd.No. 762434 (1931)
POMEROY
SANDHURST: Pink floral border
SARAH SIDDON: For the Pump Room, Chicago, where the actress frequented
SHANDON: Green leaf
THORNLEY
WHITBY
WILLOW (see Plate 319.)
YORK: Floral

Plate 316. Hotelware platter, unidentified pattern. 9 ½" x 6 ¾" wide. *Author collection* $25+

Plate 317. Hotelware, sample plate showing several variations of the pattern being offered. 9" in diameter. *Author collection* $50+

Plate 318. HANFORD, Hotelware covered sugar. 5" wide x 5" high. *Author collection* $30+

Plate 319. WILLOW, Hotelware pattern plate, 9" in diameter. *Author collection* $30+

No Flow Blue children's dishes were produced by the Grindley pottery. In the 1950s ABC cups and bowls were made, but true Flow Blue children's dishes have not surfaced. We know that children's dishes were produced in the Early Victorian period, and can be found, but the search for Late Victorian examples have been fruitless. There are those dealers who claim to have some, but under simple observation, they are determined not to be. For example, I was in a booth at an antique mall and observed what was being labeled as children's dishes, but in reality, they were demitasse cups and saucers with a relish dish being called a child's platter. I have seen 6" plates being called children's dinner plates and butter pats being called children's breakfast plates. There is further verification. Recently, I saw a children's wash set up for auction. The pitcher was about eight inches high and the body style was one typical for the 1880s. This was a very common thing for children to have in the 1880s. It was preparatory and instructional for later

life. However, it was not a Grindley pattern, or body style, but rather, the wash set had been made by Adams of Tunstall (the bottom of the bowl had "Adams" impressed), and sold by Grindley with his stamp on it (under glaze). Why was this done? It was not uncustomary for potters to order merchandise from other potters that was not in their product line – in order to fill orders for their own clients. It would have been too costly to special make one item for one customer. If you will recall, Grindley bought the Newfield Works from William Adams; they were friends. In this scenario, Grindley ordered a children's wash set from his friend at the Adams pottery, to fill a customer order for an item he did not make. Grindley was no small pottery, and if he did make children's dishes, there would be thousands of them and their presence made known. We know that children's dishes are in high demand and command a premium dollar. It's a buyer beware market and extreme caution should be taken.

Johnson Bros. Ltd.

a personal history

Robert Johnson was born circa 1824 on a farm in the rural Staffordshire area. Farming would become his life's work, the setting he would bring his bride home to, and the environment where they would raise their children. In 1909, at the age of eighty-five, Robert was still living in Oulton, England and it was said of him, "He is a splendid specimen of what the German Emperor said he would like to be, an English country gentleman."[11] It is believed his death came the following year in 1910, at the age of eighty-six.

Robert was married to Sarah Meakin, the oldest daughter of a Master Potter from Hanley, James Meakin. Sarah had five brothers in the pottery industry. They are listed below:[12]

James (1833-1885) of Darlaston, and a Master Potter of the Eagle Works.
    James was married to Emily Ridgway, who was the daughter of Edward J. Ridgway, Master Potter of the Bedford Works, Hanley.
Alfred, Master potter of the Victoria and Albert Works, Tunstall
Charles, Master Potter of Joiners Square.
William (died 1889), Master Potter of the Eagle Works.
George, Master Potter of the Eagle Works.

Of her brothers, James and George would become partners and trade under the name of, J. & G. Meakin Ltd. and Alfred would trade under the name of Alfred Meakin Ltd.

Robert and Sarah Johnson had four sons. If there were any other children, I am not aware of them. They were Henry James, Robert Lewis, Frederick George, and Alfred. In later years, these four sons would form a partnership and trade under the now famous name of Johnson Bros. Ltd.. The following is a history of the those four sons, their potteries, and the "dynasty" they created. For genealogical purposes, they will be listed in birth order.

Henry James Johnson

Henry James Johnson was born in 1851 on the family farm at Oulton in the Staffordshire district. Oulton is near Stone, just south of the potting district. This is where he would be raised until the age of seventeen, at which time he entered the pottery field.

Plate 320. Henry James Johnson, 1851 to April 28, 1931. *Reproduced with permission of Johnson Brothers, a Division of Josiah and Sons Limited, Barlaston, Stoke-on-Trent, Staffordshire, England.*

Henry became an apprentice potter in 1868 under his uncles' (James and George Meakin) direction, at their Eagle Works. He would stay there for six years learning the technical aspects of the trade through practical hands on experience. In most cases, an apprenticeship lasted for six years and began at the age of fifteen.[13] In 1874 another uncle, Alfred Meakin, purchased the Royal Albert Works, Tunstall. Henry went to work for him taking the position of general manager. While at the Royal Albert, Henry learned in great detail about and laid the bases for connection to the American trade.[14] For nearly twenty years, Henry stayed at the Royal Albert Works until in 1893, at the age of 43, he made the decision to join his brothers at the Charles Street Works. As history will show us, for the next thirty-eight years he would eventually become the main brother in the Johnson Bros. firm. Anyone who was connected to the pottery trade from all parts of the world considered Henry as the "head" of the Johnson Bros. enterprises.[15] Also, by joining the firm in 1893, it would be the first time that the four brothers would be together. Soon this infusion of interests would spawn the formation of the world's largest group of potteries. In 1931, all the works owned by the Johnson Bros. employed some 5000 workers.

Henry was known to be a man of action, a shrewd organizer, and administrator. All the while, he inspired this gift of activity in others. As a result of these attributes, he was elected unanimously as the president of the British Pottery Manufacturers' Federation. A post he accepted and held until his death. Henry did not have the opportunity to take part in public life, but was very active in the religious life of his church. His hobby was music and he was considered to be a very talented organist.[16] Henry was also a past president of the North Staffordshire Royal Infirmary.

Henry, who was living in Barlaston in September of 1928, was honored by having his name added to the roll of Freemen of the City of Stoke-on-Trent. It was the Lord mayor Alderman T. C. Wild who proposed that Mr. Johnson be given the honor of Freeman of the City, "In appreciation and in recognition of his long and eminent public services." Within recent years of receiving this honor, Henry and the Johnson Bros. firm had contributed some 30,000 pounds to the North Staffordshire Royal Infirmary and had contributed greatly to the well being of the pottery industry of the day. Henry's reply in receiving this honor was, "What little I have done to secure the prosperity and welfare of the district since I came to the potteries 59 years ago, I have always regarded as a privilege. I have seen many changes, but yet, when looking back over the years, I found in the inhabitants of North Staffordshire just the same lovable characteristics and just the same kindly and sympatic feelings animating all sections of the community." In conclusion Henry stated, "I consider being placed on the freeman role as the greatest honor of my life. In the list of freemen my name follows closely to that of Sir Oliver Lodge, a friend of many years standing, who was also in the days of his youth, associated with the pottery industry."[17]

Henry's obituary had this to say about him, "Mr. Johnson was the doyen of the British pottery industry, and in the course of his long and active life he had well earned the reputation of being one of the leading personalities of North Staffordshire. He was a man who thoroughly deserved the respect, admiration, and even affection, which was entertained towards him from all quarters, and as a generous supporter of many good causes his memory will long remain green."[18] Henry died April 28, 1931 at his residence, "The Upper House," Barlaston. At the funeral, which took place at Barlaston on May 2nd, following a service in the Parish Church the attendees were described as "every shade of the industrial and public life of the potteries district was represented, and the manifestations of sorrow in the passing of so eminent and beloved a citizen were profoundly impressive." In Henry's memory, a new main entrance with oak vestibule was added to the North Staffordshire Royal Infirmary. His two sons and four daughters survived Henry. The sons were Rev. Henry Grindley, and Frank, a director of the Johnson Bros. firm. Two sons preceded Henry in death. They were Robert Gerald and Reginald. The histories of Henry's four sons are as follows.

Note. The following sons of Henry James may not be in birth order.

Rev. Henry Grindley Johnson was the Rector of Whitmore and later became Rector of Onecote, near Leek, Staffordshire. It would appear that Henry decided his role in life was a religious one. To the best of my knowledge, Henry never took part in the pottery industry. As part of the original agreement made by the four Johnson Bros., only two sons were allowed to enter the business. For Henry James, they would be Frank and Reginald.

Frank G. Johnson was born in 1882, had joined the firm at least by 1909, and was director of the firm by 1928. It was the intent of the four senior partners initially that all of the sons that entered the business be given a comprehensive instruction on the manufacturing end before they could specialize in sales or finance. Eventually all of the sons that entered the business were given specific responsibilities.

Plate 322. Reginald T. Johnson, 1879-1915, was the son of Henry James Johnson. *Reproduced with permission of Johnson Brothers, a Division of Josiah and Sons Limited, Barlaston, Stoke-on-Trent, Staffordshire, England.*

Plate 321. Frank G. Johnson, 1882-1952, was the son of Henry James Johnson. *Reproduced with permission of Johnson Brothers, a Division of Josiah and Sons Limited, Barlaston, Stoke-on-Trent, Staffordshire, England.*

Just prior to 1913, the Johnson Bros. Directors' were focusing on Germany and decided to build a sanitary plant near Frankfurt. Reginald and his cousin Victor were involved in this plant's development and were there when it opened for business in 1913. During WWI, Reginald joined the 5th Battalion of North Staffordshire Regiment. He was killed in action in Flanders, February of 1915.

Robert Lewis Johnson

Robert Lewis Johnson was born 1856 on his father's farm in Oulton. Being raised on the family farm instilled in Robert a great love for that life. Even though he would join his brothers' in the pottery business, he would always maintain a connection to farming.

By the late 1920s, Frank had two of his sons in the business. They were Peter and Christopher F. Christopher was in production and Peter was in decorating. Before they were given these jobs, however, each son was given a comprehensive background of the manufacturing side of the business. During WWII, Peter joined the Navy and served in home waters and the Pacific. When Peter returned home in 1946, plans were made to modernize the company's factories.

I had some correspondence with Christopher back in July of 1999 and some of his remarks I found most interesting. The one that stands out for me is where he states when he went to work for the firm in the middle 1920s, he never remembers seeing the Flow Blue wares being produced. I have stated previously that Late Victorian Flow Blue went out of popularity and production in the middle 1920s. Christopher's comment, and knowing when he joined the firm, I believe helps to verify my claim.

Robert Gerald was the youngest son of Henry James and was born c.1893. Robert never took part in his fathers firm and died in June 1930, at the young age of thirty-seven. Robert had a keen interest in both cricket and football, and was an enthusiast for hunting and shooting. He left a widow and three children.[19]

Reginald T. was born in 1879, and entered the pottery firm by 1909.

Plate 323. Robert Lewis Johnson, 1856 to May 18, 1909. *Reproduced with permission of Johnson Brothers, a Division of Josiah and Sons Limited, Barlaston, Stoke-on-Trent, Staffordshire, England.*

Robert was educated at the Grammar School in Stafford. Early in life, his first interests were centered in farming. In fact, at one time, he was considered to be one of the largest tenant farmers in Staffordshire. Even though Robert had attained great successes, and an enviable reputation in farming, for reasons not disclosed, he decided in 1888 to leave farming and join his brothers in the pottery business in Hanley.

In this new endeavor, Robert brought with him his ability to breed success, and after a short internship at the pottery, he was sent to the United States as the company representative. He was living in New York, and set up his office in the same city. With samples in hand he would travel the countryside stimulating a demand for Johnson Bros. products. In a very short time, because of his congenial nature, the firm's list of customers and his list of friendships grew rapidly. There is no question that his ability to obtain friendships greatly enhanced the firm's growth in America. He was living in the states at this time with his wife Sarah (maiden name unknown) and their children, and his intentions were to remain there for several years. However, after a few short years, because of the growth in the firm's customer base that he had created, his brothers called him home to help with the increase in production. Because of the few short years he spent in the states, the Johnson Bros. firm experienced a steady increase in growth and put their wares in constant demand.[20]

Upon coming home to England, Robert took a leading role in the management of the firm, which grew not only in increased production, but in the number of potteries they owned as well. The firm was strictly owned and operated by the four brothers and members of their families. However, this did not prevent the brothers from owning other firms privately. In 1900, Robert bought the Crystal Porcelain Tile Works at Cobridge and put his son Harry in charge to run the firm. They traded under the firm name of H&R Johnson. In 1904, Robert's uncle, Alfred Meakin, died. In 1907, Robert's firm H&R Johnson bought the Highgate Works, formerly owned by Alfred, and was then currently owned by Alfred John Meakin, Alfred's son. Upon Alfred John's death in 1908, Robert bought the Royal Victoria, and Royal Albert Works in Tunstall. He paid one hundred thousand pounds for these potteries and placed his son Arthur 'Stuart' in charge. He remained there until at least 1969, and jointly with his son Reginald Stuart from about 1952.[21] These firms, after Robert bought them, continued to trade under the firm name of Alfred Meakin Ltd. Please recall for a moment, as earlier stated, the original agreement of the four brothers was to allow only two sons from each to enter the firm. Roberts way around this rule was to have separate buy-outs, and place his sons, who were not members of the Johnson Bros. firm, in charge. Of the four brothers, Robert was the most prolific, and in an effort to be a "good daddy," he made efforts to see to it that all his family was taken care of.

Robert was a man who was genuinely respected by many in the States as well as his fellow potters in England. His opinion was sought after not only by members of the Johnson Bros. firm, but of the firm's competitors as well. His influence on others was greatly enhanced because of the opportunities afforded him, by the highly successful firm he was a part of and his extensive travels in America.

Robert was bestowed many honors over his life time, but one he relished greatly was when he was given a royal warrant to supply his ware to Her Majesty the Queen Mother. Because of this warrant, and the fact that it was given for several years, gave Robert great personal satisfaction. When you consider the amount of potteries that were producing in England at this time, not only would this have been a great honor, but a very enviable one as well.

Robert's obituary had this to say of him, "The late Mr. Johnson was a disciplinarian, but was held in great esteem by all his employees, in whose welfare, on and off the works, he always took deep interest. He was a considerate employer, and many of those who have worked for him are ready to speak of his generosity. He was fond of sport, and

to the day of his death retained his love of farming pursuits. He rented a large farm at Hanchurch, from the Duke of Sutherland, which is managed by a bailiff, but Mr. Johnson found in his frequent visits to it congenial recreation from the pressing cares of business."[22]

After suffering for some time with an internal condition, Robert died at his home, Butterton Hall in Newcastle, May 18, 1909, at the relatively young age of fifty-three. His funeral, which was kept private as possible, took place at the Newcastle Cemetery on May 20th. By 1933 Roberts wife Sarah had died, and in that year, a gift of five thousand pounds from their children was given to the Staffordshire Royal infirmary in their honor. The gift coincided with the infirmary's newly built main entrance. This new entrance was constructed of oak, consisted of a vestibule and office, and was installed in the memory of Mr. & Mrs. Henry James Johnson. With the check was a letter that was read during the ceremony. It stated, "It is the desire of the children of the late Robert Lewis and Sarah Johnson to perpetuate their memory in this district, and to give the sum of 5,000 pounds for this purpose to the North Staffordshire Royal Infirmary, where they hope such a memorial is possible, and where the money so provided can be best used for the interest of the people in the district."[23] In accepting the gift, the infirmary unanimously voted to dedicate an important ward to the memory of Robert and Sarah Johnson. The history of Roberts's sons, are as follows:

Note. The following sons of Robert Lewis may not be in birth order.

Robert 'Lewis' Jr. was born in 1879, and entered the family business in 1897. Lewis was made part of the team to expand on the founder's beginnings and to further develop the overseas market. By the end of the 1920s his son, Robert 'Basil', had entered the firm. Basil specialized in all aspects of sanitary ware, and in later years, became a director of the Johnson Bros. firm.[24] Geoffrey Lewis, another son, was also made a part of the business.

Plate 324. Robert Lewis Johnson Jr., 1879 to November 1946, was the son of Robert Lewis Johnson. *Reproduced with permission of Johnson Brothers, a Division of Josiah and Sons Limited, Barlaston, Stoke-on-Trent, England.*

Plate 325. Robert 'Basil' Johnson, 1910-1969, was the son of Robert Lewis Jr., and grandson to Robert Lewis Johnson. *Reproduced with permission of Johnson Brothers, a Division of Josiah and Sons Limited, Barlaston, Stoke-on-Trent, England.*

In the obituary for Robert Lewis Jr., it was stated, "The death occurred of Mr. Robert Lewis Johnson, J.P. of Oulton Rocks, Stone, managing director and chairman of Messrs. Johnson Bros. Ltd. He was 67. Mr. Johnson's death was sudden, only a week earlier he had been taking part in the wage negotiations between the British Manufacturers' Federation and the National Federation and National Society of Pottery Works. He entered the firm in 1897, and had been a director for thirty-five years. He was a brother of Sir Ernest Johnson, and leaves a widow, four daughters and two sons, Mr. Geoffrey Lewis and Mr. R. Basil Johnson."[25]

Col. Harry Johnson was born in 1878, and began his business career with the family firm, the Johnson Bros. shortly after graduating from Bath College. In 1901, in partnership with his father, Harry founded the Crystal Porcelain Tile Works in Cobridge. Harry later added branches in Hanley and Burslem and became one of England's most important manufacturers in the tile industry.[26] Interestingly, Burslem was originally called "Butter-Pot Town," because of the glazed red clay butter-pots that were made there. They traded under the firm name of H&R Johnson. After taking over the Crystal Works, the weekly out-put of glazed tiles was two hundred thousand, but by 1955 when Harry died, the business had grown to such an extent that the weekly out-put had grown to three million.[27]

Col. Harry was a former President of the British Pottery Manufacturers Federation, and up until 1953, was Chairman of the British Ceramic Research Association. He was also a Chairman of the Potters' Insurance Company, and a Director for the Johnson Bros. firm. At the time of his death, July 11, 1955, Col. Harry was Chairman of the Johnson Bros. Ltd. At the same time as the funeral service, there was another service being conducted in the canteen of the Highgate Works. All two hundred fifty of the employees turned off their machines for two minutes of silence, and reflected on their departed president.[28]

Frank Charles, another son of Robert Lewis, to the best of my knowledge never entered his fathers business. No further information was found.

Arthur Stuart, the eldest of three brothers, was put at the helm of the Royal Victoria Works in 1908 by his father Robert, who purchased the works for 100,000 pounds.[29] At this works, thirteen biscuit and glost kilns were kept busy every day. Modern machinery replaced the potter's hands in making most of the wares including plates, cups, platters, bowls, etc. After the pieces wares were formed the green ware was placed on revolving dobbins to dry. After the wares have dried, they are placed in saggars, separated by sand for their first firing, which usually takes about one hundred hours.[30]

Alfred Johnson was another son of Robert Lewis, and was living in Stone, England. He was married to a daughter of Alfred Boote. I do not know if he entered the family business.

Sir Ernest James was born 1881. He was a long time, ardent member of the family firm and a well-known figure in the North Staffordshire potting district.

Ernest was made a member of the same team as his brother Robert Lewis Jr., but soon took over his fathers' commitments in America. While on a business trip to East Orange, New Jersey, Ernest met his future bride. They were engaged in 1906, and married that same year. Their first two years of marriage were spent at Barlaston, but in October of 1908 they moved to Altona, England, and remained there ever since.[31] Lady Johnson, Ernest's wife, was born in East Orange, New Jersey, and was the former daughter of Mr. Alfred Boote. Alfred was a native of Cheshire and later moved to America at the age of twenty. Lady Johnson's sister was married to Alfred Johnson, Ernest's brother. So here we have a case of brothers marrying sisters. Lady was a prominent member of the Committee of the Stone Nursing Association, was a worker in the cause of the Stone Hospital Saturday Fund, was associated with the St. Michael's Church Mothers' Union and was President of the Ladies Committee of the North Branch of the Commercial Travelers Association. Lady Johnson was known as a charming, modest and unassuming person, who asked for nothing and gave her all to the community.

By 1928, Ernest was a director of the Johnson Bros. ltd., and in that same year was elected president of the North Staffordshire Royal Infirmary. He succeeded Mr. S. Clowes, M. P. who had held the office for four years.[32] For four years, Ernest was the Chairman of the Stone Urban District Council, and president of the British Pottery Manufacturers' Federation from 1933-1946. Ernest was knighted in 1937 in the Coronation Honors for public services.

By the end of the 1920s Ernest's' son, F. Shepard had joined the firm. By the 1930s another son, E. James Jr. had joined. E. James was born in Stone, and was later of Oulton Cross. He was educated at Rugby, and soon took interest in the family business. Just like his father, E. James made many business trips to the American shores. These trips were meant to help consolidate their business ties with the States. He was married in 1935 and was a keen sportsman and had his father's interest in cricket. He also had interests in Rugby football, tennis, and shooting. By the middle 1930s another son, Major Stephen B. had joined the firm. Stephen joined the Territorial Army in 1939, and was absent from the firm for six or seven years.[33] Sir Ernest died December 21, 1962, at the age of eighty-one.

Plate 326. Ernest James Johnson, 1881 to December 21, 1962, was the son of Robert Lewis. *Reproduced with permission of Johnson Brothers, a Division of Josiah and Sons Limited, Barlaston, Stoke-on-Trent, England.*

Frederick George Johnson

Frederick George Johnson was born September 7, 1858 on the family farm.

He began his business career in 1883 when he joined his brothers in the purchase of the Charles Street Works from the Pankhurst family. In the beginning, there were only a few employees, but by 1923 the firm had over twenty seven hundred employees at their various works. He was widely known and recognized as an outstanding potter, and much of the firm's improvement in production techniques were contributed to him.[34] Frederick was an enthusiastic fisherman, lover of horticulture, and his generosity to institutions in need were well known. His death came September 18, 1923, and due to his heart trouble, was not unexpected. Frederick left his wife, two sons, and five daughters. At the time he was living in Clayton Hall, and after his funeral, he was buried in that same city.

Note: The following sons of Frederick George, may not be in birth order.

Herbert Clayton was a son of Frederick George, and if he was a member of the family firm is unknown to me. I have not been able to find any further information.

Frederick's second son was Frederick Victor. He was born in 1886. Victor was educated at Repton and Trinity College, Cambridge. Upon entering the firm, Victor was put on the same expansion team as his cousins, Lewis and Ernest. Victor was jovial and well liked by the staff and employees, and was held in high regard by all.[35] As part of the firm's expansion efforts, it was decided to build a new Sanitaryware plant in Frankfurt, Germany. The plant was opened in 1913 with Victor and his cousin Reginald as its directors. This new venture was abandoned when WW I broke out, and was never re-opened. Most members of the Johnson Bros. staff managed to escape without too much trouble, with the exception of Victor. While he was attempting to escape by motorcar to Switzerland, he was captured by the Germans and interned at Ruheblen, a civilian prison camp in Berlin. In the early part of 1918, Victor was released by the Germans and allowed to cross into Holland, and arrived in England towards the end of that same year. In his first year back, Victor was made a director of the Johnson Bros. firm, and held this office until his death November 13, 1928. It was widely believed that the time Victor spent in prison had a serious effect on his health, and contributed greatly to his death. Victor died at his home The Limes, Barlaston, at the young age of forty-two.[36] He left behind his wife and two children.

Plate 327. Frederick George Johnson, September 7, 1858 to September 18, 1923. *Reproduced with permission of Johnson Brothers, a Division of Josiah and Sons Limited, Barlaston, Stoke-on-Trent, England.*

Plate 328. Frederick Victor, 1886 to November 13, 1928, was the son of Frederick George Johnson. *Reproduced with permission of Johnson Brothers, a Division of Josiah and Sons Limited, Barlaston, Stoke-on-Trent, England.*

Alfred Johnson

Alfred Johnson was born in 1862 on the family farm, in Oulton. It was Alfred and his brother Frederick who first joined together in partnership when they bought the Charles Street Works in 1883. It remained this way until 1888 when brother Robert joined the firm, and then finally in 1893 brother Henry joined. This would be the first time that all four brothers were joined in partnership, but as you will see, it only lasted for about three years. It was in 1896 that Alfred left the business and moved to Queenborough and started in private business.

Plate 329. Alfred Johnson, 1862 to December 29, 1919.
Reproduced with permission of Johnson Brothers, a Division of Josiah and Sons Limited, Barlaston, Stoke-on-Trent, England.

Soon after arriving in Queenborough, Alfred started his firm of Alfred Johnson & Son Ltd. A. Johnson Tiles Ltd. Alfred's potteries were of great importance to Queenborough and helped the small town to prosper. His Sanitary Works was situated on eleven acres and had twenty-one kilns in constant use. Those same kilns burned eighteen hundred tons of coal every month and produced fifteen hundred pieces of their Pyramid earthenware every day (the largest output capacity of any firm in Europe). Electrical motive power was used throughout the manufacturing process. It was here that Alfred first invented the "casting method," and since has been adopted by countries as far away as China and Brazil. To help with their employee's housing, Alfred implemented a housing scheme, by developing the estate known as Stanley Avenue. This estate was close to the pottery and allowed the workers easy access.

In 1911 Alfred took up residence in Gore Court, Otham, near Maidstone. Here, as before, he took up a genuine and generous interest in the community. He always declined to accept any public position of authority, but during Coronation week, Alfred and his son Stanley,

entertained the whole town with festivities that were very elaborate. Alfred also donated a tract of land to be converted into a park, and a memorial to the Otham men that fell during the great war.[37] He loved the game of cricket, and formed the very successful team, Gore Court XI, who played some of the greatest teams in Maidstone and the district. Alfred loved to fish, and found great pleasure in the shooting sport of hunting.

Alfred died December 29, 1919, at his residence, Gore Court, Otham. Those of most importance who attended Alfred's funeral, which was held under inclement weather, were Stanley and Alfred J. Johnson (sons), Mr. & Mrs. Alfieri (brother-in-law & sister-in-law), Lewis, Frank, and the Rev. Grindley Johnson (nephews), Mr. Mayland (works manager at Queenborough), the whole office staff, and about seventy workmen from Queenborough, all the workmen employed on the farms at Stoneacre and Gore Court and all the leading residents of the neighborhood. The service, which included the hymn Rock of Ages, was conducted by the Vicar Rev. F. J. Blamire, and assisted by the Rev. Grindley Johnson.

Note: The following sons of Alfred may not be in birth order.

Stanley, to the best of my knowledge, never entered into his father's firm, but instead entered into politics as an Alderman for Queenborough. Stanley also volunteered for service during the Great War.

Alfred Jr. would always remain a farmer, but did join his father's firm and was the son in Alfred Johnson & Son. He took over the firm upon his father's death, but still ran and maintained his place of residence, The Holm Place Farm, Sheerness. He also, like his brother, was in politics as a Councilor of Sheerness (he won re-election in 1931), and volunteered for service during the great war.

Alfred Jr., in 1930, spent seventeen weeks traveling thirty-three thousand miles and covering two continents, New Zealand and Australia. It was done with the object of "improving and fostering" trade within the Empire. His party, consisting of sixty-one persons, left England on the 18th of January and headed by steamer to New Zealand. In passing through the Panama Canal, Alfred stated, "There is a lift of 85 feet for one line of shipping, and a fall of 85 feet for the other stream of vessels. This marvelous arrangement is worked by electric mules, and I have seldom seen so interesting a piece of ingenuity and engineering skill." He spent five weeks there visiting all parts of the country. In describing the North Island, which is mainly dairy farming, Alfred had this to say, "It has a forty-inch rainfall, and the grass grows all the year round. We saw thousands of Jersey cows there, and they feed on the grass; there is no artificial feeding of any kind. The cows are milked nine months of the year, and the milk or cream is sent to adjoining butter factories, which are all run on the co-operative system, and owned by the farmers who supply the factories."

Alfred left New Zealand and arrived at Sydney, Australia March 25th. In Australia, Alfred found that the country was suffering everywhere from the effects of severe drought, and the sheep and cattle were in starving condition. He found that seventy-five percent of the population was living in the towns, and most were unemployed. Alfred felt that the answer was developing the vast tracts of land for agriculture.

On his return trip home, Alfred received a wireless message from H. M. The King, that congratulated him on the success of his trip. He arrived home on the ship R.M.S. Narkunda, May 15, 1930.[38] Alfred led a full and varied life, just as many of the other members of the family had. When he died is unknown to me, but this brief insight to his personal life helps to flesh out the "whole" story of the Johnson Bros.

the pottery history

The Johnson Bros. company motto was, "Quality is remembered when price is forgotten." They attributed this to the fact that throughout their various departments, they made it a rule to maintain a high quality ware during production.[39] Now that you have read through the history of the people, and are about to read the history of their potteries, think of this motto often. One way to insure consistent quality is to control all aspects of the business, and this is what the firm tried to achieve. Throughout the firm, for each integral part of the business, a family member was put in charge. This gave family involvement, family control, and a system of checks and balances.

The Charles Street Works, located at the top of Charles Street where it meets Bucknall New Road, was first established by William Mellor in 1758, and was set up to produce Egyptian black.[40] This was eleven years before Josiah Wedgwood opened the Etruria Works. Toft & Keeling, who made similar wares, followed Mellor. The partnership of Toft & Keeling lasted from 1801 to 1824. In 1825, it became Toft & May, and this partnership lasted until 1829, when May alone took over. Robert May held the works in operation for only one year, at which time he sold it to William Ridgway & Co.[41] Ridgway, who was producing white ware for the American market, continued the Charles Street Works until 1834, when he sold it to J. W. Pankhurst & Co. Pankhurst continued a similar operation as Ridgway, until finally in 1883, he sold it to the Johnson Bros., a newly formed partnership. The Johnson Bros. continued the operation by producing a very similar ware as their predecessors.[42] In fact, pieces may be found marked "Late Pankhurst," which were produced by the Johnson Bros. The Johnson Bros. used the Pankhurst name in their mark because they did not continue in the potting business after the sale, and as a marketing tool to keep the past "Pankhurst" customers happy and coming back for more. My research, which made an extreme effort, has not located any photos of the Charles Street Works.

By the early 1930s, the effects of the worldwide depression found its way to the Johnson Bros., and the decision to close the now obsolete Charles Street Works was made. Eventually it was torn down, and a new office building was built to replace it. It was about the middle of the 1930s before they were back to full production.

In the late 1930s, the Johnson Brothers were changing over from the old-fashioned bottle kilns to the new tunnel method. This new method used gas or electricity instead of coal. The first tunnel was electric and was installed in the Hanley Works. This was followed by a gas fired one installed at the Imperial Works. Progress dictated that in order for the Johnson Bros. to remain successful, they had to change with the times.

In 1888, just five years after the purchase of the Charles Street Works, and the same year brother Robert joined the firm, they began construction on their second works, the Hanley Pottery. It was located on Eastwood Road, and was completed in 1889. At the Hanley Works, ordinary tableware was produced. We know that Flow Blue was produced at the Hanley Works, and probably was the main factory for this ware. Known body styles produced at the Hanley were, JB-A, JB-B, and JB-E. Patterns applied to these shapes were, ARGYLE, DEL MONTE, HOLLAND, JAPAN, JEWEL, NORMANDY, SAVOY, STERLING, TOKIO, and WARWICK. ARGYLE and DEL MONTE were produced only in Flow Blue.[43] See Plates 330, 331, 332, and 333.

Plate 330. The Hanley Pottery was first operated by the Johnson Bros. in 1883. The road by the gates is also going over the canal. The white room in the photo was used for shipping on the canal. *Courtesy of Neil Ewens, England* 1997.

Plate 331. This photo shows a fuller view of the same side of the building as Plate 330. The canal is out of site, but runs along the base of the building. If you were to continue on the canal, by going to the left, you would see first the Imperial Works on your left, and then the Eastwood Works on your right. *Courtesy of Neil Ewens, England* 1997.

Plate 332. The offices of the Johnson Bros. located at the Hanley pottery. The canal is under the low wall on the right. *Courtesy of Neil Ewens, England* 1997.

Plate 333. The Hanley pottery as it runs along Eastwood Road. *Courtesy of Neil Ewens, England* 1997.

The Alexander Pottery came next. It was built in 1889 and was named after the current Princess of Wales. This works was also set up to produce ordinary tableware, and in all probability, Flow Blue was produced there. The Alexander was located in Tunstall, on the north side of Stoke-on-Trent. The hope, by placing the factory there, was to attract employees from that area.[44] See Plate 334 for a picture of the Alexander Pottery. Also see Plate 529.

Plate 334. The Alexander Pottery was first built by the Johnson Bros. in 1889, and held until 1939. As you can see, it is now owned by Wedgwood. *Courtesy of Neil Ewens, England* 1997.

The Johnson Bros. were experiencing tremendous growth, and in March of 1891, they opened the Imperial Works. At the Imperial Works, ordinary tableware was produced, and it is strongly possible that Flow Blue was produced there. This works, as the Hanley Pottery had been, was built on Eastwood Road. Both the Hanley and the imperial Works were located within a ten-minute walk from the original Charles Street Works. The Hanley and the Imperial factories both were a series of one and two storied buildings that surrounded the bottle kilns in the center. This was standard design for pottery factories in those days, and was done to give all the factory departments a close distance to the kilns. The building design gave minimum movement of the product, and helped to prevent breakage. For pictures of the Imperial Pottery see Plates 335, 336, 337, and 338.

In 1996 the Imperial Pottery, which by then was owned by Wedgwood, was sold to Hemburymill, a Leek-based property developer. By 1999, the building had fallen into great disrepair, and had been the victim of vandals. The developer wanted to tear the building down and replace it with sixty new homes. Head teacher, Hilary Pickin

at Joiners Square Primary School, a school close to the factory stated, "The building was a blot on the landscape and a danger to the children. I feel it is a shame that we have to look at it day in, day out. Our school was built in 1879 and it still looks good." The other residents in the area also stated that they thought the building was close to collapsing.[45] Today, like so many other historic buildings in other countries, the building was razed. Sixty homes now reside where once the Imperial first stood.

Plate 336. A close up view of the front façade, showing the pottery name. *Courtesy of Neil Ewens, England* 1997.

Plate 337. In this photo we show you the back of the Imperial pottery, and the obvious deterioration of the building. *Courtesy of Neil Ewens, England* 1997.

Plate 335. The Imperial Pottery as seen in February 1999. The building is in obvious state of deterioration. *Courtesy of Neil Ewens, England* 1999.

Plate 338. One of the few remaining bottle kilns left at the Imperial. *Courtesy of Neil Ewens, England* 1997.

In February of 1896, the Johnson Bros opened the Trent Sanitary Works. This would be a new venture for them, and was located across the street from the Imperial Works. The Trent was laid out in a modern "open-plan" form as a single story building. The Trent had eleven ovens, and was devoted to their world famous "Trent Sanitary Ware." See Plate 339 for a photo of this pottery.

This factory was almost self-contained, as they made their own fittings of wood, cast iron, and brass. As a result of this quality control, their claim was "guarantee of a perfect fit and working arrangements for all goods sent out ready for erection."[46] In 1899, a new mill was erected at the Trent Works and was used not only to supply their own needs for flint and Cornish stones, but the ground stones were also supplied to other potteries. In 1909, a new mill was constructed at the Alexander Works. This new mill would be used to supply stone for that pottery, and to relieve the high production pressure at the Trent mill.

Business was going very well for the Johnson Bros., and stayed steady for them during the otherwise slow times. America in 1906, 1907, and 1908 was experiencing a financial panic that was felt all over the world. While most potteries were reflecting a slump in business, the Johnson Bros. firm was able to maintain their usual volume of trade.[47] In fact, throughout the years, the firm had achieved sales records of worldwide magnitude. From the 1890s, and well into the 1900s, the Johnson Bros. was the largest ceramic producing firm in the world. Not necessarily in Flow Blue production, but the largest earthenware manufacturers in the world.[48] Part of the success of the Johnson Bros. was that they maintained offices in New York and other countries, and made personal visits to their customers. This created opportunities to better service their accounts and for enhanced customer relations. Remember their company motto? "Quality is remembered, when price is forgotten." In a trade that has experienced many highs and lows, the Johnson Bros. firm was a true dynasty in the potting industry.

Plate 339. The Trent Works is the white building on the left. The building on the right is the Imperial Works, and the road running between them is Eastwood Road. *Courtesy of Neil Ewens, England* 1997.

pottery marks

For the marks listed below, when possible, I have given the reader "code numbers" applied to the marks from two reference works. They are: Geoffrey A. Godden, *Encyclopedia of British Pottery and Porcelain Marks*, New York, N. Y.: Bonanza Books, 1964, and Arnold A. & Dorothy E. Kowalsky, *Encyclopedia of Marks On American, English, and European Earthenware, Ironstone, and Stoneware 1780-1980*, Atglen, PA: Schiffer Publishing, Ltd. 1999.

Plate 340. Godden No. 2176 – KAD No. B1366 – The Royal Coat of Arms mark, which incorporates "Royal Ironstone China" was used c.1883-1913. This mark was used on their heavy White Granitewares, and Tealeaf/Copper Lustre.

Plate 341. Godden No. 2177 – KAD No. B1367 – This mark, with banner below the crown, Semi-Porcelain over crown and Royal above Semi-Porcelain, and England below banner was used c.1891+. If the pattern name is listed, it will be on top of the mark above Royal. This mark was used on their Ironstone/Stoneware body styles, and have Flow Blue and other colored transferware patterns applied.

Plate 342. This mark is not to be found in other reference works. The uniqueness of this mark comes mostly from the shape of its crown. It was used c.1902. We arrived at this date because it was noted on several pieces that have U. S. Patent dates representing 1902. This mark, as Plate 341, was used on Ironstone/Stoneware body styles that have Flow Blue and other colored transferware patterns applied.

Plate 343. Godden No. 2179 – KAD No. B1369 – This mark was used c.1913+, and was applied to Ironstone/ Stoneware body styles that have Flow Blue, and other colored transferware patterns applied. This mark was used on the last of the Flow Blue ware that the Johnson Bros. produced, and has been seen on pieces dating to the early 1920s.

a pottery chronology

The following is a chronology of the Johnson Bros. Ltd. Pottery. The dates listed will include all pertinent facts, as well as factory marks. Also there will be incidental dates, such as the year of entry for a brother into the partnership, and the date a brother leaves the partnership whether through free will or death. The four brothers' names are listed in bold.

1868 – **Henry James** enters pottery apprenticeship
1883 – **Frederick George** & **Alfred** join in partnership
1883 – Charles Street Works is purchased
1883 – Mark (Plate 340) is in use
1888 – **Robert Lewis** joins partnership
1888 – Hanley Pottery is built
1889 – Alexandra Pottery is opened
1891 – Imperial Pottery is opened
1891 – Mark (Plate 341) is in use
1893 – **Henry James** joins partnership
1893-1896 – Is the only time that all four brothers are together in partnership
1896 – Trent Sanitary Works is opened
1896 – Johnson Bros. becomes "limited"
1896 – **Alfred** leaves partnership
1897 – Robert Lewis Jr., son of Robert Lewis, joins firm
1897 – Ernest James, son of Robert Lewis, joins firm
1899 – New mill is built at Trent Sanitary Works
1900 - Frederick Victor, son of Frederick George, joins firm

1901 – **Robert Lewis** buys Crystal Porcelain Tile Works, headed by son Harry
1902 – Mark (Plate 342) is in use
1908 – **Robert Lewis** buys Royal Victoria Works
1909 – Reginald T. & Frank G., sons of Henry James, join firm
1909 – **Robert Lewis** dies May 18
1909 – New mill is built at Alexandra Pottery
1913 – Sanitary Plant is built in Frankfurt, Germany
1913 – Mark (Plate 343) is in use
1914 – Frankfurt Sanitary Plant is closed due to outbreak of WWI
1919 – **Alfred** dies December 29
1920s – Peter & Christopher, grandsons of Henry James, join the firm
1920s – Basil & Geoffrey Lewis, grandsons of Robert Lewis, join the firm
1923 – **Frederick George** dies September 18
1930s – F. Shepard & E. James Jr., grandsons of Robert Lewis, join the firm
1931 – **Henry James,** the last of the original four brothers, dies April 28
1932 – Charles Street Works closes as a result of being obsolete & depression
1947 – Sovereign Pottery in Hamilton, Canada is acquired
1957 – Tableware plant is built in Croydon, Victoria, Australia
1958 – Eastwood Works is acquired[49]
1965 – British Aluminum Co., Milton, Stoke-on-Trent, is acquired
1968 – Johnson Bros. Ltd is acquired by the Wedgwood Group in January

dish body styles – specifics

JB-A

Plate 344. *Courtesy of Ann Potts, Illinois*
Body Style: JB-A
Factory Name: Laurel
U. S. Patent Applied/Dated: - / -
English Registry: -
First Year Catalog: FW 1907/1908 Sears Roebuck & Co.
Late Victorian Dating Label: Transition
Flow Blue Patterns: HOLLAND, JAPAN, JEWEL, NORMANDY, and REGIS

JB-A pattern identification:

Plate 345. HOLLAND plate, 10" in diameter. *Courtesy Murray Weisberg & Mark Armstrong, California* $90-$125

Plate 346. JEWEL plate, 10" in diameter. *Anonymous collector* $90-$125

Plate 347. NORMANDY plate, 10" in diameter. *Courtesy of Shell & Jim Lewis, Illinois* $90-$125

JB-A body style shapes:

Plate 348. Butter pat, top left NORMANDY & JEWEL, bottom, HOLLAND. *Courtesy of Shell & Jim Lewis, Illinois* $50+

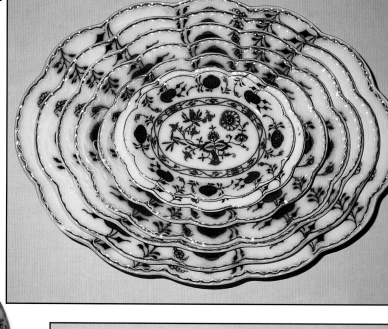

Plate 349. Oval platter HOLLAND, 7 ¾", 8 ¾", 10 ½", 12 ½", 14 ¼", 16", 18". *Courtesy of Murray Weisberg & Mark Armstrong, California* $175+, $175+, $150+, $175+, $200+, $225+, $275+ respectively

Plate 350. Round charger, NORMANDY, 12" in diameter. *Courtesy of Terry & Ann Potts, Illinois* $350+

Plate 351. Cake plate, HOLLAND. *Courtesy of Murray Weisberg & Mark Armstrong, California* $225+

Plate 352. Round/Oval covered tureen, NORMANDY. *Anonymous collector* left round $300+, right oval $275+

Plate 353. Covered soup tureen complete, NORMANDY. *Courtesy of Warren & Connie Macy, Indiana* $1500+

Plate 354. Bone dish, butter pat, & individual oval bowl, HOLLAND. *Courtesy of Murray Weisberg & Mark Armstrong, California* $95+, $50+, $90+ respectively

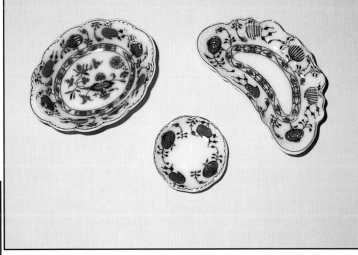

Plate 355. Covered sauce tureen complete, NORMANDY. *Courtesy of Warren & Connie Macy, Indiana* $750+

Plate 356. Covered butter, HOLLAND. *Anonymous collector $425+*

Plate 357. Gravy boat with undertray, NORMANDY. All are JB-A body style, except front right. It is JB-G body style. The double spout gravies are hard to find, and the ones with two handles, like the one back left, are very rare. *Anonymous collector $275+ back left, the rest $350+*

Plate 358. Eggcup, NORMANDY. Eggcups are universal for all body styles. The Johnson Bros. did not make a different one for each body style of dish. *Anonymous collector $200+ea due to pattern popularity*

Plate 359. Cup, NORMANDY, l to r demitasse, coffee, tea. *Courtesy of Warren & Connie Macy, Indiana $225+, $90-$125, $90-$125 respectively.*

Plate 360. Two handled cup/saucer. Used for cream soup or bouillon. *Courtesy of Murray Weisberg & Mark Armstrong, California $125+*

Plate 361. Waste bowl right, oyster bowl, NORMANDY. Please take note of the pedestal base on the oyster bowl, which is the main difference between the two bowls. *Courtesy of Warren & Connie Macy, Indiana $275-$350 waste bowl, $200+ oyster bowl*

Plate 362. Oyster bowl, NORMANDY, another study. *Courtesy of Terry & Ann Potts, Illinois* $200+

Plate 363. Covered sugar/creamer, NORMANDY. *Courtesy of Terry & Ann Potts, Illinois* $275+ sugar, $225+ creamer

Plate 364. Teapot, NORMANDY. *Courtesy of Warren & Connie Macy, Indiana* $2000+ due to pattern popularity

Plate 365. Pitcher, NORMANDY. *Courtesy of Warren & Connie Macy, Indiana* l to r $225+ creamer, $275+ pint, $300+, $350+

Plate 366. Covered mustard jar with attached undertray, HOLLAND, undertray 5" long, mustard jar 4 ¼" tall. The shape of this mustard is universal for all body styles. *Courtesy of Murray Weisberg & Mark Armstrong, California* $275-$375

Plate 367. Pedestal compote, NORMANDY. *Lee & Betty Hochstetler, Indiana* $350-$1200

Plate 368. Pedestal fruit bowl, JEWEL, 10" handle to handle by 4 ½" high. *Author collection* $500-$750

Plate 369. Pedestal fruit bowl, NORMANDY, another study. *Courtesy of Warren & Connie Macy, Indiana* $500-$750

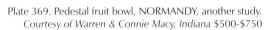

Plate 370. Punch bowl, punch cup, HOLLAND. *Courtesy of Murray Weisberg & Mark Armstrong, California* $1000+ punch bowl, $250+ cups ea.

Plate 371. Fish platter & drainer, NORMANDY, 22" long. *Courtesy of Warren & Connie Macy, Indiana* $1200+, $1500+ with drainer

Plate 372. Ladle, soup & sauce, NORMANDY. The ladles are universal for all Johnson Bros. body styles. *Courtesy of Warren & Connie Macy, Indiana* $500+ soup ladle, $275+ sauce ladle

Non-Flow Blue patterns applied to JB-A body style:
WHITE: Whiteware
WHITE: Whiteware/gold tracings

JB-B

Plate 373. *Courtesy of Ann Potts, Illinois*
Body Style: JB-B
Factory Name: Elite
U. S. Patent Applied/Dated: - / -
English Registry: -
First Year Catalog: FW 1911/1912 Sears Roebuck & Co.
Late Victorian Dating Label: Transition
Flow Blue Patterns: DARTMOUTH, MARLBORO, SAVOY, STERLING, and WARWICK

JB-B pattern identification:

Plate 374. SAVOY soup tureen undertray, 14" long. This undertray has a very distinct indent for the tureen to rest in. *Anonymous collector* $200+

Plate 376. WARWICK plate, 9" in diameter. *Courtesy of Sue Otteman, Texas* $80-$100

Plate 375. STERLING plate, 10" in diameter. *Courtesy of JoAnn Woodall & Paul Woolmer, Illinois* $90-$125

JB-B body style shapes:

Plate 377. Butter pat, top left WARWICK and SAVOY, bottom STERLING. *Courtesy of Shell & Jim Lewis, Illinois* $50+

Plate 378. Round open bowl, STERLING, 9 ½" wide. *Courtesy of Marilyn & James Holm, Michigan* $225-$325

Plate 379. Oval open bowl, WARWICK, 9" x 7" wide. *Courtesy of Bonnie Oleksa, Ohio* $175-$225

Plate 380. Gravy boat, WARWICK. *Courtesy of Debby Hagara, Washington* $150+ with no undertray

Plate 381. Oyster bowl, WHITE ware, 6" wide x 3" high. *Author collection* $30+

Plate 382. Teapot, WARWICK. *Courtesy of Warren & Connie Macy, Indiana* $750+

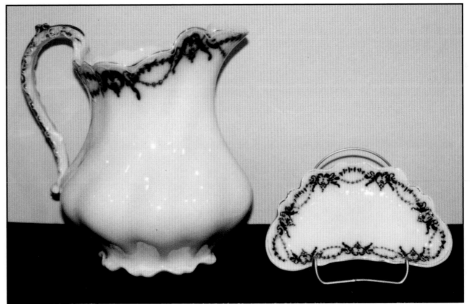

Plate 383. Pitcher & bone dish, STERLING, pitcher 7 ½" tall. *Courtesy of JoAnn Woodall & Paul Woolmer, Illinois* $350+ pitcher, $95+ bone dish

JB-C

Plate 384. *Courtesy of Ann Potts, Illinois*
Body Style: JB-C
Factory Name: The Erminie
U.S. Patent Applied/Dated: - / April 18, 1902
English Registry: Rd.No.377074 (1901)
First Year Catalog: FW 1902/1903 Sears Roebuck & Co.
Late Victorian Dating Label: Lace
Flow Blue Patterns: DOROTHY, GENT, MONTANA, REGENT, ST. LOUIS, and VENETIAN

JB-C pattern identification:

Plate 385. MONTANA plate, 10" in diameter. *Courtesy of Tom & Murline Georgeson, California* $90-$125

Plate 386. ST. LOUIS plate, 10" in diameter. *Courtesy of Don & Zan Webb, Texas* $90-$125

JB-C body style shapes:

Plate 387. Round covered soup tureen, MONTANA. *Courtesy of William & Rebecca Leach, New York* $750+

Plate 388. Round covered tureen, DOROTHY. *Courtesy of William & Rebecca Leach, New York* $300+

Plate 389. Oval covered soup tureen, ST. LOUIS. This is the only known pattern that the Johnson Bros. applied polychrome to. *Anonymous collector* $800+

Plate 390. Teapot, MONTANA. *Courtesy of Warren & Connie Macy, Indiana* $750+

Plate 391. Teapot, ST. LOUIS, another study. *Courtesy of Warren & Connie Macy, Indiana* $750+

Plate 392. Pitcher, DOROTHY, 6 ½" high. *Author collection* $300+

JB-D

Plate 393. *Courtesy of Ann Potts, Illinois*
Body Style: JB-D
Factory Name: Silver
U. S. Patent Applied/Dated: - / October 21, 1902
English Registry: RdNo417778 (1903)
First Year Catalog: FW 1904/1905 Sears Roebuck & Co.
Late Victorian Dating label: Lace
Flow Blue Patterns: CORAL, ECLIPSE, GEORGIA, KENWORTH, OREGON, and THE BLUE DANUBE

JB-D pattern identification:

Plate 394. CORAL plate, 8" in diameter. *Courtesy of Terry & Ann Potts, Illinois* $60-$80

Plate 395. ECLIPSE plate, 9" in diameter. *Courtesy of Lloyd & Sue Otteman, Texas* $80-$100

Plate 396. GEORGIA plate, 7" in diameter. *Courtesy of Jeanne Mueller, California* $40-$60

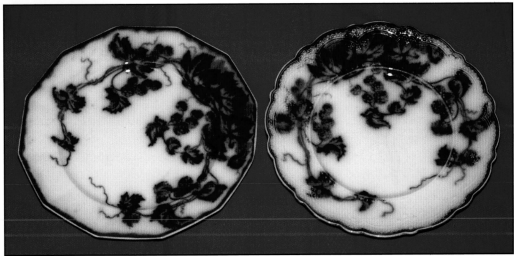

Plate 397. KENWORTH plates, 10" in diameter. This plate shows the two body styles that this pattern was applied to, the other style is JB-J. *Courtesy of Terry & Valee Lyon, Florida* $90-$125

Plate 398. OREGON plate, 10" in diameter. *Courtesy of Shell & Jim Lewis, Illinois* $90-$125

Plate 399. THE BLUE DANUBE plate, 8" in diameter. *Anonymous collector* $60-$80

JB-D body style shapes:

Plate 400. Butter pat, top OREGON, bottom left GEORGIA, right THE BLUE DANUBE. Note the similarity to these patterns. They are very close to being identical, but there are differences. This gives us an indication that this design was very popular. *Courtesy of Shell & Jim Lewis, Illinois* $50+

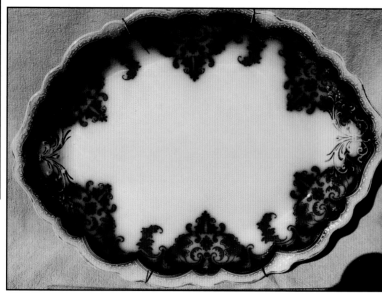

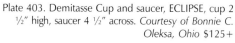

Plate 401. Platter, GEORGIA, 14" across. *Anonymous collector* $200+

Plate 402. Round covered tureen, KENWORTH. This shape came with two different styles of handles for the tureens. The style shown came about two years after the original introduction of JB-D. The original style for the handles was more of a loop shape. *Anonymous collector* $300+

Plate 403. Demitasse Cup and saucer, ECLIPSE, cup 2 ½" high, saucer 4 ½" across. *Courtesy of Bonnie C. Oleksa, Ohio* $125+

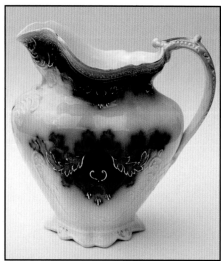

Plate 404. Pitcher, THE BLUE DANUBE, 7 ½" high. *Courtesy of Shell & Jim Lewis, Illinois* $350+

Non-Flow Blue patterns applied to JB-D body style:
WHITE: Whiteware
WHITE: Whiteware/gold tracings

JB-E

Plate 405. *Courtesy of Ann Potts, Illinois*
Body Style: JB-E
Factory Name: St. Elmo
U. S. Patent Applied/Dated: - / -
English Registry: -
First Year Catalog: -
Late Victorian Dating Label: Transition
Flow Blue Patterns: ARGYLE, DEL MONTE, and
TOKIO

JB-E pattern identification:

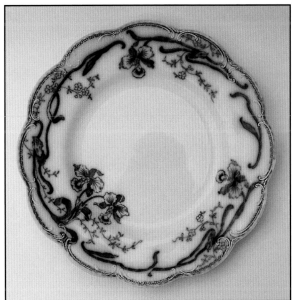

Plate 407. DEL MONTE plate, 10" in diameter. *Courtesy of Shell & Jim Lewis, Illinois* $90-$125

Plate 406. ARGYLE plate, 10" in diameter. *Courtesy of Venessa Luce, Texas* $90-$125

Plate 408. TOKIO plate, 10" in diameter. Please note the body style of this plate is JB-G. This plate is for pattern identification only. *Courtesy of Shell & Jim Lewis, Illinois* $90-$125

JB-E body style shapes:

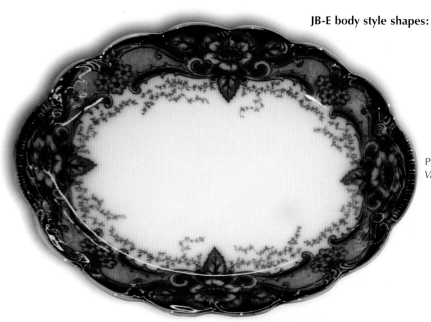

Plate 409. Platter, ARGYLE, 14" long. *Courtesy of Vanessa Luce, Texas $200+*

Plate 410. A variety of shapes, ARGYLE, front, relish dish $175+, middle left, round open bowl $225-$325, middle, platter 14" long $200+, right, oval open bowl $175-$225, two waste bowls $275-$350, top, two sizes of plates and a 8" coupe shaped bowl. *Courtesy of Vanessa Luce, Texas*

Plate 411. A variety of shapes, ARGYLE, in back, plate 10" in diameter, front left to right, berry bowl $40+, 8" coupe shaped bowl $70+, cup and saucer $90-$125. *Courtesy of Gordy & Judy Jesse, Wisconsin*

Plate 412. Cup, DEL MONTE. *Courtesy of Shell & Jim Lewis, Illinois $75+ cup only*

Non-Flow Blue patterns applied to JB-E body style:
BEAUFORT: Green floral border
WHITE: Whiteware

JB-F

Plate 413. *Courtesy of Ann Potts, Illinois*
Body Style: JB-F
Factory Name: -
U. S. Patent Applied/Dated: - / -
English Registry: -
First Year Catalog: 1903 Sears Roebuck & Co.
Late Victorian Dating Label: Scroll
Flow Blue Patterns: BROOKLYN, CLAREMONT, CLOVERLY, and FLORIDA

JB-F pattern identification:

Plate 414. BROOKLYN plate, 8" in diameter. *Anonymous collector* $60-$80

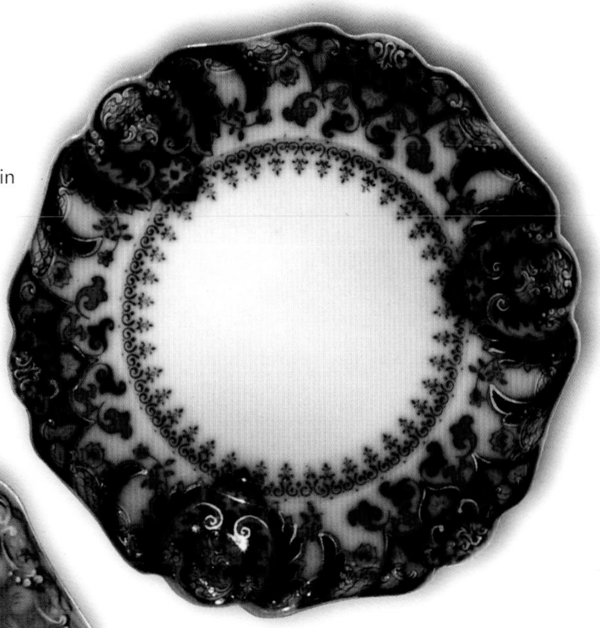

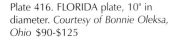

Plate 416. FLORIDA plate, 10" in diameter. *Courtesy of Bonnie Oleksa, Ohio* $90-$125

Plate 415. CLAREMONT plate, 0" in diameter. *Courtesy of Shell & Jim Lewis, Illinois* $90-$125

JB-F body style shapes:

Plate 417. Platter, CLAREMONT, 14" long. *Courtesy of Shell & Jim Lewis, Illinois* $200+

Plate 420. Eggcup, FLORIDA. *Courtesy of Shell & Jim Lewis, Illinois* $175+

Plate 418. Covered sauce tureen with true undertray, CLAREMONT. *Courtesy of Shell & Jim Lewis, Illinois* $500+ set is minus ladle

Plate 421. Teapot, FLORIDA. *Courtesy of Warren & Connie Macy, Indiana* $750+

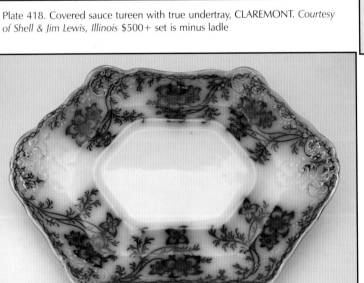

Plate 419. Undertray for sauce tureen, CLAREMONT. Another study of the undertray to show the indent for the sauce tureen to rest in. *Courtesy of Shell & Jim Lewis, Illinois* $125+

Plate 422. Teacup, FLORIDA. *Courtesy of Dolores DeBenedictis* $90-$125 with saucer

JB-G

Plate 423. *Courtesy of Ann Potts, Illinois*
Body Style: JB-G
Factory Name: -
U. S. Patent Applied/Dated: - / -
English Registry: -
First Year Catalog: -
Late Victorian Dating Label: Transition
Flow Blue Patterns: EXETER, MONGOLIA, SULTANA, THE TRIESTE, TOKIO, and TURIN

JB-G pattern identification:

Plate 424. MONGOLIA plate, 10" in diameter. *Courtesy of Patrick Rinehart, Pennsylvania* $90-$125

Plate 426. TURIN plate, 10" in diameter. *Courtesy of Sue Otteman, Texas* $90-$125

Plate 425. THE TRIESTE gravy boat with attached undertray. *Anonymous collector* $275+

JB-G body style shapes:

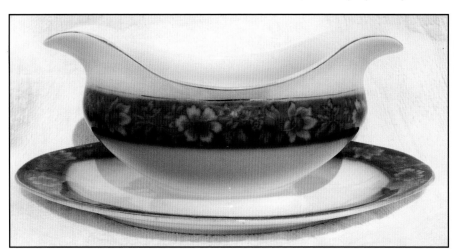

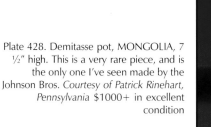

Plate 427. Gravy with double spout and attached undertray, TURIN, undertray is 9 ½" long x 6 ½" wide, gravy boat is 7 ½" long x 4" wide. *Courtesy of Bonnie Oleksa, Ohio* $275+

Plate 428. Demitasse pot, MONGOLIA, 7 ½" high. This is a very rare piece, and is the only one I've seen made by the Johnson Bros. *Courtesy of Patrick Rinehart, Pennsylvania* $1000+ in excellent condition

Plate 429. Teapot, MONGOLIA. *Courtesy of Warren & Connie Macy, Indiana* $750+

The JB-G body style was the last shape used by the Johnson Bros. for Flow Blue. This body style was produced in the late 1910s, and continued through the 1920s. During the 1920s and 1930s "Botanical Borders" became very popular, and JB-G was used extensively for many of them. The JB-G body style rivals Grindley's Gr-I in both looks and use.

Non-Flow Blue patterns applied to JB-G body style:
ARCADIAN: Yellow floral border
FRANKLIN
GOLDEIN: Whiteware/gold tracings
HAVERHILL: Art Nouveau border
NASSAU: Art Nouveau border
ORLEANS: Yellow floral
THE HEVELLA: Botanical border
THE PONTRACINA: Blue Art Nouveau border
THE VIGO: Botanical border
WHITE: Whiteware

JB-H

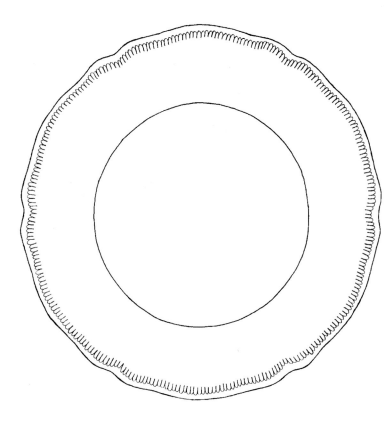

Plate 430. *Courtesy of Ann Potts, Illinois*
Body Style: JB-H
Factory Name: -
U. S. Patent Applied/Dated: - / November 11, 1898
English Registry: -
First Year Catalog: SS 1900 Sears Roebuck & Co.
Late Victorian Dating Label: Scroll
Flow Blue Patterns: PRINCETON, RALEIGH, RICHMOND, and STANLEY Flow Mulberry Patterns: RALEIGH

JB-H pattern identification:

Plate 431. PRINCETON plate, 9" in diameter. *Courtesy of Shell & Jim Lewis, Illinois* $80-$100

Plate 433. STANLEY plate 9" in diameter. *Courtesy of Terry & Ann Potts, Illinois* $80-$100

Plate 432. RICHMOND plate, 8" in diameter. *Courtesy of Jeanne Mueller, California* $60-$80

Plate 434. RALEIGH plate, 9" in diameter. Besides Flow Blue, this pattern also came in Flow Mulberry and blue green as shown. *Courtesy of Norman Wolfe, Washington* $50+ because of color

JB-H body style shapes:

Plate 435. Platter, RICHMOND, 16" long.
Anonymous collector $225+

Plate 436. Round open bowl,
STANLEY, 9" across. *Courtesy of Shell
& Jim Lewis, Illinois $225-$325*

Plate 437. A partial tea set, STANLEY. Pieces shown are in back left,
cake plate & oval platter, front left to right, covered sugar, teacup,
teapot, and pint pitcher (this pitcher is not the creamer, but the next
size larger). *Courtesy of Phyllis & Bob Butner, Ohio $750+ teapot,
$225+ cake plate, $275 covered sugar, $275 pint pitcher.*

Plate 438. A wonderful assortment of
shapes for JB-H. This plate also shows
you how well Flow Blue displays in a
cabinet. *Courtesy of Phyllis & Bob
Butner, Ohio $750+ for round
covered soup tureen, middle bottom,
$95+ for bone dish in front of teapot*

JB-H is the only known body style that a fish platter was produced
in. Patterns from other body styles are applied to this one shape.

Non-Flow Blue patterns applied to JB-H body style:
KILDARE: Botanical border
NINGPO: Botanical border
OLD MALVERN: Pink/yellow floral
UNIDENTIFIED: Purple floral
WHITE: Whiteware
WHITE: Whiteware/gold tracings

B-I

Plate 439. *Courtesy of Ann Potts, Illinois*
Body Style: JB-I
Factory Name: -
U. S. Patent Applied/Dated: - / -
English Registry: -
First Year Catalog: FW 1898/1899 Sears Roebuck & Co.
Late Victorian Dating Label: Scroll
Flow Blue Patterns: ALBANY, ASTORIA, CLARISSA, FORTUNA, and SAVANNAH Flow Mulberry Patterns: CONSTANCE, SALISBURY, SAVANNAH, and VIENNA II

JB-I pattern identification:

Plate 440. ALBANY plate, 9" in diameter. *Courtesy of Terry & Ann Potts, Illinois* $80-$100

Plate 441. ASTORIA plate, 8" in diameter. *Courtesy of Tom & Murline Georgeson, California* $60-$80

Plate 442. CLARISSA plate, 10" in diameter. *Courtesy of Leonard & Joyce Setaro, California* $90-$125

Plate 443. CONSTANCE plate in Flow mulberry, 9" in diameter. *Author collection* $50+ Price is reduced because Late Victorian Flow Mulberry, at this time, is less collectable.

Plate 444. Mark on back of CONSTANCE plate. Please note that the mark was also printed in Flow mulberry, and the letter "M" under the mark. This letter "M" is the factory code to signify this piece to be Flow Mulberry.

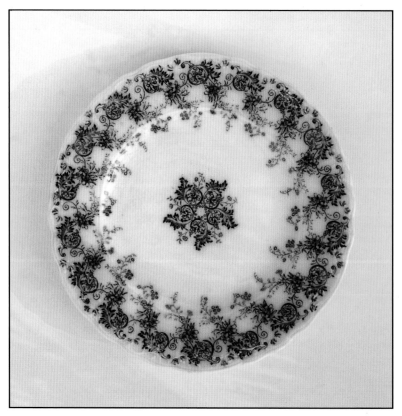

Plate 445. FORTUNA plate, 8" in diameter. *Author collection* $40+ because of color

JB-I body style shapes:

Plate 446. Platter, ALBANY, 12" long. *Anonymous collector* $175+

Plate 447. Round covered bowl, ALBANY. *Courtesy of Betty Krogh, Idaho* $300+

Plate 448. Gravy boat and undertray, ALBANY. *Courtesy of Betty Krogh, Idaho* $275+

Plate 449. Teacup, ALBANY. Please note nted sides and flared rim of cup. *Courtesy of Betty Krogh, Idaho* $90-$125

Plate 450. Coffee cup, ALBANY. Please note the straight sides of the cup, and no flared rim. *Courtesy of Betty Krogh, Idaho* $90-$125

Plate 451. Oyster bowl on pedestal base in center of photo, CLARISSA. *Courtesy of Susan Hirsch, Georgia* $200+

Plate 452. Covered sugar and creamer, ALBANY. *Courtesy of Betty Krogh, Idaho* $275+ sugar, $225+ creamer

Plate 453. Covered sugar that is in the process of being repaired. Collectors should be congratulated who take the time and money to have their damaged pieces restored. We must keep this a constant reminder, that for every piece hopelessly damaged, there is one less piece in this world to share.

Plate 454. Teapot, ASTORIA. *Courtesy of Warren & Connie Macy, Indiana* $750+

Plate 455. Pitcher, ALBANY, 8 ½" high. *Courtesy of Betty Krogh, Idaho* $400+

JB-J

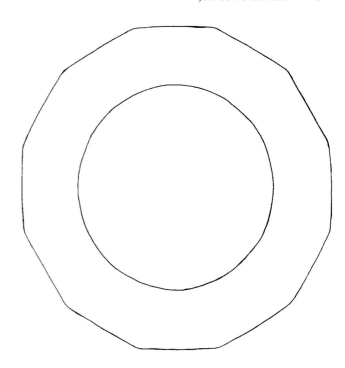

Plate 456. *Courtesy of Ann Potts, Illinois*
Body Style: JB-J
Factory Name: -
U. S. Patent Applied/Dated: - / -
English Registry: -
First Year Catalog: -
Late Victorian Dating Label: Transition
Flow Blue Patterns: KENWORTH and ROYSTON

JB-J pattern identification:

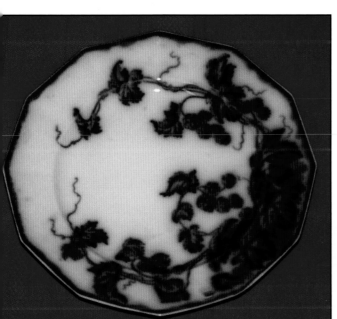

Plate 457. KENWORTH plate, 10" in diameter. *Courtesy of Lloyd & Sue Otteman, Texas* $90-$125

Plate 458. ROYSTON creamer. *Courtesy of Bob & Nancy Ferriani, Indiana* $225+

JB-J body style shapes:

Plate 459. Platters, KENWORTH, 14" x 11" wide, 12" x 9 ½" wide. *Courtesy of Lloyd & Sue Otteman, Texas* $200+ for 14" platter, $175+ for 12" platter

Plate 462. Coffee cup, two sizes, KENWORTH, large 4" x 2 ½" high, small 3 ½" x 2" high. *Courtesy of Lloyd & Sue Otteman, Texas* $125+ large, $90-$125 small

Plate 463. Waste bowl, KENWORTH, 5 ¼" x 3" high. Please note the similarity of the cup to the waste bowl. They are identical except for the handle and size. *Courtesy of Lloyd & Sue Otteman, Texas* $275-$350

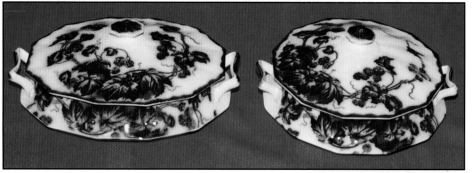

Plate 460. Oval & round covered tureens, KENWORTH, left oval 11" handle to handle x 7 ½" wide, round 9" handle to handle. *Courtesy of Lloyd & Sue Otteman, Texas* $275+ for oval, $300+ for round

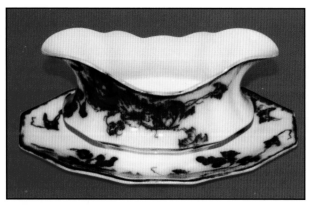

Plate 461. Gravy boat with two spouts and attached undertray, KENWORTH, undertray 9" x 5 ¼" wide, gravy boat 7 ¼" spout to handle x 3 ¼" wide. *Courtesy of Lloyd & Sue Otteman, Texas* $350+

Plate 464. Tea set, KENWORTH, covered sugar, teapot, and creamer. *Courtesy of Lloyd & Sue Otteman, Texas* $275+ sugar, $750+ teapot, $225+ creamer

Non-Flow Blue patterns applied to JB-J body style:
WHITE: Whiteware
WHITE: Whiteware/gold tracings

JB-K

Plate 465. *Courtesy of Ann Potts, Illinois*
Body Style: JB-K
Factory Name: -
U. S. Patent Applied/Dated: - / October 21, 1902
English Registry: -
First Year Catalog: FW 1903/1904 Sears Roebuck & Co.
Late Victorian Dating Label: Lace
Flow Blue Patterns: CLAYTON I, GLENWOOD, PEKIN, PERSIAN, and WAVERLY

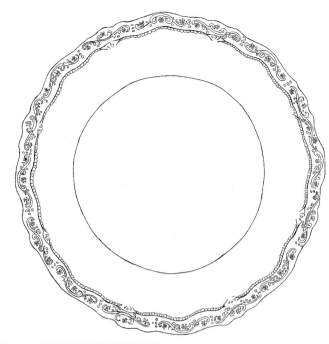

JB-K pattern identification:

Plate 466. CLAYTON plate, 7" in diameter. *Anonymous collector* $40-$60

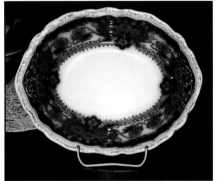

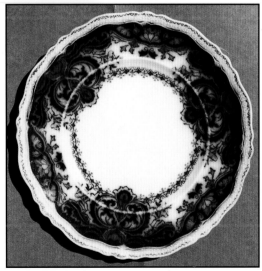

Plate 468. PEKIN platter, 10" in diameter. *Courtesy of Debby Hagara, Washington* $150+

Plate 469. PERSIAN plate, 10" in diameter. *Anonymous collector* $90-$125

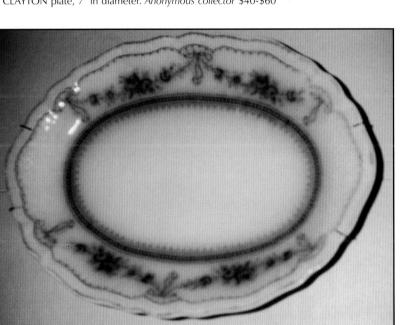

Plate 467. GLENWOOD platter, 14" long. *Anonymous collector* $200+

JB-K body style shapes:

Plate 470. Bone dish, CLAYTON. *Courtesy of Shell & Jim Lewis, Illinois* $95+

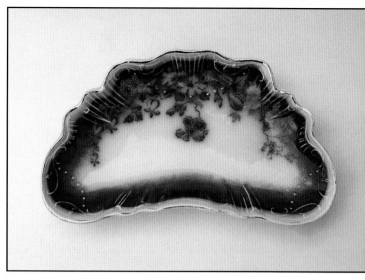

Plate 471. Platters and oval bowl, PERSIAN, platters, 14" & 16", oval bowl 9" long. *Anonymous collector* $200+ 14" platter, $225+ 16" platter, $175-$225 oval bowl

Plate 472. Cake plate, CLAYTON. *Courtesy of Shell & Jim Lewis, Illinois* $225+

Plate 473. Round covered tureen, WAVERLY. *Courtesy of William & Rebecca Leach, New York* $300+

Plate 474. Oyster bowl, PEKIN. *Courtesy of JoAnn Woodall & Paul Woolmer, Illinois* $200+

Plate 475. Covered sugar, PERSIAN. *Courtesy of Debby Hagara, Washington* $275+

Plate 476. Teapot, GLENWOOD, 7 ¾" high. *Author collection* $750+

Plate 477. Pitcher, CLAYTON, 8" high. *Author collection* $400+

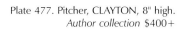

JB-L

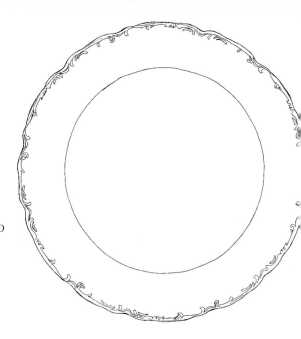

Plate 478. *Courtesy of Ann Potts, Illinois*
Body Style: JB-L
Factory Name: -
U. S. Patent Applied/Dated: - / -
English Registry: -First Year Catalog: FW 1908/1909
Sears Roebuck & Co.
Late Victorian Dating Label: Transition
Flow Blue Patterns: ANDORRA, FULTON, and OXFORD

JB-L pattern identification:

Plate 479. ANDORRA
plate, 8" in diameter.
*Courtesy of Ben & Jodie
Morris, Oregon* $60-$80

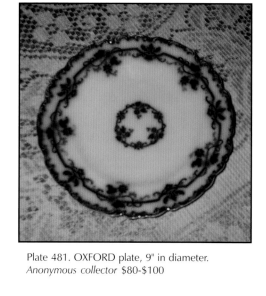

Plate 481. OXFORD plate, 9" in diameter.
Anonymous collector $80-$100

Plate 480. FULTON plate, 7" in diameter. *Courtesy of Tony &
Sharon Thraen, Nebraska* $40-$60

JB-L body style shapes:

Plate 482. Oval covered tureen, FULTON. *Courtesy of Tony & Sharon Thraen, Nebraska* $275+

Plate 483. Covered sauce tureen, undertray, & ladle, FULTON. *Courtesy of Tony & Sharon Thraen, Nebraska* $750+ complete

Plate 484. Covered butter, FULTON. *Courtesy of Tony & Sharon Thraen, Nebraska* $325+ missing drainer

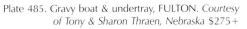

Plate 485. Gravy boat & undertray, FULTON. *Courtesy of Tony & Sharon Thraen, Nebraska* $275+

Plate 486. Coffee cup, ANDORRA. *Courtesy of Shell & Jim Lewis, Illinois* $90-$125 with saucer

Plate 487. Creamer & covered sugar, FULTON. *Courtesy of Tony & Sharon Thraen, Nebraska* $225+ creamer, $275+ covered sugar

Plate 488. Teapot, OXFORD, 9 ¼" handle to spout x 7 ½" high. *Courtesy of Terry & Ann Potts, Illinois* $750+

Plate 489. Teapot, NORMANDY. NORMANDY is normally a JB-A pattern. This teapot was part of a tea set, and all the other pieces that made up the tea set were also applied to the JB-L body style. The rest of the NORMANDY collection that this tea set came from was on its normal JB-A body style. *Courtesy of Warren & Connie Macy, Indiana* $2000+ due to pattern popularity

Plate 490. Pitcher, FULTON, 7 ½" high. *Courtesy of Tony & Sharon Thraen, Nebraska* $350+

Plate 491. Covered mustard jar, OXFORD, 4 ¼" high. *Courtesy of Arnold & Dorothy Kowalsky, New York* $275-$375

JB-M

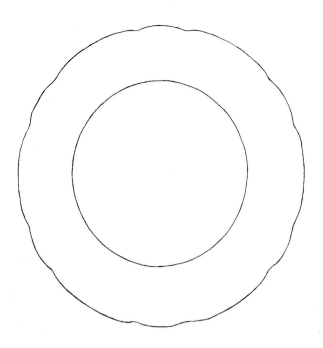

Plate 492. *Courtesy of Ann Potts, Illinois*
Body Style: JB-M
Factory Name: -
U. S. Patent Applied/Dated: - / -
English Registry: Rd.No.208595 (June 27, 1893)
First Year Catalog: c. SS 1895 Montgomery Ward & Co.
Late Victorian Dating Label: Scroll
Flow Blue Patterns: BEGONIA, CONVOLVULUS, DRESDON, PEACH, and THUMBERGER

JB-M pattern identification:

The JB-M body style was the transition shape that brought the Johnson Bros. from the 1880s to the beginning of the 1890s. One of the next body styles of dish produced was JB-N, and many, if not most of the patterns applied to that body style, may also be found applied to JB-M. Times were changing, and so was the style of dishes. Rather than waste the old JB-M blanks, they were used to help fill orders for their "new for the times," JB-N body style.

Plate 493. PEACH plate, 8" in diameter.
Courtesy of Ray & Jan Schomas, Illinois
$60-$80

Plate 494. DRESDON plate, 9" in diameter. *Courtesy of Sue Otteman, Texas*
$80-$100

JB-M body style shapes:

Plate 495. Coffee cup, PEACH. *Courtesy of Ray & Jan Schomas, Illinois* $90-$125 with saucer

Plate 496. Teapot, PEACH. *Courtesy of Ray & Jan Schomas, Illinois* $750+

Non-Flow Blue patterns applied to JB-M body style:
UNIDENTIFIED: Pink floral
WHITE: Whiteware
WHITE: Whiteware/gold tracings

JB-N

Plate 497. *Courtesy of Ann Potts, Illinois*
Body Style: JB-N
Factory Name: -
U. S. Patent Applied/Dated: - / April 14, 1896
English Registry: -
First Year Catalog: SS 1895 Montgomery Ward & Co.
Late Victorian Dating Label: Scroll
Flow Blue Patterns: BEGONIA, DRESDON, MENTONE, PARIS, PEACH, ROSEDALE, TULIP, and VENICE

JB-N pattern identification:

Plate 498. DRESDON plate, 10" in diameter. *Courtesy of Sue Otteman, Texas* $90-$125

Plate 500. TULIP plate, 10" in diameter. *Courtesy of Bill McDonnell, New Jersey* $90-$125

Plate 499. MENTONE, saucer, 6" in diameter. *Anonymous collector* $20+

Plate 501. VENICE platter, 14" long. *Anonymous collector* $200+

JB-N body style shapes:

Plate 502. Platter, DRESDON, 16" long. *Courtesy of Sue Otteman, Texas* $225+

Plate 503. Gravy boat, oval covered tureen & small round covered tureen, TULIP. *Anonymous collector* $125+ gravy boat, $275+ oval tureen, $275+ small round tureen. Price for small round tureen is because of its rarity.

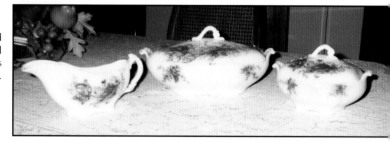

Plate 504. Teapot, MENTONE. *Courtesy of Warren & Connie Macy, Indiana* $750+

Non-Flow Blue patterns applied JB-N body style:
CONVOLULUS: Brown floral
HOP: Floral border
PRINCE: Brown floral
UNIDENTIFIED: Green floral
UNIDENTIFIED: Pink/yellow floral
WHITE: Whiteware
WHITE: Whiteware/gold tracings

I have just recently realized a new Johnson Bros. body style. This new shape is JB-O, and followed JB-N in production. So starting in the early 1890s, the first four body styles used for Flow Blue were JB-M, JB-I, JB-N, and JB-O. Because JB-O is such a recent discovery, I do not have a line drawing for it, but I do have a photo of a plate and a teapot that will give you an idea of what this shape looks like. I also do have some preliminary data for this shape. There are times when I wonder if the new discoveries will ever end.

Body Style: JB-O
Factory Name: -
U. S. Patent Applied/Dated: - / -
English Registry: -
First Year Catalog: SS 1896 Montgomery Wards & Co.
Late Victorian Dating Label: Scroll
Flow Blue Patterns: NEOPOLITAN

Plate 505. NEOPOLITAN plate, 10" in diameter. *Courtesy of JoAnn Woodall & Paul Woolmer, Illinois* $90-$125

Plate 506. Teapot, NEOPOLITAN. *Courtesy of Warren & Connie Macy, Indiana* $750+

wash set body styles – specifics

Plate 507. *Courtesy of Ann Potts, Illinois*
Body Style: JB-W1
Factory Name: -
U. S. Patent Applied/Dated: - / -
English Registry: -
First Year Catalog: FW 1899/1900 Sears Roebuck & Co.
Late Victorian Dating Label: Scroll Flow Blue Patterns: VIENNA I

Plate 508. VIENNA I, large
pitcher. *Courtesy of JoAnn
Woodall & Paul Woolmer,
Illinois* $600+

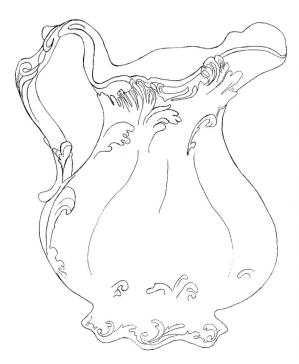

Plate 509. *Courtesy of Ann Potts, Illinois*
Body Style: JB-W2
Factory Name: -
U. S. Patent Applied/Dated: - / -
English Registry: -
First Year Catalog: SS 1900 Sears Roebuck & Co.
Late Victorian Dating Label: Scroll
Flow Blue Patterns: LILY

Plate 510. LILY pitcher & bowl. *Courtesy of Phil & Betty Baker, Kansas* $900+

Plate 511. LILY chamber pot with lid. *Courtesy of Phil & Betty Baker, Kansas* $175+

Plate 512. LILY master slop jar with lid. *Courtesy of Phil & Betty Baker, Kansas* $275+

Plate 513. LILY three items in front left to right, toothbrush holder, covered soap dish, mug. *Courtesy of Phil & Betty Baker, Kansas* $225+ toothbrush holder, $250+ three piece covered soap dish, $225+ mug

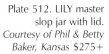

Plate 515. POPPY pitcher & bowl, mug, partial soap dish, toothbrush holder. Courtesy of Carrie & Ron Simmons, Missouri $500+ pitcher bowl, $100+ mug, $30+ bottom to soap dish, $100+ toothbrush holder. Prices are less due to color.

Plate 514. *Courtesy of Ann Potts, Illinois*
Body Style: JB-W3
Factory Name: -
U. S. Patent Applied/Dated: - / -
English Registry: -
First Year Catalog: -
Late Victorian Dating Label: Scroll
Flow Blue Patterns: POPPY

Plate 516. POPPY wash set. Another view of the same set, but with more of the bowl showing.

Plate 517. *Courtesy of Ann Potts, Illinois*
Body Style: JB-W4
Factory Name: -
U. S. Patent Applied/Dated: - / October 21, 1900
English Registry: -
First Year Catalog: -
Late Victorian Dating Label: Scroll
Flow Blue Patterns: CLAYTON II

Plate 519. CLAYTON mug, toothbrush holder, master slop jar with lid in back. *Courtesy of Adele Kenney, New Jersey* $225+ mug, $225+ toothbrush holder, $275+ master slop jar with lid

Plate 518. CLAYTON II pitcher & bowl. *Courtesy of Adele Kenney, New Jersey* $900+

Plate 520. CORNWALL JB-W5 wash set. *Anonymous collector* $1500+ as shown

The following three wash set body styles, JB-W5, JB-W6, and JB-W7 are recent discoveries and I do not have a line drawing for them. As I stated before, it can be very difficult for collectors to "loan" you their pitcher for a drawing to be done. I do, however, want you to be aware of them, and will show you what I can. I would like to encourage any collector who has any of these sets or any others that I do not show to contact me through my publisher, Schiffer Publishing Ltd., Atglen, Pennsylvania.

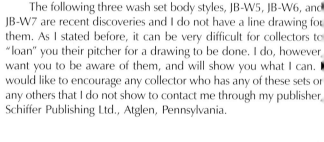

Plate 522. CLEMATIS JB-W7, toothbrush or razor holder. *Courtesy of Tom & Murline Georgeson, California* $200+ very rare piece, but the color holds the price down

Plate 521. MANHATTAN JB-W6 toothbrush holder. *Courtesy of Ron & Dee Pine, Illinois* $225+

complete pattern list

The following is a complete pattern list for Johnson Bros. Ltd. These patterns may also have been printed in other colors, but to get on this list, they must have been printed in Flow Blue, Flow Mulberry, or Slate Blue. The following information will be given, if known, for each pattern. "Pattern" is the name of the pattern. "Category" is one of the following: "AN" Art Nouveau, "F" Floral, "M" Miscellaneous, "O" Oriental, "S" Scenic. The "Body Style" is the code I have given the

body style of dish the pattern was applied to. In some cases, you may see more than one body style code. This means that this pattern was applied to more than one style of dish or wash set. The first code given will be its original, and the others will represent secondary body styles. For "Rd.No." & "(DATE)" these will show the English pattern registration number and the "start up" date it represents. Because the Johnson Bros. first started in business in 1883, all of the following patterns were produced after 1883.

PATTERN	CATEGORY	BODY STYLE	Rd.No. (DATE)
ALBANY	AN	JB-I	285152 (1896)
ANDORRA	AN	JB-L	-
ARGYLE	AN	JB-E	526896 (1908)
ASTORIA	F	JB-I	285459 (1896)
AUBREY	-	-	-
BEGONIA	F	JB-N & JB-M	-
BRITTANY	AN	-	-
BROOKLYN	AN	JB-F	-
CLAREMONT	F	JB-F	-
CLARISSA	F	JB-I	235459 (1894)
CLAYTON I	F	JB-K	396702 (1902)
CLAYTON II	F	JB-W4	355159 (1900)
CLEMATIS	F	JB-W7	Pre-1890
CLOVERLY	AN	JB-F	-
COLUMBIA	M	-	-
CONSTANCE	F	JB-I	-
CONVOLVULUS	F	JB-M	-
CORAL	M	JB-D	-
CORNWALL	F	JB-W5	-
DARTMOUTH	M	JB-B	-
DEL MONTE	F	JB-E	-
DOROTHY	M	JB-C	-
DRESDEN	F	JB-N & JB-M	-
ECLIPSE	M	JB-D	427456 (1904)
ENGLISH GARDEN	-	-	-
EXETER	F/M	JB-G	-
FLORA	F	-	-
FLORIDA	AN	JB-F	336400 (1899)
FORTUNA	F	JB-I	23???? (1894)
FULTON	AN	JB-L	-
GENT	AN/F	JB-C	-
GEORGIA	AN	JB-D	-
GLENWOOD	M	JB-K	Reg. Oct. 21, 1902
HAGUE	M	-	-
HAVERHILL	AN	-	-
HOLLAND	M	JB-A	483405 (1906)
HOPE	F	-	-
JAPAN	F	JB-A	-
JEWEL	AN	JB-A	487719 (1906)
KENWORTH	F	JB-D & JB-J	-
LILY	F	JB-W2	-
MANHATTAN	F	JB-W6	336471 (1899)
MARLBORO	F	JB-B	-
MENTONE	F	JB-N	-
MONGOLIA	M	JB-G	year 1913?
MONTANA	F	JB-C	-
NEOPOLITAN	F	JB-O	260049 (1895)
NORMANDY	M	JB-A	457271 (1905)
OLYMPIA	F	JB-W?	-
OREGON	AN	JB-D	-
ORIENTAL	O	-	-

PATTERN	CATEGORY	BODY STYLE	Rd.No. (DATE)
OXFORD	AN	JB-L	-
PARIS	F	JB-N	145660 (1890)
PARIS	F	-	re-registered 745660 (1929)
PEACH	F	JB-M & JB-N	208597 (1893)
PEKIN	M	JB-K	457719 (1905)
PERSIAN	AN	JB-K	Oct. 2, 1902
POPPY	F	JB-W3	-
PRINCETON	AN	JB-H	347009 (1899)
RALEIGH	F	JB-H	363358 (1900)
REGENT	AN	JB-C	-
REGIS	AN/F	JB-A	-
RICHMOND	F	JB-H	-
ROSEDALE	F	JB-N	-
ROYSTON	AN	JB-J	-
ST. LOUIS	F	JB-C	377107 (1901)
SALISBURY	F	JB-I	-
SAVANNAH	F	JB-I	-
SAVOY	AN	JB-B	-
STANLEY	M	JB-H	341992 (1899)
STERLING	AN	JB-B	483400 (1906)
SULTANA	AN	JB-G	-
THE BLUE DANUBE	AN	JB-D	-
THE TRIESTE	AN	JB-G	-
THUMBERGER	F	JB-M	-
TOKIO	AN	JB-E & JB-G	-
TULIP	F	JB-N	208691 (1893)
TURIN	F	JB-G	-
VENETIAN	F	JB-C	-
VENICE	F	JB-N	250791 (1895)
VIENNA I	F	JB-W1	-
VIENNA II	F	JB-I	-
WARWICK	F	JB-B	-
WAVERLY	F	JB-K	-

Now we will take this same pattern list and put it in approximate date order. For our dates, we will use known Rd.No.s, body style patent dates and catalog entry dates. This list will not be completely accurate, but it will give us a very close idea of the patterns production order.

PATTERN	BODY STYLE	Rd.No.	DATE
PARIS	JB-N	145660	1890
BEGONIA	JB-N&M	-	1893
DRESDON	JB-N&M	-	1893
PEACH	JB-M&N	208597	1893
TULIP	JB-N	208691	1893
CLARISSA	JB-I	235459	1894
CONSTANCE	JB-I	-	1894
FORTUNA	JB-I	23——	1894
SALISBURY	JB-I	-	1894
SAVANNAH	JB-I	-	1894
VIENNA II	JB-I	-	1894
VENICE	JB-N	250791	1895
MENTONE	JB-N	-	1895
ROSEDALE	JB-N	-	1895
NEOPOLITAN	JB-O	260049	1895
ALBANY	JB-I	285152	1896
ASTORIA	JB-I	285459	1896
RICHMOND	JB-H	-	1898
FLORIDA	JB-F	336400	1899
MANHATTAN	JB-W6	336471	1899
STANLEY	JB-H	341992	1899

PATTERN	BODY STYLE	Rd.No.	DATE
PRINCETON	JB-H	347009	1899
CLAYTON II	JB-W4	355159	1900
RALEIGH	JB-H	363358	1900
ST. LOUIS	JB-C	377107	1901
DOROTHY	JB-C	-	1901
GENT	JB-C	-	1901
MONTANA	JB-C	-	1901
REGENT	JB-C	-	1901
VENETIAN	JB-C	-	1901
THE BLUE DANUBE	JB-C	-	1901
CORAL	JB-D	-	1902
GEORGIA	JB-D	-	1902
KENWORTH	JB-D	-	1902
OREGON	JB-D	-	1902
CLAYTON I	JB-K	396702	1902
GLENWOOD	JB-K	-	1902
PERSIAN	JB-K	-	1902
WAVERLY	JB-K	-	1902
BROOKLYN	JB-F	-	1903
CLAREMONT	JB-F	-	1903
CLOVERLY	JB-F	-	1903
FLORIDA	JB-F	-	1903
ECLIPSE	JB-D	427456	1904
NORMANDY	JB-A	457271	1905
PEKIN	JB-K	457719	1905
STERLING	JB-B	483400	1906
HOLLAND	JB-A	483405	1906
JAPAN	JB-A	-	1906
JEWEL	JB-A	487719	1906
REGIS	JB-A	-	1906
DARTMOUTH	JB-B	-	1906
SAVOY	JB-B	-	1906
WARWICK	JB-B	-	1906
ARGYLE	JB-E	526896	1908
DEL MONTE	JB-E	-	1908
TOKIO	JB-E	-	1908
ANDORRA	JB-L	-	1908/09
FULTON	JB-L	-	1908/09
OXFORD	JB-L	-	1908/09
EXETER	JB-G	-	1913+
MONGOLIA	JB-G	-	1913+
SULTANA	JB-G	-	1913+
THE TRIESTE	JB-G	-	1913+
TURIN	JB-G	-	1913+

pattern details – additional information

The patterns below are from the complete pattern list, but with additional information. Not all patterns will be represented, as further information is not known for all patterns. The additional information will include different colors used, catalog data, and the unusual.

ARGYLE: Was produced only in Flow Blue (see chapter two endnote 43).

ASTORIA: Was first sold in FW 1898/1899 Montgomery Ward & Co. catalog under the pattern name "Richmond." It sold for two years.

BRITTANY: Also seen in slate color.

CLAREMONT: Also seen in slate color.

CLAYTON: Was first sold in FW 1905/1906 Montgomery Ward & Co. catalog under the pattern name "Cambridge." It sold for three years. In the catalog, the pattern is called a "rich Flown Blue." Also seen in a gray blue color.

CONSTANCE: Was produced only in Flow Mulberry.

CONVOLVULUS: Seen in slate or brown color.

DEL MONTE: Was produced only in Flow Blue (see chapter two endnote 43).

DOROTHY: Also seen in gray blue color.

EXETER: Also seen in a green blue.

FLORA: A cheese Stilton has been seen in this pattern. (see Plate 523.).

FORTUNA: Also seen in slate color.

GLENWOOD: Also seen in gray blue color.

HAVERHILL: Seen only in slate color. Is believed to be an 1880s pattern.

JEWEL: Was first sold in FW 1907/1908 Montgomery Ward & Co. catalog under the pattern name "Blue Windsor." It sold for two years.

MENTONE: Also seen in slate color.

OXFORD: Was first sold in SS 1909 Montgomery Ward catalog under the pattern name "Yale." It sold for three years and was pulled from the catalog for one year. In the FW 1912/1913 Montgomery Ward & Co. catalog, it was brought back for two more years.

PARIS: Was first registered Rd.No. 145660 in 1890, and re-registered Rd.No. 745660 in 1929. Also seen in slate color. (see Plate 524.).

PEACH: Was first sold in c. SS 1895 Montgomery Ward & Co. catalog under the pattern name "Peach Blossom." It sold for four years. This pattern has been mistakenly called "Peach Royal" and "Peach Blossom." The true pattern name is PEACH. In the catalog the pattern is described as "Rich Flown Blue."

RALEIGH: Was first sold in FW 1901/1902 Montgomery Ward & Co. catalog under the pattern name "Beverly." It sold for one year. RALEIGH was also produced in Flow Mulberry.

REGIS: Also seen in green.

SALISBURY: Was first sold in SS 1898 Montgomery Ward & Co. catalog under its correct pattern name. It sold for two years. It was produced only in Flow Mulberry.

SAVANNAH: Was also produced in Flow Mulberry or green color.

ST. LOUIS: Is the only known pattern that you could get two ways, with or without red polychrome.

STANLEY: Was U. S. Patented November 7, 1899.

THUMBERGER: Seen only in slate.

VIENNA I: Was first sold in FW 1899/1900 Montgomery Ward & Co. catalog, under its correct pattern name. It sold for two years.

VIENNA II: Was only produced in Flow Mulberry.

Note: All known Flow Mulberry patterns produced by the Johnson Bros., were applied to the same body styles used for Flow Blue.

other wares produced

TEA LEAF/COPPER LUSTRE: shapes
ACANTHUS
CHELSEA
ROSETTA
SQUARE RIDGED V (Ribbed)

WHITE IRONSTONE/GRANITE: shapes
ACANTHUS: Was sold in FW 1896/1897 Montgomery Ward & Co. catalog. It sold for four years under the pattern name "Josephine." (see Plate 525.)

CHELSEA: The SS 1895 Montgomery Ward & Co. catalog was their last to sell CHELSEA. Their next catalog, FW 1896/1897, ACANTHUS was being sold. (see Plate 525.)

DOUBLE SWIRL

PLAIN SQUARE

SQUARE RIDGED

TRACERY: Was sold in the SS 1900 Montgomery Ward & Co. catalog. It sold for four years. Oddly, Montgomery Ward sold TRACERY under the same pattern name of "Josephine," as they did for ACANTHUS.

WHEAT & DAISY

Plate 525. CHELSEA left, and ACANTHUS cup & saucer. *Author collection.* $25+ CHELSEA, $20+ ACANTHUS

Plate 523. Cheese Stilton, FLORA. Courtesy of Bruce & Linda Brammer, Arizona $350+

Plate 524. PARIS gravy boat, in slate color. *Courtesy of Tom & Murline Georgeson, California* $40+ due to color.

Brown Transfer, pre-1890:
COLUMBIA: Floral, seen on ACANTHUS shape.
PRINCESS: Floral, seen in "Claret Brown."
SPRING: Floral, seen in H. Leonard's Sons & Co.'s catalog for 1888.
SYLVAN: Floral, Rd.No. 123733 (1889), seen on SQUARE RIDGE shape.
UNIDENTIFIED: Floral, Rd.No. 122732 (1889).

WESTWOOD shape was first registered in 1910.[50] It has a very smooth
surface with no scallops or embossing. This shape is very similar
to JB-G, but no known Flow Blue patterns exist. Non-Flow Blue
patterns for the Westwood body style are:

CHESTER: Gold edge
COLONA
DEVON
ELSA
GOLDEN ARROW: White with gold
KENMORE
LICHFIELD
LOUISE
LORNE
NEBRASKA
ROUEN
ROSEBERY
SENORA: Supplied in olive green, silver gray
SULTANA: Supplied in peacock blue, apple green, silver gray
THE GOLDEN DART
VERONA

In 1929, the Johnson Bros. brought onto the market the first of
self-colored wares. It was a deep blue-gray color and was called
"Graydawn."[51] Its success was immediate, and was soon followed by
"Rosedawn," "Greendawn," and "Goldendawn." The purpose of this
ware was if a chip occurred, it would be unnoticeable. This was achieved
because the body was the same color all the way through.

Souvenir plates:
Note: For further reading see Arene Burgess, *Souvenir Plates*, Schiffer
publications, Atglen, Pennsylvania, 1996.

ARIZONA: Grand canyon, seal of state etc.
BOSTON: Acorn border
CAPITAL, WASHINGTON D. C.
FIRST FORT DEARBORN, 1833-1933
GEORGE AND MARTHA WASHINGTON
HANCOCK HOUSE, BOSTON, MASSACHUSETTS
HISTORIC AMERICA, U. S. Patent number 111255. Was marketed in
    the 1960s. I present this series here because of the popularity it
    has with collectors. Ralph Stevenson, 150 years earlier, first did
    the "acorns and leaves" border seen on this series. (see Plates 526
    & 527.) series include:

    Barnum's Museum
    Block House
    Boston Harbor
    Clipper Ship Flying Cloud
    Covered Wagons
    Ferry Boat
    Frozen Up
    Hudson from West point
    Independence hall
    Lowell House
    Michigan Avenue
    Natural Bridge of Virginia
    New Orleans
    Niagara Falls
    President's House
    San Francisco
    San Francisco Harbor
    Sacramento City, California
INDEPENDENCE HALL
LEWIS AND CLARK
MONTANA
MT. RUSHMORE, SOUTH DAKOTA
OLD MAN OF THE MOUNTAIN
OREGON CITY
PENNSYLVANIA GERMAN FOLKLORE SOCIETY OF ONTARIO,
    CANADA
WASHINGTON'S HEADQUARTERS AT NEWBURGH

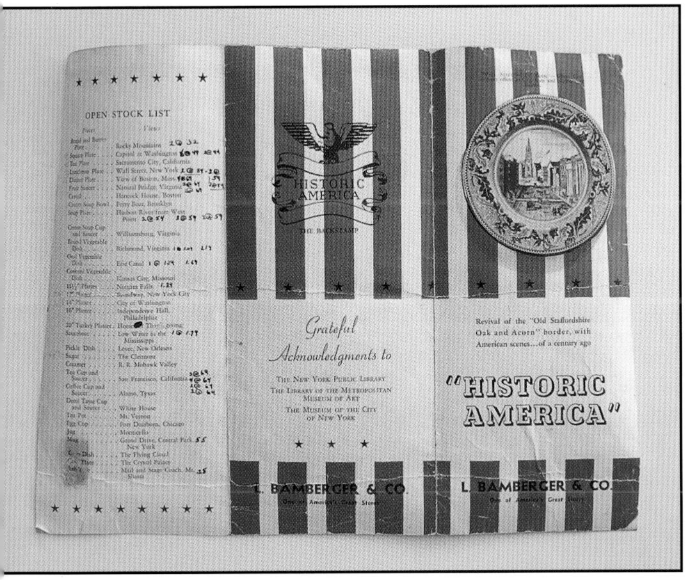

Plate 526. Old brochure depicting the Historic America, with prices.
Courtesy of Arene Burgess, Illinois This view is of the front.

Plate 527. Old brochure depicting the Historic America series. Courtesy of
Arene Burgess, Illinois This view is reverse of Plate 526.

OLD BRITAIN CASTLES: Started in 1928, was engraved by Henry Fennell (c1854-June 1934) of Hanley. Miss Fennel, Henry's daughter, did the scene drawings. She used book photographs of old steel engravings as guides. A team of ten engravers began the project in 1929, and by 1930 they had approximately forty engravings to begin production.[52] The series includes:

> Alnwich Castle in 1792
> Blarney Castle in 1792
> Bolsover Castle in 1792
> Brougham Castle in 1792
> Cambridge Castle 1792
> Canterbury Castle in 1794
> Chadsworth Castle in 1792
> Conway Castle in 1792
> Denbigh Castle in 1792
> Dudley Castle in 1792
> Haddin Hall Castle in 1792
> Kenilworth Castle in 1792
> Powderham Castle in 1792
> Rochester Castle in 1792
> Rochester Goodrich Castle in 1792
> Rugland Castle in 1792
> Ruthin Castle in 1792
> Stafford Castle in 1792

> Warwick Castle in 1792
> Windsor Castle in 1792

There are no known Johnson Bros. Flow Blue children dishes. A search through authoritative books on the subject, as we did for W. H. Grindley & Co. Ltd, shows that there are not any "known" to exist. Maureen Batkin's book, as listed below, does show that from 1900-1925 the Johnson Bros made some children's dishes. However, they were decorated with nursery rhymes and fairy tales like "Jack & the Giant Killer" and "Cinderella."

Note: For further study of children's dishes see:

Maureen Batkin, *Gifts for good children, The History of Children's China, Part, II 1890-1990*, Somerset, England: Richard Dennis Publications, 1996.

Maurice & Evelyn Milbourn, *Understanding Miniature British Pottery and Porcelain, 1730- Present Day*, Woodbridge, Suffolk, England: Antique Collectors Club Ltd., 1983.

Lorraine Punchard, *Playtime Pottery & Porcelain From Europe & Asia*, Atglen, Pennsylvania: Schiffer Publishing, Ltd., 1996.

Lorraine Punchard, *Playtime Pottery & Porcelain From the U. K. and the U. S.*, Atglen, Pennsylvania: Schiffer Publishing, Ltd., 1996.

Noel Riley, *The History of Children's China 1790-1890*, London, England: Richard Dennis Publications, 1991.

Alfred Meakin Ltd.

a personal history

We now turn our attention to the Meakins and their potteries. Many collectors in discussion simply use the term "Meakin," leaving one confused as to which one was intended. I think this exemplifies the fact of how dominant the name "Meakin" is to the ceramic industry. While many of the wares produced by the different Meakin factories are very similar, both in body content and type of ware, their identities and histories are distinctly separate.

Any discussion of the "Meakin" pottery industry must first begin with James Meakin, father of the "Meakin Legend," and a noted potter of his day. James was born in the district of Sandon of yeoman farming stock in 1807. We know little of his early years, but we do know that he began his potting career in Longton at the Stafford Street Works. In 1845, he erected the Newtown Pottery located on High Street, Longton. The market at this time was looking for cheap durable white tableware, and James provided this to the American market through his graniteware. So prolific was his marketing and production that he virtually monopolized the American market.[53]

In 1847, the record shows J. Meakin as the occupier and Jacob Stanley as the owner. James remained at the Newtown pottery for five years , and in 1850 it was passed to Stanley & Lambert. The record does not show how many ovens were at the Newtown Pottery under James's occupation, but we know in 1856 under Stanley & Lambert there were four. In leaving the Newtown, James moved to Hanley and continued business at the Cannon-Street Pottery with two of his sons, James and George. James died in 1852 after just one year of retirement, and two years after moving to Hanley. The impact he made on the pottery industry is still being explored by researchers and through modern day collector clubs such as White Ironstone China association, Inc., and the Tea Leaf Club International. James and his wife had twelve children and most, if not all of their sons, were Master Potters. One of them, Alfred, we now continue with.

Alfred Meakin

Alfred Meakin was the youngest of twelve children and was born a resident of Hanley in 1852, the same year his father died. Being raised in a family of potters made it no surprise when Alfred decided to enter the industry. He learned the technical part of the business with his older brothers, James and George, at their Eagle works in Hanley. In 1875 Alfred purchased the Royal Albert Works. In 1883, he built a second part to this work's, which was located across the street. By 1892, the two locations of the Royal Albert had been amalgamated as one with the Victoria Works, which was just to the east.[54] Alfred's business was doing very well. Sometime later the Highgate Works was acquired, which was also located in Tunstall. With this new acquisition, it added largely to Alfred's output for the American and other foreign and colonial markets. It was said of Alfred, "Mr. A. Meakin ranks with James Beech and Edward Challinor as an eminently practical business man, untiring, energetic, and able. He became one of the most notable commercial men at the latter end of the nineteenth century in Tunstall. The products are chiefly for the American market—the quality of the goods will quite maintain the celebrity the name has held for the last 50 years."[55]

Alfred, before his death, had been ill for quite some time, and to the extent that it prevented him from supervising his business as well as he had. He died January 16, 1904, at his residence, Henshall Hall, Congleton. Even with the state of Alfred's health, his death came unexpectedly early. The coroner performed an inquest. The cause of death was determined to be inflammation of the brain. Alfred's obituary had this to say about him, "Mr. Meakin was an earnest supporter of educational and charitable schemes, and his comparatively early death will be deeply regretted by a large circle of acquaintances. He leaves a widow and nine children, five sons and four daughters. The funeral took place at Mossley Church on January 21 in the presence of a large gathering of relatives and acquaintances, including many public officials, manufacturers from several pottery towns."[56] After Alfred's passing, his son Alfred John, who had been working with his father, took the helm.

Plate 528. Alfred Meakin's final resting place in the Wolstanton Church Yard, Wolstanton, England. *Courtesy of Neil Ewens, England.*

Alfred John was born c. 1875, in Congleton. His early life is not known, but after his father's death he assumed his new role as Director of Alfred Meakin Ltd. This was an enormous undertaking for a young man of twenty-nine. Especially when you consider the size earthenware and tile manufactory his father had extended the business to be and the enormity of the international framework of the company. By no means was this new task going to be an easy undertaking, but Alfred John took to it readily and with fervor. Some of the innovations Alfred John accomplished was to refurbish the Highgate, added tiles to their production line, and installed new gas fired tunnel kilns.

Before his father's death, he had gone under a severe attack of Typhoid fever, and even though he fully recovered, it left a permanent weakness to his system. His new position as director and the demands it made on him soon took its toll. Towards the end of 1907, Alfred John was suffering from an internal complaint, and it was decided that an operation was needed. He went to London for this, and it was successfully carried out, but the results showed that his condition was incurable. Even though he was enduring much pain, he remained of good cheer. At home, afterwards, he was only able to go for a short ride or walk, and that was with nursing assistance. The zeal was still there however, and just a few days before his death, he insisted on attending to some business matters. The last few days of his life he was confined to his bedroom and unable to do much.

Alfred John died Wednesday June 24, 1908 at his residence Park-avenue, Wolstanton. His funeral was held on June 26, at Wolstanton. A "friend" had this to say about Alfred's business capacity. "He was always very plucky, and this is shown very strongly by the way he has carried on the huge business which on the death of his father naturally fell to his lot. The Highgate works has been completely changed, and has now a flourishing tile trade, the business of which has gone on increasing very rapidly. The introduction of gas-firing to kilns and ovens required a good deal of pluck and energy, but this has been successfully accomplished, in conjunction with his chemist, Mr. Jackson, who was engaged by Mr. Meakin when it seemed certain that Mr. Jackson's services would be lost to the district by his going to America. He was always quick to discover a good man, confided very largely in those he trusted, and had the good sense to listen to advice and act upon it. It was while presiding at the annual dinner of the Golf Club that it was first perceived that he was unwell, and ever since his failing seemed to increase, but during the whole period of his illness he has been most plucky, and maintained a cheerfulness which was a surprise to all who saw him. A broken career, a baffled life, a tragedy for which there is no explanation, and he passes away in his youth, and we are left wondering-Why?"[57] In his passing, Alfred left a wife and two young children.

the pottery history

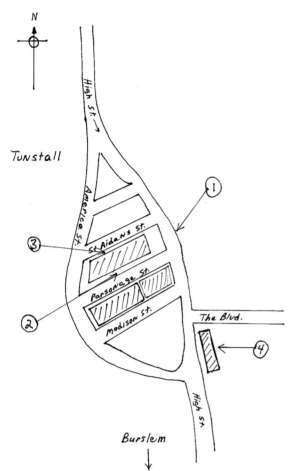

Plate 529. Free hand drawn map of the Royal Albert & Victoria Potteries, located in Tunstall. Plates 530 thru 534 were taken from Parsonage Street as shown by green arrow number 2. Plates 535 & 536 were taken behind the Royal Albert, on St. Aidans Street, as shown by green arrow number 3. The Royal Albert & Victoria Works drawing in the Alfred Meakin advertising poster, Plate 537, was apparently taken from a spot located by the red arrow number 1. The black shaded box pointed to by the black arrow number 4, is the approximate location of the Alexander Pottery, owned by the Johnson Bros.

Turner, Goddard & Co. built the first part of the Royal Albert Works on the south side of Parsonage Street (blue shaded area in Plate 529), sometime between 1858 and 1866. The record is unclear if Turner and Goddard were still there in 1875, but that is when Alfred Meakin acquired the Royal Albert. The year 1880 sees Alfred go into partnership with W. H. Grindley in the purchase of the Newfield Pottery. This partnership lasted for three years until Grindley buys out Alfred and gains sole ownership of the Newfield. In that same year 1883, on the opposite side of Parsonage Street (green shaded area Plate 529), Alfred added a second part to his Royal Albert Works. It would seem logical that with the income he received from Grindley on the Newfield buy-out, it may have encouraged Alfred to enlarge the Royal Albert.

John Tomkinson first built the Victoria Works (red shaded area Plate 529.), in 1858. A further block of building was added to the Victoria in 1911. By 1892, the Victoria had been acquired by Alfred and amalgamated as one with the Royal Albert.[58] By 1903, and probably much earlier, Alfred acquired the Highgate Works, also located in Tunstall. This was the extent of Alfred's business, until his death in 1904. Of the Royal Albert and Victoria Works, the only remaining building today is the section Alfred built on the North side of Parsonage Street in 1883. See Plates 530 thru 536.

Plate 530. Photo taken from the corner of High & Parsonage Streets looking Northeast towards the Royal Albert Works. *Courtesy of Neil Ewins*, England.

Plate 531. This photo taken a little further East on Parsonage, and showing the center façade of the Royal Albert. *Courtesy of Neil Ewins*, England.

Plate 532. Nameplate at top of center facade. *Courtesy of Neil Ewins, England.*

Plate 535. A view taken from the center of St. Aidans Street looking West towards America Street, showing the back of the Royal Albert. *Courtesy of Neil Ewins, England*

Plate 533. This photo looking through the front gates on Parsonage Street. *Courtesy of Neil Ewins, England*

Plate 536. A view taken from the center of St. Aidans Street looking East towards High Street, showing a different view of the back of the Royal Albert. *Courtesy of Neil Ewins, England*

Plate 534. Another view of the front gates on Parsonage Street. *Courtesy of Neil Ewins, England*

In 1904, the North-Western Power Gas & Electricity Corp. gained the necessary powers to supply the potteries of the Staffordshire District. In 1905, at a Hanley pottery, a large-scale experiment began using gas kilns for firing earthenware and china. Gas could be kept to a more precise control, as apposed to coal, its predecessor. The temp was controlled by a thermo scope, which was developed around 1900. In 1907, two years after the Hanley experiment and three years after Alfred's death, his son Alfred John, successfully adopted gas firing for the firm's kilns.[59]

Plate 537. Alfred Meakin Ltd. advertisement. This advertisement was placed in the Gazette one year before Alfred's death. *Courtesy of The Pottery Gazette 1903, Stoke-on-Trent, England*

Even though their production was chiefly for the American market, the Alfred Meakin firm had markets that covered the globe. In one of Alfred's advertisements, it states, "Ironstone China, White Granite, suitable for North America, South America, West Indies, the Colonies, etc."[60] We also know that they had markets in South Africa (see Plate 537.). In America, Hugh C. Edmiston was Meakin's sole agent for New York, and his wares were also sold extensively through mail order catalogs such as Sears Roebuck & Co., and Montgomery Ward & Co. In 1876, Woodward & Phelps, New York, was an importer of Meakin's White Ironstone.

Alfred Meakin was a supplier to other potteries as well, and as a result, some pieces that Meakin produced may have other pottery marks in addition to Meakin's. This will cause confusion where attribution is concerned. This can happen when a smaller pottery has a greater demand for its wares than their on hand stock could handle. Also, a pottery may not have made a heavy duty item such as Meakin did, and they would buy these heavy duty "blanks" to fill their orders. A case in point is Hollinshead & Kirkham. Even though they produced Persian pattern in earthenware, they had to buy in the heavy duty "blanks" such as spittoons from suppliers such as Alfred Meakin to complete their orders. This was nothing new, and done on a daily basis between many potteries.

When one pottery bought out another, in most cases, it bought it lock, stock, and barrel. This included the copper plates, and what shapes the former pottery made and was still left in stock. Chances are the new pottery owner would put their mark on the former owners wares, and would eventually make new shapes. However, the old ones were not wasted, they were used first. We learned this when the Johnson Bros. first bought the Charles Street Works from the Pankhurst firm. Their first wares sold are considered "Late Pankhurst." Grindley first began production in 1880 when he purchased the Newfield Pottery. Where would he have gotten his first molds and copper plates? Should we consider his first wares to be "Late Adams"? I have seen a J. & G. Meakin pattern and factory mark applied to a ladle that was a Grindley blank. These instances could, and did occur. However, in my opinion from what I have seen, at least for the larger firms such as I am covering here, the practice of "buying-in" another potteries blanks for their use was limited. A large factory had an image they projected through their wares, and to use another potteries shapes, even though they applied their own patterns and factory marks on them, would distort that image.

Another aspect to consider was the similarity of patterns produced by relatives who each had their own pottery. A case in point would be the pattern CORAL by the Johnson Bros., and the pattern COLONIAL by their uncles J. & G. Meakin. These two patterns, even though they were produced by separate potteries, and on each potteries own body style, are very, very similar, if not identical. Unless we were "there," or could view the company's records, we will never know if it was a case of uncles helping nephews, or nephews helping uncles. Another example is the pattern HARVARD produced by Charles Meakin, and the identical pattern HARVARD produced by Alfred Meakin; they were brothers.

We know trends helped to determine what new patterns were produced. We also know there were companies set up solely for the design of patterns, and that they sold them to different factories. This may explain why some factories produced similar patterns to what other potteries were producing. However, in general, for a large manufactory they had their own design departments. Most of the large factories were self-contained and protected themselves through registration, or patented their patterns and shapes. If this similarity of pattern production was within the same pottery, than this was a case of the pottery exploiting the success of one of their own "hot" patterns. A good example of this would be three of the patterns made by the Johnson Bros. for JB-D, THE BLUE DANUBE (Plate 399.), GEORGIA (Plate 396.), and OREGON (Plate 398.). Those three patterns are very similar, with only the slightest of differences. However, I believe the majority of similar pattern production by one pottery over another was nothing more than "copying" the success of another manufacturer.

In 1907, three years after Alfred's death, the Highgate Pottery was sold to H. & R. Johnson, a firm owned by Robert Johnson. H. & R. Johnson continued business at the Highgate under the trade name of Alfred Meakin Ltd. After Alfred John's death in 1908, the H. & R. firm acquired the Royal Albert and the Victoria Works for one hundred thousand pounds. They remained selling at these firms under the trade name of Alfred Meakin Ltd. In c.1913, the pottery was retitled "Alfred Meakin (Tunstall) Ltd.," but only "Alfred Meakin Ltd." shows in the factory marks. It could be a little disconcerting for someone who is a collector of Alfred Meakin wares that were made post 1908, and then to find out that they were really made under the ownership of H. & R. Johnson, but I am told that this practice was not uncommon.

Further expansion occurred when in 1918, the firm acquired the Newfield pottery from Thomas Rathbone. However, the records are confusing on this issue as they show Thomas Rathbone still working the pottery until 1923.

The firm was doing very well in the 1940s and 1950s. They had employees with thirty, forty, fifty, and more years still working there and getting satisfaction from a job well done. The Meakin factory offered music while you worked, had a canteen, a Social Club with sports field and clubhouse, cash awards for good suggestions, dances, and summer sports. The long time employees of the firm were worried that the "nuts and bolts" of the potters' craft would not be passed on when they were gone. In response, the firm also offered training schools for the young to learn the craft under the right conditions, and in the right atmosphere, a working pottery manufacturer.[61]

In October of 1969, Myott & Son, Co. Ltd. was purchased by Interpace Corporation from Parsippany, New Jersey for four-hundred thousand pounds. In 1976, five years later, Alfred Meakin (Tunstall) Ltd. (which was already owned by Interpace), was merged with Myott & Son, Co. Ltd. to become Myott-Meakin Ltd. The firm was in financial difficulties in 1980, and in 1982 the firm was restructured. March of 1991 the firm went into receivership and was offered for sale in April of that year. Two months later, in June, The Churchill Group bought Myott-Meakin from the receivers.[62]

While Alfred Meakin did not produce the quantity of Flow Blue that Grindley or the Johnson Bros. had, he did produce vast amounts. Some of his patterns are still highly sought after by collectors today. To mention a few would include, CAMBRIDGE, DEVON, KELVIN, ORMONDE, and THE HOLLAND. By 1903, Alfred had adopted the "Decalcomania" process, which was the French spelling for "Decalcomania." For this process, the pattern was lithographed onto a sheet of paper, and then transferred onto the ware. Meakin advertised that this gave "life-like" colors to his designs.

When you look at a potteries production and compare the percentage of patterns produced in either Flow Blue or Flow Slate, we find the Alfred Meakin firm very high in the Flow Slate category. In the catalogs, Meakin's Flow Slate is listed as a "Dark Pearl," and his "Canton Flow Blue" is a shade between blue and gray. Currently, Flow Slate is not as collectable as Flow Blue, but as much as Alfred produced at his pottery, he must have had a substantial market for this type of ware. It is my contention that if a particular antique item were popular in its day, then it would be a popular collectable today. People do not change. Our likes and dislikes seem to follow the same tastes as our past generations. Limited acceptance and production when it was being produced could be the reason that Flow Slate has limited popularity for collectors today. Alfred is probably better known for his Tea Leaf than anything else he produced. The comment is still made today, "If it isn't Meakin, it isn't Tea Leaf."[63]

So far we have discussed the changes made to White Ironstone and Mulberry, and how they developed as we entered the Late Victorian Period. Let's now take a look at Tea Leaf, and what changes were made there. I have sought the help of Dale Abrams, a Tea Leaf expert, to give his views on the subject.

Tea Leaf Ironstone China – An Overview

No study of English or American ironstone production would be complete without exploring the Tea Leaf story.

English ironstone production began early in the 1800s and the earliest ironstone items were generally sold after being decorated with any of a number of motifs – copies of Oriental patterns, historical blue, flow blue, mulberry, all-over luster applications, gaudy designs and numerous others. Some have irreverently claimed that this early overall decoration was intended to hide flaws in the potting process. By the 1840s, however, the quality of ironstone had, indeed, improved so significantly that undecorated white ironstone began to be sold in large quantities to the world market. All-white ironstone was a huge success with the North American consumer and sold well for scores of potters whose output was destined for the United States and Canada.

Nearly concurrent with the popularity of this undecorated white ironstone, a parallel trend emerged. Some ironstone potters began to enhance their wares with various copper luster effects and embellishments. Beginning simply with the addition of copper-colored lustre bands to pieces, the decorators eventually employed a variety of fanciful floral and geometric motifs. This copper lustre treatment was obtained by the addition of gold or copper oxide to the glazes, which the potter used in the decorating phase of the firing.

So what is Tea Leaf Ironstone China? Strictly speaking, Tea Leaf is considered to be any English or American ironstone china decorated with the traditional Tea Leaf motif consisting of three leaves and a bud (see Plate TL-1.), in copper or gold lustre. Today's collectors, however, have expanded that definition of Tea Leaf to include any white ironstone decorated with copper lustre motifs, whether those decorations be floral, botanical, geometric or simply lustre banded.

Originally introduced by Anthony Shaw in the mid-1850s, nearly 50 well-known English potters eventually adopted the Tea Leaf motif and used it on over 140 recognized ironstone body styles. While Tea Leaf popularity waned in the late 19th century, beginning in the 1880s American potters nonetheless eagerly entered the Tea Leaf market and eventually over 25 American manufacturers also employed the Tea Leaf (or close variant) motif.

The chart above shows several of the many motifs ultimately considered being in the Tea Leaf family (see Plate TL-2.).

How did Tea Leaf change from the earliest production to later wares? As was the case with the body styles themselves, early application of copper lustre to white ironstone started simply, with the addition of lustre banding or enhancement along the rims, finials, and handles of hollowware and flat pieces. Lustre-decorated pieces of the 1840s and early 1850s tend to be simple and geometric, like the copper lustre decoration itself. The ironstone body styles are usually heavy and primarily many-sided, although still often splendidly embossed. Favorite early potters employing copper lustre decorations include Edward Walley, Livesley & Powell, Jacob Furnival, T.&R. Boote and John Farrall.

The 1850s and 1860s body styles are characterized by magnificent floral and geometric embossment and the bodies themselves became rounder and less "gothic," while the copper lustre decorations also became more imaginative. Tea Leaf, Teaberry, Morning Glory and similar motifs flourished. Favorite early Tea Leaf potters include Anthony Shaw, Elsmore & Forster, Joseph Clementson, R. Cochran (the sole Scottish potter of Tea Leaf), and Wm. Davenport.

The 1870s and 1880s are characterized by more simple body styles (square and rounded) with plain or fanciful handles and finials which were no-doubt more easily (and inexpensively) mass-produced yet still satisfied the desire of the American family for this durable and practical whiteware. Even the copper lustre applications became more "standardized" and few of the Tea Leaf Variant motifs are found in these years. Body weights are slightly less dense, lighter, than earlier wares, yet still durable enough to survive difficult ocean and overland journeys. Among the most prolific Tea Leaf potters of this period are Alfred Meakin, Wedgwood & Co., John Edwards, Powell & Bishop, Thos. Furnival, Johnson Bros., Anthony Shaw & Sons, Arthur Wilkinson and others.

Tea Leaf by W.H. Grindley & Co. and J&G Meakin? Interestingly enough, W.H. Grindley & Co. and J&G Meakin came late to Tea Leaf production and the absence of much Tea Leaf ware by either of these potters can undoubtedly be explained by the fact that they began their production as the market for these copper lustre decorated wares was declining. Grindley is best known for Tea Leaf produced on both the Bamboo and Favorite (reg. 1886) body styles while J. &G. Meakin's output is simple and found mostly on their version of the Cable and Plain Round body styles. Back marks on Tea Leaf by both potters include the word "England" signifying their addition of the Tea Leaf design probably wasn't applied to the white wares until after 1891.

Evidence today suggests that Tea Leaf was a favorite of farm and working-class folks. While some of the items in a Tea Leaf set (i.e., bone dishes, butter pats, etc.) mimic elements of a more elaborate Victorian place settings, Tea Leaf is generally thought to have been "common folks" china. Interestingly enough, most Tea Leaf collectors today began their collections by inheriting a piece of Tea Leaf from a cherished family member. They remember Tea Leaf in the corner cupboards and on special-occasion tables of grandparents and great-grandparents.

By the turn-of-the-century the popularity and production of Tea Leaf ironstone had waned significantly. Although the 1960s saw a brief resurgence of Tea Leaf production by both British (Wm. Adams) and American (Red Cliff) manufacturers, at that time the Tea Leaf motif failed to capture the hearts of American consumers as had the wares of a century earlier. Today, however, the original and the more "contemporary" Tea Leaf are passionately collected. Tea Leaf, its Variant motifs and copper lustre decorated white ironstone have once again become prized for their durability, beauty, simplicity, craft and style.

Dale Abrams
Columbus, OH
April 16, 2001

Plate TL-1. Courtesy of Dale Abrams, Ohio. *Reproduced with permission of the Tea Leaf Club International.*

Plate 541. Godden No. 2589 – KAD No. B1629 - This mark has been seen mostly on Flow Slate, and other colored transfer printed wares. c.1897+ The reason I list an earlier date than other reference works is because this mark has been seen in an 1897 catalog.

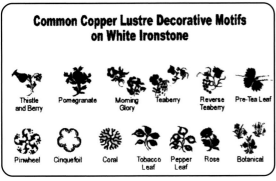

Plate TL-2. Courtesy of Dale Abrams, Ohio. *Reproduced with permission of the Tea Leaf Club International.*

Plate 542. Godden No. 2584 – KAD No. B1625 – This mark as shown c.1897+. With Ltd. deleted and England under Alfred Meakin is c.1880s[+]. This mark was used extensively on Meakin's White Ironstone, and Tea Leaf wares.

pottery marks

For the marks listed below, when possible, I have given the reader "code numbers" applied to the marks from two reference works: Geoffrey A. Godden, *Encyclopedia of British Pottery and Porcelain Marks*, New York, N. Y.: Bonanza Books, 1964.

Arnold A. & Dorothy E. Kowalsky, *Encyclopedia of Marks On American, English, and European Earthenware, Ironstone, and Stoneware 1780-1980*, Atglen, PA: Schiffer Publishing, Ltd., 1999.

Plate 543. Godden No. 2587 – KAD No. B1628 – c.1907+ This mark was used extensively for Flow Blue and other transfer printed wares.

a pottery chronology

The following chronology is of the Alfred Meakin Ltd. Pottery. The dates listed include all pertinent, as well as incidental, facts and factory marks.

1852 – **Alfred Meakin** is born.
1875 – Alfred's son, Alfred John, is born.
1875 – Acquires the Royal Albert Works.
1875 – Mark in Plate 538 in use.
1880 – Alfred enters into partnership with W. H. Grindley in the purchase of the Newfield pottery.
1880s – Mark in Plate 542 minus Ltd., and with England in use.
1883 – Second part to Royal Albert Works is added.
1883 – Alfred leaves partnership with W. H. Grindley.
1891 – Mark in Plate 539 in use.
1891 – Mark in Plate 540 in use.
1892 – By this date, the Victoria Works had been acquired and amalgamated as one with the Royal Albert.
1897 – Mark in Plate 542 as shown in use.
1897 – Mark in Plate 541 in use.
1904 – **Alfred** dies January 16th.
1907 – Mark in Plate 543 in use.
1907 – Gas fired kilns adopted.
1907 – Highgate Pottery acquired by H. & R. Johnson.
1908 – Alfred John dies June 24th.
1908 - Royal Albert & Victoria Works acquired by H. & R. Johnson.
1911 – An addition to the Victoria Works is added.
1913 – Alfred Meakin Ltd. retitled Alfred Meakin (Tunstall) Ltd.
1918 – Newfield Pottery acquired.
1976 – Alfred Meakin Ltd. is merged with Myott & Son, Co. Ltd., to form Myott-Meakin Ltd.
1991 – In March, Myott-Meakin Ltd. goes into receivership.
1991 – In June, the Churchill Group acquires Myott-Meakin Ltd.

Plate 538. Godden No. 2583 – KAD No. B1624 – This could very well be the first mark used by Alfred Meakin, and dates to c.1875-1897. It has been seen on an assortment of Flow Slate, brown, green and other colored transfer prints.

Plate 539. Godden No. 2585 – KAD No. B1626 – This mark was used on Alfred Meakin's ironstone/stoneware bodies in an assortment of Flow Blue and other transfer ware prints. Not a common mark. c.1897+

Plate 540. Godden No. 2586 – KAD No. B1627 – This mark was used extensively on Flow Blue, Flow Slate, and other colored transfer prints applied to bodya styles used for Flow Blue. c.1897+

dish body styles – specifics

AM-A

Plate 544. *Courtesy of Ann Potts, Illinois*
Body Style: AM-A
Factory Name: -
U. S. Patent Applied/Dated: - / -
English Registry: -
First Year Catalog: -
Late Victorian Dating Label: Lace Flow Blue Patterns:
KELVIN, VERNON, and VERONA

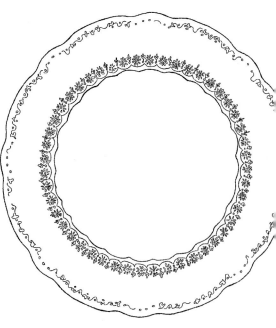

AM-A pattern identification:

Plate 545. KELVIN rimmed soup plate, 10" in diameter. *Courtesy of Jo Ann Woodall & Paul Woolmer, Illinois* $90-$125

AM-A body style shapes:

Plate 546. Butter pat, KELVIN. *Courtesy of Shell & Jim Lewis, Illinois* $50+

AM-B

Plate 547. *Courtesy of Ann Potts, Illinois*
Body Style: AM-B
Factory Name: -
U. S. Patent Applied/Dated: - / -
English Registry: -
First Year Catalog: FW 1904-1905 Montgomery Wards & Co.
Late Victorian Dating Label: Lace
Flow Blue Patterns: CAMBRIDGE, ERINA, OVANDO, OXFORD, RALEIGH, and THE HOLLAND

AM-B pattern identification:

Plate 548. CAMBRIDGE plate, 10" in diameter.
Courtesy of Shell & Jim Lewis, Illinois $90-$125

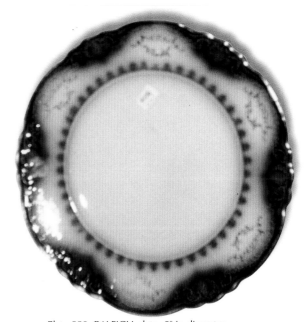

Plate 550. RALEIGH plate, 8" in diameter.
Anonymous collector $60-$80

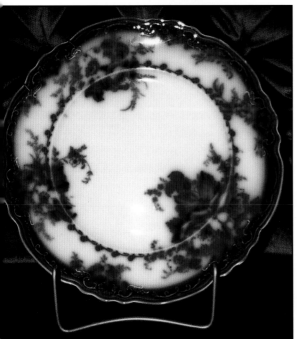

Plate 549. OVANDO plate, 9" in diameter. *Courtesy of Jean & David Stelsel, Wisconsin* $80-$100

AM-B body style shapes:

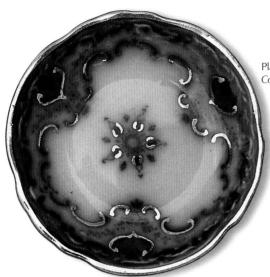

Plate 551. Butter pat, CAMBRIDGE.
Courtesy of Shell & Jim Lewis, Illinois $50+

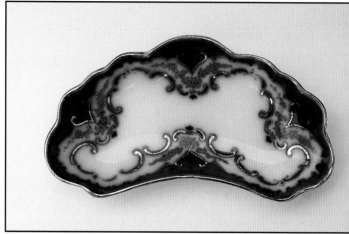

Plate 552. Bone dish, CAMBRIDGE. *Courtesy of
Shell & Jim Lewis, Illinois* $95+

Plate 553. Relish dish, THE HOLLAND, 8 ½" by 5 ¼"
wide. *Author collection* $175+

Plate 554. Platter, CAMBRIDGE, 12 ½" long. *Courtesy of Marilyn
& James Holm, Michigan* $175+

Plate 555. Round covered bowl, CAMBRIDGE, 9" across. *Courtesy of Marilyn & James Holm, Michigan* $300+

Plate 556. Covered butter, CAMBRIDGE. *Courtesy of Marilyn & James Holm, Michigan* $325+ no drainer

Plate 557. Coffee cup, CAMBRIDGE. *Courtesy of Shell & Jim Lewis, Illinois* $90-$125 with saucer

Plate 558. Spoon holder, CAMBRIDGE. *Courtesy of Charlotte Olejko, Missouri* $300+

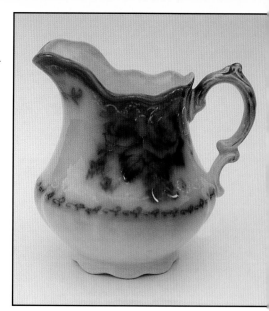

Plate 559. Creamer, OVANDO. *Courtesy of Shell & Jim Lewis, Illinois* $225+

Plate 560. Teapot, OVANDO. *Courtesy of Shell & Jim Lewis, Illinois* $750+

Plate 561. Teapot, CAMBRIDGE. *Courtesy of William Miller & Bill Byers, Illinois* $1000+ due to pattern popularity

Plate 562. Pitchers, CAMBRIDGE, 5 ½" & 6 ½" tall. *Courtesy of Charlotte Olejko, Missouri* $225+ & $275+

Plate 563. Pedestal compote, OVANDO. *Courtesy of Arnold & Dorothy Kowalsky, New York* $350-$1200

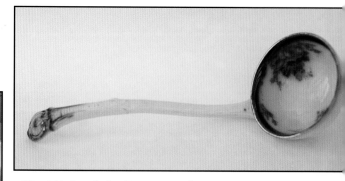

Plate 564. Soup ladle, OVANDO, 10" long. *Courtesy of Arnold & Dorothy Kowalsky, New York* $500+ Alfred Meakin only made one shape ladle for all his Flow Blue body styles.

AM-C

Plate 565. *Courtesy of Ann Potts, Illinois*
Body Style: AM-C
Factory Name: -
U. S. Patent Applied/Dated: - / -
English Registry: -
First Year Catalog: -
Late Victorian Dating Label: Lace
Flow Blue Patterns: DEVON, REGENT, and VANE

AM-C pattern identification:

Plate 566. DEVON plate, 10" in diameter. *Anonymous collector*
$90-$125

AM-C body style shapes:

Plate 568. Butter pat, DEVON. *Courtesy of Shell
& Jim Lewis, Illinois* $50+

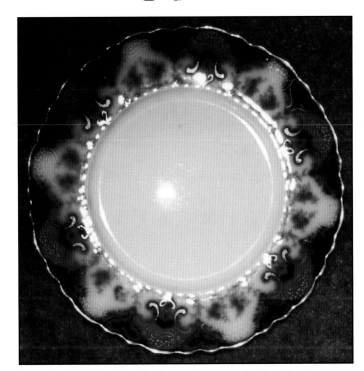

Plate 567. REGENT plate, 9" in diameter. *Courtesy of Jo Ann Woodall &
Paul Woolmer, Illinois* $80-$100

AM-D

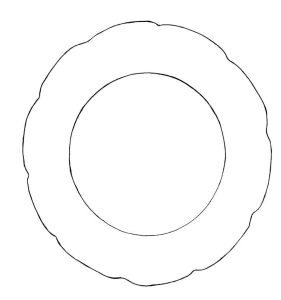

Plate 569. *Courtesy of Ann Potts, Illinois*
Body Style: AM-D
Factory Name: -
U. S. Patent Applied/Dated: - / -
English Registry: -
First Year Catalog: SS 1895 Montgomery Ward & Co.
Late Victorian Dating Label: Scroll
Flow Blue Patterns: ALBERMARLE, BELL, BLOSSOM, BRAMBLE, GREENVILLE, HUDSON, KENT, KENWOOD, LA GRANDE, LYNN, OBAN, and SEVERN

AM-D pattern identification:

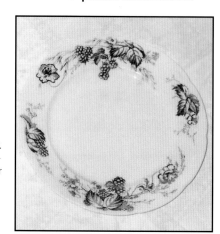

Plate 570. BRAMBLE, plate, 10" in diameter.
Courtesy of Carrie Simmons, Missouri $50+
due to color

AM-E

Plate 571. *Courtesy of Ann Potts, Illinois*
Body Style: AM-E
Factory Name: -
U. S. Patent Applied/Dated: - / -
English Registry: -
First Year Catalog: -
Late Victorian Dating Label: Scroll
Flow Blue Patterns: MEDWAY, MELTON, MESSINA, and SPRINGFIELD

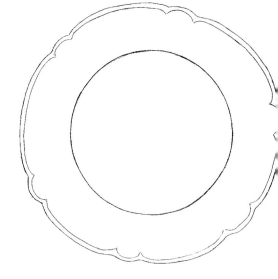

AM-E pattern identification:

Plate 572. MEDWAY butter pat. *Anonymous collector* $10+ due to green color

AM-F

Plate 573. *Courtesy of Ann Potts, Illinois*
Body Style: AM-F
Factory Name: -
U. S. Patent Applied/Dated: - / -
English Registry: -
First Year Catalog: SS 1896 Sears Roebuck & Co., and SS 1896
Montgomery Ward & Co.
Late Victorian Dating Label: Scroll
Flow Blue Patterns: BRIER, CLIFTON, and LUTON

AM-F body style shapes:

Plate 574. Creamer, CLIFTON, 4 ¼" tall. *Author
collection* $75+ due to color

Plate 575. Creamer & Covered Sugar, LUTON, creamer 4 ¼"
tall, covered sugar 5 ¼" high. *Anonymous collector* $225+
creamer, $275+ covered sugar

Plate 576. Teapot, LUTON. *Anonymous collector* $750+

Plate 577. Meakin
trade card for the
pattern LUTON.
Advertising a
pattern and body
style on a trade
card was a very
common practice
during the Late
Victorian period.
Author collection
$50+

AM-G

Plate 578. Author generated
Body Style: AM-G
Factory Name: -
U. S. Patent Applied/Dated: - / -
English Registry: -
First Year Catalog: FW 1898-1899 Montgomery Ward & Co.
Late Victorian Dating Label: Lace
Flow Blue Patterns: BELMONT II, GLENMERE, HILAMOND, ORMONDE I, and RICHMOND

AM-G pattern identification:

Plate 579. RICHMOND plate, 9" in diameter. *Courtesy of Jo Ann Woodall & Paul Woolmer, Illinois* $80-$100

AM-G body style shapes:

Plate 580. Teapot, ORMONDE I. *Courtesy of Warren & Connie Macy, Indiana* $750+

Plate 581. Teapot, BELMONT. *Courtesy of Shell & Jim Lewis, Illinois* $750+

Plate 582. Creamer, RICHMOND. *Courtesy of Jo Ann Woodall & Paul Woolmer, Illinois* $225+

AM-H

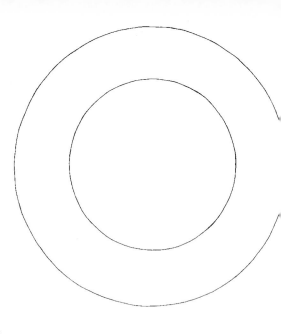

Plate 583. *Courtesy of Ann Potts, Illinois*
Body Style: AM-H
Factory Name: -
U. S. Patent Applied/Dated: - / -
English Registry: -
First Year Catalog: -
Late Victorian Dating Label: Transition
Flow Blue Patterns: COBURG, LENNOX, LUCIVILLE, NORMANDY, and ROSALINA

AM-H pattern identification:

Plate 584. LENNOX plate, 10" in diameter. *Courtesy of Norman Wolfe, Washington* $40+ due to color

Plate 585. LUCIVILLE plate, 8" in diameter. Courtesy of Carrie Simmons, Missouri $50+ due to color

AM-I

Plate 586. Author generated
Body Style: AM-I
Factory Name: -
U. S. Patent Applied/Dated: - / -
English Registry: -
First Year Catalog: FW 1900-1901 Mont-
gomery Ward & Co.
Late Victorian Dating Label: Scroll
Flow Blue Patterns: BURNS, HANWELL,
HARVARD, MELROSE, and MENTONE

AM-I pattern identification:

Plate 587. HANWELL rimmed soup plate, 10" in
diameter. *Author collection* $50+ due to color

AM-I body style shapes:

Plate 588. Platter, HARVARD, 14" long.
Anonymous collector $100+ due to color

To date, no line drawing has been generated for **body style AM-J**. I give you what facts I have.

        Body Style: AM-J
        Factory Name: -
        U. S. Patent Applied/Dated: - / -
        English Registry: -
        First Year Catalog: -
        Late Victorian Dating Label: Lace
        Flow Blue Patterns: OAKLEY

To date, no line drawing has been generated for **body style AM-K**. I give you what facts I have.

        Body Style: AM-K
        Factory Name: -
        U. S. Patent Applied/Dated: - / -
        English Registry: -
        First Year Catalog: FW 1897-1898 Montgomery Ward & Co.
        Late Victorian Dating Label: Lace
        Flow Blue Patterns: CLARIDGE, HAMILTON, and HARVEST

Plate 589. Oval open vegetable bowl, HARVEST. *Courtesy of Leonard & Joyce Setaro, California* $175-$225

Plate 590. Oyster bowl, HARVEST. *Courtesy of Terry & Ann Potts, Illinois* $200+

Plate 591. Creamer, HARVEST. *Anonymous collector* $225+

wash set body styles – specifics

To date, no line drawings have been generated for Alfred Meakin's wash set body styles. I have identified four different shapes and will give you what I have for each. Hopefully, the photos in the Plates below will give you some significant idea of the different shapes.

For AM-W3 we do not have any photos, but this shape was observed with the pattern ORMONDE II. Even though this ORMONDE II pattern is very close to the one applied to dish body style AM-G, it has not been determined if the two body styles or patterns are the same.

Plate 594. AM-W4, PEONY razor box. Any wash set that incorporated the use of a razor box, in the Late Victorian period, is very, very rare. *Courtesy of Arnold & Dorothy Kowalsky, New York* $300+

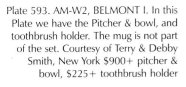

Plate 592. AM-W1, WELLINGTON. *Anonymous collector* $900+

Plate 593. AM-W2, BELMONT I. In this Plate we have the Pitcher & bowl, and toothbrush holder. The mug is not part of the set. *Courtesy of Terry & Debby Smith, New York* $900+ pitcher & bowl, $225+ toothbrush holder

complete pattern list

The following is a complete pattern list for Alfred Meakin Ltd. These patterns may also have been printed in other colors, but to get on this list, they must have been printed in Flow Blue or Slate Blue. The reason I have included Slate Blue is that I consider this color to be in very close association with Flow Blue, and many of the catalogs will call this color "flow." The following information will be given, if known, for each pattern. "Pattern" is the name of the pattern. "Category" is one of the following: "AN" Art Nouveau, "F" Floral, "M" Miscellaneous, "O" Oriental, "S" Scenic. The "Body Style" is the code I have given the body style of dish the pattern was applied to. Unfortunately, Alfred Meakin, unlike W. H. Grindley and the Johnson Bros., did not mark his wares with registration numbers or U. S. patent dates. As a result, I have none to post.

PATTERN	CATEGORY	BODY STYLE	PATTERN	CATEGORY	BODY STYLE
ALBEMARLE	F	AM-D	LUTON	F	AM-F
ALHAMBRA	-	-	LYNN	F	AM-D
ATLANTIC	F	-	MEDWAY	F	AM-E
BELL	AN	AM-D	MELROSE	F	AM-I
BELMONT I	F	AM-W2	MELTON	F	AM-E
BELMONT II	F	AM-G	MENTONE	F	AM-I
BENTICK	-	-	MESSINA	F	AM-E
BLOSSOM	F	AM-D	MILAN	F	-
BRAMBLE	F	AM-D	NORBURG	F	-
BRIER	F	AM-F	NORBURY	F	-
BURNS	-	AM-I	NORMA	F	-
CAMBRIDGE	AN	AM-B	NORMANDY	F	AM-H
CARNATIONS	F	-	OAKLEY	F	AM-J
CHESTERFIELD	AN	-	OBAN	F	AM-D
CLARIDGE	F	AM-K	ORMONDE I	F	AM-G
CLIFTON	F	AM-F	ORMONDE II	F	AM-W3
COBURG	M	AM-H	OVANDO	F	AM-B
DAISY	F	-	OXFORD	F	AM-B
DENSTONE	F	-	PEONY	F	AM-W4
DEVON	F	AM-C	PERSIAN	F	-
ERINA	F	AM-B	PORTLAND	AN	-
GENOA	-	-	RALEIGH	AN	AM-B
GLENMERE	F	AM-G	REGENT	AN	AM-C
GREENVILLE	F	AM-D	RICHMOND	F	AM-G
GROSVENOR	F	-	RIPON	F	-
HAMILTON	F	AM-K	ROMA	AN	AM-W?
HANLEY	-	-	ROSA	F	-
HANWELL	F	AM-I	ROSALINA	F/M	AM-H
HARTWELL	F	-	SELWYN	-	-
HARVARD	F	AM-I	SEVERN	F	AM-D
HARVEST	F	AM-K	SPRAY	F	AM-W?
HILAMOND	F	AM-G	SPRINGFIELD	F	AM-E
HUDSON	F	AM-D	THE HOLLAND	M	AM-B
KELVIN	F	AM-A	TOKIO	-	-
KENT	F	AM-D	VANE	F	AM-C
KENWOOD	F	AM-D	VERNON	AN	AM-A
LA GRANDE	F	AM-D	VERONA	AN	AM-A
LENNOX	F/M	AM-H	WASHINGTON	F	-
LILY	F	-	WELLINGTON	F	AM-W1
LINNELL	M	-	WESTMEATH	F	-
LUCIVILLE	F	AM-H			

pattern details – additional information

The patterns below are from the complete pattern list, but with additional information. Not all patterns will be represented, as further information is not known for all patterns. The additional information will include different colors used, catalog data, and the unusual.

ALBEMARLE: Is the same pattern as MEDWAY.

ATLANTIC: Also seen in green.

BELL: Has only been seen in slate color.

BLOSSOM: Also seen in brown, and has been seen on a ceramic cheese cutting board.

CAMBRIDGE: Also seen in slate color.

CLIFTON: Was first sold in SS 1897 Montgomery Ward & Co. catalog, and was sold under its correct pattern name. It sold for one year. Has been seen in slate or green color.

COBURG: Seen with "Flown Blue" on back with mark.

DENSTONE: Has only been seen in slate color.

DEVON: Also seen in green.

ERINA: Has only been seen in slate color.

HARVARD: Also seen in green.

KELVIN: Also seen in slate color. The pattern KELVIN was used as an advertisement hand out by W. Wood Merchant Thames.

KENWOOD: Also seen in brown.

LA GRANDE: Has only been seen in slate color.

LYNN: Has only been seen in slate color.

LUTON: Was first sold in FW 1896-1897 Montgomery Ward & Co. catalog, and was sold by the pattern name "MONSOON." It sold for three years.

MEDWAY: Is the same pattern as ABERMARLE.

MELROSE: Has only been seen in slate color.

MELTON: Has only been seen in slate color.

MILAN: Has only been seen in slate color.

NORBURG: Has only been seen in slate color.

NORBURY: Has only been seen in Flow Mulberry.

ORMONDE: Was first sold in FW 1898-1899 Montgomery Ward & Co. catalog, and was sold under its correct pattern name. It sold for two years. Also seen in green.

OVANDO: Was first sold in FW 1905-1906 Montgomery Ward & Co. catalog, and was sold under the pattern name "Blue Waterloo." It sold for five years, a very long run. The color listed in the catalog was a "Rich Flown Blue." Also seen in green.

PEONY: A cracker jar, 7"x5 1/2'," was seen in this pattern.

REGENT: Also seen in green.

ROSA: Has only been seen in slate color.

ROSALINA: Has only been seen in slate.

SPRINGFIELD: Has only been seen in slate color.

other wares produced

TEA LEAF/COPPER LUSTRE: shapes
BAMBOO
BEADED TRACERY
BROCADE
CHELSEA
CREWEL
FISHHOOK: Was being sold in H. Leonard's Sons & Co.'s catalog, for 1888.
SCROLL
SIMPLE PEAR
TWELVE PANEL

Sears Roebuck & Co. first sold Alfred Meakin's TEA LEAF in the BAMBOO shape in their SS 1896 catalog. It sold for four years. The description in the catalog gives no reference to the name "Tea Leaf." Their description is as follows, "Open Meakin's English ware. This ware is so well known that a description is hardly necessary, the decorations are of a heavy luster band, and a flower sprig in luster, which resembles gold very closely, but will not wash off as gold is apt to do."

Plate 595. TEA LEAF plate, 9" in diameter. An example of Alfred Meakin's TEA LEAF. *Author collection* $50+ depending on condition and design of motif

WHITE IRONSTONE/GRANITE: shapes
BAMBOO
BASKETWEAVE WITH BAND
BROCADE
CHELSEA
FISHHOOK: Was being sold in H. Leonard's Sons & Co.'s catalog, for 1888. Was also produced using the "Moss Rose" pattern applied.
PLAIN ROUND
PLAIN UPLIFT
WHEAT & HOPS: Seen with "Ltd." on factory mark
WHEAT & ROSE: Seen with "Ltd." on factory mark

LUSTREWARE:

An 1899 Alfred Meakin presentation jug has been documented. It was designed with copper luster borders, handle, and spout. The jug was painted with flowers and had an inscription on one side that read, "Presented by Alfred Meakin, Tunstall, England," and dated 1899. Lusterwares were not typical of the standard Meakin products, however, and very little is believed to have been made.[65]

SOUVENIRS & COMMEMORATIVES:

Alfred Meakin is very well known for these wares. For many years, the firm produced "calendar plates," which are very collectable today. For over a decade, Meakin produced pictorial souvenir ware for John H. Roth & Co., such as the "Historic Boston" plate depicting different scenes of Boston, MA.[66] These plates are considered very collectable today.

The Meakin firm also produced "Baseball Hall of Fame" souvenir plates, "French Costume," and the "Fairwinds" series, which contain
  Friendship of Salem
  Manhattan and New York Dock, 1856
  New York Harbor 1830 and Canton Port 1830
  Sailors Farewell
  USS Delaware Capturing LeCrotable
  USS Macedonia Attacking Pirate Raider

Meakin's Audubon Plate Series was reproduced from the Elephant Folio edition of Audubon's Birds of America. The series contains:
  Carolina Turtle Dove, #17
  Berwicki Wren, #18
  Cedar Bird, #43
  Passenger Pigeon, #62
  Tyrannus Tyrannus, #79
  White Crowned Sparrow, #114
  Fork Tailed Flycatcher, #168
  Band Tailed Pigeon, #367

Harmony body style: U. S. Patent #78288, 1933 Harmony patterns:
DUNKIRK: Red/yellow floral

There are no known Flow Blue children's dishes produced by the Alfred Meakin firm.

J. & G. Meakin Ltd.

a personal history

Continuing with the Meakin family, we now turn to two of Alfred's brothers, James and George, most commonly known as J. & G. Meakin Ltd. It is a rare occasion when you learn of a pottery firm, which along with its original owners, transverses through all three periods of Flow Blue production, but such is the case with the J. & G. Meakin firm. "The business of James and George Meakin survived and prospered because it was built by men of vision and integrity, and because it has kept abreast of every significant development in the techniques of production, management, and marketing."[67] The brothers had high energy and zeal for their business. They passed these attributes onto their sons, who extended the firm into modern day.

James and George first entered the trade by joining with their father, James, at his Cannon-Street Works, Hanley, in 1851. James had first acquired the works in 1850, and passed away in 1852, one year after his sons joined with him in the business. Thus began the career of the two brothers, who would guide their pottery business through all the highs and lows the market created, and extend their firm to world-class status. The two brothers together formed a partnership, but individually, they played their own separate roles in the firm's development. The firm would remain family owned for over one hundred years, and would gain a reputation for treating their employees fairly. They also gave freely to charitable organizations. The firm, for example, donated five thousand pounds towards the establishment of Hanley Park in 1892, and provided the organ for the Victoria Hall, Hanley. These two men were not only financially successful through their business, but were also down to earth realists who had a strong respect and commitment to their fellow citizens and to their community.

James Meakin

James Meakin was born in 1833, and was the first born of twelve children. Of his early years we know very little. However, at the age of twenty, he joined with his father at the Cannon-Street Works. When his father died the following year, George became the chief breadwinner for his mother and the rest of the family. He vowed to her then that he would not marry until all his brother and sisters had grown up. George was a man of his word and kept his vow to his mother. He was the last of his brothers to get married.[68]

Plate 596. James Meakin, photo taken late in life. Photo, May 2001, Courtesy of Neil Ewens, and Reprinted here with Special Permission of The Wedgwood Museum, Barlaston, Stoke-on-Trent, England.

James married Emily Ridgway, the daughter of a famous potter, and pottery line. This marriage linked two of the leading potteries of the day and created an important bond between the two firms. James and Emily's oldest son, Lionel, and his cousin John Ridgway formed the American agency, Meakin and Ridgway. Their offices were in New York, and later in Toronto, Canada. This important American agency, at one time, also represented the Grindley Pottery.

James was the stronger half of the partnership, and it was said that he was the driving force behind the firm. He was a man of strong action and integrity, but few words. James was the "practical potter, the manufacturer, organizer, and technician."[69] He first envisioned and was the planner behind their new pottery, the Eagle Works, which was completed in 1859. Because of James' practical knowledge and his ability to advance the firm through technology and good planning, he was highly esteemed by his fellow manufacturers and by his employees. They saw first hand that his innovations worked. To show their respect for James, the employees of the J. & G. Meakin firm, presented a plaque with his portrait on it that was given, "as a mark of their esteem and respect," and is now hanging in the Hanley Town Hall. In 1868, at a gathering of the working people at the Mechanics Institute, James was presented with another plaque showing their high respect for the man.

James died a very accomplished and respected man at his home Darlaston Hall in 1885, at the age of sixty-five. In one tribute to him, twenty-eight of the leading merchants in New York sent a memorial to his family that read in part, "sterling integrity, steadfast friendship, and untiring benevolence."[70]

James and Emily had eight children. Some of his children, because of James' late marriage, were younger than the grandchildren of his brothers and sisters. In addition to Lionel, who had the New York agency, two of their sons are known to have joined the firm. Their history is as follows.

Kenneth joined the firm in 1899 and played a considerable role with the firm as Director from 1905-1915. At the onset of World War I, he joined the Fifth North Stafford and was killed in action in May, 1915. This came as a terrible loss to the family, as well as the firm. The Fifth North Stafford had in its ranks several sons of famous potters. If you will recall, this is the same unit that Grindley's son, and his partner Fleming's son, were members of. They too would die in action, five months later in October. In February of 1915, Reginald, who was the son of Henry James Johnson, died in action. In many countries, horrific and tragic stories were being played out every day during World War I, but for the Staffordshire pottery district in 1915, it was especially full of tragedy and sorrow.

Bernard was younger than his brother, Kenneth, and joined the firm in 1908. As a member of the firm, his abilities and skills were in administration. In his youth, Bernard was an accomplished batsman and captain of his soccer team. The soccer teams coach was S. F. Barnes, who helped to lead the team through many successful seasons. Bernard always enjoyed sports, and soccer in particular. In later years, he remained a member of the Country Club, and its president for many years. He became Chairmen of the J. & G. Meakin firm in 1917 and held that position to 1951 and beyond. Bernard had one known son that entered into the family business. His name was Rodney, and he directed the engineering policies. Bernard's brother Lionel also had one son that entered the firm. His name was James F. and he was in charge of the reconstruction of the works.[71]

George Meakin

George Meakin was born in the mid 1830s. He was considered the ambassador of the firm and maintained an office in Boston, Massachusetts. George was the emissary to the states, selling the firm and its products. He believed in the policy of fostering trade through personnel contact between Hanley and its merchant customers overseas. George was a man of "indefatigable application to duty, meticulous, persistent, and level headed."[72]

Plate 597. George Meakin, photo taken late in life. Photo, May 2001, Courtesy of Neil Ewens, and Reprinted here with Special Permission of The Wedgwood Museum, Barlaston, Stoke-on-Trent, England.

George kept a diary, and through his words we get an insight into the man. This excerpt from his diary, dated Wednesday, January 3rd, 1855, shows his preciseness: "copied a letter in twenty minutes, a long one; took breakfast in 3 min., and walked to my office in 4 min., a distance of half a mile, received 2 orders from Canada, went to a lecture on Modern Chivalry which was very good, and retired about 9 o'clock."[73]

His whole life was regulated by his own self-inflicted preciseness to regularity. He apparently cleaned out his office every other day or so, wrote to his brother James regularly, attended church every Sunday, took regular constitution on Boston Common, called regularly upon several gentlemen, and retired about nine o'clock every night.

George was a generous giver to those charitable organizations that needed it the most. This included contributions to the new development of Hanley Park, and because he loved music, he founded the famous Meakin Concerts. He died in 1891, leaving a long legacy of excellence.

George was married in 1858 and had two sons, George Meakin and James Meakin, who entered into the family business. Their stories follow.

George Elliot was born in 1864 at Northwood House, Hanley. He was educated at Rugby and studied for a career in the army. However, at the age of nineteen, he changed his mind and returned home to enter the family business. He went into apprenticeship under his father and his uncle James at the Eagle Works. He acquired a sound and practical knowledge of the potting business, and at the end of his apprenticeship entered into partnership with his father (his uncle James having already passed away).

Plate 598. George Elliot Meakin, 1864-1926. Photo, May 2001, Courtesy of Neil Ewens, England, and Reprinted here with Special Permission of The Wedgwood Museum, Barlaston, Stoke-on-Trent, England.

In 1890, the firm became a limited liability company. After his father's death in 1891, he assumed chairmanship of the business. 1891 was also a very critical time for potteries in general. Their foreign markets population had been increasing dramatically. The United States alone went from fifty million in 1880 to seventy-five million in 1900, and along with this increase in population came changes in style.[74] Tastes were changing, and the Meakin's famous Granite/Ironstone was losing favor. Foreign markets were changing their preferences and looking away from the graceful and beautifully embossed Ironstone dinnerware. They wanted pattern and colors. Accordingly, George Elliot set the factory into motion to create, for the first time in its history, "semi-porcelain" dinnerware, and hired engravers to create new transferware patterns. At first the prints were plain transfers from engravings, but as the demand for colors increased they introduced the lithograph process. This was being done by the industry as a whole, and not uniquely by the Meakin factory. When we look at the potteries already discussed, and consider the registration numbers of their patterns and shapes, we see similar wares beginning production at this same time.

George Elliot was an accomplished potter and savvy businessman, who had the respect of his peers and of those he employed. In 1918, he was given the honor of being appointed High Sheriff of Staffordshire, and for many years was an Alderman of the City of Stoke-on-Trent. He died in 1926, at the age of sixty-two.

James Henry Meakin was the second son of George, and entered into the family business as an apprentice potter. I have no further information on James Henry except that he was made a director of the firm in 1890, and died in 1917.

the pottery history

We know that the Meakins were first instilled in the potting business by their father at the Newtown Works in 1845, and secondly the Cannon-Street Works in 1850, where James and George joined in partnership with their father. They remained at the Cannon-Street Works for only one year, and from there they removed to the Market Street Works. During my research, no photos of the Cannon-Street and Market Street Works were located. During their occupation for one year at the Cannon-Street Works, their seven years at the Market Street Works, James and George may have been known as the "Meakin Brothers."

The Market Street Works in 1831 was owned and operated by John Glass. The works at this time had two biscuit and three glost kilns, and also had a flint and color mill. Hackwood and Keeling were tenants from 1834 to 1836, followed by Samuel Keeling and Co. from 1838 to 1849. Keeling's possession ended October 20, 1849, and his partnership was dissolved a year later, with James & George taking possession in 1852. In 1859, after seven years, the Market Street Works was sold to the Taylor Brothers who held the pottery until at least 1865. By 1875, the works had been demolished.

During the seven years spent at the Market Street Works, plans were made and the subsequent building of the new Eagle Works begun, which was completed in 1859. The Eagle Works was bold and visionary, and well in advance for its day. It was erected on the moorlands on the outskirts of Hanley, and in close proximity to the canal, which gave good access to the Mersey ports.

After the completion of the Eagle Works in 1859, James and George moved their business from the Market Street Works to this new location. At this time the Meakin's main product line was white granite dinner and tea ware that imitated French porcelain in style.[75] The "Wheat Design" was an early favorite, and the majority of their wares were for the export market, primarily America. James and George were

Plate 599. An aerial view of the Eagle Works taken in the 1950s. Notice that some of the old bottle kilns are still standing. *Courtesy of Neil Ewens, England.*

"pioneers of the modern practice of production of high quality goods, in quantity, for the export markets." In fact, during the 1870s, the firm almost monopolized the trade of the United States in cheap earthenware, and because the demand was so high, the factory's maximum production could not keep up with it. As a result, much of the factory's orders were let-out to the George Jones Works, who for many years produced wares for the Meakin firm. Many of the J. & G. Meakin Flow Blue wares, with brush stroke and other type patterns applied, from the 1860s and 1870s period of production, have their names "J&G Meakin" impressed on the back. As a result of their continuing practice of upgrading their facilities, the factory was enlarged in 1868, and they remained at this pottery through 1970 and beyond. On the grounds surrounding the Eagle Works, and owned by the firm, sports fields were laid out, which included areas for Cricket and Football.

Another of the Meakin brothers, a Master potter himself, was Charles Meakin. Charles was first located at the Trent Pottery in Burslem, 1876-1882. Whether he owned the pottery is unclear, but in c.1883 he bought the Eastwood Pottery and remained there until 1889. At this time his brothers James and George bought the factory from him. It may be possible that Charles had died in 1889, because all records for him stop in that same year. With the acquisition of the Eastwood Works, the J. & G. Meakin firm became the largest in England.[76] The Eastwood Works had seven kilns that were set in line along the canal. They were known as "The Seven Sisters."

Plate 600. The Eastwood factory, now owned by Bridgewater. *Courtesy of Neil Ewens, England* 1998

Plate 601. Another view of the Eastwood Works, but from a distance to give you an idea of its surroundings. *Courtesy of Neil Ewens, England* 1999

Plate 602. This side photo of the Eastwood Works was taken from the Litchfield Bridge over the Caulden Canal. This photo clearly shows the age of this factory and how it is deteriorating. *Courtesy of Neil Ewens, England* 1998

Plate 603. This photo is looking inside the pottery from the back and clearly shows the deterioration this building is undergoing. *Courtesy of Neil Ewens, England* 1998

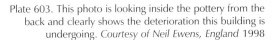

With the acquisition of the Eastwood Works, the need for other potteries to help with their production eased, and the firm also began the production of new lines of ware. 1890 was a pivot point in the style of wares produced. Consumer tastes were changing, and a thinner more delicate type of dinnerware was becoming in vogue. By 1891, both James and George the founding brothers had died, and in ushered a new era for the firm with George Elliot, George's son, at the helm. Under his leadership, "Semi-Porcelain" ware was introduced at their pottery, as well as the beginning of, if not all of the Late Victorian Flow Blue transferware patterns the J. & G. Meakin pottery produced. The term "Semi-Porcelain" may have been new to the Meakin firm, but was not new to the industry. George Grainger & Co first introduced the term in 1848.[77] The firm held the Eastwood Pottery until 1958, when it was sold to the Johnson Bros.

Around the year 1900, Francis 'Frank' Albine Potts was a freelance modeler who later became head modeler at the J. & G. Meakin firm. He started at the age of twelve and a half as a trainee modeler with his father, Thomas, at the Brownfield Pottery in Cobridge. Thomas had trained as a modeler at the Minton Works and later joined Brownfield's, then staying with them until they closed. Thomas lived at 56 Trent Terrace in Bucknail, next to the Trent River.[78]

In 1936, a major project for rebuilding and upgrading the potteries was begun. In 1938, as part of the upgrading plans, the first biscuit tunnel kiln was installed, and by 1939, the first glost tunnel oven was in operation. The old antiquated bottle kilns were being phased out.

In 1968, the J. & G. Meakin firm was merged with W. R. M. Midwinter Ltd., and they were merged with the Wedgwood Group in 1980. Today the J. & G. Meakin firm, while still trading under the Meakin name, remains a part of the Wedgwood Group, and is one hundred-fifty years old. The firm has a very long, and proud tradition.

pottery marks

For the marks listed below, when possible, I have given the reader "code numbers" applied to the marks from two reference works. They are: Geoffrey A. Godden, *Encyclopedia of British and Porcelain Marks*, New York, N. Y.: Bonanza Books, 1964, and Arnold A. & Dorothy E. Kowalsky "KAD," *Encyclopedia of Marks On American, English, and European Earthenware, Ironstone, and Stoneware 1780-1980*, Atglen, PA: Schiffer Publishing, Ltd. 1999.

Plate 604. Godden No. 2601 – KAD No. B1608 – This mark, c.1890+, was most commonly used on white ironstone/granite ware, with or without a transfer print applied.

Plate 607. Godden No. 2602 – KAD No. B1609 – This mark, c.1907+, is a variation to the mark in Plate 606. However, because of the difference in dates between Plate 605 & 606, it may be used for dating purposes.

Plate 605. Godden No. 2599 – KAD No. B1606 – This mark, c.1890+, was commonly used for Flow Blue and other transferware prints. My research also indicates that it may be an earlier mark than Plate 606., and Plate 607.

Plate 608. Godden No. 2603 – KAD No. B1611 – This mark, c.1912+, was very commonly used on Flow Blue and other transferware prints.

Plate 606. Godden No. 2600 – KAD No. B1607 – This mark, c.1890+, was commonly used on Flow Blue and other transferware prints.

Plate 609. Godden No. 2605 – KAD No. B1613 – This mark, c.1912+, was used on a wide variety of shapes and transfer prints, as well as Flow Blue. "SOL" in the mark does not indicate a shape or pattern name, but merely was used as a trade name.

a pottery chronology

The following pottery chronology is for the J. & G. Meakin Ltd. Pottery. The dates listed will include all pertinent, as well as incidental facts, factory marks, birth/death and first introduction to the business dates of the Meakin family members.

c.1807 – James (Sr.) is born in the District of Sandon.
1833 – **JAMES MEAKIN** is born.
c.1835 – **GEORGE MEAKIN** is born.
1845 – James (Sr.) erects the Newtown Pottery, Longton.
1850 – James (Sr.) sells the Newtown Works and buys the Cannon-Street Works, Hanley.
1851 – James and George join in partnership with their father, James (Sr.).
1851 – James (Sr.) retires due to health problems.
1852 – James (Sr.) dies.
1852 – James and George join in partnership and trade under the firm name, J. & G. Meakin.
1852 – J. & G. sell the Cannon-Street Works and buy the Market Street Works.
1850s – Plans are drawn up, and the building of the new Eagle Works begins.
1858 – George marries.
1859 – J. & G. sell the Market Street Works, and move into their newly erected Eagle Works, Hanley.
1864 – George Elliot, son of George, is born.
1868 – The Eagle Works is enlarged.
1870s – The firm almost monopolizes the American market with cheap earthenware.
1883 – George Elliot enters the family business as an apprentice.

1885 – **JAMES,** one of the senior partners, dies at the age of 65.
1889 – The Eastwood Works is acquired, and the Meakin firm becomes England's largest.
1890 - James Henry, son of George becomes a director.
1890 – The firm becomes Ltd.
1890 – Marks from Plates 604, 605, & 606 are now in use.
1891 – **GEORGE,** the remaining senior partner dies.
1891 – George Elliot assumes chairmanship of the firm.
1891 – The firm begins production of "Semi-Porcelain."
1899 – Kenneth, son of James, joins the firm.
c.1900 – Francis Albine Potts becomes firm's head modeler.
1905 – Kenneth becomes a director.
1907 – Mark from Plate 607 is now in use.
1908 – Bernard, son of James, joins the firm.
1912 - "SOL" ware is introduced.
1912 – Marks from Plates 608 & 609 are now in use.
1915 – Kenneth dies in the service during WW I.
1917 – James Henry dies.
1917 - Bernard becomes Chairman of the Board.
1926 – George Elliot dies at the age of 62.
1936 – Plans were begun for rebuilding and upgrading the potteries.
1938 – The first biscuit tunnel oven was in operation.
1939 – The first glost tunnel oven was in operation.
1951 – The firms Centennial was celebrated (see Plates 610, 611, & 612).
1956 – In 1956, due to the clean-air act in England, bottle kilns were deemed illegal, and ceased to operate.
1958 – The Eastwood Pottery is sold to the Johnson Bros.
1968 – The firm is merged with W. R. M. Midwinter Ltd.
1980 – Meakin and Midwinter are merged with the Wedgwood Group.

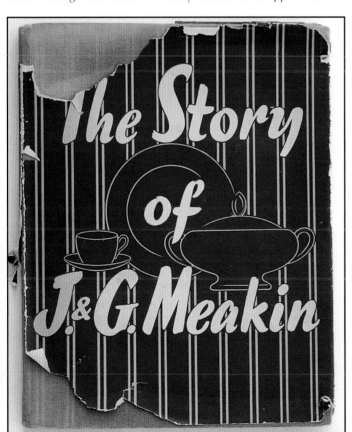

Plate 610. Bernard Hollowood wrote the book "The Story of J. & G. Meakin" in 1951, to celebrate the firm's centennial, 1851-1951. For this celebration, there were many things used for commemoration, including a ceramic cameo with a bust of the brothers on it. *Author collection*

Plate 611. Whole sets of dishes in several different patterns were produced for the centennial celebration. In this photo we have the famous INDIAN TREE pattern. *Author collection*

Plate 612. Here we see the reverse side of Plate 611, with the inscription "Centenary 1851-1951".

dish body styles – specifics

J&G-A

Plate 613. *Courtesy of Ann Potts, Illinois*
Body Style: J&G-A
Factory Name: -
U. S. patent Applied/Dated: - / -
English Registry: -
First Year Catalog: SS 1896 Sears Roebuck & Co.
Late Victorian Dating Label: Scroll
Flow Blue Patterns: ANGLESEA, BEAUVAIS, COLONIAL I,
CASTRO, FLEUR DE LIS, HAGUE, ROSINE, and
WENTWORTH

J&G-A pattern identification:

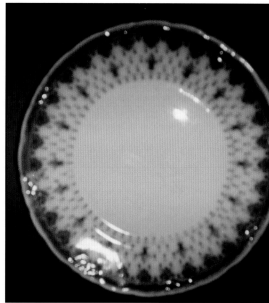

Plate 615. FLEUR DE LIS plate,
8" in diameter. *Anonymous
collector* $60-$80

Plate 614. COLONIAL plate, 10" in diameter. *Anonymous
collector* $90-$125

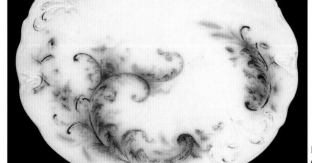

Plate 616. WENTWORTH platter, 12" across.
Courtesy of Carrie Simmons, Missouri $175+

J&G-A body style shapes:

Plate 617. Platter, COLONIAL, 16" across. *Courtesy of Terry & Ann Potts, Illinois* $225+

Plate 618. Round covered bowl, FLEUR DE LIS. *Anonymous collector* $300+

Plate 619. Teapot, COLONIAL. *Courtesy of Warren & Connie Macy, Indiana* $950+ a very collectable and rare teapot

Non-Flow Blue patterns applied to J&G-A body style:
UNIDENTIFIED, purple floral
WHITE, whiteware

J&G-B

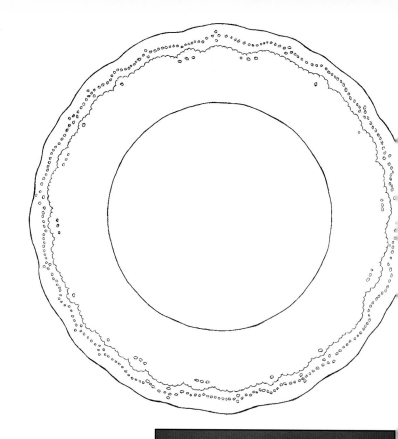

Plate 620. *Courtesy of Ann Potts, Illinois*
Body Style: J&G-B
Factory Name: -
U. S. Patent Applied/Dated: - / -
English Registry: -
First Year Catalog: -
Late Victorian Dating Label: Lace
Flow Blue Patterns: ACANTHA, BALMORAL, HOMESTEAD, JULIA, SEVRES, and SWEET PEA

J&G-B pattern identification:

Plate 621. BALMORAL plate, 9" in diameter.
Courtesy of Virginia & Michael Peterson, Iowa
$80-$100

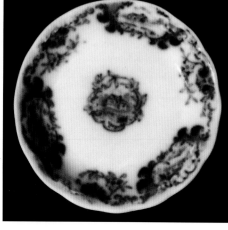

Plate 622. HOMESTEAD butter pat.
Anonymous collector $50+

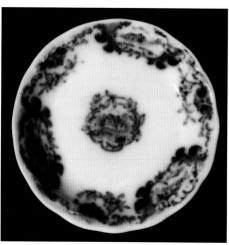

Plate 623. SWEET PEA plate, 10" in diameter.
Courtesy of Tammy Foss, Illinois $60+ due to color

J&G-B body style identification:

Plate 624. Platter, BALMORAL, 9 ½" x 12 ½" across.
Courtesy of Virginia & Michael Peterson, Iowa $175+

J&G-C

Plate 625. *Courtesy of Ann Potts, Illinois*
Body Style: J&G-C
Factory Name: -
U. S. Patent Applied/Dated: - / -
English Registry: Rd.No.503010 (1907)
First Year Catalog: -
Late Victorian Dating Label: Lace
Flow Blue Patterns: HOPE LOUISE, OLYMPIA, REGINA, and
UNIDENTIFIED I

J&G-C pattern identification:

Plate 626. HOPE LOUISE, plate, 10" in
diameter. *Courtesy of Mike & Norma
Devine, Illinois* $90-$125

Plate 628. UNIDENTIFIED I butter pat. *Courtesy of
Charlotte Olejko, Missouri* $50+

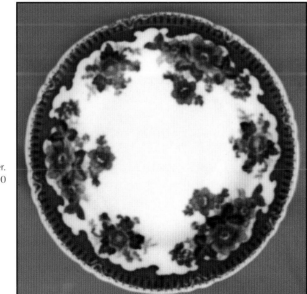

Plate 627. REGINA plate, 9"in diameter.
Anonymous collector $80-$100

J&G-C body style shapes:

Plate 629. Platter, HOPE LOUISE, 18 ¼" across. *Courtesy of Mike & Norma Devine, Illinois* $275+

Plate 630. Oval & covered bowls, HOPE LOUISE. *Courtesy of Mike & Norma Devine, Illinois* $275+ oval tureen, $300+ round tureen

Plate 631. Cup & saucer, UNIDENTIFIED I, cup 3 ½" x 2 ½" high, saucer 5 7/8" across. *Author collection* $90-$125

Plate 632. Pitcher, HOPE LOUISE, 1 pint & 3 pint size. *Courtesy of Mike & Norma Devine, Illinois* $275+ 1 pint, $350+ 3 pint

Non-Flow Blue patterns applied to J&G-C body style:
UNIDENTIFIED, violet floral
WHITE, whiteware/gold tracings

Plate 633. *Courtesy of Ann Potts, Illinois*
Body Style: J&G-D
Factory Name: -
U. S. paten Applied/Dated: - / -
English Registry: -
First Year Catalog: -L
ate Victorian Dating Label: Lace
Flow Blue Patterns: LEON, and PAGODA

J&G-E

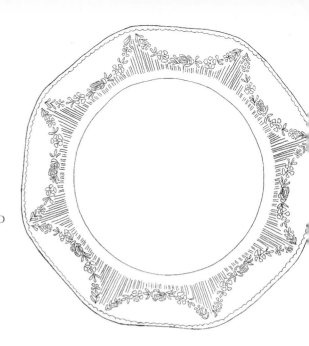

Plate 634. *Courtesy of Ann Potts, Illinois*
Body Style: J&G-E
Factory Name: -
U. S. patent Applied/Dated: - / -
English Registry: SOL RdNo391413 (1902)
First Year Catalog: -
Late Victorian Dating Label: Lace Flow Blue Patterns: STAFFORD

J&G-E pattern identification:

Plate 635. STAFFORD plate, 6" in diameter. *Author collection* $40-$60

J&G-E body style shapes:

Plate 636. Round open bowl, creamer, and platter, STAFFORD, platter 12" across. *Courtesy of Ray Woodmansee, Missouri* $225-$325 round bowl, $225+ creamer, $125+ platter.

Plate 637. Cup & saucer, STAFFORD. *Courtesy of Ray Woodmansee, Missouri* $90-$125

&G-F

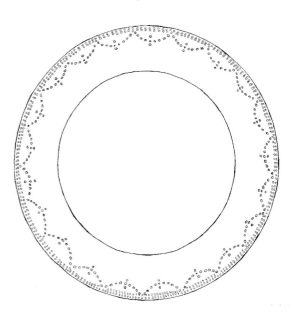

Plate 638. *Courtesy of Ann Potts, Illinois*
Body Style: J&G-F
Factory Name: -
U. S. Patent Applied/Dated: - / October 2, 1900
English Registry: Rd.No.321197 (1898)
First Year Catalog: -
Late Victorian Dating Label: Lace
Flow Blue Patterns: BURLINGTON, CHAPLET, HUDSON, REGAL, and VICTORIA

J&G-F pattern identification:

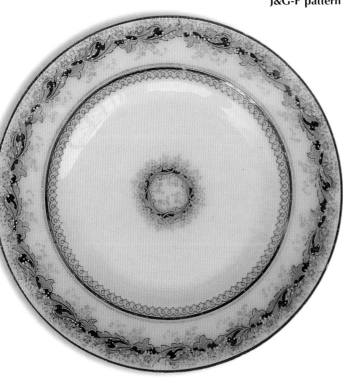

Plate 639. CHAPLET plate, 8" in diameter.
Author collection $30+ due to color

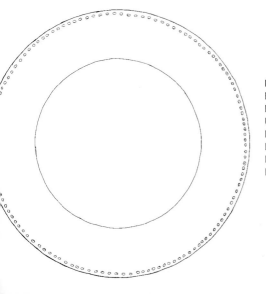

Plate 640. *Courtesy of Ann Potts, Illinois*
Body Style: J&G-G
Factory Name: -
U. S. Patent Applied/Dated: - / -
English Registry: -
First Year Catalog: SS 1896 Sears Roebuck & Co.
Late Victorian Dating Label: Scroll
Flow Blue Patterns: All UNIDENTIFIED

J&G-H

Plate 641. *Courtesy of Ann Potts, Illinois*
Body Style: J&G-H
Factory Name: -
U. S. Patent Applied/Dated: - / -
English Registry: -
First Year Catalog: -
Late Victorian Dating Label: Lace
Flow Blue Patterns: CHATHAM, DELAWARE, GENOA, and HANLEY

J&G-H pattern identification:

Plate 642. DELAWARE plate, 10" in diameter.
Courtesy of Shell & Jim Lewis, Illinois $90-$125

J&G-H body style shapes:

Plate 643. Creamer, GENOA, 5 ½" tall. *Courtesy of Joe & Nancy Padilla, Texas* $225+

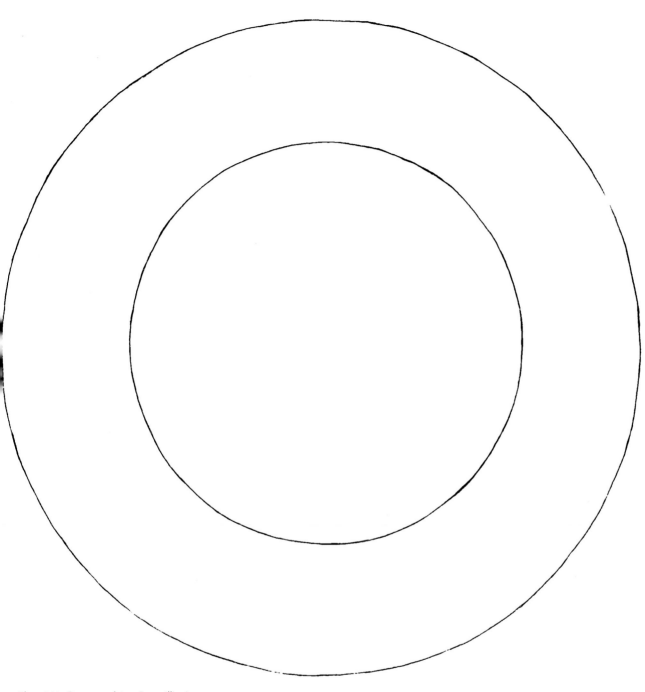

Plate 644. *Courtesy of Ann Potts, Illinois*
Body Style: J&G-I
Factory Name: -
U. S. Patent Applied/Dated: - / -
English Registry: -
First Year Catalog: -
Late Victorian Dating Label: Transition
Flow Blue Patterns: IPSWICH, and MADISON

To date, no line drawing has been done
Body Style: J&G-J
Factory Name: -
U. S. Patent Applied/Dated: - / -
English Registry: -
First Year Catalog: -
Late Victorian Dating Label: Lace
Flow Blue Patterns: GEISHA, and JAPAN PATTERN

wash set body styles – specifics

Plate 645. *Courtesy of Ann Potts, Illinois*
Body Style J&G-W1
Factory Name: -
U. S. Patent Applied/Dated: - / -
English registry: -
First Year Catalog: -
Late Victorian Dating Label: Lace
Flow Blue Patterns: MODERNA

Plate 646. Pitcher & bowl, MODERNA.
Anonymous collector $900+

To date, no line drawing has been done
Body Style: J&G-W2
Factory Name: -
U. S. Patent Applied/Dated: - / -
English Registry: -
First Year Catalog: -
Late Victorian Dating Label: Scroll
Flow Blue patterns: COLONIAL II

Plate 647. Pitcher & bowl, COLONIAL II.
Courtesy of Debby Hagara, Washington
$900+

Plate 648. Bowl, COLONIAL II. Here we show a better
view of the washbowl. *Courtesy of Debby Hagara,
Washington* $300+

To date, no line drawing has been done
Body Style: J&G-W3
Factory Name: -
U. S. Patent Applied/Dated: - / -
English Registry: -
First Year Catalog: -
Late Victorian Dating Label: Scroll
Flow Blue patterns: FORTUNA

To date, no line drawing has been done
Body Style: J&G-W4
Factory Name: -
U. S. Patent Applied/Dated: - / -
English Registry: -
First Year Catalog: -
Late Victorian Dating Label: Scroll
Flow Blue patterns: ZUYDER

To date, no line drawing has been done
Body Style: J&G-W5
Factory Name: -
U. S. Patent Applied/Dated: - / -
English Registry; -
First Year Catalog: -
Late Victorian Dating Label: Scroll
Flow Blue patterns: ILLINOIS

complete pattern list

The following is a complete pattern list for J. & G. Meakin Ltd.. These patterns may also have been printed in other colors, but to get on this list, they must have been printed in Flow Blue, Flow Mulberry, or Slate Blue. There are no known Mulberry patterns produced by the J. & G. Meakin pottery. The following information will be given, if known, for each pattern. "Pattern" is the name of the pattern. Pattern names in "quotes" are given names for identification. "Category" is one of the following: "AN" Art Nouveau, "F" Floral, "M" Miscellaneous, "O" Oriental, "S" Scenic. The "Body Style" is the code I have given the body style of the pattern was applied to. Patterns may have been applied to multiple body styles. For "Rd.No." & "(date)" these will show the English pattern registration number, and the "start up" date it represents. Pattern names in "quotes" represent given names for identification purposes. If a pattern has a body style code of "J&G-W?," it means that this pattern was applied to a wash set, but the correct code number has not been determined. If (-) appears, it means that information has not been determined.

PATTERN	CATEGORY	BODY STYLE	Rd.No. (DATE)
ACANTHA	F	J&G-B	-
ANGLESEA	AN	J&G-A	-
BALMORAL	AN	J&G-B	-
BEAUVAIS	F	J&G-A	-
BOLIVIA	F	J&G-W?	-
BURLINGTON	M	J&G-F	-
CAIRO	-	-	-
CASTRO	M	J&G-A	-
CHAPLET	M	J&G-F	-
CHATHAM	AN	J&G-H	479912 (1906)
CLARIDGE	F	-	-
COLONIAL I	M	J&G-A	-
COLONIAL II	F	J&G-W2	-
COLUMBIA	F	J&G-W?	-
CORINTHA	F	J&G-W?	-
DELAWARE	F	J&G-H	410010 (1903)
DEVON	F	J&G-W?	-
DIANA	M	-	-
DUCHESS	F	-	-
DUNROBBIN	F	J&G-W?	-
ELYSE	F	-	-
FLEUR-DE-LIS	M	J&G-A	-
FORTUNA	M/F	J&G-W3	-
GEISHA	M	J&G-J	-
GEM	F	-	-
GENOA	F/AN	J&G-H	-
HAGUE	F	J&G-A	-
HANLEY	S	J&G-H	-
HAREBELL	F	-	-
HARVEST	F	-	-
HOMESTEAD	S	J&G-B	-
HOPELOUISE	F	J&G-C	503011 (1907)
HUDSON	F	J&G-F	352830 (1899)
ILLINOIS	F	J&G-W5	-
IPSWICH	AN	J&G-I	-
JACKSON	AN	-	-
JAPAN PATTERN	F	J&G-J	545904 (1909)
JULIA	M	J&G-B	-
LEON	F	J&G-D	-
LOMBARDY	F	J&G-W?	-
LOUVRE	M	-	-
MADISON	M	J&G-I	-
MODERNA	F	J&G-W1	409774 (1903)
"MOUNTAIN STREAM"	S	-	-
NONPARIEL	F	-	-
OLYMPIA	F	J&G-C	-
PAGODA	M	J&G-D	-
QUEEN	-	-	-
REGAL	AN	J&G-F	332826 (1899)
REGINA	F	J&G-C	-
ROSALIE	F	-	318994 (1898)
ROSINE	F	J&G-A	-
SEVRES	F	J&G-B	-
"SPINACH"	M	-	- (see Plates 649 & 650.)
STAFFORD	F	J&G-E	-
SWEET PEA	F	J&G-B & J&G-W?	-
TENNERIFFE	S	J&G-W?	-
THE CARLYLE	F	J&G-W?	-
UNIDENTIFIED I	M	J&G-C	-
VICTORIA	M	J&G-F	-
VIRGINIA	S	-	-
"WATERFALL"	S	-	-
WELLINGTON	F	J&G-W?	-
WENTWORTH	M	J&G-A	-
"WOMAN"	AN	-	- (see Plate 651.)
YORK	M	-	-
ZUYDER	M	J&G-W4	-

Plate 649. "SPINACH" plate, 8" in diameter. J. & G. Meakin did produce Flow Blue during the Early & Middle Victorian Periods. Here we show a brush stroke pattern c.1860s. *Author collection* $100+ due to age

Plate 650. "SPINACH" cup & saucer. This cup & saucer comes from the same set of dishes as Plate 649. *Author collection* $125+

Plate 651. "WOMAN" platter, 16" across. This Art Nouveau/Art Deco pattern was made into a set of dishes, as other pieces to the set have been seen. *Courtesy of Arnold & Dorothy Kowalsky, New York* $300+ due to uniqueness of pattern

pattern details – additional information

The patterns below are from the complete pattern list, but with additional information. Not all patterns will be represented, as further information is not known for all patterns. The additional information will include different colors used, catalog data, and the unusual.

ACANTHA: Also seen in slate color.

BALMORAL: Also produced with red polychrome. This pattern was named after "BALMORAL" Queen Victoria's castle home in Scotland.

CASTRO: Is the exact same pattern as COLONIAL I.

CHAPLET: Also seen in green color.

CHATHAM: Also seen in green color.

COLONIAL I: Is the exact same pattern as CASTRO. A spoon holder has been seen in this pattern. Was sold in FW 1897/1898 Montgomery Ward & Co. catalog, and under its correct pattern name. It sold for three years.

DIANA: Also seen in green color.

DUCHESS: Also seen in slate color.

GEISHA: The Missouri Glass Co., St. Louis, MO, also gave This pattern away as a premium.

HUDSON: Also produced with red polychrome.

JULIA: Also seen in green color.

MADISON: Is very similar to the pattern TOURAINE by Henry Alcock.

SEVRES: Also produced with red polychrome.

STAFFORD: Has "SOL" trade name included in factory mark.

SWEET PEA: Also seen in green color. A spoon holder has been seen in this pattern. The exact same pattern was used for a wash set.

VICTORIA: Also seen in slate color.

other wares produced

TEA LEAF/COPPER LUSTRE
CERES SHAPE
CABLE & RING

WHITE IRONSTONE/GRANITE
ACORN
BLOCK OPTIC
BORDER OF LEAVES
BOW KNOT
BUDDED VINE
CABLE & RING: Was sold in the 1895 Sears Roebuck & Co. catalog. It sold for four years.
CHAIN OF TULIPS
CHERRY SCROLL
FERN
FERN WITH MEDALLION
FRUIT OF THE VINE
FUCHSIA
GARDEN SPRIG
MINIATURE SCROLL

MOSS ROSE
ONE LARGE & TWO LITTLE RIBS
PANELLED LEAVES
PANELLED LEAVES WITH BERRIES
PEARL SYDENHAM
PIECRUST
PLAIN ROUND
PLAIN (UPLIFT)
PLUM DECAGON
RIBBED BERRY WITH BLOOM
SAFETY PIN
SQUARE MELON/RIBBED
STRAWBERRY
WHEAT
WHEAT & BLACKBERRY

Patterns seen on White Ironstone/Granite body styles:
CRESWELL, in brown
GENOA
MOSS ROSE
WASHINGTON, floral with impressed mark "Parisian Granite"

Non-Flow Blue Body Styles & Patterns
American Legend: No patterns identified

Romantic England Series:
HADDON HALL

Renaissance: No patterns identified

Country Life: No patterns identified

Sterling:
BLUE NORDIC, onion pattern, and one of the most prolific of Meakin's contemporary patterns
Commemorative Ware, A plate was done to commemorate the 1939 World's Fair held in New York City

Willow:
BLUE WILLOW: Booths variant pattern. Was produced especially for Neiman Marcus and sold by catalog.
GREEN WILLOW

No Flow Blue children's dishes have been discovered. However, in the 1880s & 1890s, J. & G. Meakin did produce children's dishes, but all were non-Flow Blue patterns. They include:
    Family Life Themes, children scenes
    Early Day Themes, boy eating pigeon pie
    Kids Playing Series, two boys playing on seesaw titled "Good Experience," young adults playing Cricket

Additional potteries and pattern lists

Henry Alcock & Co. Ltd.

Henry Alcock was an English potter starting in the potting business late in the Early Victorian Period. Henry experienced great success and guided his firm through the Middle and Late Victorian Periods, and beyond. He is descended from the famous Alcock family of potters, who were so well known in the Staffordshire potting district. There were nine children born to Thomas and Katherine Alcock, yeoman farmers from Kingsley, in the later half of the eighteenth century. Two of those children were known potters, John, and Samuel who was born in 1799. The first record of Samuel as a potter came in 1822-1823 Kings Street, Burslem. Samuel died in 1848.[79] Samuel had two potteries. His smallest was the Cobridge China Works and his Hill Pottery in Burslem. By 1833, between his two factories, he had twenty kilns.

Samuel's brother, John, started a legacy of his own. Two of his sons, John and George, joined in partnership and traded under the firm name J. & G. Alcock. John and George began their potting business c.1839 in Cobridge, Staffordshire. Two of the most famous Flow Blue patterns produced by this manufactory were SCINDE and SOBRAON.

Henry was the son of one of those brothers and had his beginning in 1861, at the Elder Pottery, Cobridge. The Elder Works was formerly owned by John Alcock, who had started in business there c.1850. Henry continued his business there until 1910 when he relocated to the Clarence Works, Stoke, Staffordshire. Henry stayed at the Clarence until c.1935.

On the back of Henry's wares, during the period 1861-1880, his initials "H.A. & Co." can be seen. For his White Ironstone/Granite ware he used the trade names "Ironstone China" and "Parisian Porcelain." His most famous Flow Blue pattern, in all probability, was TOURAINE that was first registered in 1898. This pattern was produced for many years by Henry, and was later continued during the 1920s and 1930s by the Stanley Pottery Co. of Middleport, Burslem c.1909-1937.

Flow Blue, Patterns

PATTERN	CATEGORY
ALMA	AN
BEVERLY	AN
BOUQUET	F
BURMESE	AN
CLARENDON	AN
CLIVE	-
DELAMERE	AN
DRESDEN FLOWERS	F
GEM	M/AN
GRENADA	F
HERALD	F
MANHATTAN	F
MINWOOD	M
MIRA	F
OLD CASTLES	S
ORIENTAL GARDEN	O
"ROYAL PREMIUM"	-
SYBIL	F
TOURAINE	F
VINE	F

TEA LEAF/COPPER LUSTRE, shapes
BLANKET STITCH [PIECRUST]
JUMBO

WHITE IRONSTONE/GRANITE, shapes
CHINESE SHAPE, John Alcock first patented this shape,   March 20, 1857.
DRAPED LEAF
FORGET-ME-NOT
JUMBO
OXFORD [FLORAL RAY]
PARIS SHAPE
PIE CRUST [BLANKET STITCH]
PRUNUS BLOSSOMS
RIBBED BERRY
SQUARE RIDGED
STYLIZED FLOWER
TRENT SHAPE, This shape was also first patented by John Alcock.
WHEAT PATTERN SHAPE

Burgess & Leigh Ltd.

Originally founded in 1851 under the name Hulme and Booth, it wasn't until 1877 that the name changed to Burgess and Leigh. The partners were **William Leigh** and **Frederick Rathbone Burgess**. Frederick was a descendant of the famous Rathbone potting family from Tunstall. The firm's first place of manufactory was the Central Pottery, Burslem. With the expansion of their business, Burgess and Leigh moved to the Hill (Top) Pottery, formerly owned by Samuel Alcock. However, their business continued to grow and it was determined to build a new larger pottery. By 1889, the construction of the Middleport Pottery was complete and was situated along the Trent and Mersey canal for ease of shipping to the export markets. Today the old bottle kilns have been replaced, with the exception of one that still stands as a reminder of the past.

Plate 652. The Middleport Pottery, Burslem. Founded in 1889, and is still in use today. *Anonymous contributor*

With the deaths of William Leigh in 1889 and Frederick Rathbone Burgess in 1898, their sons, Edmund Leigh and Richard Samuel Burgess, continued the business. Richard was an engineer and designed several pieces of equipment for the pottery, which included photographic equipment. Edmund was the salesman and traveled extensively in America, Canada, Australia, New Zealand, and South Africa creating new trade with these countries.

In 1905, Thomas Wood Heath was asked to go to Australia and represent Burgess and Leigh, of which he did. Through his two grandsons', Barrie and Tom Heath, this business relationship lasted for over ninety years.

Richard Burgess died in 1912, and Edmund Leigh acquired the entire business. In 1924 Edmund died and his sons continued the firm on. As of 1999, all the members of the board of directors were descendants of the original partner, William Leigh. However, in that same year, the company entered into hard times and entered into receivership. In August of 1999, Rosemary and William Dorling saved the financially hurting company, and today the firm is called Burgess, Dorling, and Leigh.[80]

Three of their most collectable Flow Blue patterns are LEICESTER, NON-PAREIL, and VERMONT that was registered in 1895. The pattern MILFORD has the registration number 567187 (1910). The pattern DALMENY has the registration number 366038 (1900). There are no known Tea Leaf or White Ironstone/Granite ware produced by the Burgess and Leigh Ltd. Pottery.

FLOW BLUE, Patterns

PATTERN	CATEGORY	PATTERN	CATEGORY
ALEXANDRA	-	HALIA	-
APSLEY PLANT	F	ITALIA	F
ATHOL	F	IVY	F
BELVOIR	AN	LEICESTER	AN
BRIAR	F	LEIGHTON	AN
BURLEIGH	AN	LILAC	F
CELESTE	P/O	MABELLE	F
CRANESBILL	F	MILFORD	AN
CRANSTON	F	NANKIN	O
DAISY	F	NAPOLI	F
DALMENY	AN	NEWLYN	AN
DERBY	F	NON-PAREIL	S
DRESDEN	AN	PREMIER	-
DRESDEN FLOWERS	F	RALEIGH	AN
ERIE	-	RICHMOND	M/AN
EATON	F	ROSETTE	-
FLORENTINE	-	SELWYN	AN
FLORETTE	AN	STRATFORD	AN/F
FLORIAN	F	SWEETBRIER	F
FLORIDA	F	VENICE	F
GARLAND	F	VERMONT	F
HAARLEM	AN	WINDFLOWER	F
HALFORD	-		

Doulton & Co. Ltd.

John Doulton was taken into partnership with the widow Martha Jones who had inherited her husband's pottery in Lambeth, which was situated south of London along the Thames in 1815. With the inclusion of her foreman, John Watts, the firm became known as Jones, Watts, and Doulton. John Doulton had served his apprenticeship at the famed Fulham Works, founded by John Dwight. This was the beginning of what, in later years, would be known as the Royal Doulton, or Doulton & Co. Ltd. Pottery.

However, it was John's son, Henry Doulton, who carried the firm to its world-renowned status. By the time Queen Victoria began her reign, the Doulton factory was well established as a manufactory of domestic and industrial products; produced in a stoneware body that would compare to any in Europe. By 1846, the Lambeth Works was becoming one of England's leading producers of sanitary ware, which was due to Henry's foresight and hard work.

In 1882, Henry acquired the Nile Street Works, Burslem, which was formerly Pinder Bourne & Co. Burslem was considered the "mother town" of the Staffordshire potting district, and Henry's entering into business there from the south was not looked on favorably by the other Burslem potters. In referring to his predicament there Henry stated, "In their view we Southerners know little about God and nothing at all about potting." Henry's business venture in Burslem was not an easy one, nor profitable, but through his domestic and art wares made in earthenware, decorated with what limited colors were available, and applied under a lead glaze, soon realized the success for which he was looking. Henry invested his money wisely by hiring only the finest team of modelers, decorators, and painters. By 1884, Henry was gaining international fame that extended well into the twentieth century.

Henry was the first potter to be knighted by Queen Victoria, and in 1901 King Edward VII gave him a double honor. Not only was he given a royal warrant for his wares, but also the specific right to use the title "Royal." Thus we see today "Royal Doulton." Henry also received honors at the international exhibit at Chicago and Paris. Beside tablewares, Henry is well known for his art pottery, ornamental, and commemorative ware. In 1955, the trade name was retitled Doulton Fine China Ltd.[81]

In consideration of Doulton's Late Victorian Flow Blue, his version of the Blue Willow pattern is the only one known, and recognized to be actual Flow Blue. A few of his better-known patterns used for toilet, and tableware are, EDGERTON, GENEVA, GLORIA DE DIJON; Rd.No.307815 (1897), MADRAS, and PERSIAN SPRAY; U.S. registered in 1906.

FLOW BLUE, Patterns

PATTERN	CATEGORY	PATTERN	CATEGORY
ADELAIDE	F/AN	KLEMSCOT	F
ADDERLEY	F	MADRAS	O
AMOY	O	MATSUMAI	F
ARUNDEL	F	MELBOURNE	M
AUBREY	AN	MELROSE	F
BABES IN THE WOODS	G	MORRISAN	G
BEVERLY	F	NANKIN	S
BRIAR ROSE	AN	NANKING	F
BUTTERCUP	F	NORBURY	F
CLIFTON	-	NORFOLK	S
DAFFODIL	F	OXFORD	F
EDGERTON	AN	OYAMA	O
EGLINTON TOURNAMENT	H	PAISLEY	AN
EMPIRE	M/S	PERSIAN SPRAY	M
FESTOON	F	POPPY	F
FLORA	F	PROVENCE	-
FRUIT & FLOWERS	F	RABBITS	S
GENEVA	S	SANDHURST	AN
GENEVESA	O	SIMPLICITAS	AN
GIBSON WIDOW	S	SUTHERLAND	F
GLADIOLUS	F	SWITZERLAND	S
GLOIRE DE DIJON	F	THE CHASE	S
GLOIRE DE GULIAN	F	THE TEMPEST	L
HOWARD	AN	TURKEY	-
IRIS	F	VERNON	F
ISTHMIAN GAMES	H	VERONICA	AN
JACOBEAN	M	VIRGINIA	F
JEDO	O	"VOLGA-VILLA"	S
JESSICA	F	WATTEAU	S
KENSINGTON	AN	"WILLOW" PATTERN	O
KENT	AN	WILLOW & ASTER	AN

J. H. Weatherby & Sons Ltd.

Henry Weatherby, a potter's turner, was born in 1818, and married Ann Clews in 1838. They produced three offspring: Rachel born in 1839, Jane in 1841, and John Henry Weatherby born in 1843. Henry died of pneumonia in 1845 at the age of twenty-seven. Ann, his widow, died in 1885. John Henry was fatherless from the age of two, and never had a chance to learn the potting trade from his father. However, a strong interest in the field must have been deeply imbedded, because at the appropriate age, John Henry became apprenticed to his uncle, William Wood, of Wood and Company, Albert Street, Burslem.

In 1864, John Henry married Mary Mawdesley, and to them were born four children, two sons and two daughters: Samuel Mawdesley born in 1866, John Henry Jr. in 1869, Mary, and Jane Ann.

In 1882, John Henry decided to leave the employ of his uncle William Wood, and to go into partnership with two others at the Hallfield Pottery, Festing Street, Hanley. The firm he joined was called Whittaker, Edge & Co. Nine years later, in 1891, this partnership was dissolved, and John Henry decided to go it alone. He wanted to build his own factory but concerns from the surrounding neighbors about the smoke pollution, ended that dream. He decided to lease an established firm, and with the support of his family they opened a trade at the Pinnox Works, Pinnox Street, Tunstall. So 1891 would be the first year that J. H. Weatherby & Sons began their trade in ceramics. In their first year their union jack label was designed and was still in use when they closed. However, due to leasing problems and wages, John Henry was forced to stop business and after one year of court battles, John Henry was finally released from his lease agreement. He was determined though to reenter the trade he loved.

It was in 1892, with the support of his family, and on a shoestring, he opened for business at the Falcon Pottery on High Street (today its Old Towne Road), Hanley. The Falcon pottery actually consisted of two potteries combined together, the Gelson Works and the Cobden Works, which dated to 1779.[82] The first few years were very difficult, but history tells us that John Henry did make a success of his pottery. The Falcon Works did not produce many patterns of Flow Blue, but they did have one very successful pattern that was kept in production, non-stop for fourteen years. That pattern was BELMONT. This transfer print pattern was applied to their Empress body style and was available in Flow Canton, Pea Blue, Sage Green, and with or without gold. Mr. F. Clough and Mrs. Charlotte Slack were the printers for the life of this pattern.

In 1924 John Henry and his wife celebrated sixty years of marriage with a "Tea and Social Evening" at the Princess Hall, Burslem. November 1929, five years later, Mary died, and John Henry died April 30, 1933 at the age of ninety. Their two sons, Samuel and John Henry Jr., continued the business, and their sons after them, and then their sons after them. This is one of the few potteries in England that began family owned and stayed family owned to the end. The end came in 2000, after one hundred nine years of production. It was Christopher Weatherby, the great great grandson of the company founder, who made the decision to cease trading and close the doors. In an article in the Sentinel Newspaper Christopher blames cutthroat competition in the hotelware business for the firm's decline. He further stated, "Basically we've decided to close down before someone else forced us to – while we are solvent rather than insolvent."[83]

FLOW BLUE, Patterns

PATTERN	CATEGORY
BELMONT	M/F
SANDON	-
WELBECK	F (1905)

WHITE IRONSTONE, Shapes

WHEAT

Endnotes - Chapter Two

[1]William Scarratt, *Old Times in the Potteries* (Stoke-on-Trent, England 1906)

[2]Editors, *Staffordshire Sentinel* (Stoke-on-Trent, England March 9, 1926)

[3]Geoffrey A. Godden, *Ironstone Stone & Granite Wares* (Suffolk, England: Antique Collectors' Club 1999),249

[4] Editors, *Pottery Gazette and Glass Trade Review* (Stoke-on-Trent, England April 1, 1926)

[5]J. Arnold Fleming, *Scottish Pottery* (Glasgow, Scotland: Maclehose, Jackson & Co. 1923),115

[6]William Scarratt, *Old Times in the Potteries* (Stoke-on-Trent, England 1906)

[7]Editors, *The Pottery Gazette and Glass Trade Review* (Stoke-on-Trent, England April 1, 1926),645

[8]William Scarratt, *Old Times in the Potteries* (Stoke-on-Trent, England 1906)

[9]Rodney Hampson, *The Northern Ceramic Society, Newsletter No.115, Pottery Jotteries* (Stoke-on-Trent, England September 1999)43

[10]Wolf Mankowitz & Reginald G. Haggar, *The Concise Encyclopedia of English Pottery and Porcelain* (London, England: Andre Deutsch, Ltd. 1968)279

[11]Editors, *The Pottery Gazette* (Stoke-on-Trent, England, June 1, 1909)701

[12]Josiah C. Wedgwood, M.P., C.C., *Staffordshire Pottery And Its History* (New York, McBride, Nast & Company 1913)194

[13]Department of Commerce, *The Pottery Industry* (Washington DC: Washington Printing Office 1915)49

[14]Editors, *The Pottery and Glass Record* (Stoke-on-Trent, England, April 1921)241

[15]Editors, *The Pottery Gazette and Glass Trade Review* (Stoke-on-Trent, England, June 1, 1931)

[16]Editors, *The Pottery and Glass Record* (Stoke-on-Trent, England, April 1921)241

[17]Editors, *The Pottery and Glass Record* (Stoke-on-Trent, England, October 1928)317

[18]Editors, *The Pottery Gazette and Glass Trade Review* (Stoke-on-Trent, England, June 1, 1931)

[19]Editors, *The Pottery Gazette and Glass Trade Review* (Stoke-on-Trent, England, May 1, 1930)840

[20]Editors, *The Pottery Gazette* (Stoke-on-Trent, England, June 1, 1909)701

[21]Rodney S. Hampson, M.A., *Churchill China*, Staffordshire Heritage Series Volume 5 (Stoke-on-Trent, England, Department of History, Keele University 1994)129

[22]Editors, *The Pottery Gazette* (Stoke-on-Trent, England, June 1, 1909)701

[23]Editors, *The Pottery Gazette and Glass Trade Review* (Stoke-on-Trent, England, November 1, 1933)1357

[24]Robert Shively, research article, *The Story of the Johnson Bros.* (Kansas City, Kansas, May 1983)3

[25]Editors, *Pottery Gazette and Glass Trade Review* (Stoke-on-Trent, England, November 1946)38

[26]Editors, *Pottery Gazette and Glass Trade Review* (Stoke-on-Trent, England, August 1955)1230

[27]Edited by Denis Stuart, *People of the Potteries, Vol. 1* (Keele, England Department of Adult Education, University of Keele, 1985)130

[28]Editors, *Pottery Gazette and Glass Trade Review* (Stoke-on-Trent, England, August 1955)261

[29]Rodney S. Hampson, M. A., *Churchill China*, Heritage Series Vol. 5 (Keele, England: The Centre for Local History, Department of History, University of Keele, 1994)129

[30]J. F. Blacker, *The ABC of English Ceramic Art* (London, England: Stanley Paul & Co. Ltd. 1911)243

[31]Editors, *The Stone Guardian* (Stone, England, The Stone Guardian Local Newspaper, June 19, 1937)

[32]Editors, *The Pottery and Glass Record* (Stoke-on-Trent, England, February, 1928)55

[33]Robert Shively, research article, *The Story of the Johnson Brothers* (Kansas City, Kansas, May 1983)3

[34]Ibid., 2

[35]Editors, *The Pottery and Glass Record* (Stoke-on-Trent, England, November 1928)331

[36]Editors, *The Pottery Gazette and Glass Trade Review* (Stoke-on-Trent, England, December 1, 1928)1958

[37]Editors, *The Guardian and East Kent Advertiser* (Kent, England, January 10, 1920)

[38]Editors, *Sheerness Times* (Sheerness, England, May 22, 1930)

[39]Editors, *The Pottery Gazette* (Stoke-on-Trent, England, April 1, 1909)446

[40]G. Woolliscroft Rhead, *British Pottery Marks* (London, England: Scott, Greenwood & Son 1910)152

[41]Arnold A. & Dorothy E. Kowalsky, *Encyclopedia of Marks On American, English, and European Earthenware, Tea Leaf, and White Ironstone* (Atglen, Pennsylvania: Schiffer publishing Ltd. 1999)352

[42]G. Woolliscroft Rhead, *British Pottery Marks* (London, England: Scott, Greenwood & Son 1910)153

[43]Editors, *The Pottery Gazette* (Stoke-on-Trent, England, April 1, 1909)446

[44]Robert Shively, research paper, *The Story of the Johnson Brothers* (Kansas City, Kansas, May 1983)1

[45]Editors, *The Staffordshire Sentinel* (Stoke-on-Trent, England, September 17, 1999)14

[46]Editors, *The Pottery Gazette* (Stoke-on-Trent, England, April 1, 1909)446

[47]Ibid., 446

[48]Wolf Mankowitz & Reginald G. Haggar, *The Concise Encyclopedia of English Pottery and Porcelain* (London, England: Andre Deutsch, Ltd. 1968)

[49]Kathy Niblett, *Dynamic Designs British Pottery Industry, 1940-1990* (Stoke-on-Trent, England: City Museum and Art Gallery 1990)83

[50]Editors, *The Pottery Gazette* (Stoke-on-Trent, England, April 1, 1910)421

[51]R. G. Haggar, A. R. Mountford, and J. Thomas, *The Staffordshire Pottery Industry, Well Street Pottery* (An Extract from The Victoria History of the County of Stafford, Vol. II, Staffordshire, England: Reprinted by Staffordshire County Library, Edited by M. W. Greenslade & J. G. Jenkins, 1981)33

[52]Mary J. Finegan, *Johnson Brothers Dinnerware* (Statesville, North Carolina: Signature Press, Inc. 1993)38

[53]Rodney Hampson, *Longton Potters 1700-1865* (Stoke-on-Trent, England: City Museum & Art Gallery, Journal of Ceramic History Vol.14)

[54]J. G. Jenkins, *A History of the County of Stafford, Vol. VIII* (London, England: Oxford University Press 1963)101, endnote: 90

[55]William Scarratt, *Old Times in the Potteries* (Stoke-on-Trent, England)

[56]Editors, *The Pottery Gazette* (Stoke-on-Trent, England, February 1, 1904)163

[57]Editors, *The Pottery Gazette* (Stoke-on-Trent, England, July 1, 1908)819

[58]J. G. Jenkins, *A History of the County of Stafford* (London, England: Oxford University Press 1963)101, endnote: 90

[59]R. G. Haggar, A. R. Mountford, & J. Thomas, *The Staffordshire Pottery Industry, Well Street Pottery* (An Extract from The Victoria History of the County of Stafford, Vol. II, Staffordshire, England: Reprinted by Staffordshire County Library, Edited by M. W. Greenslade & J G. Jenkins, 1981)

[60]Geoffrey A. Godden, *Ironstone Stone & Granite Wares* (Suffolk, England: Antique Collectors' Club Ltd. 1999)282

[61]Govia Starey, *The Story of Alfred Meakin (Tunstall) Ltd.* (London, England: Ruthier Publications Press, November, 1949)

[62]Rodney S. Hampson, M.A., *Churchill China Great British Potters Since 1795* (Stoke-on-Trent, England: The Centre for Local History, Department of History, University of Keele, 1994)128, 129

[63]Jean Wetherbee, *White Ironstone: A Collectors Guide* (Dubuque, Iowa: Antique Trader Books, 1996)157

[64]Ernie & Bev Dieringer, *White Ironstone China, Plate Identification Guide 1840-1890* (Atglen, Pennsylvania: Schiffer Publishing Ltd., 2001)139

[65]Geoffrey A. Godden and Michael Gibson, *Collecting Lustreware* (London, England: Barrie & Jenkins, 1991)

[66]Frank Stefano, Jr., *Pictorial Souvenirs & Commemoratives of North America* (U.S.A.: Dutton-Sunrise, Inc., a subsidiary of E. P. Dutton & Co., Inc. 1976)68

[67]Bernard Hollowood, *The Story of J. & G. Meakin* (Derby and London, England: Bemrose Publicity Co. Ltd., 1951)5

[68]Ibid., 14

[69]Ibid., 12

[70]Ibid., 19

[71]Ibid., 29,30

[72]Ibid., 20

[73]Ibid.

[74]Barbara W. Tuchman, *The Proud Tower, a portrait of the world before the war: 1890-1914* (New York, New York: The Macmillan Company, 1966)119

[75]G. Woolliscroft Rhead, *British Pottery Marks* (London, England: Scott, Greenwood & Son, 1910)219

[76]Steve Birks (web site: netcentral.co.uk/steveb)

[77]Arnold A. & Dorothy E. Kowalsky, *Encyclopedia of Marks On American, English, and European Earthenware, Ironstone, and Stoneware 1780-1980* (Atglen, Pennsylvania: Schiffer Publishing, Ltd. 1999)577

[78]Keith Potts, for *The Northern Ceramic Society*, Newsletter No.114 (Stoke-on-Trent, England: self published, June, 1999)13

[79]Arnold A. Kowalsky, for *Northern Ceramic Society Journal*, Volume No.17 (Stoke-on-Trent, England: self published, 2000)24-26

[80]Steve Birks (web site: netcentral.co.uk/steveb)/potteries/burgess

[81]Ibid., /potteries/doulton

[82]Susan Jean Verbeek, *The Falcon Ware Story* (London, England: Pottery Publications, 1996)7

[83]Steve Birks (web site: netcentral.co.uk/steveb)/allpotters/1057

Chapter Three — The Wares: An Anatomy

Table Service

Americans always want to know, "What is it?, and What was it used for?" It really seems to be an American "thing" to want to label each piece. In this chapter, we will deal with those two questions. The answers are not always easy to obtain, however. For what we have is not so much a language barrier, as much as a difference in cultures. The vast majority of Late Victorian Flow Blue was manufactured by the British and Germans, and purchased by the American market. So we find that there are the purists who believe that if the British made the pieces, we should use their terms. Then there is the American public that was the consumers, who had their own terms for each piece that "they" used. To further segment the American version, we find different cultures within our American ranks, as well as the developing of individual family customs when it came to dining. This can cause havoc to researchers, such as myself, who try to decipher and sort out this whole array of terms. I firmly believe that there are no wrong answers.

The English are much more simplistic in their approach to this subject. They call it a dish, Americans call it a breakfast plate. If the British call a piece an oval plate, and we Americans call the same piece an oval platter – who is using the wrong term? When Americans are listening to an English speaker on ceramics, you can feel the tense confusion immediately when the inevitable questions are asked; "What is this piece called?" So for this chapter on terms, rather than deciding on one specific label for each piece (which would throw both the English and Americans into constant debate), I have decided to list the terms used by both sides of the Atlantic, when available.

I have listened to American Antique dealers, viewed American and Canadian catalogs, listened to individual collectors, read British books and listened to their speakers, and have read an array of ship manifests in helping me to accumulate this list of terms. The one thing that I find confusing, but very interesting, is the varying terms used by Americans for each piece; these terms will vary, depending on what source you are viewing. To illustrate this I was reading one catalog that called the six inch oval bowl an "individual vegetable," and another called the same piece a "baker"; in actuality, both are correct. The consumer in this case would name the piece dependant on what "they" used it for. It is my hope, for this chapter, that a certain amount of order will come from this massive amount of confusion, and help given to your need to know, "what is this piece called."

Plates

Plates are the most basic pieces in a set of dishes. There are generally five sizes of plates available: six, seven, eight, nine, and ten inch. This is not to say that all ten-inch plates are exactly ten-inches, or nines are always exactly nine-inches etc. As needed, a pottery would occasionally change their molds (which always seemed to be smaller), and in cost cutting maneuvers, plates were reduced somewhat in size. Thus you may find a ten-inch plate that has an actual measurement of nine

and three quarters. If you collect one pattern long enough, you will come to realize the actual dimensions of the five plates available for your set of dishes. Also, for plates, there is a very slight foot rim that it rests on.

In researching some catalogs, the sizes can be confusing because of the English potteries marketing ploy to reduce the tariff charged when their products entered the states. The tariff paid was based on size, thus it would be less if the eight-inch plate were advertised as a six-inch plate. It's all in how you measure the plate. To down size an eight-inch plate from an actual ten inches, they measured from one side to the plate well edge on the other side. The British call the six and seven-inch plates, muffin plates. Eight-inch plates were twifflers, nine-inch plates were supper plates, and table plates were the ten-inch. Other names used for plates would be:

Six-Inch: Pie Plate, Dessert Plate, and Bread Plate
Seven-Inch: Pie Plate, Dessert Plate, and Tea Plate
Eight-Inch: Breakfast Plates, Luncheon Plates, and Salad Plates
Nine-Inch: Supper Plates
Ten-Inch: Dinner Plates, and Jumbo Dinner Plates

Another form of plate was the individual butter pat. They are generally about three inches across and were used expressly for a pad of butter. Butter pats are exclusive to the Late Victorian period and were first introduced because of the demand created by the American consumer, in the 1880s. They finally went out of vogue in the 1930s, but butter pats will be remembered as an exquisite refinement to individual pampering that the Late Victorians were so fond of. Other names given to the butter pat are:

Butter Chip, Butter Plate, Butter Saucer, and Individual Butters

Cups and Saucers

Cups are basically either tea or coffee. Is there a difference? Yes indeed! The differences are two fold, size and shape. The teacup is wider than it is tall, and the rim will flare out. Typical dimensions for a teacup are four inches across and two inches high. A coffee cup will generally be the same dimensions in width and height, and the cup will be straight sided – with very little, if any flare of the rim. In England, the coffee cup is sometimes referred to as a coffee can. The saucers will have an indent for the cup to rest in, and be about six-inches in diameter. For the English description of the tea and coffee cup, we note, George Savage & Harold Newman, *An Illustrated Dictionary of Ceramics* (London, England: Thames & Hudson Ltd., 1992)

Teacup: Usually of semi-spheroid form (a shape resembling a flattened sphere), with one handle, and accompanied by a saucer, used for drinking tea; it holds about four ounces.

Coffee cup/can: A straight sided cylindrical cup shaped like a mug. It has a slight foot ring, and is about two and one half inches in both height and width. The shape was introduced by Sevres, and was widely copied elsewhere.

Plate 653. Coffee cup left, FLORIDA, teacup, MELBOURNE. Both patterns are by Grindley, and represent the Gr-B body style. Note the rim flare, the squatty look to the teacup, and the straight sides of the coffee cup. *Author collection* $90-$125 each, with saucer.

With few exceptions, all cups were made for use with the right hand. You will notice the small design that is put inside the cup rim can be viewed when holding the cup with the right hand. Also, the top of the cup handle is slanted towards you when held with the right hand. These are minor points, but its all part of the cup anatomy.

The teacup and coffee cup each come in two sizes with the largest being about one half inch larger in height and width. The saucers for these cups are about six and one half inches in diameter. The largest coffee cup is considered the Breakfast cup, or farmer's cup as some will call it. In England, this large coffee cup is sometimes referred to as the breakfast can. The largest of the teacups is just that, a large teacup. For some body styles, it seems like the only cups you see are the large and small teacups. As a result, many people mistakenly call the large teacup a coffee cup. And quite frankly, it may have been purchased and actually used for this purpose. It is all very possible, however, you cannot rewrite history and state with accuracy, that the large teacup is a coffee cup. In other words, you can call it what you want, but the historical shape of the cup dictates that it is a teacup. I personally have seen the teacup and coffee cup for every body style that W. H. Grindley and the Johnson Bros. produced during the Late Victorian period. If a coffee cup (or any other piece in the set) was made for a body style, then I maintain, any pattern applied to that style of dish could potentially have the coffee cup (or other piece you are searching for). Because you have not seen one yet, does not mean that they don't exist.

The Late Victorian potteries also produced a pedestal punch cup, demitasse cup, and cream soup cups. All are very difficult to find. I have yet to see a Grindley punch bowl, yet he did produce punch cups. All of the punch cups that I have seen, regardless of who the potter is, are all set on a pedestal base. Demitasse cups are small versions of the normal size tea or coffee cup. These small cups are generally about two-inches high, and two and one half inches across (sizes will vary), with the saucers being about four and one half inches in diameter. The cream soup cups are very easy to detect because they have two handles opposite of each other. They are similar in shape to the teacup, but have two handles, instead of one.

Round and Oval Bowls

All of these bowls were designed not to have a lid, and they can be for either individual or table use. All of the round bowls are considered nappies, and the oval bowls are considered bakers; now let me explain. In H. Leonard's Sons & Co.'s catalog for 1888, they list the round bowls as nappies, scallops, or scalloped nappies.

In each of the two categories of open bowls, the smaller ones are for individual use, and the larger ones would be for table use. The question is asked, "How do I know which ones are for individual use

and which ones are for table use?" For the round bowls, the answer is quite simple. The round open bowls intended for table use will have tab handles. The smaller round bowls, intended for individual use, will not have tab handles. This method of using tab handles was standard for the industry. However, some body styles produced by a pottery do not incorporate the use of tab handles. Examples of these would be Gr-C and Gr-I produced by Grindley. In those particular cases, where a body style does not incorporate the use of tab handles, the dimensions I list for you and common sense will help you determine the use of each bowl.

The round open bowls will range in size from five-inches, and progress by one-inch increments to as much as twelve-inches across. The separation point between individual and table service bowls is about nine-inches in diameter. The largest of these round bowls are considered to be potato bowls. Many of the round bowls have their own name, and in many of the catalogs they are listed with those names. However, in many instances, the round bowls are merely listed as nappies by size only. Below is listed the names used for some of the round open bowls.

Five-Inch: Berry Bowl, Desert Bowl, Fruit Saucer, and Sauce Bowl

Six-Inch: Cereal Bowl, Ice Cream Bowl, and Salad Bowl

Eight-Inch: Coupe Soup, Soup Bowl

Another form of round open bowl is the flanged soup plate, or flat soup. These are shaped exactly like a plate, but have a deep well. They can be found in increments of one-inch, and ranging in size from seven to ten-inches. Some of the larger potteries, the Johnson Bros. in particular, made flanged bowls as small as five and six-inches. You will find in most instances that the larger potteries manufactured a larger variety of pieces, and sizes.

The oval open bowls, from the smallest to the largest, all have tab handles. They come in increments of one-inch, and range in size from six to about eleven-inches. This use of tab handles on oval bowls confused me at first, until I realized that all oval bowls were considered bakers by many catalog lists. As we stated for round bowls, in catalogs you can find the oval bowls listed individually by name, or merely as bakers by size only. The English use the larger ones for baking meat pies and the smallest for a sweet dish at teatime. In America, we use the smallest oval bowl as an individual vegetable, but I have heard it being called a baked potato dish. In the beginning this term puzzled me, until I realized it was considered a baker, the tab handles, and its size, which would be perfect to bake a potato in.

Round and Oval Covered Bowls

There are five basic covered bowls for a set of dishes. All are standard for the industry. They are the round and oval vegetable, round and oval covered soup, and the oval covered sauce. There is a sixth one, and we will cover it after we discuss the five mentioned above. When I say round or oval, my meaning of those terms is the representation of the basic shape of the piece. I do not mean that they are perfectly smooth in either the round or oval form.

The covered vegetable bowls, round and oval, are smaller in size than the covered soup tureens. In most cases, they are referred to as covered vegetables. The round one, however, in many circles is referred to as a covered casserole. The round and oval soup tureens are much larger than the covered vegetable bowls, and the lids for the soup tureens will have a slot for the ladle to extend through. The round covered soup tureen in some cases is referred to as a chowder bowl, or stew tureen. The oval covered sauce tureen is smaller than the covered vegetables, and will have a slot in the lid for the sauce ladle to extend through. A round covered sauce tureen, during the Late Victorian period, is practically not existent, if they were produced at all. The oval covered soup and sauce tureen could be bought with, or without a stand. The stand was nothing more than an under tray that the tureen sat on, and used to catch any drips. I will not say that they do not exist, but I have never seen an under tray for the round covered soup tureen.

The sixth covered bowl I mentioned before is the small round covered vegetable. There must have been a demand for a smaller cov-

ered vegetable, and because the sauce tureen was oval, they made this one the same size as the covered sauce tureen, but round in shape. I have seen this small round tureen called the newlywed size, small round covered vegetable, apartment size, and individual covered vegetable.

Plate 654. Oval covered vegetable, KEELE by W. H. Grindley & Co. This oval tureen incorporates the use of loop handles for the bowl as well as the lid. *Courtesy of Shell & Jim Lewis, Illinois* $325+ due to popularity of pattern.

Plate 655. Oval covered vegetable, CLARENCE by Wood & Sons. This oval covered vegetable bowl incorporates loop handles for the bowl, and a knob handle for the lid. *Courtesy of Shell & Jim Lewis, Illinois* $225+

Plate 656. Oval covered soup tureen right, and oval covered sauce tureen, NORMANDY by Johnson Bros. The two covered tureens shown have all four parts available; lid, bowl, ladle, and stand. *Courtesy of Warren & Connie Macy, Indiana* $1000+ oval soup tureen, due to popularity of pattern, $850+ sauce tureen, due to popularity of pattern.

The way you can tell if the round or oval bowl you have was intended "not" to have a lid is quite simple. For the open bowls, whether round or oval, the main part of the pattern decoration will be on the inside of the bowl, and a token amount of pattern on the outside. For covered bowls, the main part of the pattern will be on the outside of the bowl, and a small part of the pattern design is placed on the inside wall of the bowl. This outside decoration of the open bowls and the inside decoration of the covered bowls is not always done, whether through intent or just missed by the worker applying the transfer print.

The way you can tell if the bowl was intended to have a lid is quite easy. The bowl will have either loop or knob styled handles. The open vegetables in most cases will have tab handles to use for holding.

Round and Oval Platters

There are two basic shapes for serving platters, round and the most common, oval. The rectangle shaped platters faded from use as we entered the 1890s. The oval platters range in size from about six-inches, and progress by two-inch increments up to and including, twenty-one inches. The smallest six-inch platter is considered an individual meat platter. The next size up, the eight-inch platters, are what we call the relish dish, and are quite common to find. In England, the oval platter is referred to merely as an oval plate or tray, or simply as a dish. In America, we can get more specific when it comes to naming the platters. In the H. Leonard's Sons & Co.'s catalog for 1888, they list the platters as follows:

Ten-Inch: Cold Meat platter
Twelve-Inch: Steaks Platter
fourteen-Inch: Small Roast Platter
Sixteen-Inch: Large Roast Platter
Eighteen-Inch: Roast Turkey Platter

The fish platter is another form of the oval platter, and is generally about twenty-two inches long. It has a shape very similar to a cigar. Many of these fish platters were sold as sets, which included six to eight, eight-inch plates. American potteries produced many of these sets, and in many cases they included a fish decal on the platter and plates.

The round platters, for most, are called round chargers. The design for many round chargers was to be hung on a wall for display, and are printed with a scenic view. Those are easily recognizable though, because on the back there are two holes in the ceramic to hang them with. The round charger came in only three known sizes: ten-inch, twelve-inch, and fourteen-inch. These sizes are approximate, and your actual size may vary somewhat. The largest of the chargers, as you will see in the chapter on marketing, were at times part of a chocolate set. The smaller ten-inch charger was normally used as a cake plate. Now the question is asked, "If I collect a body style that does not incorporate tab handles, how will I know if it is a cake plate, or a normal ten-inch plate?" Here's how you can tell. The edge of the cake plate will be cupped upwards more than the dinner plate, and the foot ring will be much more pronounced. Names used for the round platters, in addition to charger, would include:

Ten-Inch: Bread Plate, Cake Plate, and Dessert Plate
Twelve-Inch: Chop Plate, and Round Tray
Fourteen-Inch: Chocolate Set Tray, Chop Plate, and Round Tray

Bone Dishes

Bone dishes are crescent or kidney shaped side dishes. These dishes first made their debut on the Late Victorian table during the 1880s. They are reminiscent of the old style of dining, where you had a common center tray with food, and small crescent shaped dishes that would surround this center tray. When the family ate their dinner, each person would take one of the crescent shaped dishes to eat from. For the Late Victorian dining table, they were crescent shape so they could fit neatly along side ones plate. They are most commonly called bone dishes, but could have been used for any table scraps. During the 1880s and through the 1930s, they were very commonly sold in catalogs with a dinner set, but starting in the 1940s they faded from use. This dish is another example of the Late Victorians elegant attention to the individual diner.

Oyster/Waste Bowls

Oyster bowls are different from oyster plates, and first came into usage in the 1880s. Research through catalogs will clearly demonstrate their shape, and to some doubters, their existence. They were sold in two sizes, with the one-pint size being the most commonly found. No matter who the potter, the basic shape is standard. A point to make here is an oyster bowl is an individual dish. For a service of twelve, you would need twelve. This is also how they were marketed, by the dozen.

Plate 657. Oyster bowl, OLYMPIA by W. H. Grindley & Co. The basic dimensions for an oyster bowl are six in diameter, and three-inches high. The bowl and pedestal each are one and one half inches high. *Author collection* $200+

The waste bowl was either sold with the dinner set, or with a tea set. Their main use was to hold the used tealeaf dredges. Some people get confused between the oyster bowl and the waste bowl as to what purpose they serve. In most cases they believe the oyster bowl is a waste bowl, when in fact it is not. The waste bowl, and this is standard for the industry, is shaped exactly like either the teacup, or the coffee cup, just larger and minus the handle. Two sizes of waste bowls were made, with the larger one being the most common. Plate 657 will show you the shape of the oyster bowl, and plates 658 and 659 will demonstrate the waste bowl shape.

Plate 658. Waste bowl right, and coffee cup, ARGYLE by W. H. Grindley & Co. This plate clearly shows the similarity of shape between the waste bowl, and the coffee cup. *Author collection* $275-$350 waste bowl, $90-$125 coffee cup with saucer

Plate 659. Waste bowl left, and teacup, TOURAINE by Henry Alcock. This plate further demonstrates the similarity of the waste bowl to the cup, but in this case it is the teacup. *Courtesy of Terry & Ann Potts, Illinois* $275-$350 waste bowl, $90-$125 teacup with saucer

Covered Sugar/Creamers/Pitchers

Late Victorian Flow Blue sugars can come in a wide variety of shapes, but one thing they all have in common, is that they are smaller in size than their Early, and Middle Victorian cousins. Most, if not all, were made with a lid. I know of no Late Victorian "open" sugar. The English will call them a sugar basin, sugar can, or sugar jar. I know of no other American term used other than covered sugar. Depending on the body style (some are and some are not) the teapot lid and the sugar lid are the same size. A teapot lid may not always have the small stay, which holds the lid on when you pour, but it will have the small steam hole punched in by the potter. It can be a little disconcerting to purchase an expensive teapot, only to find out at a latter date that your teapot lid is actually a sugar lid.

Plate 660. Sugar and small creamer, KEELE by W. H. Grindley & Co. *Courtesy of Terry & Ann Potts, Illinois* $500+ for the set

Creamers for a set of dishes came in two sizes, small and large. The small creamer is about four-inches high, and the large creamer is about five-inches high. I have examined the small and large creamer for every Late Victorian Flow Blue body style that W. H. Grindley, and the Johnson Bros. produced. They all have two sizes of creamers, with the exception of one, and that is Grindley's Gr-C body style. I also have viewed the same for many other body styles produced by other English potteries. Some body styles may not have the two creamers, but I have seen enough to tell me that the two creamer series was standard for the industry. The pitcher next in size, is the pint size pitcher, and in many cases this pitcher is confused with, and labeled a creamer. It may have been bought as, and used as a creamer, but for the purist, it is not a creamer.

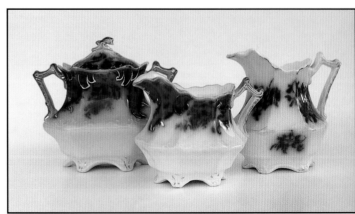

Plate 661. Large creamer, small creamer, and covered sugar, GIRONDE left, and ARGYLE by W. H. Grindley & Co. Even though we show two different patterns, they both were applied to the same body style of dish. *Author collection* $225+ creamers, $275+ sugar

There are seven pitchers available for a set of dishes, which includes the two creamers. The seven pitcher series would seem to be standard for the industry, with the smaller pitchers being used for milk or cream and the larger pitchers being used for water. If you collect one pattern, and do not have all seven, that does not mean that they do not exist. To have all seven pitchers in the series for today's collector to find, they would have to have been bought when they were produced. I know a collector that has collected the pattern MELBOURNE by W. H. Grindley & Co. for thirty years and does not have the largest pitcher in the series. Could it be possible, that when that pattern was being produced and sold, that no one ever bought one? For me, this just adds to the intrigue and mystery of collecting antiques.

Plate 663. Eggcups, r to l FULTON, ST. LOUIS, NORMANDY, and HOLLAND, all by Johnson Bros. The two eggcups on the left are singles, and the two on the right are considered double eggcups. *Courtesy of Shell & Jim Lewis, Illinois* $175+ ea. NORMANDY $225+ due to pattern popularity

Plate 662. Seven pitcher series, TOURAINE by Henry Alcock. A very rare sight indeed! *Courtesy of Terry & Ann Potts, Illinois* $3000+ for the set

The dimensions I list below for you are merely guidelines. Some body styles are tall and thin, while others are short and squatty, and as a result your actual dimensions will vary. For our purposes, let's give them numbers one through seven, with number one being the smallest.

Number One: Four-Inches
Number Two: Five-Inches
Number Three: Five 1/2 Inches
Number Four: Six 1/2 Inches
Number Five: Seven 1/2 Inches
Number Six: Eight 1/2 Inches
Number Seven: Nine 1/2 Inches

Eggcups

If you collect one particular pattern, what could be more elegant than to own several eggcups to match your set? They are exquisite pieces that demand attention. In researching catalogs, I cannot recall seeing a set of dishes that included eggcups. They always seem to be sold latter in the ceramic section with other separate and unique pieces. They can be found as a double eggcup, which includes a large cup on one end and a much smaller cup on the other end. They also can be found in a much smaller version, considered a single. The single eggcup sits on a pedestal base. Eggcups in Europe, where eggs are more a part of the diet, were more popular than in America. Most eggcups sold in the states were done through special order.

For many potteries, the large double eggcup seems to have been a universal style. By this I mean the potteries manufactured one shape, no matter what body style of dish it was to go with. When the pottery received an order for eggcups, the "one" shape was used, no matter what pattern had been requested or body style that pattern was normally applied to.

One notable pottery that was an exception to this rule was W. H. Grindley & Co. For every one of his Flow Blue body styles, the double eggcup was made to match that style of dish. However, as with most other potteries, the small eggcup was produced with one shape. This one shape was used for all patterns and body styles they were applied to. Here is a way to tell if you have the proper Grindley eggcup, for a pattern you collect, even though it has the correct pattern on it. For the double eggcups produced by Grindley, the embossing design he puts along the edge of a plate in a given body style, will show up on the edge of the large cup.

There is a third styled eggcup. This one "looks" like a napkin ring, but is in fact a large eggcup with no pedestal base. This eggcup can fool you because there is a hole that extends through the cup. The give away, which is also the way to tell if it is an eggcup, is its shape. It will be shaped just like the "cup" of the eggcup, but missing its base.

Gravy/Sauce Boat

The gravy boat has a shape similar to a boat with a handle. In every marketing catalog I viewed, it was sold with a stand (under tray). This under tray had an indent for the boat to stand in, and the obvious use for the under tray, was to catch any drips. The gravy under tray, and the relish dish are very similar in size, but, the relish does not have an indent and the under tray is about one half inch wider. Many times you will see today, a gravy boat being sold sitting on top of a relish dish, and it being advertised as the under tray. For most body styles, the gravy boat will not fit right when set on a relish dish. It will rock. When the set was originally purchased, the customer may have only bought the gravy boat and relish dish. The idea here would be to save money, and to use the relish dish in a dual role, relish and under tray. For the purist, the relish dish is not a true gravy under tray.

You can find the gravy boat produced with two handles, with attached under tray, and with two handles and two spouts. There are those that say the two handled/two spout gravy boats were marketed with a fish set. This may be true, and would be an excellent reason why some do call this a fish sauceboat. Any gravy boat is also called a sauceboat. In many marketing catalogs, two were sold with a set of dishes.

Ladles

Ladles are so elegant, delicately fragile, and yet, asked to do their job day in and day out. How did any of them survive? To complicate the survival rate of a ladle, is the underlying fact that the handles are hollow. Thousands were made in their day, and so few of them remain for today's collector to find. If you collect one particular pattern, and you have a covered soup tureen and undertray, the picture is never really complete without the ladle; it is the finishing touch.

Plate 666. Soup ladle, MELBOURNE left, ARGYLE by W. H. Grindley & Co. Compare the shape of these ladle with those in Plate 667. *Author collection* $800+ ea. due to pattern popularity

Plate 664. Soup and sauce ladle, NORMANDY by Johnson Bros. Compare the shape of these ladles to Plate 665, which was also made by the Johnson Bros. *Courtesy of Warren & Connie Macy, Indiana* $1000+ for large soup ladle, $500+ for sauce ladle, both due to popularity of pattern.

Plate 667. Sauce ladles, l to r PORTMAN, MELBOURNE, and ARGYLE by W. H. Grindley & Co. These patterns represent three different body styles, yet all are the same shape ladle. *Author collection* $325+ ea. due to pattern popularity

Plate 665. Soup ladle, FLORIDA by Johnson Bros. *Courtesy of Arnold & Dorothy Kowalsky, New York* $500+ despite its condition

Every pottery made two sizes of ladles; large for the two soup tureens, and small, shorter one for the sauce tureen. The handles for the large ladles are about ten-inches long, and the bowl about four and one half inches in diameter. The handles for the sauce ladles are about five to six-inches in length, and the bowl is three-inches across.

In all my research, I have never seen a pottery make a different styled ladle for each of its body styles. Each pottery produced their own shape, but that shape was used for all body styles produced by that factory. Grindley used the same shaped ladle for every set of dishes he made from his starting in business, till the day he retired. This statement also includes his Tea Leaf, White ironstone wares, and non-Flow Blue transfer patterns.

The knowledge of knowing what a potteries ladle looks like can be very beneficial. Most ladles are not marked, and in many cases the pattern is reduced because of the smaller area. If you own a ladle and are not sure of the pattern, but you know by the shape which pottery produced it, you have narrowed your search considerably and are close to solving the pattern mystery.

Pedestal Compote

The pedestal compote can be found in two sizes. Both are about ten-inches in diameter, with the tall one being about four and one half inches tall, and the other about three-inches tall. They look exactly the same, but the pedestal base for one is shorter. The top part or tray of the compote resembles a round charger or cake plate to some degree, but there is more of a bowl effect to the compote.

In Denmark, the compote is referred to as a desert dish, or tray. In England, it is mostly called a comport. In many of the American catalog ads, it is referred to as a comport or cake stand. A term I have heard the compote being called, that I think is incorrect, is pedestal fruit compote. The pedestal fruit bowl has a shape all its own, and has a bowl that is much deeper than the compote. See Plate 669 for an example of a pedestal fruit bowl.

Pedestal Fruit Bowl

The pedestal fruit bowl is a distinctly shaped bowl, which is easy to identify once you have seen one. The bowl can be oval or round in shape and will have tab handles. The pedestal base it sits on resembles the same pedestal base, used for the covered tureens in the same body style.

You can understand why the pedestal fruit bowl has a deeper bowl than the pedestal compote when you consider the size and shape of fruit. Besides the PORTMAN fruit bowl, I have seen one other that was produced by Grindley. The pattern is GRACE, and the bowl was the correct Gr-E body style for that pattern. Two are known for the Johnson Bros., JEWEL and NORMANDY, and they were applied to their correct JB-A body style. One is known for Burgess & Leigh, and it was the pattern VERMONT applied to its correct body style. Current research shows two that were produced by the Bourne & Leigh pottery. One pattern is MILTON, and the other unidentified. It would appear that the pedestal fruit bowl was not manufactured universally by the different factories, but rather, by individual body style.

Plate 668. Pedestal compote, MELBOURNE by W. H. Grindley & Co., 9 ½" in diameter x 4 ½" high. This Plate shows the typical shape of a pedestal compote. *Author collection* $350-$750

Plate 669. Pedestal fruit bowl, PORTMAN by W. H. Grindley & Co., the bowl is 12 ½" x 9" x 4" tall including pedestal base. *Author collection* $500-$750

Jam Jars

Jam jars are small cup shaped bowls with a slotted lid, and either sits on or has an attached undertray. Most of the jam jars I have seen have the undertray attached. All but one that I have seen has been produced on individual body styles, as opposed to one that was used universally for all patterns. If they came with a spoon, and I assume they did, I have never seen one.

This piece has also been called a mustard jar, and a condiment jar. I doubt if it was used for mustard because it is too large for that purpose. Some even have called it a honey jar, but the slot in the lid spoils that theory. Honey jars were made without a slot in the lid in order to keep the honey bug free. I believe the best term for this piece is either a jam or jelly jar.

Honey Jar

A honey jar looks very similar to a covered sugar, but smaller and with slight differences. We draw the description of a honey jar from George Savage & Harold Newman's *An Illustrated Dictionary of Ceramics*, Thames & Hudson Ltd., 1992 (reprint): "A small jar of pottery or porcelain for serving honey; it is usually cylindrical and provided with a cover, some examples being made to simulate a beehive. Some jars have a fixed saucer-like stand." The lids for honey jars will not have a slot. They were made that way to prevent contamination by insects. Note: see Plate 688 for an example.

Spoon Holder (Toothbrush Holder?)

As for the term "spoon holder," or "spooner" as many will call it in America, I think spooner is merely a slang version of spoon holder. With this is mind it is not justified to discuss each term's meaning; quite simply, they are the same piece.

Plate 670. Jam jar, HAMPTON SPRAY by W. H. Grindley & Co., 5" to top of finial. It is very rare to find a jam jar in this mint condition. *Courtesy of Arnold & Dorothy Kowalsky, New York* $275-$375+

Plate 671. Spoon holders and Toothbrush holder, r to l CLARENCE, ARGYLE, spoon holders, SYRIAN toothbrush holder, all by W. H. Grindley & Co. Note the similarity in shape of the CLARENCE spoon holder, and the SYRIAN toothbrush holder. *Author collection* $300+ spoon holders, $225+ toothbrush holder

Plate 671 shows the item in question, and the two shapes it will come in. The one on the left is the straight sided, and the other two have the two curled tangs (similar to a spout) on either side of the upper rim. Just spending a little time researching books on china that were printed in England, you will find out very quickly that in England the "spoon holder" does not exist. It simply was not a product that they used. That does not, however, close the door on our belief that spoon holders were made, and by the British. In researching the 1890s marketing catalogs, such as Sears Roebuck & Co., you will find pictures of, and sale ads for, spoon holders. Spoon holders were more popularly sold in glass, silver, and silver plate, but in an effort to compete, the British also produced them in porcelain and ironstone/stoneware. You can talk to many collectors today, and they will tell you stories of seeing, as a child, spoon holders with spoons in them, sitting on their grandparent's kitchen table. There is no question that in this country there was a need for, and did exist, spoon holders. We must remember that marketers such as Sears Roebuck & Co., and Montgomery Ward & Co. did not invent, nor make the products they sold. But we must also remember that as marketers, what they sold, and what they called it were a reflection of the American wants and needs. English potters, such as W. H. Grindley & Co., recognized this need, and as producers, gave the American public what they wanted. Let's face it. They were in the business to make money. There was only one question each English Potter had to ask himself. What piece do I supply them with? Let's now explore what W. H. Grindley decided on. Let's look at Plate 671 for a moment. Grindley produced all three pieces, and all look like they could be either a spoon holder, or a toothbrush holder. From left to right we have, ARGYLE Gr-A spoon holder, CLARENCE Gr-C spoon holder/toothbrush holder, and SYRIAN Gr-W1 toothbrush holder. How do I know this? What are the differences? Read on.

Every piece in a wash set, with the exception of the bowl, matches the exact same lines as the pitcher from the bulbous rim, handle, and the exact same embossing marks. Every Grindley pitcher and bowl set that I have ever seen, will follow this rule. Grindley aside, all potteries made their wash sets to match. That quite simply is how they were made, standard for the industry. For a wash set, the toothbrush holder can be found in either the straight sided, or double spout look. This is your answer to why I know the SYRIAN piece is a toothbrush holder; the pattern is applied to body style Gr-W1, a known wash set body style.

Let's establish something here before we continue. Grindley produced body styles strictly used for his wash sets, and body styles that he used strictly for his dish sets. Of his dish sets, three are known to have been used for wash sets as well. They are Gr-B (Gr-W4), Gr-C (Gr-W5), and Gr-E (Gr-W6). I have seen all three of those body styles, as a pitcher and bowl set, in white and/or white with gold tracings. The only spoon holders (with the two tangs on them) seen with a flow blue dish pattern applied were in every case one of these three body styles. All other spoon holders seen with a flow blue pattern on them, irregardless of body style, are of the straight-sided variety.

Even though there was a wash set body style produced from the Gr-C body style (Gr-W5), the pattern CLARENCE, to date, has only been seen on a set of dishes. If per chance, you owned a CLARENCE set of Gr-C dishes, and were able to find a CLARENCE Gr-W5 wash set, the CLARENCE piece in Plate 671 would go perfectly with either set. The shape would be exactly the same because it is the exact same piece.

Here is how I know that the ARGYLE piece, shown in Plate 671, is a spoon holder. When I first bought my ARGYLE spoon holder, I studied it very closely. To my amazement, there wasn't a single scallop or embossing mark on it that matched the ARGYLE Gr-A body style. Then I spotted the exact same piece, but in the pattern ROSE that is normally applied to the Gr-D body style. That's when everything started to make sense to me. If one of the body styles used for Grindley's flow blue dishes were also used for a pitcher and bowl set, then the spooner for your dish pattern would be the two-tang variety. For all the other styles, because Grindley did not have a toothbrush holder to sub for a spoon holder, he created the straight-sided version. So, in affect, the straight-sided version (a universal piece) is the only true spoon holder Grindley made specifically for that purpose.

I realize that there are no absolutes in this world of ceramics. However, to date, nothing has surfaced that would alter my thoughts on this subject. If a collector bought any or all of the pieces in Plate 671 and called them either a spoon holder, or a toothbrush holder, he would basically be right and not many would argue their claim. However, with the knowledge of a potteries body styles, he would know exactly what each of the three pieces was used for, and what to call it.

Wash Sets

Pieces that comprise a Flow Blue wash set are some of the most sought after by collectors. Each piece is a jewel that is cherished by the lucky collector. I think part of the reason for this is the history wash sets represent and the "homey" feeling they convey. In the early days when money was less plentiful wash sets were "shared," but as we entered into the Late Victorian period more money was available and etiquette dictated more sets for individual use.

In describing the pieces that comprise a wash set, one must go very cautiously. They are so embedded in our societies history that each piece is warmly referred to as individual cultures dictate. In England, they are called an ewer and basin, jug and basin, and simply a toilet set. In America, they are referred to as a chamber set, toilet set, pitcher and bowl, or a wash set. The pieces that comprise a "complete" set are all standard for the industry. Some pieces may have been manufactured by some potteries a little differently than others, but the basic shape and use remain constant. Twelve pieces were manufactured for a complete wash set:

> Large Pitcher
> Wash Bowl
> Small Pitcher
> Master Slop Jar and Lid
> Chamber Pot and Lid
> Covered Soap Dish: Base, Drainer, and Lid
> Toothbrush Holder
> Mug

Large Pitcher

The large pitcher was used to hold cold water that was poured into the bowl to wash with. For Late Victorian wash sets, the large pitcher will range in size from eleven to as much as thirteen-inches in height. With this dimension in mind, there is no confusion with a pitcher from a dish set, because they stop around nine and one half inches in height. The size of the large pitcher is very typical of its development as it passed through the Early and Middle Victorian periods. This development saw the large pitcher go from a shorter, thinner version in the Early Victorian times, to a taller, wider, and rounder main body in the Late Victorian era.

Wash Bowl

The washbowl can come in three shapes: rectangle, oval, and round, which are the most common. It was used to hold the water for washing with. When the washing was complete, the dirty water was poured into the master slop jar and discarded. The Late Victorian version of the washbowl is much larger in diameter and stands taller than in earlier times.

Small Pitcher

The small pitcher is an exact replica of the larger pitcher, and was used to hold hot water, thus the name hot water pitcher most commonly spoken. The small pitcher is generally about seven to eight-inches in height, and can be confused with pitchers from a dish set of the same size. That is unless you are familiar with dish and wash set body styles. This is one area where this book can be very beneficial. It can help you determine your pitchers use. By using the line drawings provided, you can determine if your pitcher belongs to either a dish or wash set.

Master Slop Jar and Lid

The master slop jar was used for transporting the dirtied water from the washbowl and the contents from the chamber pot outside to be discarded. It consists of two pieces, the main basin and the lid. In some case a pottery manufactured the slop jar with three pieces. The third piece was a liner/drainer that rested on top of the main jar, and the lid would rest on the liner/drainer when stored. This liner/drainer would hold the used washcloth in an effort for it to air dry. The three-piece system for the slop jar was not commonly used. There would be two handles on the slop jar, and they would be the same shape fashioned after the pitcher handle. While not in use the slop jar would be placed on the floor next to the washstand that held the rest of the set.

Chamber Pot and Lid

The chamber pot was the evening toilet of its day. If at night, nature called, the chamber pot was used rather than venturing outside to use the outhouse. I'm sure on many a cold night, it was much appreciated. In the morning the contents were emptied into the main slop jar, cleaned, and placed back under the bed for storage. The lid for the chamber pot is shaped exactly like the slop jar lid, and the handle is shaped after the pitcher handle. It was in this way that a wash set looked like a set; uniformity of shape for the lids, handles, continuity of body, and usage of embossment.

Covered Soap Dish: Base, Drainer, and Lid

The covered soap dish was used to hold the homemade or store bought soap and can be found in either oval or round shapes; the

Plate 672. Complete wash set, LILLY by Johnson Bros. This plate shows every piece available for a wash set. Back row left to right, master slop jar and lid, large pitcher and washbowl, and chamber pot with lid. Front row left to right, toothbrush holder, mug, covered soap dish, and small pitcher. *Anonymous collector* $2500+

over-all shape of the wash set determined this. The lid for the soap dish will be fashioned after the other the lids in the set, as will the handles. The drainer for a Flow Blue wash set will most commonly have a part of the pattern applied. Rarely will it be all white. It can occur, but for the drainer to be consistent with the set, in most cases it contained part of the pattern. The drainer will have a one half-inch whole in the center, with several smaller holes surrounding the larger. Their purpose was to allow the soap to "drain" after use. Drainers, whether from a wash or dish set, are the most fragile pieces of all, and the hardest to find.

Toothbrush Holder

The use of the toothbrush holder, as the name indicates, was the holding receptacle for the family's toothbrushes. It can also be called a brush holder, brush vase, and brush jar. They can be found in two shapes, and are the same as spoon holders shown in Plate671. The shape of the spout on the double spout version of the toothbrush holder will be fashioned after the pitcher. The purpose of the spout was to give the toothbrush holder a higher extension for the toothbrushes to rest on when held in storage. It is styled very similarly to a spoon holder, but because its shape matches the wash set body style, its use and purpose becomes a toothbrush holder.

Mug

The most controversial piece in a wash set is the mug. What was it used for and what to call it is the reason for the controversy. The mug, like the toothbrush holder, comes in two shapes.

The shape of the CHATSWORTH mug, in Plate 673, is why some collectors confuse it with being a creamer for a set of dishes. As we have seen for the toothbrush holder, spouts can have more use than to pour with. In many of the catalogs, the mug is called a drinking mug. Most dealers and collectors I questioned consider it a shaving mug. I think there is one thing we can determine with certainty, and that is, whatever its purpose, or given name, its use must have been something that would associate it with the wash set or else why would it be part of the set. We also know through catalog ads that shaving mugs were sold separately and with a more unique shape than the one sold with a wash set. See Plate 674, for an interesting view of the wash set mug.

Shaving mugs are more valuable to collectors than a regular mug, and this maybe why some call it so; or is shaving its real purpose? I wonder, if a woman purchased a wash set, what she would have called the mug and what she would have used it for? Could it be that the mug was a utilitarian piece and had several uses that could have been applied? Could the term "mug" be the best term to use for this piece? Whatever the name, or its use, the mug will remain an integral part of a wash set, and highly collectable.

Plate 673. Mug showing the two shapes it comes in, right is CHATSWORTH with two spouts on Gr-W12 body style, and ALBANY with basic straight sides on Gr-W11 body style. Both were produced by W. H. Grindley & Co. *Author collection* $225+ ea.

Plate 674. Mugs from a wash set, BOSTON right, from Gr-W3 body style, and CHATSWORTH from Gr-W12 body style. W. H. Grindley & Co. manufactured both of these mugs. This photo, especially for the CHATSWORTH mug, shows how they may have been used for a shaving mug. Also, because of the double spouts effect on the CHATSWORTH mug, it would be very difficult to use as a drinking mug. *Author collection* $225+ ea.

Chapter Four — Common & Rare: What to look for

An item may be quite rare for one collector, and be commonly collected by another. Rarity may be determined by region, the item or pattern collected, and how extensive a collectors search is. The country of Denmark tends to favor floral patterns, so a search there for Art Nouveau may be fruitless. New York may favor Art Nouveau, the Midwest floral, and the west coast may prefer trendy patterns. Some collectors enjoy acquiring oyster bowls, and thinking regionally, would consider the east coast as their best option for searching. If you think in terms of where it "should " be, and center your search in that area, you will never find it. The popularity in collecting Flow Blue today is known worldwide. In today's market, Late Victorian Flow Blue is everywhere, and highly sought after. The original distribution of Flow Blue has been distorted completely as items are bought here and sold there.

This chapter then, is about true rarity of individual items and patterns and how it can affect values. If you collect one particular pattern, it will help you to set up your own value chart for items needed to complete your set. Let me explain that last sentence further. There are collectors that will only buy pieces in "mint" condition, which is fine for that collector. However, if they have not acquired a teapot in their pattern as yet, and have passed on one that had some damage, they may, but the chances are better that they will never see one again. The English have a wonderful attitude towards collecting antique china. They acquire pieces for what they represent in history. The item may have been broken in five pieces and wired together, and they will buy and cherish it for what it represents. Remember this, if you see a damaged item you have been looking for to add to your collection, and you know it to be extremely rare, buy it! You can always sell it "if" you find a better one. The pleasure you will have viewing that item in "your" home will be worth it.

Collecting antiques is by choice, and the collection acquired will be by individual values, tastes, and income. The one main thing that will benefit all collectors is acquiring knowledge of the items they collect. In the field of collecting, knowing what is rare, and what is reasonably common, is a major factor in knowing and selecting items to add to your collection.

Why are some items or patterns rare, and some are not? It is my belief that if a particular pattern was popular in its day, than it will be just as popular in today's market. Likes and dislikes seem to stay constant from one generation to the next. The thought is, that with the popularity of a pattern in its day, then more would have been bought, and there should be more for collectors today. This is a reasonable theory, and we find that it does tend go this way, but not always. An example of this would be the Grindley pattern GRACE, produced on dish body style Gr-E. The shape of this body style, in addition to the patterns popularity, makes it extremely collectable and sought after by many. Now try and collect a set of it; very difficult.

What if you are collecting a pattern that was not so popular when it was originally sold? Then your acquiring a complete set can be complicated by availability. This can be further complicated when you learn of the rarity of some items, as opposed to other items in a set of dishes. The dedication of a collector may help them locate an item, but it does not determine the items rarity. If an item is extremely rare, then it will be that way for all collectors.

In the 1880s and 1890s, glass and silver or silver plate, was gaining enormously in popularity. It was a wealthy emulation for a middle class family to have ceramic dinnerware and a silver-plated tea set. With the increased sale of silver-plated tea sets, the sale of Flow Blue teapots saw a decrease. This lessens the availability of Late Victorian tea sets today. Late Victorian teapots are about as rare as you can get for this reason. In actuality, it is easier to locate an Early Victorian Flow Blue teapot than it is for a Late Victorian one. There are some reasons for this. In 1784, the Commutation Act reduced the tax on tea from 119% to 12-1/2%. This eliminated smuggling and the adulteration of mixing tea with other leaf substances. In addition a tax was imposed on silver that made buying a ceramic tea set more attractive.

With the increase in sales of glass pitchers, the sale of ceramic pitchers saw a decline. It is almost harder to locate Late Victorian Flow Blue pitchers today than it is to locate a Late Victorian Flow Blue teapot. Late Victorian teapots and pitchers are very rare items, in any condition.

I have polled many collectors and dealers, studied the internet auction sites, and recorded what items were being sold. In my extensive travels I keep a watchful eye for what is being offered for sale, and what I am *not* seeing for sale. I may determine bone dishes to be very rare, but in your locality, they are not. This chapter should not be considered an absolute, but rather a guideline. There will be those who disagree with my findings. Take the information listed, combine it with your own locality and experience, and form your own personalized list to better serve your collection.

The following list is of items and patterns separated by the rarity of each "individual" item or pattern. The emphasis is on items, rather than patterns. The lists are not so extensive that they will cover every pattern produced by every pottery. This would take a volume by itself. I have selected some patterns to include here, however, because I know of their rarity. I would not assume the knowledge of the availability of all patterns produced. It is suggested that you take the information on the patterns listed merely as information for "those" patterns. A particular pattern may be listed as common, and an item in that pattern will be listed as extremely rare; this can happen. As we went through the different body styles we gave each shape a dating label. Through that dating system, we will categorize whole blocks of patterns pursuant to their dating label. In so doing, we can better emphasize when the bulk of Late Victorian Flow Blue was produced.

The listed categories (*Common, Scarce, Rare, Vert Rare,* and *Extremely Rare*)are relevant to collecting Late Victorian Flow Blue. As a commodity, all Flow Blue is a rare. So when you see the common category, it merely means that those pieces or patterns are somewhat easier to find than others. We must also remember, that for every piece irreparably damaged, there is one less for collectors to choose from. The rarity of old Flow Blue is continuously changing. Because it no longer is produced, it only has one direction to go, and that is to become even more rare as time, and damage through accident and mishandling, takes its toll.

232

Common

Dish Set Items

Covered Sugar
Creamers
Gravy Boat
Oval Open Bowl
Plate 7"
Plate 9"
Platter 14"
Platter 16"
Saucers (small)

Patterns – Grindley
BEAUTY ROSE
HADDON
LORNE
ROSE
SPRING

Patterns – Johnson Bros.
HOLLAND
NORMANDY
STERLING

Dating Labels & Body Styles

Lace
AM-D
Gr-B
Gr-C
Gr-I
J&G-H

Scarce

Dish Set Items

Berry Bowl
Butter Pat
Cake plate 10"
Oval Covered Bowl
Platter 10"
Platter 12"
Relish Dish

Patterns – Grindley
ARGYLE
CLARENCE
DENTON
DERWENT
LAWRENCE
MELBOURNE
THE HOFBURG

Patterns – Johnson Bros.
DEL MONTE
DOROTHY
ECLIPSE
JEWEL
ST. LOUIS

Dating Label & Body Styles

1880s
AM-A
AM-B

AM-C
AM-I
Gr-A
JB-A
JB-B
JB-K
J&G-B
J&G-F

Rare

Dish Set Items

Bone Dish
Coffee Cup (small)
Gravy Boat/Attached Undertray
Oval Soup Tureen
Pitcher 5 ½"
Pitcher 7 ½"
Plate 8"
Round Charger 12"
Round Open Vegetable
Teacup (small)
Waste Bowl

Plate 675. Round Charger 12" in diameter, MELBOURNE. *Author collection $350+*

Patterns – Grindley
ALASKA
ALBANY
BEAUFORT
GIRONDE
PORTMAN
PROGRESS
SHANGAI
THE MARQUIS

Patterns – Johnson Bros.
CLAYTON
CORAL
FLORIDA
GEORGIA
GLENWOOD
PEACG
PRINCETON
SAVOY

Dating Labels & Body Styles

Transition
AM-G
Gr-D
Gr-F
Gr-H
Gr-J
Gr-N
JB-C
JB-E
JB-F
JB-H
JB-L
J&G-A
J&G-D

Wash Set Items

Mug
Pitcher (small)
Toothbrush Holder

Very Rare

Dish Set Items

Coupe Soup Bowl 8″
Covered Butter
Covered Sauce Tureen
Gravy Boat/Undertray
Oyster Bowl
Pedestal Compote (large)
Pitcher 6 ½″
Pitcher 8 ½″
Plate 10″
Platter 18″
Round Covered Bowl
Saucers (large)
Teacup (large)
Two Handle Cream Soup Cup
Undertray (oval soup tureen)
Undertray (sauce tureen)

Patterns – Grindley

CELTIC
CHATSWORTH
CLOVER
DOVER
FLORIDA
JANETTE
WAVERLY

Patterns – Johnson Bros.
ALBANY
BROOKLYN
MONGOLIA
NEOPOLITAN
THE BLUE DANUBE
WARWICK

Dating Labels & Body Styles

AM-E
AM-F
AM-H
Gr-G
Gr-M
Gr-O
JB-G
JB-I
J&G-C
J&G-I

Wash Set Items

Chamber pot
Covered Soap Dish

Extremely Rare

Dish Set Items

Baker 6″ (individual vegetable)
Butter Drainer
Coffee Cup (large)
Covered Jam/Jelly Jar
Covered Sauce Tureen/Attached Undertray
Demitasse Cup/Saucer
Demitasse Teapot/Sugar/Creamer
Double Salt
Eggcup
Fish Platter
Covered Honey Jar
Ladle (soup/sauce)
Meat Drainer 14″+
Original Packaging
Oval Platter 20″+
Pedestal Compote (small)
Pedestal Fruit Bowl
Pitcher 9 ½″
Pitchers (whole set for one pattern)
Plate 6″
Platter 6″
Punch Bowl
Punch Cup
Round Charger 14″+
Round Covered Bowl (small)
Round Soup Tureen
Salad Bowl

Sauce Boat Double Handle/Spout
Saucers (demitasse)
Spoon Holder
Teapot
Waste Bowl (small)

Patterns – Grindley
ALTON
ASHBURTON
ASTRAL
BALTIC
BURTON
CRESCENT
DELMAR
GIRTON
GLENMORE
GRACE
KEELE
KENT
MARLBOROUGH
SOMERSET

Patterns – Johnson Bros.
ASTORIA
ARGYLE

CLAREMONT
KENWORTH
PERSIAN

Dating Labels & Body Styles
Gr-E
Gr-K
Gr-L
Gr-P
JB-J
JB-M
JB-N
J&G-E
J&G-G

Wash Set Items
Drainer Soap Dish
Master Slop Jar
Pitcher & Bowl

Find below a few Plates showing examples of the *extremely rare* items. These gorgeous items emphasize the exquisite beauty of Late Victorian Flow Blue.

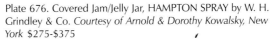

Plate 676. Covered Jam/Jelly Jar, HAMPTON SPRAY by W. H. Grindley & Co. *Courtesy of Arnold & Dorothy Kowalsky, New York* $275-$375

Plate 678. Demitasse teapot/sugar/creamer, IDRIS by W. H. Grindley & Co. Demitasse pot is 3 ½" to top of finial. It is extremely rare to have complete set. *Author collection* $1500+ set

Plate 677. Covered sauce tureen with attached undertray, MELBOURNE by W. H. Grindley & Co. *Author collection* $850+

Plate 679. Demitasse sugar & creamer, SHANGHAI by W. H. Grindley & Co. *Courtesy of Arnold & Dorothy Kowalsky, New York* $500+ set

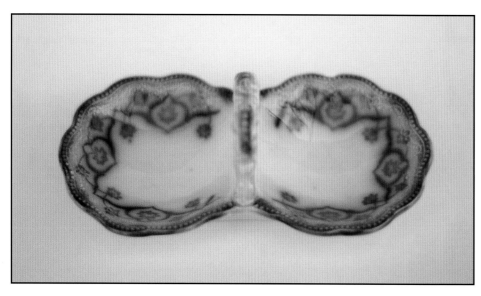

Plate 680. Double salt, HADDON by W. H. Grindley & Co. *Author collection* $250+

Plate 681. Pedestal fruit bowl, JEWEL by Johnson Bros. *Author collection* $500-$750

Plate 682. Complete set of seven pitchers, TOURAINE by Henry Alcock. Back for an encore; an extremely rare sight. *Courtesy Terry & Ann Potts, Illinois* $3000+ set

Plate 683. Platter 6", BEAUFORT left, ANTIQUE both by W. H. Grindley & Co. *Author collection* $125+ BEAUFORT, $50+ ANTIQUE due to color

Plate 684. Charger 15", GRACᴱ by W. H. Grindley & Co. *Author collection* $350+

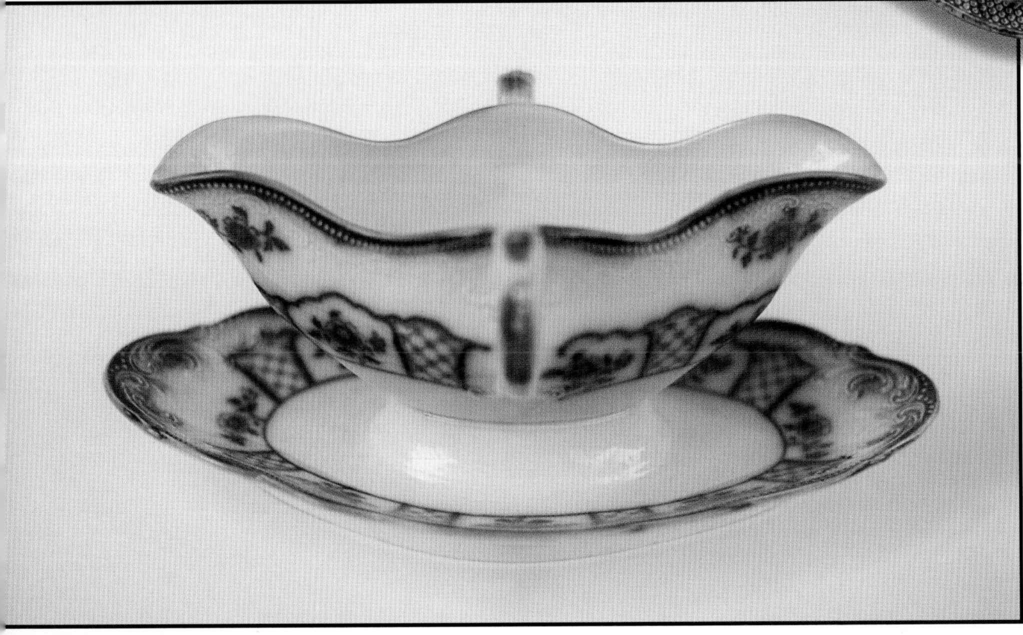

Plate 685. Sauce boat with double handles & spouts, MELBOURNE by W. H. Grindley & Co. *Author collection* $350+

Plate 686. Waste bowl, ARGYLE large on right, DENTON small both by W. H. Grindley & Co. Large waste bowl 5 ½" in diameter x 3 ½" tall, small waste bowl 5" in diameter x 3" tall. The small waste bowls are extremely hard to find, if you can find them at all. *Author collection* $275-$350 large waste bowl, $275-$400 small waste bowl

Plate 687. Fish platter, NORMANDY by Johnson Bros. Ltd. A magnificent example of a fish platter, with intact drainer. Due to the lack of pattern on the drainer there is some doubt if it is a set, but I am told it fits perfectly. This also could mean that drainers came with or without the pattern applied. *Courtesy of Warren & Connie Macy, Indiana* $2000+ for set

Plate 688. Honey jar on right and CELTIC covered sugar, both in Gr-E body style. Note the difference between the Gr-E normal body style sugar, and the honey jar made for the same body style. The body bulbous rim is higher on the honey jar, which is similar to the tureens for Gr-E. Honey jar. *Author collection* $350+

Plate 689. Box used for original packaging. See Plate 690 for contents.

Plate 690. Inside of box used for packaging a six cups and saucers in NORMANDY by the Johnson Bros. Ltd. This is an exceptionally rare find. *Courtesy of Warren & Connie Macy, Indiana* $unlimited

The Pottery Worker

Once a sight was selected for construction of a new pottery, the industrious entrepreneur did not always find a friendly reception from the local residents. Before the invention of gas or electric fired continuous tunnels, the old coal or wood fired bottle kilns were strong pollutants, and this is what the residents feared. Conditions would improve in the early 1900s, but the smog from the coal fired bottle kilns was horrendous during the 1880s. John Henry Weatherby discovered this when he left Tunstall in 1891 to build a pottery in Hanley. The local residents, because of their concerns of air pollutants, rebuked him.[1] Even after a site was agreed upon and construction was completed, there was not always a ready pool of willing workers to choose from. Harold Owen, *The Staffordshire Potter* writes: "The topography of the potteries is very varied. You may pass down a street to find that its exit is barred by a mound of ashes, higher than the houses, gathered from furnace fires long since extinct, or of shale, raised from a coal-pit."[2] Yet, the lively-hood of the potteries was so dependant on coal, they would shut down if the coal miners went on strike. Harold Owen states: "The traveler passing from one town to the other would see no interval between the six towns of which it is composed, and Tunstall ends, as Longton began, the pilgrimage, in a view of the walls of manufactories lining the main streets and the side streets – the conical tops of smoking ovens peeping over and behind them – with frequent interludes of two-storied shops and rows of cottage houses."[3] The coal fired bottle kiln did not punch the time clock. It stayed burning for the duration of its cycle, night and day. The air in and around "The Potteries," was filled with the black billowing and lingering smoke. It was not uncommon for the sun to be virtually blacked out by the smoke. In the early 1850s, the use of coal by the potteries in Stoke-on-Trent was set at 468,000 tons annually, and for the collieries and mills an annual use of 282,000 tons. This is a total annual use of 750,000 tons of coal. At this same time, the estimated annual value of earthenware produced by the potteries was 1,700,000 pounds, and 1,300,000 pounds of that value was exported. The value of the gold used on this earthenware was valued at 36,000 pounds.

Many of the pottery workers lived in "The Potteries" only with the hope of making enough money to move out of it. In reference to the carts delivering coal to the potteries Owen writes: "These coal-carts are followed by poor and ragged little boys and girls, sent out by their mothers – and often accompanied by them – to pick up in baskets, buckets, or folded dress-fronts, the small coal which falls from the carts."[4] These scenes were played out time and again throughout the potteries. If you were born and raised in the Potteries, it was life as usual. England was not unique in this. Similar scenes of poverty could be observed everyday in other parts of Europe, and the big cities in America as well.

Working at a pottery was a demanding job that required the employee to keep a timely schedule. Mike Mcphail in *The Northern Ceramic Society, April 1996* relates a story that takes place in August of 1896. It is about a twenty-six year old woman painter who worked at a large factory in Stoke-on-Trent. She lived in a small town and her job

at the factory was enameling, or filling in color on wares that already had been transfer printed. Mr. McPhail writes: "On entering the work shop which is a very large one with whitewashed walls and great beams I am greeted with the smell of turpentine, oil, and tar that we use for our work. There are fifty-four painters and gilders in the shop each sitting on a three-legged stool opposite tables ranged under the windows, which stretch the whole length on either side. Then we have a designer who makes the patterns and coloring, and a manager who has to see that they are executed accordingly, besides a lady who we take orders from and counts our work when it is finished."[5] Her working hours were: "Our hours generally are from half-past nine to six, but when we are very busy from eight till seven…if not there we get sent back for the day." Her breakfast break: "I have now painted a few flowers and it is nine o'clock which from then top half past is our breakfast time and if we should happen to work a minute after the manager will pop out of his office and call: 'Now you girls do know what time it is?' Which means we must stop work at once because if the inspector should find us working during meal times we are liable to a very heavy fine." When enameling toilet sets she writes: "At seven o'clock I have completed my four toilet sets which consists of from six to ten pieces each, the ewers and basins being very heavy to hold with one hand while working with the other. For this I can earn the sum of two shillings and eight pence."[6]

Even though the working conditions were not always the best, each factory had their share of dedicated employees who were the second, and third generation of their family to work at the same pottery. Susan Jean Verbeek writes of many such stories in her book *The Falcon Ware Story*. William Smith was a slip maker that worked for the J. H. Weatherby & Sons Ltd. pottery for at least forty years, beginning in 1898; his father worked for the company before him. Mrs. Florrie Wakefield retired from the Weatherby factory at the age of 84, in 1985, after working in the pottery industry for seventy-one years, starting at age thirteen, which was common in those days. Frank Clough was a flat plate printer who completed fifty years service in 1945, when he received his retirement check. John Woodward was a biscuit and glost fireman. In those bottle oven days this was an art in itself. The heat had to be carefully controlled and coal added every three hours. This was a vital part of the production as a quantity of weeks potting could be ruined by either over-firing or short-firing. Jack was the expert in this particular field, and was one of the highest paid workers at the time, earning 4.8 pounds per week. He fired glost ovens every fortnight, as well as the biscuit oven that took eighty hours. All sorts of tricks of the trade were used to achieve the correct temperatures, and working constantly in the heat and dust of the ovens must have been exhausting. He retired in 1945 having completed fifty years service with the J. H. Weatherby factory.[7]

H. Leonard Jones, the Vice-Chairman of J. & G. Meakin Ltd. in 1951, had already given a lifetime of service with over sixty-years. Bernard Hollowood in his book *The Story of J. & G. Meakin*, lists eighteen men who had fifty or more years of service at the Meakin factory. Some were sons of former employees. The eighteen men had a combined total of nine hundred forty-seven years between them. James and George Meakin, the co-founders, at one time had their homes inside the Eagle factory walls.[8] This was just recently made aware to me, and a subsequent photo was taken.

Plate 691. The two brick homes just inside the gates were the homes of James & George Meakin, co-founders of J. & G. Meakin Ltd. *Courtesy of Neil Ewens, England, May 2001.*

The information leading to the identity of the two Meakin homes came from an employee of the Wedgwood Museum, who at one time, was assigned to the Eagle Works. The dates when the two Meakin brothers were living in these homes are not known.

Many children were used as laborers at the potteries. The book *Adams Ceramics Staffordshire Potters and Pots, 1779-1998* gives us a little insight into this subject. "Despite the general improvements in trade, working conditions remained miserable almost beyond bearing and labor remained restless. Children from age six, girls and boys, did the simpler jobs and often had to endure the same long hours as older workers. On the other hand, better machinery meant job losses. Either way the workers had cause to feel threatened. Resulting riots were brutally put down. Parliament eventually reacted and in 1831 began a process of investigation. It commissioned inspections of mines and factories with particular reference to the employment of women and children. In 1833 Parliament compelled employers to give their child workers sufficient time off to obtain a basic education."[9]

Many conflicts arose as a result of the worker's union and management's constant bickering over conditions and wages, and there never seemed to be an equitable answer. In the beginning, the owners wanted to pay their potters good from oven, which certainly was a great idea from their standpoint. The workers felt the wares passed through too many hands before its final firing in the glost oven. They wanted pay to be based on good from hand, and eventually, this is how it went. Over the years the worker did gain ground, and in the 1880s at some potteries, the balance scale had tipped the other way in favor of the worker. *Adams Ceramics Staffordshire Potters and Pots* gives a little insight for the Adams Works, during the 1880s. "The late 1880s brought a recession in United Kingdom business and talk of higher import tariffs in the United States. Material and production costs were rising. Working conditions continued to improve gradually. Working

hours were fewer and wages rose so that each worker cost more and produced less in a given time. There had to be improvements in the factory, transport, communications, and selling to counter these other costs."[10]

The pottery owner, besides dealing with employee disputes, faced many other challenges in keeping his business profitable. Inflation, recession, wars, foreign tariffs, and keeping a good supply of raw materials are but a few. This, however, is an extensive subject and would take its own volume to be dealt with properly. For a further study see: Harold Owen, *The Staffordshire Potter*, Redwood Press Ltd., 1901, Bath, England and John Thomas, *The Rise of the Staffordshire Potteries*, R & R Clark Ltd., 1971, Bath, England.

Let us now take a look at the percentage of male, female, and child workers, and how it related to the pottery workforce. In 1901, there were four hundred factories in the Staffordshire District. They employed twenty-one thousand males, sixteen thousand females, and thirteen thousand children less than eighteen years of age.[11] The chart below shows the percentage of male and female workers in different countries for 1910, but does not separate out a figure for children under eighteen. It does, however, clearly show England and Austria as leaders in employing women.[12]

Country	Percent Male	Percent Female
United States	80.87	19.13
England	49.58	50.42
Germany	65.78	34.22
Austria	44.63	55.37

The following chart for the years 1901 and 1911, shows further detail on the percentage of male, female, and child worker by age. This chart is based on England's statistics only.[13]

Age	1901 Male	1901 Female	1911 Male	1911 Female
10-13 Years	44	28	1	-
13 Years	556	583	502	737
14 Years	848	1,202	739	1,254
15 Years	(a)	(a)	780	1,362
16 Years	(a)	(a)	748	1,374
17 Years	(a)	(a)	804	1,506
18 Years	(a)	(a)	720	1,448
19 Years	4,147	7,088	651	1,336
20-24 Years	3,767	4,954	3,164	5,103
25-34 years	6,705	4,164	5,450	5,140
35-44 Years	4,619	1,915	4,765	2,543
45-54 Years	2,860	888	2,962	1,129
55-64 Years	1,279	342	1,387	403
65+ Years	378	84	375	106

(a) Were not separately listed.

In 1901, for the chart above, of the 21,248 female employees, 14,711, or 69.2 percent were unmarried, the remainder being married or widows. For 1911, of the 23,441 female employees, 15,683, or 66.9 percent were unmarried, 6,739 were married, and 1,019 were widows. For 1911, this chart also shows that of the total employees, children under 18 represented 21.09 percent, and for all employees under the age of 35, women are favored.

Below is a chart for 1907. It shows the average number of persons employed in China and Earthenware factories at workshops in England, Wales, and Ireland. It is separated by male, female, and under or over the age of eighteen. Of those numbers listed below, over two-thirds represent the Staffordshire pottery district.

Type Employee	Male 18+	Female 18+	Male 18-	Female 18-
Wage earner	29,000	19,364	5,790	7,509
Salaried persons	3,015	286	299	84

The following chart shows the principal jobs at a pottery and what number, from an English group of potteries, held each position.[14]

Occupation	Men	Women	Boys	Girls
Plate Makers	68	-	-	-
Mold Runners	-	-	91	17
Towers (finishers)	-	24	-	68
Cup Makers	1	35	-	-
Batters-out	-	-	1	46
Mold Runners	-	-	-	44
Spongers	-	58	-	-
Casters	36	-	-	38
Saucer Makers	23	16	-	-
Batters-out	-	-	-	58
Mold Runners	-	-	53	8
Spongers	-	61	-	-
Machine Dish Maker	27	1	-	-
Mold Runners	-	-	24	-
Spongers	-	20	-	9
Hand Dish Makers	13	-	-	-
Hand Hollow-ware Pressers	106	-	-	-
Hollow-ware Jiggerers	33	-	-	-
Mold Runners	-	-	32	-
Spongers	-	40	-	15

The following chart shows a pay scale for 1910, and compares the United States with England, Germany, and Austria. The figure shown for the United States is the rate paid in cents for each job, and the figure given for the other countries is the percent the U. S. was paying higher per job over that countries rate. This chart clearly shows one of the reasons why the United States had problems competing against foreign trade.[15] Labor costs were creating too large a debit before the wares were even sold, thus creating higher market prices. This chart further shows significantly the higher wage paid to men over women in both skilled, and unskilled jobs.

Occupation	United States	England	Germany	Austria
Skilled Men:				
Jiggerman	45.66	146.94	206.24	303.71
Dish Makers	44.43	136.71	163.21	-
Pressers	36.54	138.05	209.66	161.19
Casters	38.91	180.74	142.88	390.05
Dippers	62.34	235.16	402.34	660.24
Mold Makers	51.45	138.75	220.96	393.76
Saggar Makers	45.28	222.28	223.43	361.57
Skilled Women:				
Banders and Liners	29.27	314.06	334.27	287.68
Unskilled Women & Girls:				
Finishers	25.78	315.14	-	368.73
Ware Dressers	16.29	305.22	256.46	279.72
Decalcomania Transferrers	20.42	276.06	323.65	341.99
Dippers' Helpers	16.55	187.83	388.20	292.18
Unskilled Men & Boys:				

Slip Makers	28.64	30.36	131.34	308.56
Batters-out	23.19	493.06	485.61	629.25
Mold Runners	18.74	432.39	373.23	462.76

The work at times was very hard, and there were many health hazards to be considered. At times a town, or given area would get stagnant with lack of available, or willing workers. This was realized, for example, when the Johnson Bros. in 1889 looked away from Hanley to build the Alexandra Works in Tunstall. The hope with this project was to draw employees from that area.[16] However, always present on the mind for the employee, and in union negotiations with the pottery owners, were the ever-present health hazards that existed for the pottery worker. Of those hazards the two greatest threats to the pottery worker was from the dust that permeated throughout the workplace, and from the smog created by the coal fired kilns.

In the beginning of the twentieth century, efforts were begun to improve this situation. In 1901, the Grimwades Ltd. Works of Stoke is credited with employing the first gas fired continuous kiln; it was called a "climax kiln." Beneficial by-products from this system, that the pottery owners would eventually realize, were that gas was cheaper to burn and gave better heat control. In this kiln, the ware was fired while packed in an iron cage on wheels, and it was possible to remove the ware mechanically without drawing the fire. It was claimed that the climax kiln was practically smokeless and reduced fuel consumption by eighty-two percent. For its use to be economic, however, the climax kiln had to be employed continuously day and night so that its use was restricted to the larger firms, and it was not in fact generally adopted.[17]

Because of rising coal costs, a genuine interest came for the use of gas which the pottery owners assumed at that time would be cheaper. The earliest experiments in gas firing made in North Staffordshire were undertaken by Blair & Co. of Anchor Road, Longton, before 1904. In that year, the North-Western Power-Gas & Electricity Corporation obtained the necessary powers to supply the Potteries. In 1905, it began to lay down plant at a Hanley factory for a large-scale experiment in the firing of china and earthenware by means of gas. Two years later, Alfred Meakin Ltd., Tunstall, successfully adopted gas firing for its kilns.[18]

Between 1910-1913 Conrad Dressler took out a series of patents for a kiln built in the form of a straight tunnel through which the ware to be fired passed on a series of loaded cars. The first tunnel kiln in the Potteries seems to have been that which Dressler installed at the timeworks of J. H. Barratt & Co. Ltd., Stoke, in 1912. Eventually, the continuous tunnel became the standard for the industry.

When considering the two main health hazards, the dust created by the manufacturing processes remained the worst for the pottery worker. For example, the glaze on Early Victorian Flow Blue contained about twenty-two percent lead. When you consider the about of Flow Blue produced, you realize the enormity of the situation. Through improvements in formulas and innovation, lead was eventually left out of the glaze. However, before that occurred it was the inhalation of a very fine dust from clay, grinding the flint stone, and carbonate or oxide of lead from the glaze that created the atmosphere for lead poisoning. Some steps were taken such as using water when grinding the flints and lead, and eating habits were corrected so that the employee did not eat where lead was present.

The lead poisoning was called "potters rot," and came from manual contact and dust in the air. The disabling affect comes very slowly, but is steadily progressive.[19] In the years of 1896-1898 there were 4,703 pottery workers working with lead, of those 1,085 were certified to be suffering from lead poisoning.[20] The average age at death in the year 1900 for a working potter was 46 ½, and for non-pottery workers it was fifty-four. This excess mortality was due to an increase in disease of the respiratory system.[21] They also found that the women employees had a higher rate of infantile mortality than women who were non pottery workers.[22]

An investigation was made by the departmental committee of the Home Office of the British Government, which sat from 1908-1910, and was appointed to "inquire into the dangers attendant on the use of lead in the manufacture of earthenware and china." The committee reported that in 1907 there were 63,000 persons employed in the manufacture of pottery in Great Britain, and of these, 48,000 were employed in North Staffordshire. It was found that 6,865 persons were employed in dangerous processes involving contact with lead that 23,000 were daily incurring danger from breathing dust, and that eleven percent of all pottery workers were exposed to the possibility of lead poisoning.[23] Below is a chart showing the number of cases of lead poisoning among dippers (glaze), dippers assistants (glaze), ware cleaners (which were the occupations most closely associated with the lead used in the pottery manufacturing processes), and also a break down by sex of those affected in Great Britain, 1899-1909 and 1912.[24]

Year	Dippers	Dipper Ass't	Ware Cleaners	Total Male	Total Female
1899	55	34	36	54	71
1900	41	32	50	51	72
1901	23	15	24	24	38
1902	15	15	21	16	35
1903	17	24	18	25	34
1904	28	20	26	20	54
1905	16	19	17	19	33
1906	28	23	19	28	42
1907	27	14	17	22	36
1908	27	25	22	28	46
1909	18	10	13	15	26
1912	15	9	14	19	19

As a result of the departmental committee of the Home Office of the British Government's investigation, a set of regulations was adopted and dated January 2, 1913. Most of the Staffordshire Potteries accepted these regulations, but some pottery owners did take them to arbitration. Soon, however, these regulations were part of standard practices. Some of the regulations adopted from this agreement were the use of a leadless glaze, and exclusions were incorporated for children and women for certain occupations requiring the handling of lead, such as dippers, dippers assistants, and ware cleaners. No sanding was done before a piece was hardened, absolute power was given to the pottery certified district "Surgeon," which allowed him to suspend or reinstate an employ back to work by certificate, and periodical medical checkups that could, depending on the occupation, be as much as once a month. Some jobs were designated that the worker must wear a respirator, and work areas had to be thoroughly ventilated. Because of this committee's foresight and involvement, the pottery industry as a whole is a safer place today.

Note: The complete set of regulations is very detailed and lengthy. I suggest for a complete study of this agreement, for those interested, see, U.S. Department of Commerce, *The Pottery Industry*, Washington D.C., Government printing office, 1915.

The Canals

The canals today represent an historic monument to the "communications revolution," but their beginnings were essential to the growth of the ceramic industry of "The Potteries." The Potteries is a landlocked area, and with the Trent and Mersey canal forming the "grand trunk" of the canal waterways, it gave the pottery owners a direct route to Liverpool, the countries main eastern shipping port. The main Grand Trunk runs from the Trent southwest of Nottingham to the Bridgewater Canal near Runcorn where it gains access to the Mersey.

Before the six towns (known as the Potteries) joined together to form the city of Stoke-on-Trent, they were small individual urban areas. Stoke became a borough in 1874, Hanley in 1857, Longton in 1865, and Burslem in 1878. Fenton and Tunstall were created urban districts in 1894, and in 1910 the six towns joined together to form the County Borough of Stoke-on-Trent. A few years later, in 1924, Stoke-on-Trent became a city.

In the middle 1700s, when the canals were first begun, trains had not been invented. It was very expensive to land carry the earthenware to England's shipping ports, and with their newly established competitors in France and America, a simpler, more economical means of transporting the finished goods was essential. With the canals in place, the ceramic industry and the Potteries as a whole were given a future and helped England to expand their world market. They were intended not only to ship the finished goods from the potteries, but also for shipping raw materials to them. The canals were successful because they were cheaper. For example, land transportation was 10d per ton per mile, and the canal reduced that cost to 1 1/2d per ton. The canal tolls were 27,142 tons in 1774 before the whole stretch was opened, and had risen to 123,707 tons by the time the railway opened in 1848. In the beginning years of the canal system, the original investors realized an impressive return on their money.[25] Their initial 200 pounds per share investment. By the time the mid 1780s had arrived, those shares had grown to 600 to 700 pounds.

The idea for the canals came from the brilliance of two men, Josiah Wedgwood, the goodwill ambassador who obtained the help and cooperation of landowners and politicians, and James Brindley, who engineered the project and actually had begun surveying the route as early as 1758. Although in at least one reference, Thomas Bentley, Josiah Wedgwood's partner, is credited with dealing with the Parliament and the conflicting views of the landowners or traders along the canal route.[26]

In 1766, an Act of Parliament authorizing the canals was issued, and Josiah Wedgwood, July 26th of that same year, cut the first sod which was located at a point half way between Tunstall and Burslem. Many people were present for this inauguration of the canals, and afterward a whole ox was roasted to celebrate. It is also known that Enoch Wood of Burslem was in attendance for this celebration. A canal committee was set up, and the following officers were appointed who would oversee the canal construction:

James Brindley - Survey General
Hugh Henshall - Clerk of the works
T. Sparrow - Clerk to the proprietors
Josiah Wedgwood - Treasurer

The canal is twenty feet wide on the top, sixteen feet on the bottom, and four foot six-inches deep. In all, the Trent and Mersey Canal is ninety-three miles long, with seventy-five locks and five tunnels. The canal was completed in 1777, eleven years later at a cost 300,000 pounds.[27] It was designed to carry boats seventy feet long, six feet wide drawing two feet six-inches and carrying twenty tons. One of the truly remarkable engineering feats of the project was the construction of the Harecastle Tunnel at Kidsgrove, which is located just north of Tunstall. The narrow tunnel was actually a hole dug through a hill and was 2880 yards long. The only way a barge could be "powered" through the tunnel was by the ship's crew, lying on their backs on the ship's deck. They would literally put their hands on the top of the tunnel and "walk" the barge through. Thomas Telford, an associate of Brindley's, modernized the tunnel in 1827. Telford built a new wider tunnel alongside it. It was wide enough to include a towpath. The canals, as designed by Brindley, were constructed with no calculations or drawings. Thus, no records exist today but the canals themselves. In all, James Brindley was responsible for engineering 360 miles of the canal network.

James Brindley was married December 8, 1765 to Anne Henshall at the Wolstanton Church. Two daughters were born to this marriage and one son, John Bennett (1760-1799) from whom Arnold Bennett the novelist descended. James died September 27, 1772, and never did see his project completed. Hugh Henshall, James Brindley's son-in-law, was the engineer who completed the project after James' death.

The reality of the economic changes left little doubt of what the canals meant to the ceramic industry in the potteries district, and all along plans were being made for additional Grand Trunk feeder canals. The Caldon was one of the additional canals built and connected with the main trunk at Etruria. Originally begun in 1773, and authorized by The Act of 1776, the Caldon Canal as it leaves the grand trunk at the Etruria Junction passes an easy route to Milton, Stockton Brook Locks, through the eastern rim of the North Staffordshire coal fields into the Churnet valley near Hazelhurst, and finally down to Froghall. The canal was first opened in 1777. Shortly after the Caldon Canal leaves the Etruria Junction, a mile or two out it passes by four famous potteries we have discussed earlier. In order they are the Eastwood Works, Hanley Pottery, Imperial pottery, and Eagle Works. Please see Plate 692 for a view of the Caldon Canal as it passed by the J. & G. Meakin Eastwood Works in Hanley. Also see Plate 693 for a further view of the Caldon Canal as it passes between the Eastwood and Imperial Potteries.

Plate 692. The boat "ALICE" being loaded for shipping to Liverpool, at the J. & G. Meakin Pottery. Note the two forms of packaging, crates and barrels used for shipping the wares. c.1900. *Courtesy of Bernard Hollowood, The Story of J. & G. Meakin, England.*

There were quite a large number of smaller canals that later became feeders to the Grand Trunk. In addition to the Caldon Canal, there are six other small stretches of canals in the pottery district that were incorporated into the Grand Trunk line. Below is a list of those canals and when construction was begun:
Newcastle Canal from Stoke to Newcastle – 1759
Caldon Canal from Shelton to Leek and Froghall – 1773
Froghall Canal from Froghall to Uttoxeter – 1797
Longport-Burslem Branch of the Grand Trunk – 1797
Shelton-Cobridge Branch of the Grand Trunk – 1797
Stoke to Lane End Canal – 1797
Newcastle Junction Canal – 1798

The canals did have problems with delays caused by repairs in the summer and frost in the winter. For example, canal traffic from Birmingham and Liverpool was closed for fifty-four days in 1820. Thirty of those days were due to winter frost. Even though the canals were cheaper than land carriage, they were slow and subject to stoppages. If goods were held up along the canal enroute to America, they were warehoused along the way at Runcorn and Anderton. Ninety-five percent of all Flow Blue exported to America left via Liverpool. The three major U. S. ports that England shipped to were Boston, New York, and Philadelphia.[28]

In 1836, 61,000 tons of earthenware and bricks and tiles were shipped to Liverpool via the canals for shipment to America and other Foreign Countries, and to Ireland, Scotland, and others. An additional 123,500 tons were shipped to other destinations using the canal system. In all, the Potteries for 1836, shipped 184,500 tons of earthenware from their factories. The railway system opened in 1848, and its initial purpose and use was to transport coal to the potteries. The new rail system was pretty much completed between the years 1868-1894, and in the beginning was not a real threat to the canals. Its initial affect, in competition with the canals, was on the passenger traffic. However, from its very beginning, it began to eat away at the amount of cargo being shipped via the canals. The chart below shows graphically how over time the rail system was cheaper, faster than the canals, and had fewer delays. The rail system eventually overcame the canals as the main shipping system for the potteries. The figures below are for weight of goods shipped, and are shown in 1,000 tons.

Canal	Rail	Year
1370	-	1819
1286	-	1840
1356	-	1849
1259	273	1850
1595	1245	1860
1563	2324	1870
1244	3369	1880
1076	4309	1890
1168	5587	1900
1130	6515	1906

Today, the Staffordshire canal network serves mostly the tourism trade and used for leisure by the local residents and sport fisherman. It also offers a scenic view of the countryside when traveled by boat, or casual walk along the towpaths. Many old and historic buildings, as well as many of the old potteries still standing, can be viewed on such excursions. Below are several plates showing different locations along the Trent and Mersey Canal, as well as the Caldon Canal as it leaves the Etruria Junction and passes by the Eastwood Works area. All of the following views were taken in August of 2000.

Plate 693. A view of the Caldon Canal in 1998, as it passes between the J. & G. Meakin Eastwood Works on the right, and the back of the Johnson Brothers Imperial Works to the left.

The following views were taken in the vicinity of Tunstall.

Plate 694. The Trent and Mersey Canal looking north, north of Tunstall. *Courtesy of Neil Ewins*, England.

Plate 696. This view is farther south towards Tunstall, and showing from the canal, the Tunstall District in the horizon. *Courtesy of Neil Ewins*, England.

Plate 695. This view is from the same point as Plate 694, but looking south towards Tunstall. *Courtesy of Neil Ewins*, England.

Plate 697. The same area as Plate 696, but looking north away from Tunstall. *Courtesy of Neil Ewins*, England.

The following views were taken farther south in Longport District.

Plate 698. The Trent and Mersey Canal as it passes by the Price & Kensington Pottery, Longport. *Courtesy of Neil Ewins*, England.

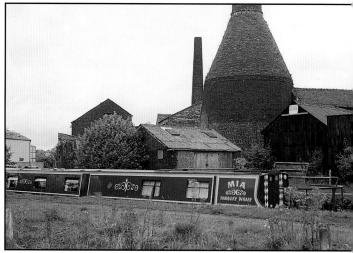

Plate 700. Another view of the Price & Kensington Pottery. In this view we see one of the original bottle kilns, and on the canal the excursion boat "MIA". *Courtesy of Neil Ewins*, England.

The following views were taken a little further south in the Longport District.

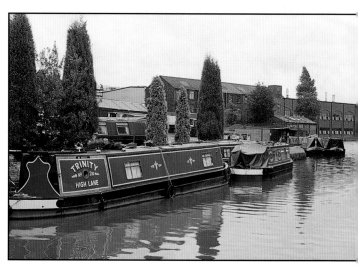

Plate 701. South of the Price & Kensington pottery the canal passes by the Dale Hall Pottery. We see the excursion boat "TRINITY" close by. *Courtesy of Neil Ewins*, England.

Plate 699. Another view of the Price & Kensington Pottery, as seen from the canal. *Courtesy of Neil Ewins*, England.

Plate 702. Another view of the same area as Plate 701. *Courtesy of Neil Ewins, England.*

The following views were taken still further south at the Etruria Junction; where the Caldon Canal enters the Trent and Mersey Canal.

Plate 705. Same point as Plate 704, but looking the other direction towards the Trent and Mersey Canal. Also showing two boats moored along the canal path. *Courtesy of Neil Ewins, England*

Plate 703. The Etruria Locks on the Trent and Mersey Canal, at the Caldon Canal junction. *Courtesy of Neil Ewins, England.*

Plate 706. The old Etruria Mill located at the Etruria Junction. *Courtesy of Neil Ewins, England*

Plate 704. The Etruria Locks going down to the Trent and Mersey Canal. *Courtesy of Neil Ewins, England.*

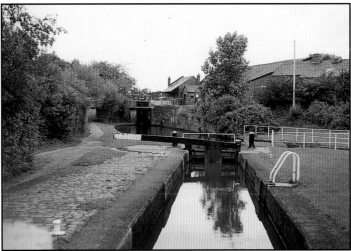

Plate 707. Here is another of the series of locks the boats pass through to get from the Caldon to the Trent and Mersey, or vice versa. *Courtesy of Neil Ewins, England*

The following views were taken going west on the Caldon Canal, from the Etruria Junction, and in the vicinity of J. & G. Meakin's Eastwood Works.

Plate 708. The Caldon Canal as it passes by the Eastwood Works. The canal is to the right of the building. *Courtesy of Neil Ewins, England*

Plate 709. A closer view of the Caldon Canal as it passes the Eastwood Works. *Courtesy of Neil Ewins, England*

Plate 710. This view is from the same point as Plate 709, but looking more to the right and showing the Johnson Bros. Imperial Works. *Courtesy of Neil Ewins, England*

Plate 711. Looking west on the Caldon Canal, and at a point further west from the Eastwood Works. *Courtesy of Neil Ewins, England*

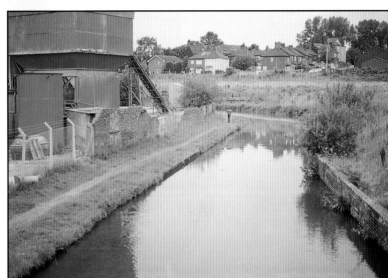

Endnotes – Chapter Five

[1] Susan Jean Verbeek, *The Falcon Ware Story* (London, England: pottery Publications, 1996)7

[2] Harold Owen, *The Staffordshire Potter* (Bath, England: Redwood Press Limited, 1901)339

[3] Ibid., 337

[4] Ibid., 338

[5] Mike McPhail for *The Northern Ceramic Society, Newsletter #102* (Stoke-on-Trent, England, April 1996)12

[6] Ibid., 13

[7] Susan Jean Verbeek, *The Falcon Ware Story* (London, England: Pottery Publications, 1996)18

[8] Bernard Hollowood, *The Story of J. & G. Meakin 1851-1951* (Derby & London, England: Bemrose Publicity Co. Ltd., 1951)31

[9] David A. Furniss, J. Richard Wagner, Judith Wagner, *Adams Ceramics Staffordshire Potters and Pots, 1779-1998* (Atglen, Pennsylvania: Schiffer Publishing Ltd., 1999)12

[10] Ibid., 13

[11] Josiah Wedgwood, M.P., C.C., and Thomas H. Ormsbee, *Staffordshire Potter* (New York, New York: McBride & Co., 1947)211

[12] Department of Commerce, E. E. Pratt, Chief, *The Pottery Industry* (Washington, D.C.: Government Printing Office, 1915)44

[13] Ibid., 423

[14] Ibid., 425

[15] Ibid., 45

[16] Robert Shively, research article, *The Story of the Johnson Brothers* (Kansas City, Kansas, May 1983)1

[17] R.G. Haggar, A.R. Mountford & T. Thomas, *The Staffordshire Pottery Industry, Well Street Pottery*, An Extract from The Victoria History of the County of Stafford, Vol.II, (Staffordshire, England: Reprinted by Staffordshire County Library, Edited by M.W. Greenslade & J.G. Jenkins, 1981)39, 41

[18] Ibid.

[19] Harold Owen, *The Staffordshire Potter* (Bath, England: Redwood Press Limited, 1901)274-5

[20] Ibid., 297

[21] Ibid., 278-9

[22] Josiah Wedgwood, M.P., C.C., and Thomas H. Ormsbee, *Staffordshire Potter* (New York, New York: McBride & Co., 1947)211

[23] Department of Commerce, E. E. Pratt, Chief, *The Pottery Industry* (Washington D.C.: Government Printing Office, 1915)440

[24] Ibid., 441

[25] Editors, *The Making of the Six Towns* (Hanley, Stoke-on-Trent, England: City Museum and Art Gallery)30

[26] Editors, *Thomas Bentley 1730-1780* (New York, New York: The Wedgwood Society of New York, 1975 reprint)44

[27] Josiah Wedgwood, M.P., C.C., and Thomas H. Ormsbee, *Staffordshire Potter* (New York, New York: McBride & Co., 1947)98

[28] Niel Ewins, *Journal of Ceramic History Vol. 15, Supplying The Present Wants Of Our Yankee Cousins...Staffordshire Ceramics and the American Market 1775-1880* (Stoke-on-Trent, England: City Museum and Art Gallery, 1997)91

Chapter Six — Marketing: Selling the Wares

Worldwide and U. S. Import Comparison

During the seventeenth century, making wares and selling them were much easier than during the Late Victorian period. Additionally the wares were produced on a much smaller scale. "The potter's oven at this period was small and dome-shaped, about 8 feet high and 6 feet in diameter; it was probably an up-draught kiln with several firemouths similar to that used in medieval times. Unglazed pottery such as butter pots and glazed flat wares, stacked with small pieces or 'bits' of broken pottery between, were exposed to the naked flame of the oven. Glazed hollow-ware pieces were placed in saggars to protect them 'from the vehemence of the fire which else would melt them down, or at least warp them'. The oven took twenty-four hours to fire and ten hours to cool before it could be drawn. It was lagged with clods of turf to conserve heat."[1] "The potter sold his ware to traveling crate men who carried it on their backs. Butter pots were made specifically for the dairymen using Uttoxeter market; these pots, which were unglazed, were not more than 6 lb. in weight and of 14 lb. capacity. A system of reckoning was already in existence in Plot's time which for hollow ware was based on content 'so that six pottle or three gallon bottles make a dozen, and so more or less to a dozen as they are of greater or lesser content'. Flat ware was 'reckoned by pieces and dozens' according to the 'different breadths'."[2] "It is evident that the North Staffordshire potter was dependent upon local materials and made utility articles for farmhouses and cottages rather than for the tables of the great houses; that he turned aside from making steens and piggins, kegs and pitchers to produce christening goblets, posset pots, and show dishes only when he received special orders for them. In manufacture he was probably assisted by members of his family and by a few laborers who worked on his farm or small holding, reserving to himself the dangerous but expensive operations of 'leading' because of the high cost of lead. Plot records this as 6 pounds or 7 pounds a ton. In his will John Colclough or Rowley (d. 1656) left to Thomas Wedgwood all his potting boards, implements, and materials 'belonging to the trade of potting' with the exception of 'lead and lead ore'. The potter-farmer probably did his own firing too because of the risk of heavy losses."[3]

For any form of manufacturing, with ambition, the business will evolve. As times change, a business will develop new and varied products, and new marketing techniques to sell them. For an English pottery to be successful, they not only had to keep up with current trends in designing their wares, but they also had to keep pace with marketing trends, less they be out-witted by their competitor. In England, the canal system, and later the railway lines were both moves towards increasing their world market. These two export conveyances were used to decrease the time it took to get the finished product to the consumer. As the ambitions of the North Staffordshire pottery owners grew, so did their line of wares. With the increase in the export market, new and varied means of marketing was inevitable, if not essential. Many of the English potteries during the last half of the eighteenth century, for marketing purposes, were using British merchants. One of the greatest problems with this system was a decrease in profit. This occurred because the British merchants were adding costs by being the middlemen in the business transaction.

As we entered the nineteenth century, American importers and American based marketing agencies, which in many cases were factory based, took on a more important role. The importance of the potteries dealing either through merchants or directly with American importers was all the influence needed when making decisions on new shapes or designs. "In McKendrick's 1964 study of Josiah Wedgwood's marketing techniques, considerable emphasis was placed on the role of Thomas Bentley who, as a merchant-partner, provided the necessary information on market trends. Subsequent writers have tended to over-emphasize this method of marketing, not explaining that few manufacturers had the benefit of merchant-partners to provide market information. In the case of some manufacturers with an extensive American trade, family representatives were sent to east-coast cities, or agencies with American importers were established. It was through links such as these that a thorough knowledge of market preferences was gained and a means of promoting wares was provided, which was vital to meet the increasing demand. Nonetheless, the proportion of manufacturers who had the benefit of direct American links was comparatively small. It is not a foregone conclusion that a direct link was established between all manufacturers and the American market."[4]

Apparently the J. & G. Meakin firm was ahead of their time, or at least experimenting by acting as their own agent. As early as 1854, they already had their own Boston outlet. This put the Meakin firm in a position to promote their own wares.[5] Although this outlet only lasted one year, and was not established again until the 1860s, it does give us a sense of direction that the marketing trends were taking. One of the problems in having a pottery "family" office was competing with the established American agencies. J. G. Meakin, through their Boston office, generated a little over 3,904 pounds worth of business, and was transacted with fifteen different American and Canadian importers; of which, only three came from the city of New York with an average value of 198 pounds. When you compare these figures with the well-established American firm of John C. Jackson based in New York, who had an average value of 420 pounds with his New York customers, it seems pale.[6] This does give cause as to why many Staffordshire manufacturers, even large concerns, tended to use established American importers as agents.

The first half of the 1800s was an experimental time for the Staffordshire potter as far as selecting the best marketing situation for their firm. Whatever the choice selected, the Staffordshire outlets in America functioned by using varied means. They would invite buyers to the office, travel with ceramic patterns to other districts, distribute printed circulars, newspaper advertising, and selling by auction were favored methods used. Links to American customers also provided for market research.[7]

The following chart shows the extent, and direction, of the English Foreign trade for 1911. It also shows, by value, the importance of the North American trade. The figures shown are in thousand pounds.

Country	Pound Value
United States	428,000
Canada	395,000
Australia	309,000
Argentina	279,000
India	232,000
Brazil	210,000
South Africa	133,000
New Zealand	125,000
France	87,000
Germany	81,000
all other countries	751,000
Total=	3,030,000

In the chart below, we draw a comparison between England and other leading ceramic producing countries that imported to the United States. The values shown are for china, Porcelain, earthenware, Parian, and bisque ware that were decorated, gilded, or ornamented, and are given in American currency. This chart was selected because the comparison involves a good part of the Late Victorian time period. The years covered are from June 30, 1892 to June 30, 1913.[8]

Year	Germany	England	France	Japan	Austria/Hungary
1892	1,597,304	2,659,490	1,081,900	330,495	6,344,708
1893	1,745,727	2,756,363	1,195,243	395,332	755,852
1894	1,418,906	2,011,395	830,931	332,656	521,850
1895	1,782,463	2,803,417	1,030,466	193,896	656,885
1896	2,501,743	3,249,761	1,276,548	386,376	727,553
1897	2,886,319	2,673,880	1,339,429	439,088	627,677
1898	1,986,974	1,917,128	767,358	312,337	486,937
1899	2,130,058	2,032,415	1,200,365	286,540	478,076
1900	2,619,737	2,225,128	1,269,071	371,038	495,545
1901	3,199,065	2,285,320	1,364,030	445,854	563,280
1902	3,423,975	2,130,177	1,399,618	468,104	642,976
1903	3,677,125	2,203,093	1,637,744	508,696	669,801
1904	4,400,803	2,330,159	1,684,616	710,879	767,690
1905	4,320,061	2,097,611	1,454,457	955,869	808,589
1906	4,736,641	2,129,022	1,708,459	1,523,870	931,604
1907	4,677,895	2,344,706	1,606,177	1,971,456	851,130
1908	4,856,892	2,397,234	1,869,660	1,448,594	910,224
1909	3,129,822	1,846,014	1,397,088	1,078,123	775,429
1910	3,510,159	2,129,555	1,488,114	1,250,202	735,350
1911	4,097,214	1,958,609	1,517,063	1,241,376	611,940
1912	3,564,028	1,692,851	1,258,549	1,227,561	576,714
1913	3,235,517	1,909,756	1,470,520	1,192,163	534,425

The chart below is for the same type of wares as the chart above, but here they are *not decorated, gilded or ornamented*. The years covered are the same as the above chart, June 30, 1892 to June 30, 1913.[9] When combining the totals from these charts, for each country, England's dominance becomes quite evident, with the exception of the war years.

Year	Germany	England	France	Japan	Austria/Hungary
1892	63,411	1,447,143	327,673	4,797	45,225
1893	82,277	1,567,569	331,227	10,541	51,168
1894	61,313	944,632	206,153	2,803	38,505
1895	90,503	1,628,563	284,629	1,135	43,978
1896	91,074	1,377,968	284,287	937	45,191
1897	92,011	1,120,123	253,671	835	30,400
1898	59,233	634,138	110,097	1,172	21,301
1899	63,181	720,059	190,403	3,335	17,511
1900	92,567	784,699	172,294	1,774	24,301
1901	122,403	645,175	179,686	2,212	43,866
1902	164,022	522,950	208,462	187	47,421
1903	194,573	558,704	226,374	5,728	42,528
1904	272,259	657,128	262,494	324	75,719
1905	263,550	512,990	255,477	994	80,380
1906	290,481	454,389	246,645	1,170	82,935
1907	347,407	509,615	271,612	2,506	87,919
1908	357,122	517,150	290,079	1,607	80,031
1909	338,424	343,090	274,652	1,005	79,208
1910	424,238	351,705	297,520	3,447	87,708
1911	473,925	302,660	260,417	2,549	82,325
1912	428,956	211,427	217,644	1,418	77,678
1913	508,001	238,083	226,523	2,728	117,346

In comparison, when considering the Late Victorian period as defined by 1880-1925, there were fewer avenues of marketing for manufacturers than there is for today's marketing. The Late Victorians were not fortunate enough to have massive magazine, radio, and television advertising campaigns. The English were able to market their wares in several ways. They are, but not limited to, advertising articles in the English pottery trade magazines, *The Pottery and Glass Trade Review*, *Pottery Gazette* from 1879, and its annual *Pottery Gazette Diary* from 1882, plus the ceramic trade magazines in America. They maintained, for any customer who requested them, factory sales catalogs with descriptions, and prices. The use of "trade cards," which depicted a new shape or pattern, was extensively used. There were also shows, like the great Philadelphia Exhibition of 1876, where many Staffordshire potteries were present and displaying a wide array of their ceramic wares. They also had advertising and sales offices in America, which were either an American based agency or in many cases, factory (family) based. American mail-order catalogs were available in the 1870s and 1880s, which advertised and sold English wares. These catalogs were beginning to be a way of life for many American city dwellers, urban areas, and the expanding western territory. Mail-order catalogs were most likely the greatest avenue that the English had in getting their wares to the rural American consumer. For each sale there was the hope, that through the word of mouth from a satisfied customer, a new one would be created. For the rural customer, leafing through mail-order catalogs was like dream weaving, and most certainly was their "wish book" connection to the big city life.

However the English potteries chose to market their wares, there were other entities that determined the success of the manufacturer. They also had to contend with slow times created by wars, diplomatic relations, economics, and tariffs imposed by the host country exported to. Tariffs could, and were intended to either increase or suppress goods being imported into the tariff-imposed country. In 1895, the Wilson Tariff Act reduced the amount charged to English ceramics from the McKinley Tariff Act of 1892. Because of this reduction, it was the hope of the English pottery worker to receive more pay. The American pottery workers in that same year (February 1895), suggested and offered that the English and American pottery workers joined together and form a common pottery union. They felt the common bond would force the pottery owners of both countries to increase their wages. Their efforts failed and this common union was never formed.[10] The chart below compares the McKinley and Wilson Tariff Acts.

Type of Ceramics	McKinley Tariff Act 1892	Wilson Tariff Act 1895
Decorated	60%	35%
Plain Ware	55%	30%

Below is a complete list of the years through 1913 that the United States imposed a tariff:

July 4, 1789
August 10, 1790
May 2, 1792
June 7, 1794
March 27, 1804
April 27, 1816
July 14, 1832
September 1, 1841
August 30, 1842
July 30, 1846
March 3, 1857
March 2, 1861
July 14, 1862
June 30, 1864
June 6, 1872
March 3, 1883
October 1, 1890
August 27, 1894
July 24, 1897
August 5, 1909
October 3, 1913

The pottery owners and their retail outlets knew in advance of the forthcoming McKinley Tariff Act. As a result, production was increased and sales were very brisk before the tariff was officially enacted. The 1892 tariff also emphasizes the bold move made by J. H. Weatherby when he opened the Falcon pottery for business in that same year. Something to note here also is nowhere in this book will you find a pattern or body style with a registration number that has an 1892 date. The McKinley Tariff created some fear and a slow period for the Staffordshire potteries, but these concerns were not prolonged. In 1893, we see many new dish and wash set patterns being registered, and put into production. Some of these patterns may have been designed in 1892, and their registry withheld until the following year. As several years passed and the news came for the Wilson Tariff Act of 1895, which reduced by almost half the amount of tariff added to imported ceramics, we find a tremendous increase in new body styles being registered 1895-1898 by the English potters. Let me emphasize this point. For the years 1895-1898 Grindley registered at least two new wash set body styles, three new dish body styles, and at least twenty-five new pattern designs. The Johnson Bros. comes close to matching those numbers. Many of the other potteries I have researched will also show dramatically increased production for

this period. It was only by recording registration numbers for body styles and patterns that we can first be made aware of what we have just discussed. I always have considered that my recording of registration numbers was the most important part of my research. Everyday, when new data is made clearer as a result, my theory is proved once again.

Catalog Marketing

Marketing is techniques used by wholesalers to sell more products. If through catalog marketing, they sold a set of dishes as a service of twelve, instead of a service of six, it meant a greater volume sale and more profit to the wholesaler. If they sold enough of those services for twelve dishes, not only did their volume and profit go up, but also their price from the manufacturer went down because their volume was up. This is just simple math, and basic business practices, as well as the backbone of the mail-order catalog trade, such as Sears Roebuck & Co. Their whole premise, in convincing their rural customer to buy a product through their catalog, unseen, was through cheaper prices. Cheaper prices, however, was only one point of a three point selling technique catalogs used. The three points are *name brand products*, *cheaper prices*, and a *solid guarantee*.

Plate 712.1903 Sears Roebuck & Co. catalog No.113, page 677. This is an excellent example of how Sears Roebuck & Co. formatted their catalog when marketing a set of dishes. It also lists all the pieces available for each of the four optional ways to purchase the set. *Reproduced with special permission from Sears Roebuck & Co. Archives, Hoffman Estates, Illinois*

In Plate 712 we see a typical ad from the 1903 Sears Roebuck & Co. catalog. If you look to the upper left corner of this ad headed "Our Reputation," there are two interesting things to note. As you read through this paragraph it lists for you, however unintentionally, who England's competition was. It states, "…would be of the very best grade of ware, made at the oldest established and best known potteries in England, France, Germany, or America." Just a small casual statement, but one providing evidence we can use to corroborate our theory of England's competition. The companies that produced these mail-order catalogs knew what would sell, and knew that name brand products (or a 'high profile' country name if you will) would help to sell those products faster. The second item in this paragraph to note is, "…we know that when our dinnerware or glassware is compared with any other dealers offer, our customers will find, quality for quality, our goods represent a savings of at least 25 to 50 percent." Marketers knew that to compete with city retail stores, they had to sell a product of equal or better quality, and sell it cheaper! Without this premise, the mail-order catalog business would never have survived.

To complete their three point selling technique, look to the paragraph in the upper right corner headed, "Our Binding Guarantee." It states, "We guarantee that if you order one of our sets of dinnerware or glassware, and do not find it in every respect better in quality and lower in price than what you could procure the same grade of ware for from any other dealer, upon return of the goods we will refund your money in full." This statement is quite interesting in that it notes all three points of the selling technique, *better in quality*, *lower in price*, and *refunds your money*. What a powerful statement, and due to the success achieved by mail-order catalogs, it worked!

Most items produced for sets of dishes or a wash set during the Late Victorian period were standard for the industry. When a pottery produced a new dish body style, they designed and produced every standard item for that new shape. However, when it came time to sell it to the wholesaler, it was sold by the piece. Most mail-order catalog houses took those individual pieces, and in most case, marketed them as a service of twelve with some variance as to what pieces were included. Today, with families having fewer children, twelve place settings seems hardly appropriate. However, during the Late Victorian period a service of twelve was very much appropriate.

This ad also depicts for us the four different versions Sears marketed their sets of dishes. If you bought any set of dishes from this 1903 catalog, you could only buy it in either a 100, 101, 56, or 80-piece set. The 100, 101, and 80-piece sets, which had a variance of pieces offered, were for a service of twelve, and the 56-piece set was for a service of six. The cost was kept down by leaving out some specialty items such as covered soup tureens, eggcups, and covered sauce tureen. Some marketed sets did include the soup and sauce tureens, but many times they were bought from the "also available" list. Most of the catalogs included a list of all items available, but to buy "only" from this list, the customer had to buy a certain minimum dollar amount.

In comparing the 100 and 101 piece sets, we see only a slight variation. Apparently, the 101-piece set was geared more for meals with soup as it includes soup plates. Below we show the differences between these two sets:

100-piece set	101-piece set
12 Breakfast plates	12 Soup plates
1 Covered Vegetable (2 Pieces)	2 Covered Vegetables (4 pieces)
1 Quart Size pitcher	None

The eighty-piece set is smaller because it only includes two sizes of plates, and does not include a covered butter, covered sugar, creamer, or any pitchers. Obviously, this set was designed for the customer who wished to buy a silver plated tea set, which was popular at the time, instead of the ceramic version produced by the pottery.

The fifty-six piece set was simple, basic, and provided for those desiring a service for six. The set was purchased by those with smaller families, or as an "add on" to the service of twelve for larger families. It becomes apparent that the catalog marketers tried to cover their entire customer base by providing an assortment of dinner sets to fill the need of every family, whether that family was small or large.

Late Victorian Flow Blue, in mail-order catalogs, was included and sold under their category of "Crockery Department." In this section, in addition to dinner sets, we find the different methods catalogs used to market individual items, as well as other types of sets. To form these groupings, the marketers selected from the available dinner set items (remember the potteries sold their wares individually), grouped them together, and called it something else. Below is a list of "dinner set items" that was marketed separately, and are listed as they appeared in the catalogs.

Fancy Tea or Coffee Cups/Saucers
Bone Dishes
Butter Plates (Pats)
Berry Dishes (Bowls)
Cake plates
Large Round Vegetable Bowls (Used for master berry bowls)
Relish Dishes
Covered Sugar/Creamer sets
Pitchers
Teapots
Cracker Jars
Covered Mustard pots
Eggcups
Covered Butter Dishes

Find below a list of different "sets" marketed, and the items, from an ordinary dinner set, selected to form them. These sets are unique only because of the names given to them by the marketers. If you have a Flow Blue set of dishes, that include to the items in the sets listed below, you could segment them out and called them the same name as the catalogs stated. There would be no difference.

Marketed Set	Items Used
Tea Set	Teapot, Sugar, & Creamer
Tea Set	* Waste Bowl, Teacup/saucers, 7" Plates, Pitcher, Cake Plate
Tea Set	* 15" Charger Tray
Berry Sets	Large Round Open Vegetable Bowl, 6 Berry Bowls
Ice Cream Sets	14" Platter, 6" or 7" Plates 12 ea.
Chocolate Sets	Chocolate pot, Sugar/Creamer, Cup/Saucers, 15" Charger
Oatmeal Sets	Cream Pitcher, ½ Pint Bowl (Berry), 8" Plate

Note: * same as above, but with these items included

The genius of marketers was in their simplistic approach. The marketers took common standard for the industry items, and simply grouped them together to form specialty sets. These sets were sales techniques that worked beautifully because they were formed for the ordinary man and their "customs" of the day. It was customary for people to enjoy ice cream, so they marketed an ice cream set. People enjoyed tea at a customary, specified time of the day, so they marketed a tea set.

Wash sets were marketed similarly as dish sets. They combined all, or some of the twelve pieces available, and formed what they hoped to be a marketable product. By combining fewer pieces in a set, the price would naturally be lower. Their purpose, with this approach, was that their catalog could then offer a product that was affordable by all. It was, after all, better to sell something rather than nothing. If they restricted themselves to selling only complete sets, they may not have been able to sell to the average customer. Below are most of the ways a wash set was sold and single items marketed separately. There may have been different ways, but these seemed to have been the most common. We must note here that all pieces were counted separately. For example, a chamber pot has two pieces, pot and lid. The soap dish could be sold two ways, with or without lid and drainer. In some very rare cases, a master slop jar was made with three pieces. The third piece was a drainer that fit into the top of the slop jar, and the lid rested on the drainer. This drainer was used to store the washcloth and allow it to dry. The three-piece master slop jar apparently had limited acceptance by the average consumer, and thus had very limited production. It is important to note here also, and this applies to dish sets as well, the items and sets listed here are for the American buyer. Thus, the terms used are those most commonly used by Americans. Other countries may have other pieces available and may have used different terminology.

Pieces in Set   Items Included

6 piece   Wash Bowl, Pitcher, Chamber/Cover, Soap Slab, Mug
10 piece * Small Pitcher, Brush Vase, Soap Dish (3 pieces)
12 Piece * Master Slop Jar/Lid
Note: * Same as above, but with these items included.

Single Items Marketed Separately

Soap Slab
Covered Soap Dish/Drainer
Chamber Pot/Lid (two sizes)
Master Slop Jar/Lid

Endnotes – Chapter Six

[1] R.G. Haggar, A.R. Mountford & T. Thomas, *The Staffordshire Pottery Industry, Well Street pottery*, An Extract from The Victoria History of the County of Stafford, Vol.II, (Staffordshire, England: Reprinted by Staffordshire County Library, Edited by M.W. Greenslade & J.G. Jenkins, 1981)4

[2] Ibid.

[3] Ibid., 5

[4] Neil Ewins, *Journal of Ceramic History Vol. 15, Supplying The Present Wants Of Our Yankee Cousins…Staffordshire Ceramics and the American Market 1775-1880* (Stoke-on-Trent, England: City Museum and Art Gallery, 1997)105

[5] Ibid., 126

[6] Ibid., 97

[7] Ibid., 101

[8] Department of Commerce, E.E. Pratt, Chief, *The Pottery Industry* (Washington, D.C.: Government Printing Office, 1915)85

[9] Ibid.

[10] Harold Owen, *The Staffordshire Potter* (Bath, England: Redwood Press Limited, 1901)241-246

Chapter Seven

Dating by Body Styles & Other Methods: Aging the Wares

This chapter brings together what we know about Late Victorian Flow Blue for dating purposes, which includes registration numbers, pottery marks, shapes, and body styles. This knowledge was combined to formulate a way to date the majority of Late Victorian Flow Blue. It only came after putting the different patterns in registration numerical order. By also categorizing the patterns and body styles, the full potential for this formula was made evident. First, the typical ways that a collector can date their antique china are discussed, and then the dating formula is presented. In most instances, it will prove very reliable.

Factory Marks

In most cases factory marks are applied under glaze. This is done at the same time and in the same application as they do for the pattern design. The mark is nothing more than a designed monogram that represents the producing pottery and as a symbol used for identification or ownership, as in identifying the pottery that produced the pattern and body style. A factory will from time to time, change their mark. When they did, it would be recorded in the English registries. The registries were not only a way of officially recording a mark, but were also done to protect themselves from "copy-cat" potteries. With an official registry in place, a researcher can go through them, year by year, and record the dates for each pottery and their marks; they are then able to write a book of marks. A book on marks will give you circa dates for the initial, and last dates of use for each mark. A mark will always be listed with a circa date because no one could be that accurate without using factory records. This window of time, from when the mark was first put in use to its last recorded use, represents its dating "window" of time. If a mark, for example, was first used in 1890 and its last recorded use was 1898, than this particular mark has a dating "window" of nine years. What this means to a collector who may own an item with this mark is with this knowledge they can now date their piece, "c.1890." There are other ways of dating this same piece, but for now your first basic step is by using the factory mark. If your piece does not have a factory mark, then you have discovered one of the reasons I have written this book, which is for pattern and body style identification. (Note: See paper written by Arnold A. & Dorothy E. Kowalsky on attribution at the end of this section.)

Now the question arises, "Why do I have two factory marks on my piece?" There are two reasons for this. One is the producing pottery may only have manufactured the piece and applied their mark, and then it was sold to another pottery, for their decorating application

and they also applied their factory mark. This was done quite often. A lesser pottery that did not have all the facilities necessary bought unfinished wares from larger potteries, and finished them with their own form of decoration.

The second reason for two factory marks comes as a result of a delay in the manufacturing process. In many cases, because of the popularity of a particular pattern for example, a backlog of pieces may have been produced in the bisque state. The pattern and factory mark would have been applied, but the final glost (glaze) firing had not been completed. If, for these pieces, a new factory mark was placed in use before the final glost firing, that new mark was added to the second mark, and the glost firing was done. Rather than take off the first (old) mark, it was left in place and the newer mark was placed along side of it. To date a piece with two factory marks, you would use the latest one. However, because of the second mark, you would know that the piece was produced towards the end of the "dating window" of the first, or oldest mark. Using factory marks is what I call "window dating," and even though marks are not specific to a single year, they are an excellent way to date your antique china to within a reasonable time period.

This next dating situation is not uncommon and was frequently done. In most cases when a pottery put a new pattern (lets call this new pattern "A" with a start-up date of 1893) into production it was applied (assigned) to a current body style, and in most cases, it was a "marriage" for the life of that pattern. Pattern "A" would have a normal two-year to five-year run, in some cases longer, and then go out of production. Then, five to ten years later, the pottery designs a new body style of dish, lets say 1901. They put it into production, design several new patterns for this new shape, and for what ever reasoning the pottery has it brings back pattern "A" and applies it to this new style. The factory will treat this pattern as though it were a new one. The pattern name and its original registration number will be applied to the back of each piece. How do you date such a piece?

This dating scenario brings out the importance of knowing a factories body styles, and what patterns were applied to them. The answer is quite simple. You have an 1893 pattern applied to a 1901 body style. So the piece would date to 1901. Remember, dating is when that particular piece was made. It could not have been made in 1893, as the pattern would suggest, because the style of dish was not in production at that time.

Attribution is a key aspect of dating Late Victorian Flow Blue. Following is an article written by Arnold A. & Dorothy E. Kowalsky:

Attribution – A Continuing Riddle

The English potting industry of the nineteenth century contains many uncertainties with regard to shapes, designs and manufacturer of origin. Although marked, in most cases, with an individual printed or impressed back mark – which often included the potter's name or initials and pattern name – the origin of the piece may not be that of the potter's name on the back mark or may be mis-attributed.

The first anomaly to consider is that nineteenth century earthenware/ironstone and graniteware manufacturers came in many sizes, from small to large, from one kiln to twenty or more kilns. The smaller the potter the less likely that he employed the use of individual workshops (on-site) capable of producing designs, colors, molds, shapes, coppers, etc. He would have, in all likelihood, gone into the open marketplace to procure his coppers, molds, etc. from specialized firms or individuals. In his *Staffordshire Chimney Ornaments*, Pitman Publishing Corp, New York, 1955, pp. 130-133, Reginald G. Haggar's *The Concise Encyclopedia of English Pottery and Porcelain*, Andre Deutsch, Ltd. England, 1968, Appendix II, pp. 276-289, contains an extensive listing of engravers.

The engravers, modelers, colorists, and mold makers helped to supply much of the coppers and models for molds for these smaller companies. As a result, a whole industry evolved to supply these smaller companies with their needs. It was not beyond these entrepreneurs of the nineteenth century to sell the same designs and molds to other potters that they supplied to the small ones. In his *Godden's Guide to Stone and Granitewares*, Antique Collectors Club, England, 1999, Mr. Godden notes four designers/modelers who not only registered their shapes but sold their designs: J. Chetwynd, George Sander; G. W. Reade; and Ralph Scragg. Amongst the potters who purchased these designs were J. Meir, George Wooliscroft, Hulme & Boote, Livesley & Powell and George Bowers.

The next conundrum to solve when considering back marks is: There were firms that continued on over long periods of time, even though there was change in family ownership. Examples that come immediately to mind are: Samuel Alcock; the various partnerships of Mason through to Ridgway, Ashworth, etc. It is known that even when partnership configurations change, many times patterns and shapes continued on. This is evidenced through T. J. & J. Mayer who evolved into Mayer & Elliot and thereafter Liddle Elliot & Son; the firm of Joseph Clementson's evolution to Clementson Brothers; and William Davenport's transition into the company of Henry Davenport,

et. al. Hereto, with Davenport and interesting occurrence is noted. John Wedge Wood and his brother Edmund T. Wood were brothers-in-law to William Davenport. Possibly over a drink of ale, John Wedge Wood asked William Davenport for permission to use his Union Shape (registered January 14, 1853), and upon payment of the bill [sic John Wedge Wood] Davenport may have said "why not."

John Wedge Wood and Edmund T. Wood were uncles to Henry Davenport, who also gave permission for one of his shapes to be used by the firm of John Wedge Wood. A shape registered by Davenport, Banks & Co. on January 12, 1863 titled "Corn on the Cob" was re-registered by Edmund T. Wood on October 31, 1863. As a side comment here, John Wedge Wood died in 1857 and his brother Edmund took over and continued the name of the pottery (i.e., John Wedge Wood) until 1876. Continuation of existing pottery names often occurs upon the death of a principal. The estate or partner may continue the trade name or style until termination of the business.

There has been very little research done on the late Victorian period and early twentieth century particularly as it relates to pottery histories and acquisition of potteries by owners other than the original. A potter who acquired a working pottery would often continue the successful patterns of his predecessor. Examples of this are the New Wharf Pottery, which was acquired by Wood & Son(s) Ltd. in 1894 with the pattern Conway being continued. Wood & Son(s) acquired the Stanley Pottery Ltd. in 1931 and continued the Touraine pattern. Additionally, potteries may have contracted out the manufacturing of pieces or even of entire patterns and lots. J. & G. Meakin (1851+), a high successful manufacturer during his time, commissioned George Jones (1861-1863) to manufacture all of his white graniteware and mark it accordingly.

One can go on and on with these examples and never even touch the surface or solve the riddle of proper attribution. When potters received orders that they could not fill they contracted them out. In Audrey M. Dudson's *Dudson, A Family of Potters Since 1800*, Stoke-on-Trent, England, Dudson Publications, 1985, Ms. Dudson notes that Dudson will often ask the client whose name he would like affixed to the piece; yours, mine or none. Cases like these abound and are cited in specialized books.

To the collector, the backstamp, shape and registry of your pieces definitely have a history of their own which – one that must be looked into!

Arnold & Dorothy Kowalsky
April, 2000

Registration Numbers: Patterns & Body Styles

Pattern and body style registration numbers are a great way to date your china, and it will be a smaller "dating window." This registration system came as a result of "The Patents, Designs & Trade Marks Act of 1883." These numbers were not only for the ceramic industry, but apply to a whole range of items except textiles. In the ceramic trade from time to time, a pottery would bring on to the market either a new pattern design, or a new body style of dish, which could be a wash set, a dish set, or a single item. In order to protect their new pattern or body style from being copied, the pottery owner, or his representative, would register the new design with the English registries. Upon proper verification, a number would be assigned to the pattern or body style. In many cases, the pottery owner would advertise this new pattern, or body style in one of England's ceramic and glass trade magazines. These registration numbers for us can be specific to a single year. If you were to research the official registration record, you could realize the month and day it was registered. The chart below shows the amount of years the new pattern or body style was protected by its registration number, and what years the protection window was increased.

Year	Length of Protection
1842	3 Years
1883	5 Years
1907	10 Years (plus additional 5 Years at Comptroller's direction)

These registration numbers are very reliable. Although, it is possible that the pottery owner had already manufactured the new pattern or body style somewhat earlier, or later, than it was registered officially. Also, a pattern may have been bought by another pottery, and registered or reissued at a latter date. This can happen. But without the official factory records, this is the best and most reliable data we have. The tragedy is that all pieces are not marked with their registration number. There are ways, however, even without a registration number that we can still date a piece, and within a smaller dating window than using factory marks. This will be discussed a little latter in this chapter.

Generally the registration number seen on an item will represent the pattern and will be printed under glaze, and placed on the back or underside of the item. A typical registration number will look something like this: Rd.No.123654. In some cases, and seeming to have occurred more in the 1910s and 1920s, the number may represent the body style. Body styles were registered, but not many of these numbers appear on the item. This is why, for the body style segment of each pottery covered, I included its registration number if known. This hopefully will lift the cloud of confusion for some body styles and pattern registration numbers.

Below is a chart showing registration numbers on the left, and the "dating window" it represents on the right. This chart is very accurate, and can be used with confidence. To further explain its use, the numbers on the left are a range of registration numbers recorded for patterns and shapes. The dates those registration numbers represent are shown to the right. This form of registration was first put into use January 1, 1884, and replaces the old "diamond mark" system that was in use 1842-1883. To give you an example, the registration number for the pattern ARGYLE by W. H. Grindley & Co. is Rd.No.289457. If you look at the chart below, you will notice that this Rd.No. fits in between the numbers 289,291-311,177. When you look to the right of those numbers, you will see the dates of Nov.28, 1896-Dec.22, 1897. This tells us that this pattern was registered between those dates, and would indicate to us the dating window for the pattern ARGYLE. Let's carry this scenario a step further. Because the registration number 289457 is so close the first number listed, 289,291, it would be reasonable to assume that ARGYLE was probably registered in December of 1896. If instead the number for ARGYLE was 311,167, it would be reasonable to assume that it was registered December 1897.

Registration Numbers	Dates Registered
1-18,868	Jan.1, 1884-Dec.15, 1884
18,869-39,953	Dec.15, 1884-Dec.21, 1885
39,954-63,874	Dec.21, 1885-Dec.21, 1886
63,875-87,324	Dec.21, 1886-Nov.17, 1887
87,325-114,048	Nov.17, 1887-Nov.17, 1888
114,049-139,295	Nov.17, 1888-Nov.29, 1889
139,296-165,353	Nov.29, 1889-Jan.27, 1891
165,354-185,824	Jan.27, 1891-Jan.5, 1892
185,825-205,137	Jan.5, 1892-Dec.30, 1892
205,138-224,604	Dec.30, 1892-Dec.28, 1893
224,605-247,418	Dec.28, 1893-Jan.9, 1895
247,419-266,237	Jan.9, 1895-Nov.21, 1895
266,238-289,290	Nov.21, 1895-Nov.28, 1896
289,291-311,177	Nov.28, 1896-Dec.22, 1897
311,178-329,512	Dec.22, 1897-Nov.28, 1898
329,513-348,670	Nov.22, 1898-Nov.4, 1899
348,671-367,216	Nov.4, 1899-Dec.6, 1900
367,217-384,526	Dec.6, 1900-Dec.12, 1901
384,527-401,621	Dec.12, 1901-Dec.3, 1902
401,622-424,184	Dec.3, 1902-Jan.5, 1904
424,185-447,602	Jan.5, 1904-Jan.3, 1905
447,603-471,608	Jan.3, 1905-Jan.3, 1906
471,609-491,472	Jan.3, 1906-Nov.19, 1906
491,473-517,231	Nov.19, 1906-Dec.7, 1907
517,232-530,717	Dec.7, 1907-Dec.29, 1908
530,711-552,897	Dec.29, 1908-Nov.20, 1909
552,898-570,588	Nov.20, 1909-Sep.26, 1910
570,589-592,431	Sep.26, 1910-Nov.17, 1911
592,432-610,963	Nov.17, 1911-Nov.23, 1912
610,964-629,940	Nov.23, 1912-Dec.22, 1913
629,941-644,055	Dec.22, 1913-Nov.24, 1914
644,056-648,254	Nov.24, 1914-May 6, 1915
648,255-656,583	May 6, 1915-Jul.5, 1916
656,584-660,416	Jul.5, 1916-May 16, 1917
660,417-664,322	May 16, 1917-May 28, 1918
664,323-672,512	May 29, 1918-Nov.6, 1919
672,513-680,282	Nov.7, 1919-Jan.11, 1921
680,283-688,220	Jan.11, 1921-Feb.16, 1922
688,221-696,323	Feb.16, 1922-Mar.2, 1923
696,324-709,012	Mar.2, 1923-Nov.6, 1924
709,013-717,778	Nov.6, 1924-Dec.15, 1925
717,779-726,866	Dec.15, 1925-Jan.27, 1927
726,867-740,897	Jan.27, 1927-Oct.3, 1928
740,898-749,695	Oct.3, 1928-Oct.30, 1929
749,696-758,458	Oct.31, 1929-Oct.4, 1930
758,459-771,135	Oct.4, 1930-Feb.5, 1932
771,136-779,893	Feb.6, 1932-Jan.24, 1933
779,894-788,498	Jan.25, 1933-Dec.17, 1933
788,499-797,486	Dec.17, 1933-Oct.26, 1934
797,487-806,973	Oct.27, 1934-Oct.5, 1935
806,974-815,888	Oct.7, 1935-Oct.19, 1936
815,889-825,248	Oct.20, 1936-Jan.4, 1938
825,249-834,429	Jan.5, 1938-Mar.3, 1939
834,430-837,945	Mar.4, 1939-Apr.10, 1940
837,946-843,242	Apr.10, 1940-Mar.22, 1945

Below is a chart showing *the use of the diamond mark system*. This system was in use from 1842-1883. Because this book defines the Late Victorian Period as 1880-1925, the last three years of the diamond mark registry is the first three years of the Late Victorian Period. For this reason, I have included it here and will only show the codes for those four years.

Plate 713. Here we see the diamond mark as used for the pattern IDEAL II by W. H. Grindley & Co. The date it represents is deciphered as follows. The "IV" at the top of the diamond represents what class the item is. In this case it is "Ornamental designs in earthenware (and porcelain), ivory bone, and other substances". The number "6" on top is the day of the month. The number "2" at the left of the diamond is the parcel number. The letter "K" to the right is the year it was registered, and the letter "B" on the bottom is the month it was registered. So for our example, using the chart below, the date would be October 6, 1883.

Year Code
J - 1880
E - 1881
L - 1882
K - 1883

Month Code
A - December
B - October
C - January
D - September
E - May
G - February
H - April
I - July
K - November
M - June
R - August
W - March

Because most of the potteries covered in this book were mainly in the export trade, there was a need to protect the body style sold in the exported country. When an English pottery brought out a new body style for sale in the U. S., in most cases, the pottery owner would apply for a U. S. Patent. In so doing, a dated application was filled out, and after a period of time to confirm the legitimacy of the application, it was approved and a patent number was issued. These U. S. patent applied for and issue dates are another excellent way to date an item. It is possible to find pieces marked with either the patent application date, or the date that the patent was officially issued. It has been my experience that the U. S. Patent date will correlate very closely with English pattern registration numbers. For obvious reasons, if the item had the application date on it, it would make it an older piece than one with the issue date applied.

For an illustration of how all the dates can correlate with one another, let's look at the pattern ARGYLE by W. H. Grindley & Co.:

Pattern Rd.No.	Body Style	U.S. Patent Applied	U.S. Patent Issue
Rd.No.289457	(Dec.1896)	Dec. 28, 1896	February 2, 1897

With this kind of corroborating dates, we can very accurately date the inception of the pattern ARGYLE, by using its Rd.No. However, we know that a pattern could have a one, five, or more years of a production run. So any piece of ARGYLE, even though its inception date was December of 1896, could in reality, have been produced one, two, three or more years after this date. This is where the date applied for can make a difference. Pieces with this date applied for on them can be dated very close to the original start up date. I personally have six, six-inch plates in the pattern ARGYLE that have the patent applied for date on them. I feel that I can date those six plates between December 28, 1896 (patent applied for date), and February 2, 1897 (patent issue date). Below see Plate 714 for an example of a U. S. Patent pertaining to Gr-A, the body style ARGYLE was applied to.

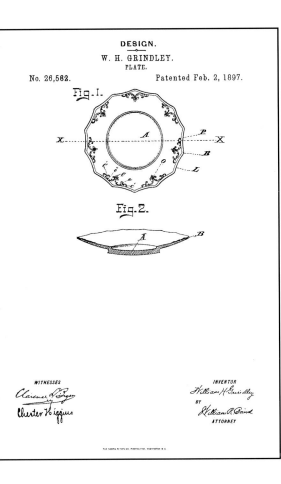

DESIGN.

W. H. GRINDLEY.

PLATE.

No. 26,582.   Patented Feb. 2, 1897.

Fig.1.

Fig.2.

WITNESSES   INVENTOR

Clarence L. Bryan   William H. Grindley

Chester Higgins   BY

                                                 William R. Baird

                                                 ATTORNEY

UNITED STATES PATENT OFFICE.

WILLIAM H. GRINDLEY, OF CONGLETON, ENGLAND, ASSIGNOR TO WILLIAM
S. PITCAIRN, OF NEW YORK, N. Y.

DESIGN FOR A PLATE.

SPECIFICATION forming part of Design No. 26,582, dated February 2, 1897.

Application filed December 28, 1896. Serial No. 617,276. Term of patent 3½ years.

To all whom it may concern:

Be it known that I, WILLIAM H. GRINDLEY, a citizen of Great Britain, residing at Congleton, in the county of Chester, England, have invented a certain new and original Design for a Plate; and I do hereby declare the following to be a full, clear, and exact description of the same, reference being had to the accompanying drawings, forming a part hereof.

In the accompanying drawings, which form part of this specification, Figure 1 is a top plan view of a plate embodying my design, and Fig. 2 is a section of the same on the plane of the line x x in Fig. 1.

The following are the leading features of my design:

The dish has a circular depression A at its center. Its outer edge is in the shape of a many-sided polygon, each side of which, as P, is slightly concave, and which is slightly rounded at each angle, as B. Just within the edge of the dish and parallel therewith is a slightly-depressed continuous line L. At each corner of the polygon is an embossed ornamentation O, raised very slightly above the surface of the dish. This ornamentation O consists in each case of a trifoliate figure C, supported from beneath on each side by a reversed curved scroll C', terminating in a long and short branch, as c and c', and the main boundary line of which is interrupted by small projections, as c''.

What I claim is—

The design for a dish substantially as shown and described.

In testimony whereof I have signed this specification in the presence of two subscribing witnesses.

WILLIAM H. GRINDLEY.

Witnesses:

WENDELL C. WARNER,

JOHN H. COPESTAKE.

Plate 714. Here we show an actual patent applied for by William H. Grindley for his body style Gr-A. It shows the application date of December 28, 1896, and the issue date of February 2, 1897. It is interesting to note the detail, as far as measurements, that went into this application. *Courtesy of Deborah Joiner, Texas*

Shapes/Body Styles

        The main purpose of chapter seven is to give you tools that will help you to date Late Victorian Flow Blue. So far we have discussed factory marks, and various ways to use registration numbers; these are all obvious ways of dating. This particular section, Shapes/Body Styles, is prefatory to the last section in this chapter. Its main purpose is to show the differences between Early, Middle, and Late Victorian Flow Blue. This will be accomplished by descriptive, as well as visual differences. Generally when discussing ceramics, shapes and body styles would be one and the same. However, for this section, and the last, there is a difference. The goal here is for you to be able to recognize Late Victorian dishes (not necessarily Flow Blue) through its shape (over all look of the piece), and the dishes body style (embossing, edge treatments like scallops etc.). Many of you already know most of what we are about to discuss, but in an effort to be thorough, I will take it step by step.

        Think of Early, Middle, and Late Victorian Flow Blue as three distinct entities, because they are. Each period of Flow Blue's production had its own particular shape that we can see. For the three periods of production, for the sake of this exercise, consider the Early as "primitive," Middle as "coming of age," and Late as "refined." This analogy is a little raw in its make-up, and even over simplified, but it makes a point. The point made here is whatever elegant design Late Victorian Flow Blue evolved too came from the development of the Early, and Middle periods of production. What these styles are, and when they changed, becomes a point of interest were dating is concerned. Another analogy that we can use is a comparison to autos. If we look at the style history of the same model of car, from any manufacturer, and select the 1950, 1980, and the 2000-year models, you would see three distinctly different automobiles. As time, styles, and the world around us changes, so does the style of autos. Dishes are no different; they evolved because style and change demanded it. Below are two charts. The first one restates the years of production for each of the three periods of Flow Blue production. I have put 1920s as the ending date for Late Victorian because this is when I believe the end came for Flow Blue. I know it was still in production, however limited, as late as the 1930s+, but 1920s seems to be the cut-off period. The second chart brings out descriptively the visual differences between the three periods. For each characteristic, I have put what I consider to be the most commonly or typically seen.

Early Victorian, 1835-1840 to 1850s
Middle Victorian, 1860s to 1870s
Late Victorian, 1880s-1890s to 1920s

Characteristic Trait	Early Victorian	Middle Victorian	Late Victorian
Embossed Beading	None	Minimal/Large	Small/Prolific
Body Thickness	Thickest	Medium	Thinnest
Bone Dishes	No	No	Yes
Butter Pats	No	No	Yes
Cup Plate/saucer	Yes/Yes	Yes/Yes	No/Yes
Cup Shape	Paneled	Paneled	Round/Embossed
Embossing	Limited	Limited	Profuse
Glaze	Pitted/Ruff/Glassy	Smooth/Glassy	Smooth/Glassy/Depth
Handled Cup	Limited	Limited	Mostly
Handles	Ornate	Ornate/Plain	Plain/Embossed
Hollowware Shape	Paneled	Paneled/Oval	Oval/Rounded
Pattern Design	Oriental	Esthetic/Floral	AN/Floral
Plate Edge	Paneled	Paneled/Smooth Round	Embossed/Scalloped
Platters	Paneled Rectangle	Paneled Rectangle	Rectangle/Oval
Scalloped Edge	None/Hint	None/Faint	Faint/Deeply
Stilt Marks	Top/Bottom	Top/Bottom	Bottom
Sugar/Creamer	Large/Paneled	Medium/Paneled	Oval/Embossed
Tureen Lids	Paneled/Embossed	Paneled/Embossed	Scalloped/Embossed

Below are some photos that will visually demonstrate the differences of style in shapes and body styles. I do have one minor glitch here, but one I think we can overlook easily enough without too much distraction. There was such little Middle Victorian Flow Blue produced, and as a result, I have no pictures to exhibit. However, the Middle period of production resembles the Early period more than the Late. The differences in style are greater between the Middle and Late than the Middle and Early. With this thought in mind, once you get the visual differences established between the Early and Late style of dishes, you will have reached the point this section is trying to accomplish. I would also make a further point, that a certain amount of continued personal comparison would help to establish the differences more firmly for you.

Plate 715. Early Victorian plate, AMOY by W. Davenport & Company, 10" in diameter. This plate was produced c.1844 and displays beautifully the Early "look". *Courtesy of Terry & Ann Potts, Illinois* $150+

Plate 716. Now we show you the same plate as Plate 715, but have added a Late Victorian plate for comparison. Notice the paneled edge of the AMOY plate, and the scalloped edge of the MELBOURNE plate. Also notice the difference in patterns, the difference in "flow", and that the MELBOURNE plate has embossing on the edge with the AMOY plate having none. MELBOURNE plate 8" in diameter. *Author collection* $60-$80

Plate 717. Here we show a tea set in SCINDE by J. & G. Alcock. This Plate gives you a good visual look of the teapot, sugar, creamer, paneled plates, cups and saucers, and platter. *Author collection*

Plate 718. Late Victorian platter for comparison with the platter in Plate 717. NORMANDY by Johnson Bros. Ltd., 16" across. Notice the scalloped embossed edge. *Courtesy of Terry & Ann Potts, Illinois* $225+

Plate 719. Early Victorian pitcher, AMOY by W. Davenport & Company. Please note the paneled look, and no scallops on rim. *Courtesy of Terry & Ann Potts, Illinois* $400+

Plate 720. Late Victorian pitcher, NORMANDY by Johnson Bros. Ltd. 7 ½" tall. Take note of round bulbous shape, and scalloped embossed edge of spout rim. *Courtesy of Terry & Ann Potts, Illinois* $400+ due to pattern popularity

Plate 721. Three styles of cups. right to left MELBOURNE (Late 1903) cup & saucer, MALTA (Late 1880s) cup & saucer, and AMOY (Early) cup, saucer & cup plate in front. This is such a great example, with excellent distinction of how the Early period of dishes evolved to the Late. MELBOURNE & MALTA, *Author collection.* AMOY, *Courtesy of Terry & Ann Potts, Illinois.*

Plate 722. right, Late Victorian teapot, PORTMAN by W. H. Grindley & Co. Ltd., 6 ½" to top of finial, and Early Victorian teapot, AMOY by W. Davenport & Company. Please note the differences in the finials, handles, the paneled look of the Early teapot, and the scalloped embossed look of the Late teapot. PORTMAN, *Author collection* $650+. AMOY, *Courtesy of Terry & Ann Potts, Illinois* $800+

Dating Formula

Now that you have gained a good understanding of and seen the visual differences of the three periods of Flow Blue production, we now can take that knowledge and move forward with the learning process by concentrating our efforts on Late Victorian for dating purposes.

Throughout my years of research, I have accumulated as many registration numbers for patterns and body styles as I could locate. I started with the Grindley pottery, and as I completed the research for that firm, I began to put all of his pattern and body styles in registration, numerical order. As this list grew in quantity, certain trends became evident. At first I thought maybe these trends were only unique to the Grindley pottery, but then I did several years of research on the Johnson Bros. factories. After I put their patterns and body styles in the same numerical order, I found their wares to be following the same style trends. I wondered why it was so evident at that point, and had not shown up before. The reason is because all I had previous to categorizing, was a hodge-podge pattern list with no order to it. I continued my research with the J. & G. Meakin and Alfred Meakin firms, and even though there were slight differences (mostly with Alfred Meakin), they both followed the same style trends as I had seen with the other two potteries researched. It was through these style trends, and the changes they caused on Late Victorian dishes, that my dating formula became evident. The formula is very simplistic in its design and readily understood.

There seem to be four trends that the Late Victorian period followed in design; so the formula is divided into four dating sections:

1880s
Scroll (1890-1899)
Lace (1899-1907)
Transition (1906-1925+)

Starting in 1837, when her reign began, Queen Victoria of England was creating most style trends. Her affect was far reaching and included the Arts, furniture, cloths, homes, etiquette, and mannerisms, as well as the dishes Victorians used to eat with. There were other style trends that coexisted with the Victorian style. La Belle Époque, meaning "The Beautiful Epoch," refers to the era starting in the 1870s, and continued up to World War I. It was a time when there was an illusion of peace and prosperity that pervaded in America and most of Europe, and throughout this period many new styles of decoration were introduced. As we moved into the 1880s, the "aesthetic movement" that began in the 1860s, was gaining in popularity. Many people had grown tired of the gaudy and unpractical designs so much apart of the Victorian style. The aesthetic movement seemed to be tied to beautiful designs, graceful lines, and in many of the patterns, simple geometric designs were used.

1880s

Aesthetic and simple floral type patterns were in demand, and very much apart of the 1880s. Of the four dating sections, the 1880s is the one most distinctly different in both style and pattern design. The 1880s dish was still somewhat thicker in body than the other three, and would remain this way until c.1890. The color choice for many of the 1880s style of pattern was brown, green, and slate blue, although many beautiful Flow Blue patterns can also be found for the 1880s. Below is a series of Plates depicting the 1880s shapes and aesthetic look in an assortment of items and patterns.

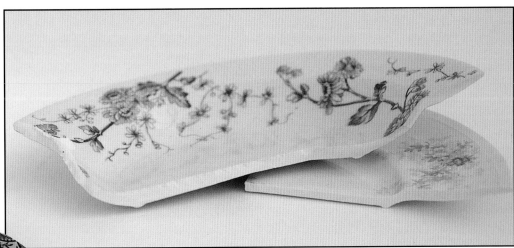

Plate 723. This Plate shows graphically the difference in the body thickness between the 1880s style, and the other three dating sections of the Late Victorian period. The top plate section is SPRING (1886), unknown floral on Gr-P body style (1900). *Author collection*

Plate 724. DAISY (1885) aesthetic pattern on typical 1880s body style. *Author collection*

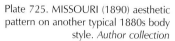

Plate 725. MISSOURI (1890) aesthetic pattern on another typical 1880s body style. *Author collection*

Plate 726. JAPANESE (1880) right, SHAKESPEARE (1882) plates. The brown colored patterns on these two plates, represent the aesthetic movement quite well. *Author collection*

Plate 727. Here are two gravy boats, right in whiteware in Gr-G body style (c.1906), MALTA (1887) showing the typical square body the wares often came in during the 1880s. Both were produced by W. H. Grindley & Co. Ltd. Take note of the extreme differences in style that occurred in the 19 years that passed, between the manufacture of these two gravies. *Author collection*

Plate 728. Square open vegetable bowl, SPRING (1886) by W. H. Grindley & Co. Ltd. During the 1880s most open vegetable bowls were either square or rectangle, instead of round and oval shaped. *Author collection*

Plate 729. Pedestal compote, MERSEY (1889) pattern by W. H. Grindley & Co. Ltd. Take note of the square look of this compote. *Author collection*

Plate 730. Teapots, right PORTMAN (1899), and MALTA (1887), both by W. H. Grindley & Co. Ltd. Notice the square look to the MALTA teapot, but the beginnings of the round or oval shape that will predominate the later part of the Late Victorian period. *Author collection*

1890s

In his book, *The Story of J. & G. Meakin*, Bernard Hollowood states, "Between 1890 and the end of the First World War the pottery industry suffered severely from cyclic fluctuations in trade. This was a period of intense competition between potter and potter, nation and nation. Years of boom, full employment and profit were followed by years of depression, cutthroat prices and loss: the pottery industry moved by fits and starts and many businesses failed to stay the course. The worst sufferers were, as always, those firms that devoted most of their energy to the export trade, for in a slump the overseas markets are the first to shut their doors and cancel orders."

Competition during the 1890s was very sharp indeed, and for a pottery to "stay the course," it had to pay particular attention to what their customers wanted. In the United States by 1890, women were gaining in civil rights, and were looked to more by manufacturers as the decision makers and especially when it came to the home. In the book *This Fabulous Century 1870-1900* by the editors of Time Life Books, New York, New York, they discuss the beginnings of Marshall Fields & Co. From Marshall Fields very beginning as a store retail clerk, he learned very quickly how to deal with his female customers. Marshall was so gifted at selling to women, that he soon started his own firm using the motto, "Give the Lady what she wants." By 1890, Marshall Fields was doing thirty-five million in annual sales.

Women were becoming more aware of their figures as well. The year c.1890, saw for the first time, dresses being made without the customary "bustle." What were women of the 1890s telling the firms that manufactured products for them? "Thin, was in." The English potteries picked up on this very quickly, because we see starting in the beginning of the 1890s the body of their wares becoming very thin, and ads in the catalogs for their wares were advertising, "extremely thin, yet strong and endurable." Yet, at the same time, there was still a market for the heavier White Ironstone/Stoneware, but its popularity was beginning to fade.

In 1892, George Elliot Meakin took over the J. & G. Meakin factory from his father who had died. This came at a most difficult time for the factory, for it was a time when competition was very fierce. George took a long look at the market, and what the public was demanding from the ceramic producers. In that same year, without further adieu, he set the factory to work on developing a formula for a "semi-porcelain" body; "give the lady what she wants," thin, yet strong and endurable. Look back to Plate 723, and you will see the dramatic difference of thickness that occurred almost overnight. The successful potteries were responsive to what their customers were saying. Below is a chart that compares the characteristic traits of the four dating sections of Late Victorian production.

Trait	1880s	Scroll	Lace	Transition
Embossed Beading	Large/Minimal	Small/Prolific	Small/Prolific	Rare/None
Body Thickness	thickest	Thinner	Thinnest	Thinnest
Embossing	Limited	Profuse	Profuse	Limited
Glaze	Smooth/Glassy	Glassy/Depth	Glassy/Depth	Glassy/Depth
Hollowware	Square/rectangle	Oval/Round	Oval/Round	Oval/Round
Scalloped Edge	Faint	Small	Large/Pronounced	Faint/Small
Sugar/Creamer	Largest	Medium	Smaller	Smallest
Type Patterns	Aesthetic/Floral	AN/Floral	AN/Floral	AN/Floral

The Scroll Dating Period, 1890-1900

Once we reach c.1890, the Scroll dating period begins. Platters and bowls are now round and oval in shape, and plates will now have gentle scallops and simple scroll type embossing on the edges. Teapots, sugars, and creamers are reduced in size. The body of the wares is thinner than the 1880s. Patterns are usually floral with some Art Nouveau that became popular c.1890. The Scroll dating period extended for about ten years.

The Lace Dating Period, 1900-1907

In late 1899, the Lace dating period begins with Grindley's Gr-C body style. The Gr-C body style first appears in the SS 1900 Sears Roebuck & Co. catalog. It states, "The design is the first for this pottery, and was produced to compete against the Haviland China Co.; of which, up to this day, was the only pottery to produce such a style of dish." The Gr-C body style was the first of this style to be made, or at least advertised in the catalogs. The differences in style between the Lace and Scroll dating period are the extensive embossing of the plates for the Lace period and the deeply scalloped edge. Grindley quickly followed with more Lace type body styles, which included Gr-B, Gr-K, and Gr-L.

The Lace period, with some overlap, was produced from Oct. 1899-1907. Plate 731 is from the 1903 Sears Roebuck & Co. catalog, and shows the Lace type body style. Even though you have seen many examples of Late Victorian dishes already, the other Plates that follow will show further representations from the four dating periods.

Plate 731. Page 685 from the 1903 Sears Roebuck & Co. catalog shows us the look of the Lace style of dish. The top set of dishes is Grindley's Gr-B body style, in the middle is the Johnson Bros. JB-C body style, and the bottom one is the Johnson Bros. JB-K body style. Note the pattern MELBOURNE being sold in the Sears catalog for the first time. The catalogs from 1900-1907 are full with the Lace type of body style. *Reproduced here with special permission from Sears Roebuck & Co. Archives, Hoffman Estates, Illinois*

Plate 733. Lace, right, berry dish, PORTMAN, 1880s berry dish, MOSS ROSE on Favorite body style. Both by W. H. Grindley & Co. Ltd. *Author collection* $40+

Plate 734. Lace plate and cup, MELBOURNE by W. H. Grindley & Co. Ltd. This plate shows the embossed Lace edge on the plate, and rim of the cup. *Author collection*

Plate 732. Transition Creamer, TOKIO by Johnson Bros. *Courtesy of Terry & Ann Potts, Illinois* $225+

Plate 735. l to r, Lace 6" oval bowl, PORTMAN (1899), 1880s 6" rectangle (oval) bowl, FLORA (1890), Scroll 6" oval bowl, ARGYLE (1897), all by W. H. Grindley & Co. *Author collection*

Plate 737. Lace series of pitchers in assorted patterns. Gr-B body style by W. H. Grindley & Co. Ltd. *Author collection*

Plate 736. Transition series of pitchers in assorted patterns. Gr-I body style by W. H. Grindley & Co. Ltd. *Author collection*

Plate 738. Lace series of pitchers in assorted patterns. Gr-C body style by W. H. Grindley & Co. Ltd. *Author collection*

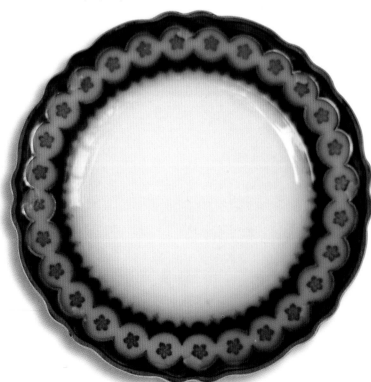

Plate 739. Transition plate, GRANBY (Gr-O, 1906) by W. H. Grindley & Co. Ltd. *Author collection*

The Transition Dating Period, 1907-1925+

The Transition dating period follows the Lace. It is named transition because there are body styles from that period that date from the true Victorian look to the look of modern times; they are transitional. In the Transition period we see that scalloped edges, for the most part, completely disappear. There is very little embossing on the plate edge, and the hollowware becomes smoother, has much less embossing, and is more cylindrical in shape. Many of the plates are now completely smooth and round. The transition style of plates once again resemble the 1880s style, but are now thinner in composition, and the patterns applied to them are differently styled and have a newer "modern" look.

The Dating Label

Below is a chart listing the dating label for each body style produced by the four main potteries covered in this book:

W. H. Grindley & Co. Ltd.

Scroll	Lace	Transition
Gr-A	Gr-B	Gr-H
Gr-D	Gr-C	Gr-I
Gr-E	Gr-K	Gr-N
Gr-F	Gr-L	Gr-O
Gr-J	Gr-P	
Gr-M		

Johnson Bros. Ltd.

Scroll	Lace	Transition
JB-F	JB-C	JB-A
JB-H	JB-D	JB-B
JB-I	JB-K	JB-E
JB-M		JB-G
JB-N		JB-J

Alfred Meakin Ltd.

Scroll	Lace	Transition
AM-D	AM-A	AM-H
AM-E	AM-B	
AM-F	AM-C	
AM-I	AM-G	

J. & G. Meakin Ltd.

Scroll	Lace	Transition
J&G-A	J&G-B	J&G-I
J&G-G	J&G-C	
	J&G-D	
	J&G-E	
	J&G-F	
	J&G-H	

The old catalogs show how the start-up dates for these four dating periods fit year-by-year as the catalogs progress in date. There is overlap. The key is the year each body style first went into production. These dates demonstrate the current trends for the trade. Some body styles were favored and kept in production for long periods, and there were patterns sold as open stock. Also, some of the well-to-do firms may have been farther advanced than their competitors, and some lesser potteries may not have been able to keep up with the trends. However, you can feel confident dating Late Victorian dishes by using the tools given; consider it a bonus if they are well marked, including the registration numbers. Sometimes we have unmarked pieces that are questionable, such as a plate in which the body style is round and smooth on the edge (and you believe it to be a Transition dating period) but the thickness of the body is more like the 1880s dating period. In this scenario, thickness rules; it belongs to the 1880s dating period.

Embossed beading seems to be the hardest for some to date. If the beads are large and the body is thick, it belongs to the 1880s dating period. If the beading is small, and the body is thin, it belongs to the Lace dating period. Before you can attribute a piece to a particular dating period, it must have at least some of that period's attributes, and none of another's.

There will be "gray area" pieces that will be difficult to date, and even impossible, but the method works.

Bibliography

Batkin, Maureen, *Gifts for Good Children, The History of Children's China, Part II 1890-1990*, Ilminster, Somerset, England: Richard Dennis Publications, 1996.

Birks, Steve, *web site: netcentral,co.uk/steveb*, England.

_____, */allpotters/1057*.

_____, */potteries/burgess*.

_____, */potteries/doulton*.

Binns, Charles F., *The Story of the Potter*, Strand, England: George Newnes Limited, 1898.

Blacker, J.F., *The ABC of English Ceramic Art*, London, England: Stanley Paul & Co. Ltd., 1911.

Bunt, Cyril, G.E., *British Potters and Pottery Today*, Leigh-on-Sea, England: F. Lewis Publishers Ltd., 1956.

Burgess, Arene, W., *A Collector's Guide to Souvenir Plates*, Atglen, Pennsylvania: Schiffer Publishing, Ltd., 1996.

Cluett, Robert, *George Jones Ceramics, 1861-1951*, Atglen, Pennsylvania: Schiffer Publishing, Ltd., 1998.

Collard, Elizabeth, *Nineteenth-Century Pottery and Porcelain in Canada, Second Edition*, Kingston & Montreal, Canada: McGill-Queens University Press, 1994.

Conroy, Barbara J., *Restaurant China, Volume 1*, Paducah, Kentucky: Collector Books, 1998.

Copeland, Robert, *Blue and White Transfer-Printed Pottery*, Pembrokeshire, England: CIT Printing Services Ltd., 1982.

_____, *Spode's Willow Pattern and other designs after the Chinese*, Essex, England: Studio Vista, 1980.

_____, *Spode & Copeland Marks*, and Other Relevant Intelligence, London, England: Studio Vista, First Edition 1993, Second Edition 1997.

Dieringer, Ernie & Bev, *White Ironstone China, Plate Identification Guide 1840-1890*, Atglen, Pennsylvania: Schiffer Publishing Ltd., 2001.

Dudson, Audrey M., *Dudson, A Family of Potters Since 1800*, Stoke-on-Trent, England: Dudson Publications, 1985.

Editors, *The Guardian and East Kent Advertiser*, Kent, England: January 10, 1920.

Editors, *The Making of the Six Towns*, Hanley, Stoke-on-Trent, England: City Museum and Art Gallery.

Editors, *The Pottery and Glass Record*, Stoke-on-Trent, England: April, 1921.

_____, February, 1928.

_____, October, 1928.

_____, November, 1928.

_____, August, 1955.

Editors, *The Pottery Gazette*, Stoke-on-Trent, England: February 1, 1904.

_____, July 1, 1908.

_____, April 1, 1909.

_____, June 1, 1909.

_____, April 1, 1910.

Editors, *The Pottery Gazette and Glass Trade Review*, Stoke-on-Trent, England: October 1, 1923.

_____, April 1, 1926

_____, December 1, 1928.

_____, May 1, 1930.

_____, June 1, 1931.

_____, November 1, 1933.

_____, November, 1946.

_____, August, 1955.

_____, February, 1963.

Editors, *Sheerness Times*, Sheerness, England: May 22, 1930.

Editors, *The Sentinel*, Stoke-on-Trent, England: Newspaper, March 9, 1926.

_____, September 17, 1999.

Editors, *The Stone Guardian*, Stone, England: Newspaper, June 19, 1937.

Editors, *This Fabulous Century 1870-1900*, New York, New York: Time-Life Books, 1970.

Editors, *Thomas Bentley 1730-1780*, New York, New York: The Wedgwood Society of New York, 1975.

Ewins, Neil, *Journal of Ceramic History Vol. 15, Supplying The Present Wants Of Our Yankee Cousins…Staffordshire Ceramics and the American Market 1775-1880*, Stoke-on-Trent, England: City Museum and Art Gallery, 1997.

Finegan, Mary J., *Johnson Brothers Dinnerware*, Statesville, North Carolina: Signature Press, Inc., 1993.

Fleming, J. Arnold, *Scottish Pottery*, Glasgow, Scotland: Maclehose, Jackson & Co., 1923.

Furniss, David A., J. Richard Wagner, Judith Wagner, *Adams Ceramics Staffordshire Potters and Pots, 1779-1998*, Atglen, Pennsylvania: Schiffer Publishing Ltd., 1999.

Gaston, Mary Frank, *A Collector's Encyclopedia of Flow Blue China*, Paducah, Kentucky: Collectors Books, 1983.

_____, *Collector's Encyclopedia of Flow Blue China, Second Series, Identification and Values*, Paducah, Kentucky: Collectors Books, 1994.

Glendenning, Sharon and Janice Kobach, *Flow Blue Handbook*, Privately Published, Vol. I, 1994, Vol. II, 1995.

Godden, Geoffrey A., *Ironstone & Granite Wares*, Suffolk, England: Antique Collectors' Club Ltd., 1999.

_____, *Encyclopedia of British Pottery and Porcelain Marks*, New York, New York: Bonanza Books, 1964.

Godden, Geoffrey A. and Michael Gibson, *Collecting Lustreware*, London, England: Barrie & Jenkins, 1991.

Haggar, R.G., A.R. Mountford, and J. Thomas, *The Staffordshire Pottery Industry, Well Street Pottery*, An Extract from The Victoria History of the County of Stafford, Vol. II, Staffordshire, England: Reprinted by Staffordshire County Library, Edited by M.W. Greenslade & J.G. Jenkins, 1981.

Hampson, Rodney S., M.A., *Churchill China*, Heritage Series Vol. 5, Keele, England: The Centre for Local History, Department of History, University of Keele, 1994.

_____, *Churchill China Great British Potters Since 1795*, Stoke-on-Trent, England: The Centre for Local History, Department of History, University of Keele, 1994.

_____, *Longton Potters 1700-1865*, Stoke-on-Trent, England: City Museum & Art Gallery, Journal of Ceramic History Vol. 14.

_____, *The Northern Ceramic Society, Newsletter No.115, Pottery Jotteries*, Stoke-on-Trent, England: September, 1999.

Henrywood, R.K., *An Illustrated Guide to British Jugs, From Medieval Times to the Twentieth Century*, England: Swanhill Press, 1997.

Hoener, Norma Jean, *Flow Blue China: Additional Patterns and New Information*, Flow Blue International Collectors' Club, 1996.

Hollowood, Bernard, *The Story of J. & G. Meakin 1851-1951*, Derby & London, England: Bemrose Publicity Co., Ltd., 1951.

Jenkins, J.G., *A History of the County of Stafford, Vol. VIII*, London, England: Oxford University Press, 1963.

Kowalsky, Arnold A., for *Northern Ceramic Society Journal*, Volume No. 17, Stoke-on-Trent, England: self published, 2000.

Kowalsky, Arnold A. & Dorothy E. Kowalsky, *Encyclopedia of Marks On American, English, and European Earthenware, Tea Leaf, and White Ironstone*, Atglen, Pennsylvania: Schiffer Publishing, Ltd., 1999.

Mankowitz, Wolf, & Reginald G. Haggar, *The Concise Encyclopedia of English Pottery and Porcelain*, London, England: Andre Deutsch, Ltd., 1968.

McPhail, Mike, for *The Northern Ceramic Society*, Newsletter #102, Stoke-on-Trent, England: April, 1996.

Milbourn, Maurice and Evelyn, *Understanding Miniature British Pottery and Porcelain, 1730 – Present Day*, Woodbridge, Suffolk, England: Antique Collectors Club, Ltd., 1983.

Miller, George L. *A Revised Set of Index Values for Classification and Economic Scaling of English Ceramics from 1787 to 1880*, Vol. 25, No. 1, Williamsburg,

Virginia: Williamsburg Foundation, Historical Archaeology, 1991 London, England: Pottery Publications, 1996.

Montgomery Ward & Co., Catalog, Chicago, Illinois, Years 1895 – 1915.

Niblett, Kathy, *Dynamic Designs British Pottery Industry, 1940-1990*, Stoke-on-Trent, England: City Museum and Art Gallery, 1990.

Owen, Harold, *The Stafforshire Potter*, Bath, England: Redwood Press Limited, 1901.

Perrott, E. George, B.A., *Pottery & Porcelain Marks, European, Oriental and USA in Chronological Order*, Bath, England: Gemini Publications, Ltd., 1997.

Potts, Keith, for *The Northern Ceramic Society*, Newsletter No. 114, Stoke-on-Trent, England: self-published, June, 1999.

Pratt, E.E., Chief, *The Pottery Industry*, Department of Commerce, Washington, D.C.: Government Printing Office, 1915.

Punchard, Lorraine, *Playtime Pottery & Porcelain From the United Kingdom and the United States*, Atglen, Pennsylvania: Schiffer Publishing, Ltd., 1996.

Rempel, Gerhard, Professor, *Article: The Industrial Revolution*, Department of History, Western New England College.

Rhead, G. Woolliscroft, *British Pottery Marks*, London, England: Scott, Greenwood & Son, 1910.

Riley, Noel, *Gifts For Good Children, The History of Children's China 1790-1890*, London, England: Richard Dennis Publications, 1991.

Roberts, Gaye Blake, Editor, *True Blue, Transfer Printed Earthenware*, the catalogue of an exhibition of British Blue Transfer Printed Earthenware to celebrate the 25th Anniversary of the Friends of Blue. Held at The Wedgwood Museum, Barlaston, Stoke-on-Trent, Staffordshire, March 21 to July 12, 1998, Oxfordshire, England: Friends of Blue Publishers, 1998.

Savage, George & Harold Newman, *An Illustrated Dictionary of Ceramics*, London, England: Thames & Hudson Ltd., 1992 (Reprint).

Scarratt, William, *Old Times in the Potteries*, Stoke-on-Trent, England: 1906.

Sears, Roebuck & Co., Catalog, Hoffman Estates, Illinois: Years 1894 – 1920.

Shively, Robert, research article, *The Story of the Johnson Bros.*, Kansas City, Kansas, May, 1983.

Snyder, Jeffrey B., *Fascinating Flow Blue*, Atglen, Pennsylvania: Schiffer Publishing, Ltd., 1997.

_____, *Flow Blue: A Collector's Guide to Patterns, History and Values*, Atglen, Pennsylvania: Schiffer Publishing, Ltd., 1992, revised editions 1996 and 1999.

_____, *Historic Flow Blue, With Price Guide*, Atglen, Pennsylvania: Schiffer Publishing, Ltd., 1994.

_____, *Historical Staffordshire, American Patriots & Views*, Atglen, Pennsylvania: Schiffer Publishing, Ltd., 1995.

_____, *A Pocket Guide to Flow Blue*, Atglen, Pennsylvania: Schiffer Publishing, Ltd., 1995.

Starey, Govia, *The Story of Alfred Meakin (Tunstall) Ltd.*, London, England: Ruthier Publications Press, November, 1949.

Stefano, Frank, Jr., *Pictorial Souvenirs & Commemoratives of North America*, U.S.A.: Dutton-Sunrise, Inc., a subsidiary of E.P. Dutton & Co., Inc., 1976.

Stuart, Denis, Editor, *People of the Potteries, Vol. 1*, Keele, England: Department of Adult Education, University of Keele, 1985.

Towner, Donald C., *English Cream-coloured Earthenware*, London, England: Faber and Faber, 1957.

Tuchman, Barbara W., *The Proud Tower, a portrait of the world before the war: 1890-1914*, New York, New York: The Macmillan Company, 1966.

Verbeek, Susan Jean, *The Falcon Ware Story*, London, England: Pottery Publications, 1996.

Wedgwood, Josiah, M.P., C.C., and Thomas H. Ormsbee, *Staffordshire Potter*, New York, New York: McBride, & Co., 1947.

Wetherbee, Jean, *White Ironstone: A Collectors Guide*, Dubuque, Iowa: Antique Trader Books, 1996.

Williams, Petra, *Flow Blue China An Aid to Identification*, Jeffersontown, Kentucky: Fountain House East, 1971.

_____, *Flow Blue China II*, Jeffersontown, Kentucky: Fountain House East, (Revised Edition), 1981.

_____, *Flow Blue China and Mulberry Ware, Similarity and Value Guide*, Jeffersontown, Kentucky: Fountain House East, (Revised Edition), 1978.

Yearbook & Directory, Queenborough, England: Years 1915, 1922, and 1933.